COMPETITIVE MARKI
STRATEGY FOR EURO

COMPETITIVE MARKETING STRATEGY FOR EUROPE

DEVELOPING, MAINTAINING AND DEFENDING COMPETITIVE ADVANTAGE

Linden Brown
and
Malcolm H. B. McDonald

ROB BROUGHAM.

First published 1994 by
THE MACMILLAN PRESS LTD
Houndmills, Basingstoke, Hampshire RG21 2XS
and London
Companies and representatives
throughout the world

ISBN 0–333–61350–3 hardcover
ISBN 0–333–61351–1 paperback

A catalogue record for this book is available
from the British Library.

Typeset by Cambrian Typsetters, Frimley, Surrey

Printed in Great Britain by
Antony Rowe Ltd, Chippenham, Wiltshire

Contents

List of Tables

List of Figures

Acknowledgements

The authors and publishers wish to thank the following for permission to use copyright material:

American Marketing Association for material from B. H. Booms and M. J. Bitner, 'Marketing Strategies and Organisation Structures for Service Firms' in *Marketing of Services*, eds J. Donnelly and W. R. George, 1981; Amstrad plc for material from their 1992 Annual Report and Accounts; The Boston Consulting Group, Inc. for material from 'Perspectives on Experience', 1970; Steve Burt for material from J. Dawson and S. Burt, 'The Evolution of European Retailing', Institute for Retail Studies/ICL, 1988; Butterworth-Heinemann Ltd for material from M. McDonald, *How to Prepare Marketing Plans*, 1989; The Free Press, a division of Macmillan Inc., for material from Michael E. Porter, *Competitive Strategy: Techniques for Analyzing Industries and Competitors* – copyright © 1980 by The Free Press; Glaxo Holdings plc for material from their 1992 Report and Accounts; Bernard Matthews plc for material from their 1992 Report and Accounts; MCB University Press for material from A. Meenaghan and P. W. Turnbull, 'Strategy and Analysis in Product Development', *European Journal of Marketing*, 15, 5, 1981, and from D. T. Browlie and C. K, Bart, *Products and Strategies*, 1985; Next plc for material from their 1992 Report and Accounts; Prentice Hall International (UK) Ltd for material from D. Knee and D. Walters, *Strategy in Retailing*, 1985; Signet Group plc for material from Ratners 1992 Annual Report and Accounts, Interim Report; Tesco Stores Ltd for material from their 1992 Annual Report and Accounts and Interim Report; Thorntons plc for material from their 1992 Annual Report and Accounts; West Publishing Corporation for material from G. S. Day, *Strategic Market Planning*, 1984, figs 7.3, 5.6, 3.1 – copyright © 1984 by West Publishing Company, and from G. S. Day, *Analysis for Strategic Market Decisions*, 1986, 7.4, A.7, A.10, 6.8, 7.3, 3.1 – copyright © 1986 by West Publishing Company; John Wiley and Sons Inc. for material from D. A. Aaker, *Strategic Market Management*, 1992; Yoram Wind for material from *Product Policy: Concepts, Methods and Strategy*, Addison-Wesley, Inc., 1982.

Every effort has been made to trace all the copyright holders but if any have been inadvertently overlooked the publishers will be pleased to make the necessary arrangement at the first opportunity.

Above all, this book would not have been possible without the extremely efficient and timely help of Clare Argent, a Cranfield MBA. Her attention to detail kept us both on the rails throughout the production of the book. Furthermore, her insight, vision and continuous advice helped turn what may have been an adequate book into what we believe is now a very good one.

CHAPTER 1

Competitive Marketing Strategy: Concepts and Application

This book is about competitive advantage – establishing, building, defending and maintaining it – and the strategies required to do that in a competitive environment. What those strategies should be will depend upon an organisation's existing competitive position, where it wants to be in the future, its capabilities and the competitive market environment it faces. The pertinent concepts are explored and their application examined in the European context by example, illustration and case study.

■ The Task of Competitive Marketing Strategy

Effective action is preceded by four interrelated steps: audit, objectives, strategies and plans for implementation. Following a situation review, objectives specify what is to be achieved, usually in terms of revenue, profit and market share. Strategies set out the route that has been chosen – the means for achieving the objectives. Plans for implementation provide the vehicle for getting to the destination along the chosen route.

In a competitive environment, the starting point is to identify the competitive position, set business objectives, which will comprise revenue, market share and profit requirements, then formulate the strategies necessary to achieve the new position.

Under these conditions, marketing strategies are the centrepiece.

The task of competitive marketing strategy is to move a business from its present position to a stronger competitive one. This must be done by adapting and responding to external trends and forces such as competition, market changes and technology, and developing and matching corporate resources and capabilities with the firm's opportunities (see Figure 1.1).

Recognition of the complexity of this task, especially for large diversified companies, has led to the development of theories, concepts and techniques that prescribe the process of strategy formulation in a systematic manner. This has become known as the strategic planning process.

The Strategic Planning Process

Strategic planning is the process of formulating longer term objectives and strategies for the entire business or business unit by matching its resources with its opportunities. Its purpose is to help a business to set and reach realistic objectives and achieve a desired competitive position within a defined time. It aims to reduce the risk of error and place the business in a situation in which it can anticipate, respond to, and even create, change to its advantage.

Evolution of the Process

In the sixties, strategic planning, known then as corporate planning, was essentially a financial plan of the business extrapolated from a base year. It worked well as a planning tool when demand exceeded supply, markets were growing and external change was minimal. When major external changes hit companies and industries in the late sixties and the seventies, however, this type of planning was no longer adequate. The successful challenge to retail price maintenance, for example, changed the nature of the food manufacturing industry, and the lowering of tariffs and provision of import quotas on many categories of goods changed local industries.

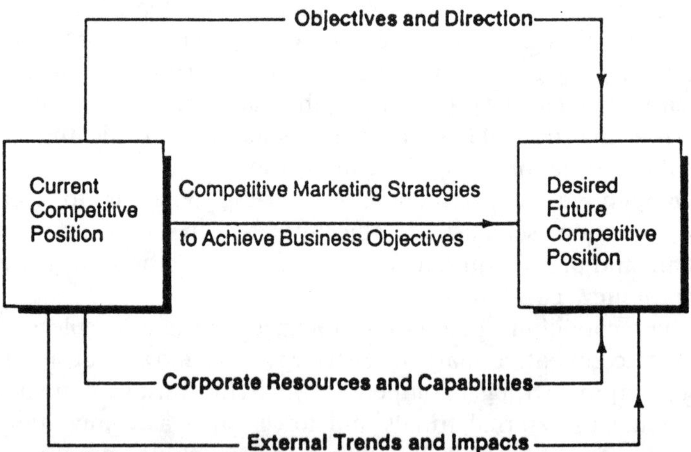

Figure 1.1 Strategies to achieve future position

Table 1.1 Evolution of Management Systems

	Budgeting/ Control	*Long-Range Planning*	*Strategic Planning*	*Strategic Market Management*
Management emphasis	Control deviations and manage complexity	Anticipate growth and manage complexity	Change strategic thrust and capability	Cope with strategic surprises and fast-developing threats/ opportunities
Assumptions	The past repeats	Past trends will continue	New trends and discontinuities are predictable	Planning cycles inadequate to deal with rapid changes
The Process	←———	Periodic	———→	Real Time
Time period associated with system	From 1900s	From 1950s	From 1960s	From mid-1970s

D. A. Aaker, *Strategic Market Management*, 1992, p. 10.

Increasing competition, more demanding customers and changing markets have forced more commitment to marketing to enable firms to capitalise on competitive advantages. Some companies now manage resources, markets and competition through a multi-level system of objectives and strategies.

Aaker depicts the evolution of management systems. The current stage is a strategic market management approach in which the firm adopts a planning and review process that aims to cope with strategic surprises and fast developing threats and opportunities.[1] This is shown in Table 1.1.

In response to evolving external factors such as technology and market maturity, firms changed their products and markets, sold and acquired businesses and reorganised. This required them to redefine their business scope because of the need to commit resources to new businesses and market development. Courtaulds, for example, originally in textiles, is now in paints and industrial plastics; ICI, originally in bulk chemicals, is in pharmaceuticals and the banks present insurance and financial services. Allied Breweries moved into hotels and leisure centres and W H Smith has a DIY chain, Do-it-all.

■ Steps in the Process

In reality, firms adopt a hybrid of management systems depending upon their size, diversity, position in the market, rate and type of external change, resource commitments and management attitudes to planning.

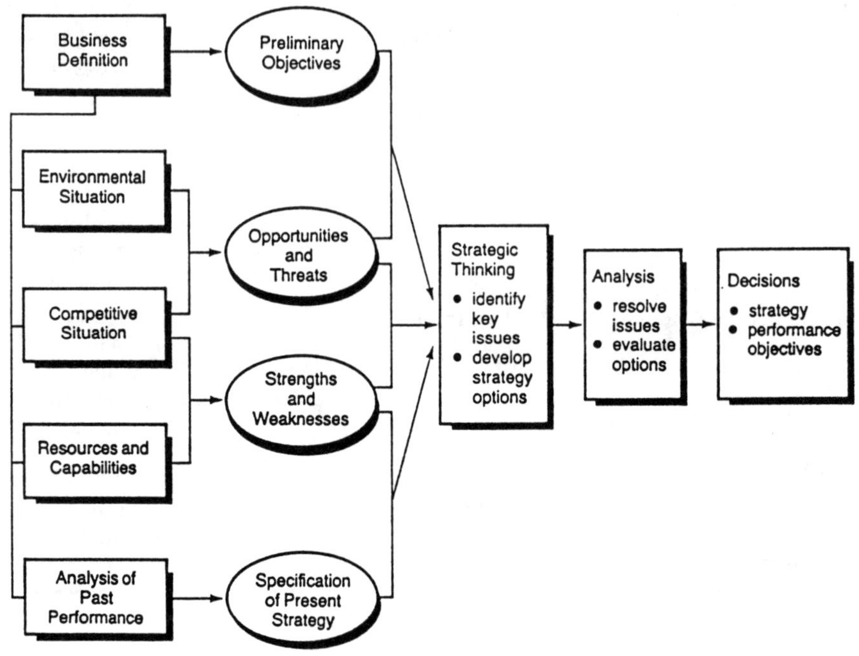

Figure 1.2 Strategy formulation process

Source: G. S. Day, *Strategic Market Planning*, 1984, p. 49.

What is important, however, is to recognise that a series of systematic steps can be useful in formulating strategies when the stakes are high and the resource commitment is significant to the firm. It reduces the risk of leaving out key issues, and it highlights the assumptions on which strategies are based and resources are committed.

A series of interrelated steps are involved in formulating strategies. Day shows a typical strategy formulation process in Figure 1.2.[2]

The basic steps are:

- business definition – scope of planning activities;
- situation assessment – analysis of internal and environmental factors;
- preliminary performance objectives – based on past performance and initial corporate expectations, constrained by achievement reality;
- strategic development – identification and evaluation of strategic options and choice of an option;

- implementation – includes action programmes, functional budgets and timetables; and
- monitoring of performance against objectives.

In essence, an analysis of internal and external factors helps to develop the business definition, relative competitive advantage and broad objectives. The central issues must be identified, the strategy options set out and evaluated. Strategic decisions are taken by selecting the strategy and relevant performance objectives. Aaker expands some of the elements in this process.[3]

The analyses by Day and Aaker relate primarily to strategy development for the Strategic Business Unit (SBU). McDonald[4] looks at planning with a more highly focused marketing perspective and views the marketing planning process within a corporate framework.

They see the steps as:

- corporate (business) objectives;
- marketing audit – analyses of external environment and internal elements, including the marketing mix;
- SWOT analysis and planning assumptions, including key determinants of marketing success or failure;
- marketing objectives and strategies, including objectives for products and markets and strategies for each part of the marketing mix;
- programmes containing details of timing, responsibilities and costs, with sales forecasts and budget; and
- measurement and review.

The development of competitive marketing strategies needs to draw from both. The SBU level provides tools of strategic analysis that are applicable to the development of marketing strategies and cut across the whole business. The functional marketing level helps define the elements that make up a marketing strategy for each of the product lines and market segments. Specific brand positioning and marketing mix decisions become more narrowly defined at the product market level of analysis. The SBU level provides tools of strategic marketing analysis, while the functional marketing level helps define the elements that make up a marketing strategy.

■ The Planning Process and Conceptual Analysis

There is a considerable number of strategic analysis concepts, methods and techniques from which to draw guidelines for competitive marketing strategies. The problem is to determine which are the most useful and relevant. It is important to recognise that each concept or technique provides only part of the picture and should not be relied upon as the only guide to strategy formulation. These concepts have evolved from the field of marketing, and in recent years, the area of strategic planning.

Much of the literature focuses on competitive analyses[5] as the key to identifying competitive advantages, and on the need to develop global strategies such as those that have been successfully implemented by Japanese corporations.[6] Many attempt to provide guidelines and general principles for the selection of strategies under different conditions. Indeed, the links between strategy and performance have been the subject of detailed statistical analysis by the Strategic Planning Institute. The PIMS Project identified six major links from studies of more than 2600 business. From this analysis, principles have been derived for the selection of different strategies depending upon industry type, market conditions and competitive position of the business.[7]

A reaction against theoretical approaches to strategic planning has occurred in recent years, however, with particular focus on the limitations of portfolio planning.[8] Some writers argue that there are no valid generalisations about strategy and criticise strategy consultants, who, they claim, have misled managers by making recommendations based on excessively broad principles. Lubatkin and Pitts[9] compare a 'policy perspective' with the 'PIMS perspective'. They suggest that a policy perspective assumes that no two businesses are exactly alike and therefore there are few specific formulae for achieving competitive advantage. They suggest that the PIMS perspective involves a mechanistic application of formulae to complex management problems, resulting in potentially misleading prescriptions for strategy.

What is agreed, however, is that strategic planning represents a useful process by which an organisation formulates its strategies, but it should be adapted to the organisation and its environments. The basic steps relevant to all business are:

- Analysis of external and internal trends;
- Review of past and current strategies;
- SWOT and issues analysis;
- Objective setting;
- Strategy selection;
- Action plans;
- Implementation; and
- Performance review and evaluation of performance.

These steps are generally agreed to include the most prominent features of strategic planning. They include, in summary form, the steps proposed by Day, McDonald and Aaker.

In practice, the weakest and often most difficult parts of this process are in strategic planning analysis and strategy selection.

Strategic Analysis Concepts

The range of concepts relevant to the analysis of competitive marketing strategy emanate from a number of disciplines, including marketing, sociology, economics, financial management and the new area of strategic management. Some of the principal concepts are described in the remainder of this chapter.

The Product Life-Cycle

One of the first attempts to form an analytical framework for determining marketing strategy was the product life-cycle theory.

The Concept

The product life-cycle concept describes stages in the sales history of a product category or form. Most representations of the life-cycle have the following characteristics:

- A product has a limited life.
- Its sales history follows a 'S' curve until sales eventually decline.
- The inflection points in the sales history locate the stages known as introduction, growth, maturity and decline. Some representations show an additional stage of competitive turbulence or shakeout once the growth rate slows.
- The life of the product may be extended.
- The average profit per unit (of the industry) rises, then falls over the life-cycle.

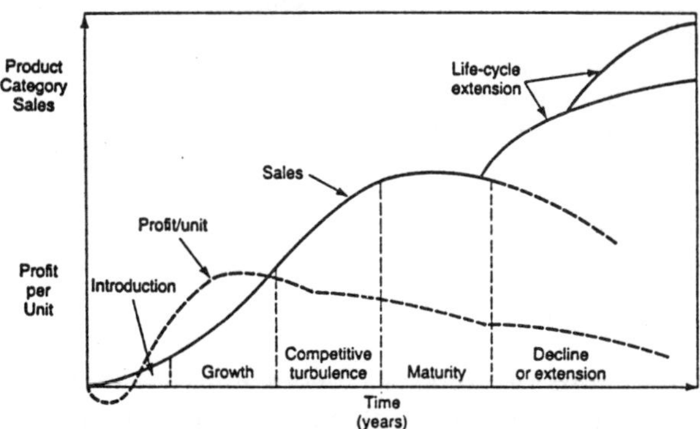

Figure 1.3 Life-cycle of a typical product

Source: G. S. Day, *Analysis for Strategic Marketing Decisions*, 1986, p. 60.

Figure 1.3 shows the idealised product life-cycle, which includes curve and unit profit trends.[10] It also shows market extension of the life-cycle.

Underlying the life-cycle is the diffusion process and associated adopter categories which are classified according to their timing of entry onto the market. Figure 1.4 indicates the proportion of the total market of each category and the idealised diffusion pattern.

Innovators represent that 2.5% of the market that will immediately accept the new product and try it. The early adopters are those who will 'make or break' the product depending upon their experiences and opinions. If these are favourable, acceptance grows rapidly and most of the market enters quickly. The last group to accept the product, the laggards, buys for the first time, often when innovators and early adopters have moved to alternative products.

Each stage of the life-cycle represents different marketing challenges. At the introductory stage, the task is to create awareness and achieve acceptance by opinion leaders within the early adopter group. During growth, the challenge is to maintain supply and quality consistency while establishing brand identification and market position. At the mature stage, the firm needs to maintain or improve its profit, defend its position and look for growth segments of the market. In decline, cost reduction, pricing and target is important to profitability, and planning is required to determine exit timing.

Examples of current products at different life-cycle stages in Europe in the early 1990s are shown in Table 1.2.

Table 1.2 Products at Different Life-Cycle Stages

Introduction	*Growth*	*Maturity*	*Decline*
Filmless cameras Computer scanners Stress wave sensing Expert systems	Compact disc players Facsimile transmission Lap-top computers	Microwave ovens Washing machines Brandy	Draught ale Typewriters

☐ *Strategic Implications*

The strategic implications of life-cycle theory are that each stage warrants different objectives, marketing mix, strategies and different management focus. Both Wasson[11] and Day[12] have conducted comprehensive analyses of life-cycle management and propose marketing strategy guidelines for each stage. Each author adds an intermediate stage between growth and maturity, termed 'competitive turbulence', which recognises the implications of the effects of a

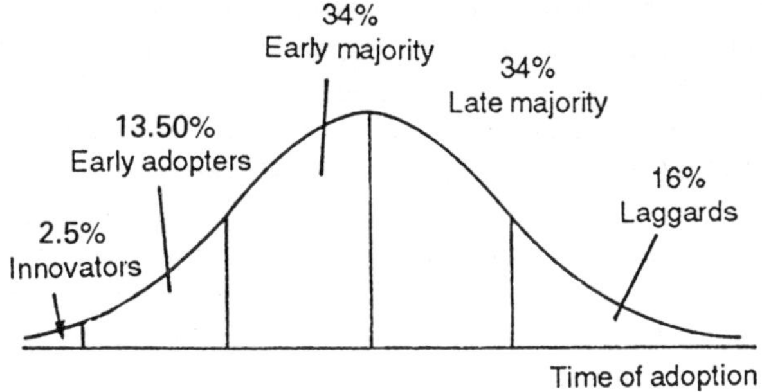

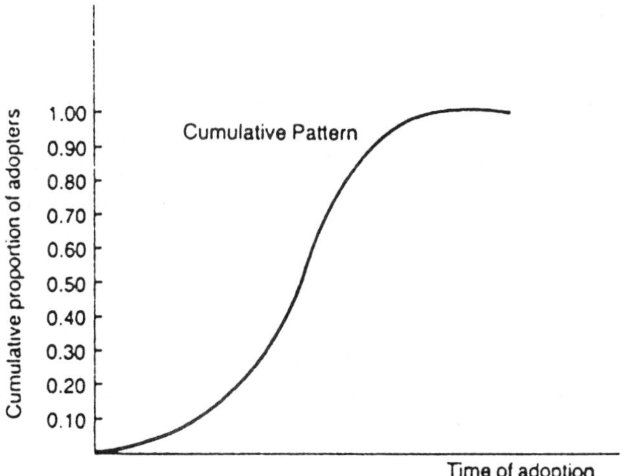

Figure 1.4 Diffusion pattern and adopter categories

Source: Y. J. Wind, *Product Policy: Concepts, Methods and Strategy*, 1982, p. 28.

slowdown in market growth and over-supply, brought on by the entry of new competitors and increase in capacity by existing ones. Day[13] and Wasson[14] provide a summary of the general strategic implications of life-cycle theory all of which are described in this book.

An example of this occurred in the British telex market. When it was introduced, telex offered an efficient, quick text transfer service as an alternative to the postal service. It rapidly became an essential business communication tool with maximum market penetration in the early 1980s. British Telecom implemented life-cycle extension strategies by adding features to telex terminals, enhancing user capabilities, allowing text transfer to computers and targeting non-user segments such as small businesses. However, the rapid growth of facsimile systems since the mid-1980s has brought about the decline of telex and a need for British Telecom to change its strategy to retain profitability and to plan for either product divestment or reformulation to enable future profit to be made on much lower telex volumes.

The introduction, growth and rationalisation of video hire shops is another example of predictable product market evolution. The rapid expansion of retail outlets resulted in over-supply, a shakeout of competitors, and now more stable competition.

□ *Variations on a Theme*

Life-cycle patterns vary in practice. Some new products skip the introductory stage and grow rapidly from the outset. These are usually products that are readily understood by the market and for which a latent demand exists, such as colour television and cellular mobile telephones. New fads exhibit only rapid growth and rapid decline because of a novelty appeal, seasonality and associations with special events. Some products show a decline, then a regrowth pattern. Industrial and consumer durables, such as farm machinery and refrigerators, reveal this cyclical pattern. Other products fail and hardly register a blip on the life-cycle chart. A number of different variations to the life-cycle theme are depicted in the box shown in Figures 1.5–1.8.[15]

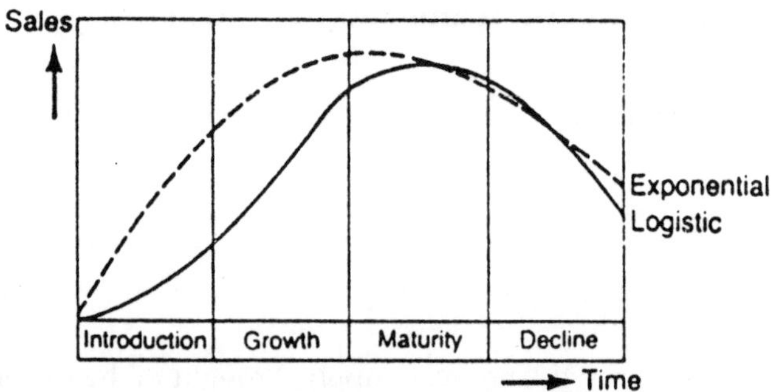

Figure 1.5 Basic product life-cycle stages

Source: A. Meenaghan and P. W. Turnbull, *Strategy and Analysis in Product Development*, MCB Publications, vol. 15, no. 5, 1981, p. 2.

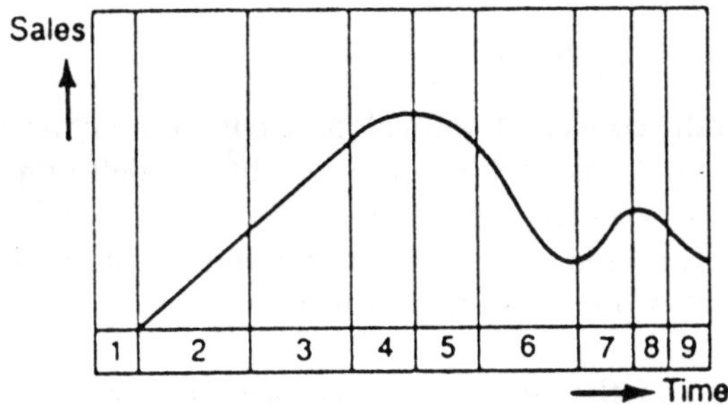

Figure 1.6 Alternative life-cycle shape and stages

Source: Meenaghan and Turnbull, *op. cit.*, p. 2.

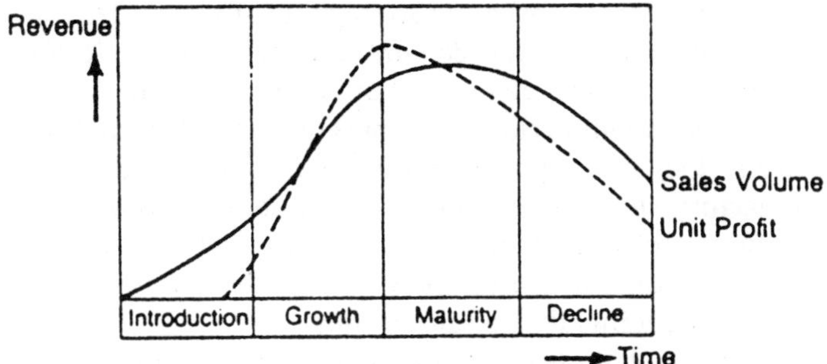

Figure 1.7 Profit-volume relationship over the life-cycle

Source: Meenaghan and Turnbull, *op. cit.*, p. 5.

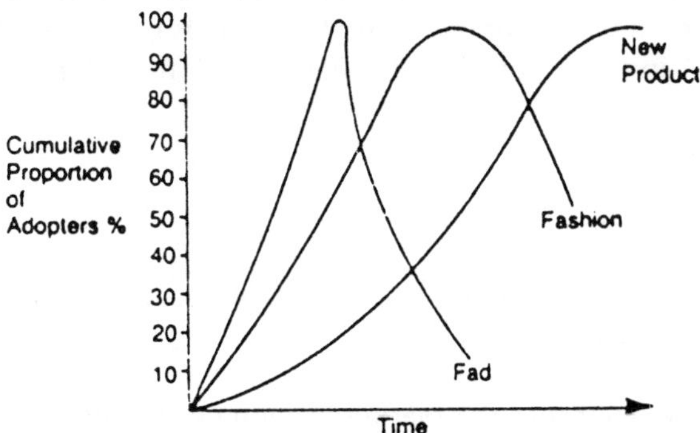

Figure 1.8 Generalised diffusion pattern for a fad, a fashion and a new product

Source: Meenaghan and Turnbull, *op. cit.*, p. 11.

□ *Limitations to its Application*

The limitations of the concept, for developing competitive marketing strategies, depend on the variations of life-cycles, problems defining the appropriate market, and the focus on strategies that tend to be applicable to the dominant firm in the market and inapplicable to competitors holding different positions. Brownlie[16] highlights the issues in this way:

1 Clear definition of the market is necessary. This requires aggregation of product market segments, which can be misleading where market boundaries cannot be delineated accurately. In practice, it is more common for markets to be defined in terms of several competing brands within a product category. The key question, posed by Weitz and Wensley,[17] is: Which level of aggregation best captures the changing nature of the environment to which marketing strategy must respond?
2 As a prescriptive tool, it is too general to enable the application of specific strategy guidelines to a given product or brand. It is difficult to predict when the turning points will occur, based purely on market analysis.
3 The concept does not explicitly allow for the influence of uncontrollable external factors such as technology, economic conditions, competitors' position and strategies and the overall capacity of the industry in relation to demand. Conditions of short supply affect sales patterns and can reflect artificial turning points in the sales trends.
4 It is not clear how far a firm can influence the shape of the life-cycle by its marketing strategies and at which stages there is potential for greatest influence. It is likely, however, that the pioneering firm and dominant players have a significant impact, particularly at the introduction, early growth and maturity stages.
5 The length of stages varies within and between markets. Now, for most product types, duration of the entire life-cycle is becoming shorter because of the increasing pace of technological innovations and introduction of new products.

□ *Practical Significance*

The life-cycle concept brings into focus a number of market factors that are important for strategic planning.

- The notion of evolution of a market bringing changing market conditions, represented by a variety of warning signs, is a valuable contribution to marketing strategy formulation.
- Recognition of a finite limit to market potential for a product type sets the market size dimension. Penetration and usage levels at any point provide an indication of future potential.

- The distinction between market sales and a firm's product sales highlights the importance of market share trends and maintaining a focus on the total market. As the market matures, focus on sales trends and cycle stages of individual segments is useful.
- The dynamics of the diffusion process provide useful targeting insights. Target customer groups change over time. It is easier to obtain market share growth during the growth stage of the life-cycle as customers form opinions of brands and try alternatives. As the market matures, customers become more knowledgeable and their perceptions of the product type, and brands within it, change. Distinctions between brands are reduced and the product type becomes 'ordinary', having lost its newness and mystique. Customers progressively develop a 'commodity' view of the product. Figure 1.9 depicts the commodity slide which characterises the maturity of some markets, particularly those in which weaker competitors try to retain profit margins by withdrawing advertising support.

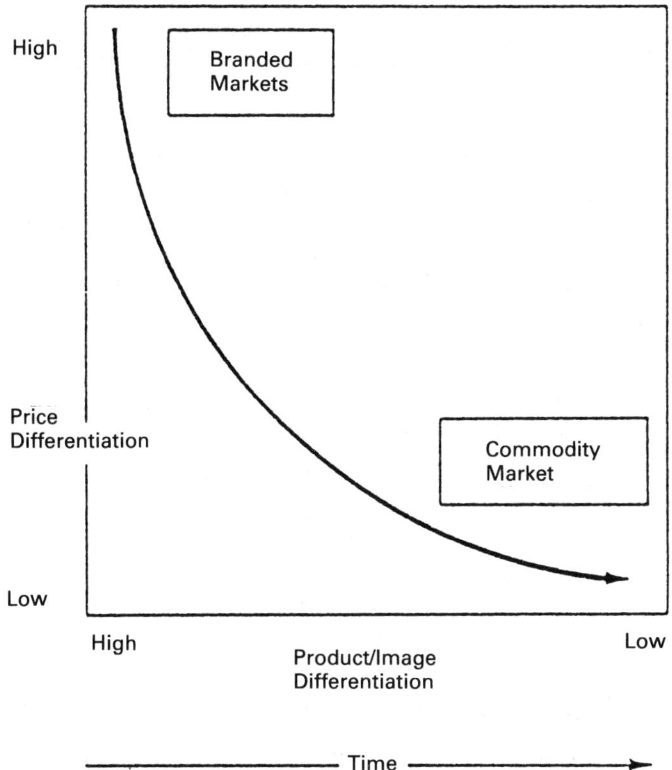

Figure 1.9 The commodity slide

Source: M. McDonald, *Marketing Plans*, Butterworth-Heinemann 1989.

- Identification of products within a firm's range which are in markets at different life-cycle stages provides an indication of the balance of products according to their future growth prospects.
- Recognition of the changing pattern of competition and different types of competitive strategies that may evolve at each stage is a useful contribution to strategic thinking.

The Experience Curve

The Concept

The results of the Boston Consultancy Group's (BCG) studies of cost and price changes in relation to accumulated volume or experience across a variety of industries, highlight cost dynamics and their impact on prices, particularly in rapidly growing markets.[18] Change in market share can produce change in cost differentials between competitors, enabling a firm which is gaining market share to lower prices faster than its profit margin declines. The per unit cost experience curve, plotted over time in relation to accumulated volume, declines, owing to efficiencies from learning, technological improvements and economies of scale.

Figure 1.10 shows that cost declines with total accumulated volume – this takes the form of a curve on the linear scale. On a log-log scale, it shows a percentage change as a constant distance on the graph; that is, a percentage change in one factor results in a corresponding percentage change in the other. In the case of cost-volume or price-volume slopes, the plotting of data about costs or prices and accumulated experience for a product on log-log paper in

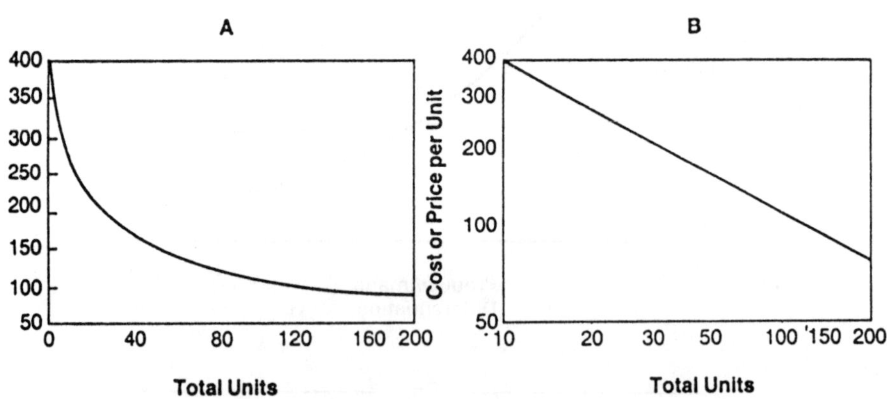

Figure 1.10 Experience cost relationships

Source: The Boston Consulting Group, 1970, p. 13.

the BCG studies produces straight lines, reflecting a consistent relationship between experience and costs and experience and prices. Across a variety of industries the BCG found that with each doubling of accumulated volume, costs dropped between 20 per cent and 40 per cent, depending upon the industry.

In response to industry cost declines, the BCG found varying price trends – some stable, others unstable. These are shown in Figures 1.11 and 1.12.

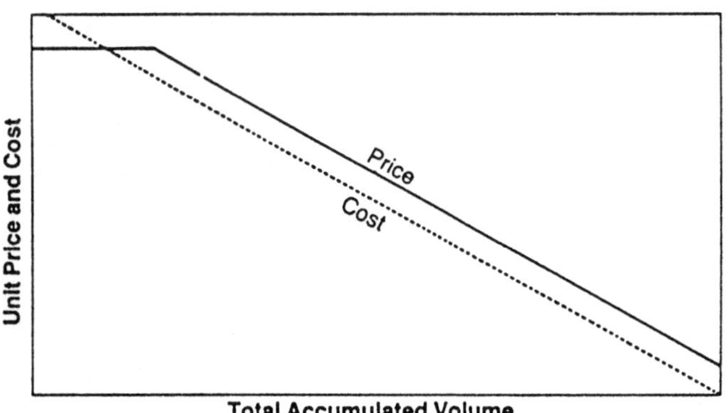

Figure 1.11 A typical stable pattern

Source: The Boston Consulting Group, 1970, p. 19.

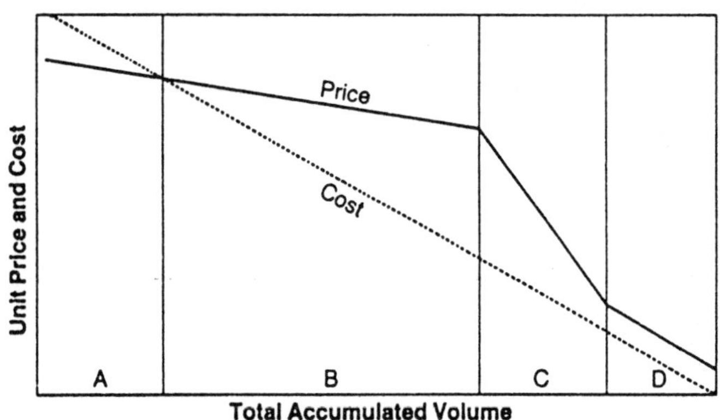

Figure 1.12 A characteristic unstable pattern after it has become stable

Source: The Boston Consulting Group, 1970, p. 21.

□ *Strategic implications*

Learning experience, and its impact on costs and price levels, has important implications for strategic planning.

There is a minimum rate of cost decline required for survival by firms in an industry where learning experience affects costs and prices. This is reflected in Figure 1.13.

Pricing strategies of leading competitors in a market where learning experience affects costs, will create a stable or unstable competitive environment. When a substantial gap develops between average unit price and average

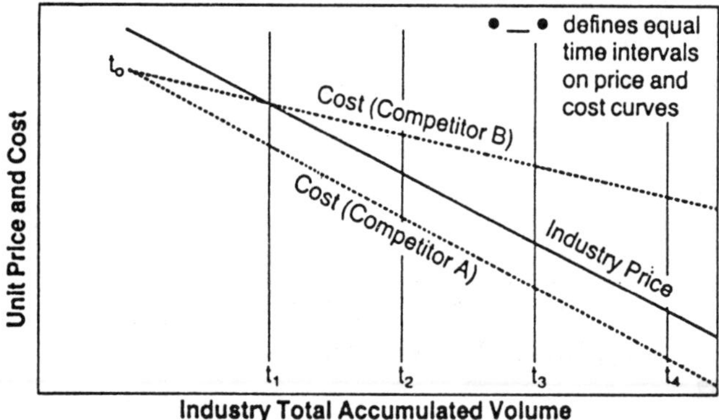

Figure 1.13 Competitor and industry price experience

Source: The Boston Consulting Group, 1970, p. 24.

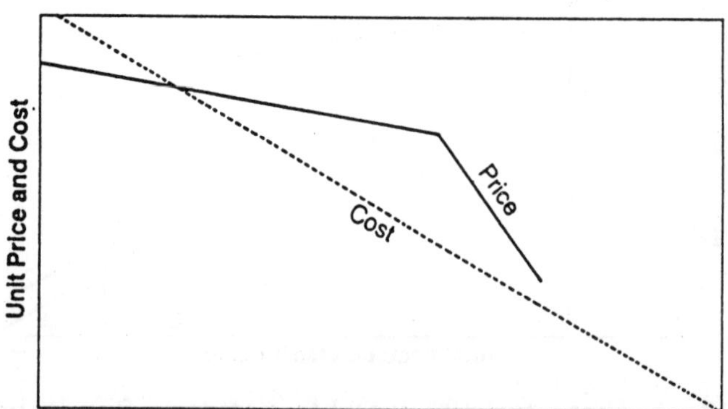

Figure 1.14 Unstable price gap

Source: The Boston Consulting Group, 1970, p. 20.

unit cost, opportunities exist for lowering prices and gaining more volume. This is usually done by smaller competitors. Figure 1.14 shows this pattern.

The major strategic implication is that firms should seek market share dominance during the growth stage of the life-cycle so that cost advantages can be reflected in price advantages, which, in turn, lead to market share increases. If this is done aggressively, using price penetration strategies it is assumed that the firm will end up with the lowest unit costs, highest market share and an ability to lead the market during its mature phase.

Texas Instruments adopted this strategy in the digital watch market, only to find that its prices ended at a point below its unit costs as the market matured and, despite its dominance, it was unable to make a profit. Clearly, this strategy requires confidence in the fact that volume growth is sufficient to achieve substantial cost reductions and that the firm can achieve, and can sustain, a lowest cost position in the industry.

□ *Limitations of the Concept*

1 The experience curve applies to broad categories of basic products such as television receivers, electric ranges or semi-conductors. When the definition is narrowed into sub-categories of these groups, the relationship applies only to the value added component. At the individual product or brand level, this becomes difficult to apply because of the high proportion of joint costs involved.
2 Variations in accounting practice can substantially distort reported costs as they affect experience curves and cost-volume analysis. Allocated costs can distort actual product costs. Cost comparisons between competitors are difficult to make for both practical and accessibility reasons. It is difficult, therefore, to gain consistent and reasonably accurate product cost trends.
3 An appropriate inflation index is necessary to ensure cost trends are measured in real terms. This is not always readily available for the product type under review.
4 Experience can be readily transferred in ways other than accumulated volume. Hiring of experienced staff, licensing of technology, franchising arrangements and acquiring 'experienced' companies in the field of interest, enable firms with low volume experience to operate on a low unit cost structure. Davidow[19] refers to 'toothpaste technology' in high-tech industries, where the demands of customers, governments and industry associations are forcing companies to base their products on identical technologies. More and more products are being built from identical 'product genes' which are now widely available technologies.
5 Some markets do not respond to massive price cutting because of the nature of the industry. Insurance, furniture removals and medical services are based on trust, and low prices can be perceived in a negative light. Other markets respond to price reductions but, once set in motion, products

become low-margin commodities with very little profit. Some generic labels sold by supermarkets exhibit these characteristics, where constant price specials are necessary to generate sales.

□ *Practical Significance*

Despite its appeal and empirical support, the experience curve applies only in certain situations. The earlier broad generalisations have been replaced with applications where the tool is recognised as one of a number of analytical methods. It does, however, focus on some key issues for strategic planning.

Costs require deliberate management to ensure competitiveness as industries, markets and cost structures change. British Leyland found in many of its manufacturing businesses, for example, that it could no longer remain cost competitive, because of lack of economies of scale, and it divested many of its manufacturing companies during the 1980s.

The competitive marketing strategies adopted by firms in an industry have an impact on industry costs and cost trends. The experience curve concept focuses attention on cost/price/volume dynamics and indicates the importance of forecasting future costs, prices and profits in the industry.

The return on investment from improved market share can be high. The variables affecting profitability are profit margin, market share and market size. In a rapidly growing market, all three are more important in the future than in the present. The strategist needs to determine when to trade profit today for future market share and vice versa.

When experience effects do occurs, competitors need to achieve an advantage on those cost elements that are important to particular market segments. These cost elements may differ significantly between segments, allowing specialists to dominate niches against broad line competitors. Davidow, in an account of marketing strategies relevant to high technology industries, illustrates the importance of competitive cost differences and how costs and margin goals affect price,[20] and demonstrates that small differences in costs and margin objectives yield significant differences in prices that can be charged by competitors.

■ The Growth-Share Portfolio Model[21]

The product portfolio concept has its origin in finance theory, where a variety of risk-returns investments is balanced as a portfolio to provide required return to the investor. Some investments are geared to immediate income at a low risk, some to capital growth with low immediate income, and others as higher risk ventures with potentially high future returns. In order to provide for both present and future cash flow, it is desirable to have a balanced portfolio.

When applied to marketing, this concept views products as investments that either require or yield cash according to their position in the portfolio. Some products, especially new ones, will have potentially high future cash flow but are high-risk investments. These may require substantial cash investment during development. Others may be declining and represent candidates for deletion. Some products within the range may yield high cash flow, which is used to fund new developments.

Portfolio models, such as the BCG's growth-share matrix, have been almost synonymous with the development of strategic planning concepts.

Frequently referred to as the BCG* matrix, the growth-share portfolio model classifies each business or product by the rate of present market growth and by a measure of market share dominance. Market growth serves as a proxy for the need for cash, and relative market share is used to reflect profitability and cash generation. Relative market share is the ratio of the product's share to the share of its largest competitor in the same market.

The logic of this model is based on the dynamics of the product life-cycle (market growth rate) and the experience curve effect (the importance of relative market share and dominance).

In its simplest form, the model depicts growth and relative share as either low or high. To reflect its future prospects and risks, each product classification is named – star, cash cow, dog and problem child/question mark.

The model uses this matrix to suggest market share and investment objectives for each category.

- **Stars**: invest to hold or increase market share.
- **Cash cows**: maintain or milk to provide cash for problem child products and research and development.
- **Dogs**: reformulate to provide positive cash flow, reduce costs, or divest.
- **Problem child/question mark**: invest in share growth in those that show positive prospects; divest others.

Figure 1.15 indicates the cash-flow position of each type and provides measures for placing products in the matrix. The market dominance axis measures the firm's market share relative to that of the largest competitor.

□ *Strategic Management Guidelines*

Brownlie, in a review of the BCG model, provides a useful summary of strategic guidelines.[22]

The main guidelines are as follows:

- **Star** products require continued heavy investment during growth. Low margins may be essential to defer competition and consolidate competitive position.
- **Cash cows** are managed for cash, but some investment is required to reduce costs and maintain market dominance. Future market prospects will determine how long an investment in maintaining dominance is pursued and when the product is harvested to make the most profit.

* The name is derived from the Boston Consulting Group that developed the concept.

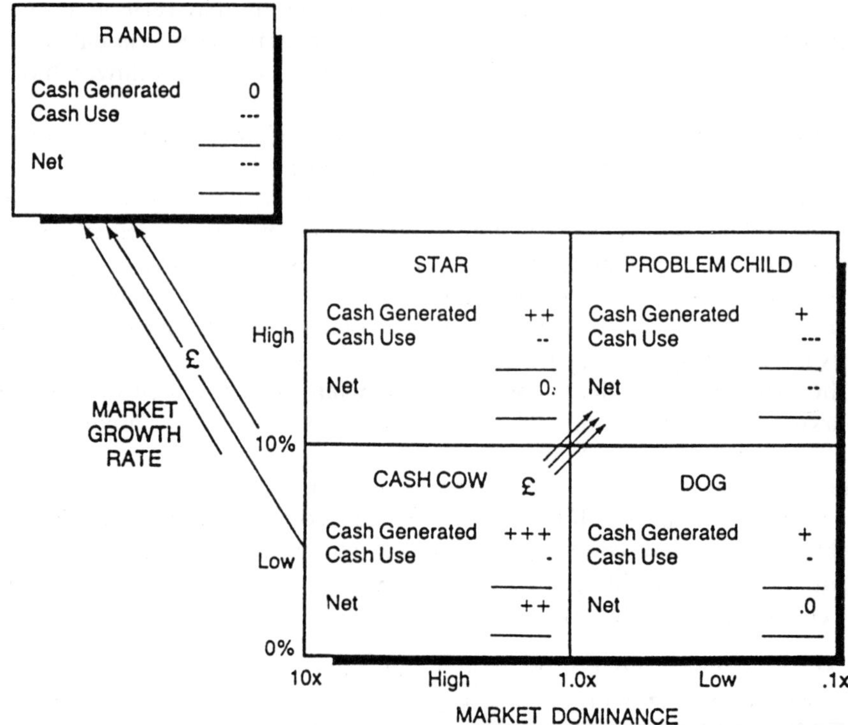

Figure 1.15 Portfolio positions and cash flows

- **Problem children** are managed to gain market share. Where star potential is not evident, divestment is recommended.
- **Dogs** have weak competitive positions in low-growth and mature markets. Most have little potential for share growth and are unprofitable. Liquidation of dog products is usually recommended.

The successful strategy sequence requires the development of a question mark product to a star, which in turn becomes a cash cow as the market matures. This may move towards dog status as it is milked for cash, but it should be withdrawn before negative cash flows occur.

An appropriate balance of cash cows, stars and question marks, enables the business to produce positive cash flows and profit, while continuing investment in future profitability.

□ *Limitations*

The major weakness of this model is its simplification of complex situations and the glib guidelines that flow from it. Measurement and definition problems must be overcome for it to be useful. Narrow definitions of the market are usually necessary to identify a useful portfolio of products. An analysis of Unilever's detergent products undertaken for the detergent market revealed that they were all 'dogs' but, in effect, they were really 'golden retrievers', which returned large cash flows and profit. When the analysis was repeated at the market segment level, it showed that Unilever had a number of 'stars' and 'cash cows'.

Another limitation is the tendency of this type of analysis to limit vision and narrow the focus to a range of options that may be inappropriate. The notion, for example, that 'cows are for milking' does not distinguish between large share products in mature markets that have long-term profit and cash flow prospects and require re-investment and defence of share position and those that do not have future prospects and should be harvested for maximum short-term profit and cash.

A further danger is that share may be seen as an end in itself, rather than as a means to achieving profitability. As Heinz discovered in the 1970s, a single-minded focus on dominating markets and maximising share, does not necessarily bring with it long-term profitability.

□ *Practical Significance*

The portfolio concept developed by the BCG does make a practical contribution to strategic planning, so long as its limitations are realised.

1 It is a useful conceptual tool for understanding where products fit in relation to each other in a portfolio and identifying those that require significant investment to improve their market positions. It helps to focus attention on problem products for which management decisions are necessary.
2 In common with the product life-cyle, it suggests a competitive evolution of a product from problem child to star to cash cow as the market matures, and it highlights the importance of building market share while the market is growing.
3 By drawing attention to cash generation and cash use of products, it emphasises the desirability of a balanced portfolio, so that new initiatives can be funded and cash generators protected.

■ Attractiveness – Competitive Position Models

The problems posed by the simplified and generic structure of the BCG model are overcome by development of models tailored to the conditions affecting the firm or industry. A number of large corporations use a nine-box matrix to identify the positions of their businesses according to market/industry attractiveness (of which market growth rate in the BCG model is one factor) and business strengths/competitiveness position (of which relative market share is one factor).

General Electric with McKinsey pioneered this model, making use of many variables to assess each dimension. The dimensions used for assessing position are believed to be representative of the significant elements of the internal and external environment from which strengths, weaknesses, opportunities and threats arise. However, the relative importance of these dimensions varies between firms and industries. GE's Business Assessment Matrix, through qualitative analysis, assesses a business as being strong, medium or weak in terms of business strength, and assesses its industry attractiveness as high, medium or low. In common with the BCG model, general strategic guidelines are provided for investment, divestment or selective growth or harvesting strategies.

The Shell Chemical Company developed a similar portfolio model called the Directional Policy Matrix, using as its two main assessment criteria Competitive Capabilities (similar to GE's Business Strengths) and Prospects for Sector Profitability (analogous to GE's Industry Attractiveness).

More recently, the authors of the book have developed a simpler four box version of the Directional Policy Matrix, for which they have developed computer software which enables practising managers to quantify the axes and include circles which accurately represent the relative importance of the contribution to the organisation of the products, services, or markets represented on the matrix.

□ *Strategic Implications*

These models have the advantage of taking account of specific factors relevant to the industry. Generic strategy guidelines, however, also emanate from them. Table 1.3 shows a number of strategic options depending upon a business's position in terms of market attractiveness (high, medium or weak). Figure 1.16 indicates directions relevant to four different business positions depending on objectives, resource availability and risk.

□ *Limitations*

The main practical difficulty is the selection and weighting of relevant criteria for assessing a business's position on the matrix. Also, when assessing businesses in different industries, the success factors usually differ, and unless separate calculations are worked out for each, direct comparisons of different businesses on the same matrix may be inappropriate. There are often strategic reasons for staying in a business when the financial indications suggest divestment. For example, Hoover's assessment of the vacuum cleaning market and its array of low-price international competitors, is that manufacturers are prepared to lose money long term in this market because it acts as an entry point to the household for a wide range of appliances and electronic products –

Table 1.3 Generic Strategy Options

MARKET ATTRACTIVENESS	PROTECT POSITION	INVEST TO BUILD	BUILD SELECTIVELY
high	• invest to grow at maximum digestible rate • concentrate effort on maintaining strength	• challenge for leadership • build selectively on strengths • reinforce vulnerable areas	• specialise around limited strengths • seek ways to overcome weaknesses • withdraw if indications of sustainable growth are lacking
medium	BUILD SELECTIVELY • invest heavily in most attractive segments • build up ability to counter competition • emphasize profitability by raising productivity	SELECTIVITY/ MANAGE FOR EARNINGS • protect existing program • concentrate investments in segments where profitability is good and risk is relatively low	LIMITED EXPANSION OR HARVEST • look for ways to expand without high risk; otherwise, minimise investment and rationalise operations
low	PROTECT AND REFOCUS • manage for current earnings • concentrate on attractive segments • defend strengths	MANAGE FOR EARNINGS • protect position in most profitable segments • upgrade product line • minimise investment	DIVEST • sell at time that will maximise cash value • cut fixed costs and avoid investment meanwhile
COMPETITIVE POSITION	strong	medium	weak

Source: G. S. Day, *Analysis for Strategic Market Decisions*, 1986, p. 204.

the vacuum cleaner being one of the first products bought by new homemakers.

□ *Practical Significance*

An important insight from these models is the strategic significance of competitive position as measured by relative business strengths, capabilities and market share. For instance, a market may be very attractive with rapid

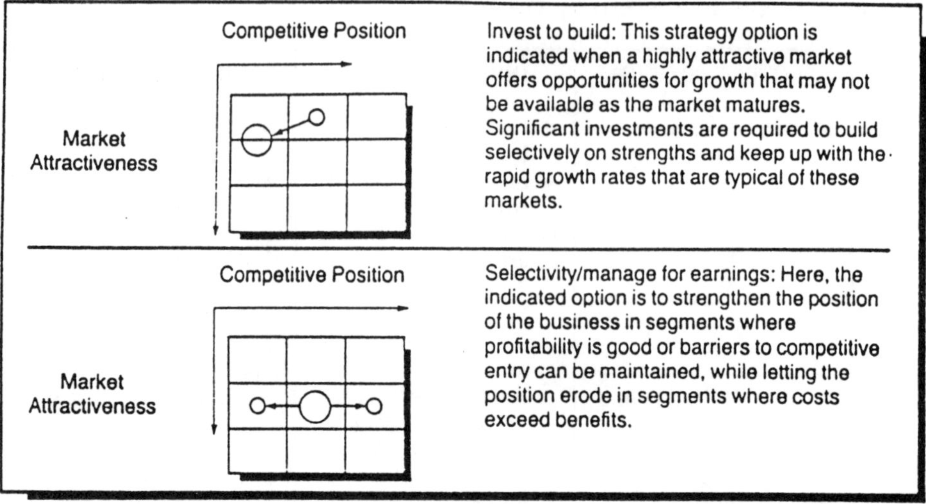

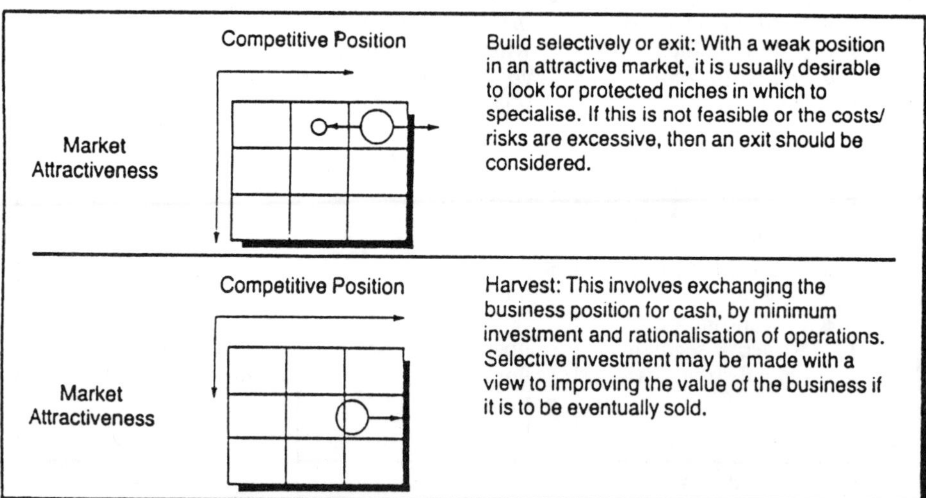

Figure 1.16 Strategy direction

Source: G. S. Day, *Analysis for Strategic Market Decisions*, 1986, p. 205.

growth prospects and a wide range of opportunities, but the business's relative competitive position is weak and competitive advantages are difficult to find and risky to implement. Alternatively, the business may have a strong competitive position in an unprofitable, declining market with poor long-term prospects. The implication is that the firm's competitive strength should be used to restructure the industry on a profitable basis or plan to divest from part or all of the business.

Ansoff's Product-Market Growth Model

Igor Ansoff, a pioneer in strategic thinking, introduced the concept of the planning gap by first charting expected future sales or return on investment (ROI) based on no change to current strategies, then charting potential sales or ROI based on market potential.[23] In Figure 1.17 two gaps are identified between expected sales from present strategies and maximum sales growth potential – a competitive gap indicating sales potential from the existing business and a diversification gap suggesting sales potential from new businesses. Figure 1.18 modifies this concept to show the top-line sales trend to represent management objectives with the task of the marketer to develop strategies to close the gap.

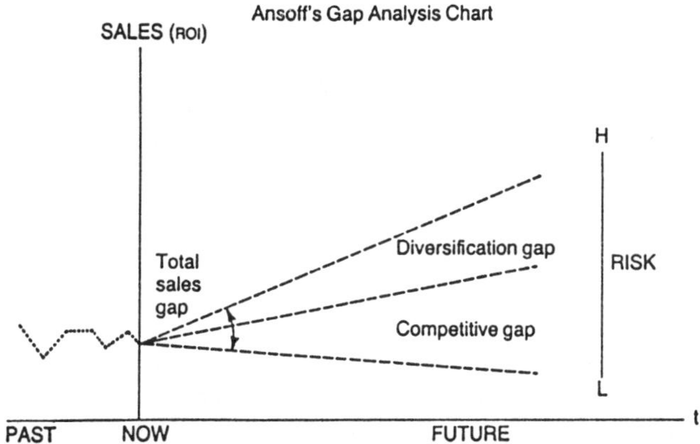

Figure 1.17 Product market directions

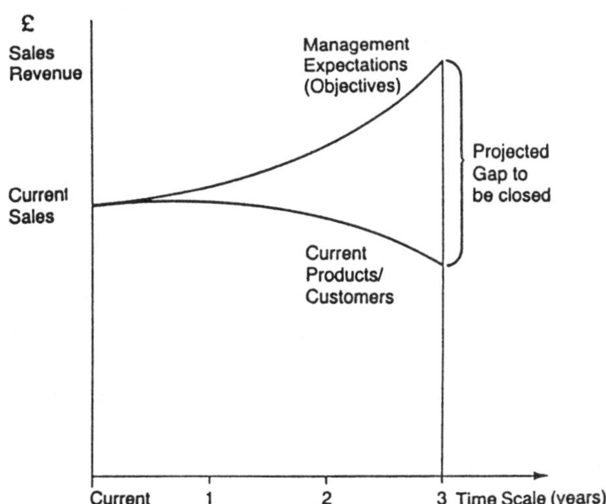

Figure 1.18 Gap analysis

Ansoff proposes options for closing the gap in this Growth Matrix based on a matching of present and new products with present and new markets, shown in Table 1.4. A market penetration strategy using products in present markets involves increasing market share and consumption or use from existing customers. Market development requires the targeting of products into new market segments and converting non-users to customers.

Table 1.4 Ansoff's Growth Vector Matrix

Product / *Market*	*Present*	*New*
Present	Market penetration	Product development
New	Market development	Diversification

Source: D. T. Brownlie and C. K. Bart, *Product and Strategies*, 1985, p. 29.

Product development enables the firm to grow from new products offered to its existing markets. Diversification requires new products for new markets, which may be related or unrelated to the existing business.

The strategic and relevant options will depend upon the size of the gap and the firm's competitive position in its markets. For instance, a high market share, in existing markets, such as Asda's stores' position in the north of England, suggests that growth will be sought from new markets such as the south and from new product ranges.

□ *Strategic Implications*

The product-market growth model has implications for objectives and strategies. Table 1.5 indicates alternative directions for growth from the established business, where market penetration is the current strategy. Depending upon the firm and its environment, product development, market development or a higher risk move to diversification will be pursued. French and German supermarket groups have expanded into other EC markets as their position in their home markets have become saturated. Coca Cola, who for decades followed a policy of market extension, has recently moved along the product development route. BAT industries has diversified away from the original core business of tobacco into a number of unrelated growth industries.

Table 1.5 Using the Ansoff Matrix in the Objective Setting Process

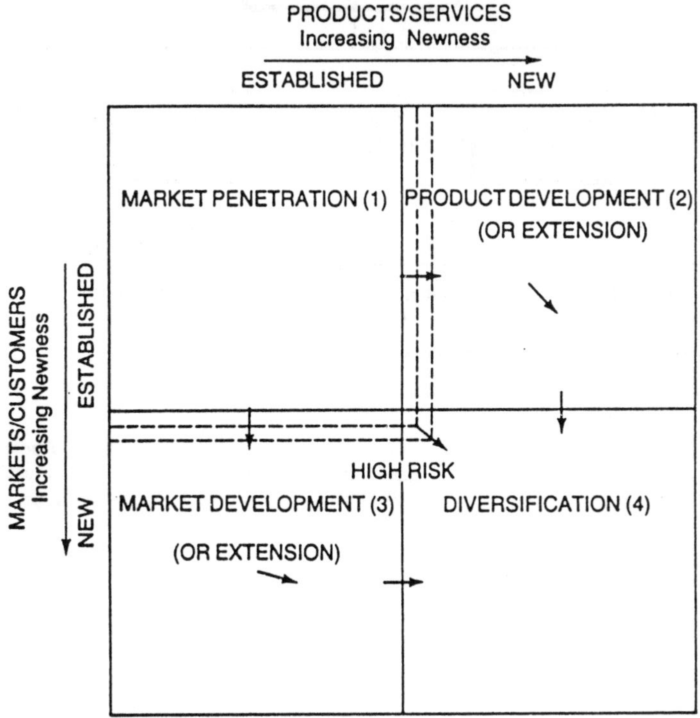

Brownlie[24] suggests that the sales or profit gap or both can be closed by one or a combination of three major strategies – sales growth, productivity improvement and redeployment of capital resources. Figure 1.19 depicts these options.

□ *Practical Application*

Although a simplification of the issues involved, the planning gap and product-market growth concepts are a good starting point for identifying the strategic analysis task and providing broad indicators for strategic direction. It can indicate widely different growth or profit expectations from those that are realistic and therefore highlight problems to be addressed by management.

Sometimes, the gap analysis approach will show that the momentum of present strategies will take sales higher than is desirable given the limited supply capabilities of the firm.

In general, we find that companies have difficulty meeting demand during the rapid growth stage of the life-cycle. The results of customer complaints,

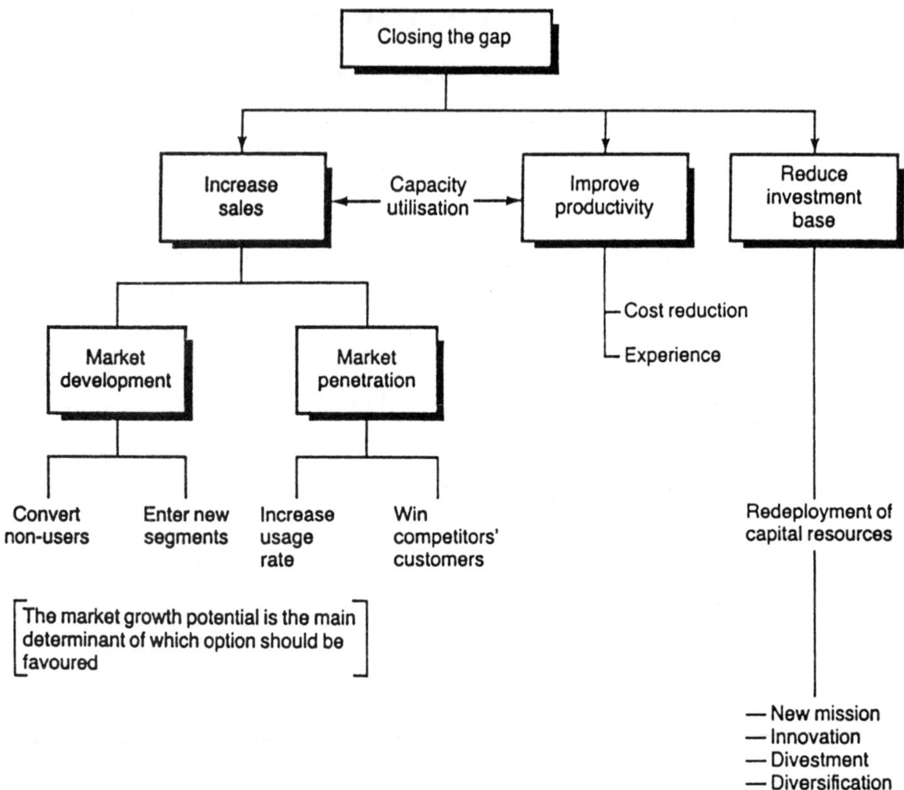

Figure 1.19 Strategy alternatives for closing the gap

Source: D. T. Brownlie and C. K. Bart, *Products and Strategies*, 1985, p. 14.

poor service and decline in quality in an effort to meet demand, weaken the firm's competitive position.

The significance of these concepts is that market growth should be managed in line with capabilities to achieve realistic objectives. Strategic planning should, therefore involve managing opportunities and capabilities to meet objectives. The setting of appropriate objectives is just as important as selecting appropriate strategies.

■ Strategy Experience Models – The PIMS Model

The basic premise underlying the pooling of business experience is that the conduct of a large series of strategy experiments on companies in a similar competitive position will provide guidelines on successful and unsuccessful strategies that will be useful in evaluating options under review by a company.

Also, the analysis of strategic experience of businesses under different market, competitive and operating conditions, helps to identify the strategic factors that primarily determine profitability. Statistical analysis and computer modelling of the data identify relationships between strategy and performance and provide guidelines for strategic planning. This approach has been adopted by the Strategic Planning Institute in Boston with its PIMS (Profit Impact of Market Strategies) programme, which was initiated in the early seventies.

The PIMS approach seeks guidance from the collective experience of a diverse sample of successful and unsuccessful businesses. Since 1972 it has compiled a data base from more than 450 corporations comprising analysis of over 2800 business units. Statistical analysis and computer modelling of the data base provides member companies, who subscribe to and provide information for PIMS, with strategic guidelines based on pooled experience of many different strategic situations in a diverse range of industries.

Two concepts are essential to the data base:

- The business unit – a division, product line or profit centre.
- The served market – a portion of the total market in which the firm competes.

The PIMS analysis measures changes in the firm's competitive position, the strategies employed to achieve it and the resulting profitability.

Analysis reveals that three sets of factors are persistently influential in affecting business profitability. One set describes competitive position, which includes market share and relative product quality. A second describes the production structure, including investment intensity and productivity of operations. The third reflects the relative attractiveness of the market growth rate and customer characteristics. Together, these variables account for 65 to 70 per cent of the variability in profitability in the sample.

The purpose of the PIMS project is to apply this experience to specific strategic questions. These questions include:

- What rate of cash flow and profit is 'normal' for this type of business, given its market environment, competitive position and the strategy being pursued?
- If the business continues as at present, what market share and profitability performance could be expected in the future?
- How will this performance be affected by a change in the strategy?
- How have other firms in the same industry or in different industries facing the same conditions and similar competitive position performed, given different types of strategies employed?

Answers to these questions can help the strategies to evaluate alternative options under consideration.

The PIMS data base is represented by many different industries, products, markets, and geographic regions. Most of these are located in North America, although about 600 of the 2800 businesses are in the UK, Europe and a scattering of other countries.

□ *PIMS Findings*

This analysis has resulted in observed links between strategy and performance. These general relationships can provide help for managers to understand and predict how strategic choices and market conditions will affect business performance. These are the most common links between strategy and performance:

1 In the long run, the most important factor affecting a business unit's performance is the quality of its products and services, relative to those of competitors.
2 Market share and profitability are strongly related.
3 High investment intensity acts as a powerful drag on profitability.
4 Many so-called dog and question mark businesses generate cash, while many cash cows are dry.
5 Vertical integration is a profitable strategy for some kinds of businesses, but not for others. For small-share businesses, return on investment is highest when the degree of vertical integration is low. For businesses with above-average share positions, return on investment is highest when vertical integration is either low or high.
6 Most of the strategic factors that boost return on investment also contribute to the long-term value of the business.[25]

Some selected PIMS findings are shown in Table 1.6. These findings provide some empirical guidelines supporting the use of the Market Attractiveness – Competitive Position models reviewed earlier.[26] The cash flow implications of investment intensity (measured by investment as a percentage of sales) and marketing intensity (measured by marketing expenses as a percentage of sales) are given an empirical foundation. The strategic importance of market share and product quality in contributing to profitability is identified.

□ *Limitations of PIMS*

Criticisms of PIMS range from definitions of variables, data collection methods and data accuracy, to the non-causal relationships found between variables. Many of these criticisms are valid and should alert the user to treat the findings with care. The PIMS type of analysis can give the user a false sense of accuracy and predictive power. It should be viewed as another source of ideas for strategic planning to be put beside the strategist's own experience, judgement and analysis.

Table 1.6 Some PIMS Findings

Attractiveness of Industry – Market Environment
Market share is most profitable in vertically integrated industries.
R & D spending is most profitable in mature, slow growth markets.
A narrow product range in the early or middle stages of the life cycle is less profitable than at maturity.
Capacity utilisation is important when investment intensity (investment/value added) is high.
High relative market share (> 75 per cent) improves cash flow; high growth (> 7 per cent) decreases it.
Competitive Position
High relative market share (> 62 per cent) and low investment intensity (< 80 per cent) generate cash; low share (< 26 per cent) and high investment intensity (> 120 per cent) results in a net use of cash.
High R & D spending (> 37 per cent sales) depresses ROI when market share is low (< 26 per cent).
High marketing spending (> 11 per cent sales) depresses ROI when market share is low.
High R & D and marketing spending depresses ROI.
A rapid rate of new product introductions in fast growing markets depresses ROI.
Capital Structure
Low or medium industry growth (< 9 per cent) coupled with low investment intensity (< 80 per cent) produces cash; high growth (> 9 per cent) and high investment intensity (> 120 per cent) is a cash drain.
A low level of new product introductions and low investment intensity (< 80 per cent) produces cash.
High investment intensity and high marketing intensity (> 11 per cent sales) drains cash.
Harvesting when investment intensity is low produces cash.
Building market share when investment intensity is high uses cash.

Source: D. T. Brownlie and C. K. Bart, *Products and Strategies*, 1985, p. 47.

□ *Practical Application*

The argument that the structure of an industry, the competitive position of the business, its costs/margins/investment structure and the competitive strategies it employs have a fundamental impact on profitability, has strong intuitive appeal.

Practitioners know that a dominant market leader position in a growing market with attractive margins and moderate investment requirements, will bring high profitability. Alternatively, a business ranked third or fourth in competitive position in a mature market with low margins, frequently yields low profitability or losses.

PIMS demonstrates that these structural attributes have a significant effect on business profitability and that firms should seek competitive structures and positions that provide them with a profit advantage.

The specific PIMS models and strategic relationships are useful in providing a 'reality test' for the competitive strategies under consideration. They answer questions such as:

- Does this strategy make sense in the light of the experience of others in a similar competitive structure and position?
- Are sufficient resources committed to achieve the desired competitive position and profitability?
- Are the business objectives unrealistic?
- What type of competitive pattern and future competitive structure is likely if this strategy is adopted?

These are important issues to raise, and PIMS analysis helps strategic thinking in these areas.

Industry Structure Models and Competitive Strategy

Micro-economic theory focuses on market structure and competitive position as determinants of competitive behaviour. The significance of monopolistic and oligopolistic structures, in shaping competitive strategies, is recognised by economists in their theories of competition.

Developments by Michael Porter extend this thinking substantially and provide a practical analytical framework for developing competitive strategies involving the structural analysis of industries.[27] He identifies the main structural forces driving industry competitors – industry competition, supplier and customer concentration, availability of substitutes and the threat to entry of new competitors – and suggests that industry profit is affected by these forces.

Porter indicates that the purpose of competitive strategy is to find a position where the company can best defend itself against these forces or influence them in its favour. He studies different industry structures at different stages of evolution and provides guidelines for competitive strategy. Porter goes on to identify the elements of a business that can be used to create and sustain competitive advantage. He considers defensive and offensive strategies for maintaining or improving the firm's market position.

This type of analysis is useful in assessing strategic opportunities and competitive threats and is developed in Chapters 2, 3, 4 and 5, where particular application is found in the case studies presented.

In order to influence the structure of an industry or market, it is necessary to identify the important elements of its structure and seek to affect the competitive forces that determine profitability.

□ *The Porter Model*

Porter[28] suggests that five major forces drive industry competition. These are shown in Figure 1.20. He proposes that the structure of the industry itself, its suppliers and its buyers have a major influence on the evolution of the industry and its profit potential. The threat of substitutes and new entrants also influence the appropriate strategies to be adopted.

The implication is that the competitor should influence the balance of forces through strategic moves, thereby strengthening the firm's position. Alternatively, the strategist might reposition the firm so that its capabilities provide the best defence against the array of competitive forces. A further approach is to anticipate shifts in the factors underlying the forces and respond to them, thus exploiting change by choosing a strategy appropriate to the new competitive balance before competitors recognise it.

A vast range of structural elements may potentially affect these competitive forces. In any particular industry, a small number of factors will be relevant. In the compressed cylinder gas market, for example, the strategic elements for management by BOC, the market leader, are the distribution system, the

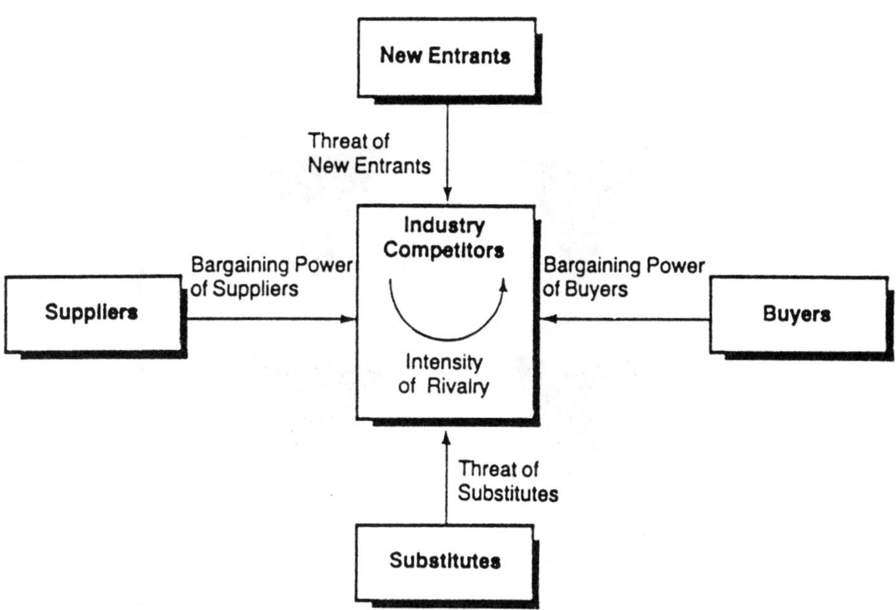

Figure 1.20 The five competitive forces and elements of industry structure[29]

Source: M. E. Porter, *Competitive Strategy*, 1980, p. 4.

fragmentation of the customer base and the control of cylinder production and supply.

Evolution of an industry is also affected by the life-cycle stage of its main markets. The large body of life-cycle literature provides marketing strategy guidelines for competitors at each stage. During the growth stage, it is appropriate for market leaders to adopt offensive strategies, whereas in maturity and decline, defensive strategies may be more appropriate. Effective strategies for smaller competitors, however, are different. Where the real opportunities lie for a competitor to restructure the market, will depend upon the industry value chain and the contribution of each of the companies at different levels of the supply/distribution/customer system. The value chain concept is explained in Chapter 4.

Porter examined industries in different stages of evolution, from emerging product-markets to declining ones. Porter considers that in the long term, the extent to which the firm is able to create a defendable position in an industry is a major determinant of the success with which it will out-perform its competitors. He proposes generic strategies by means of which a firm can develop a competitive advantage and create a defendable position:

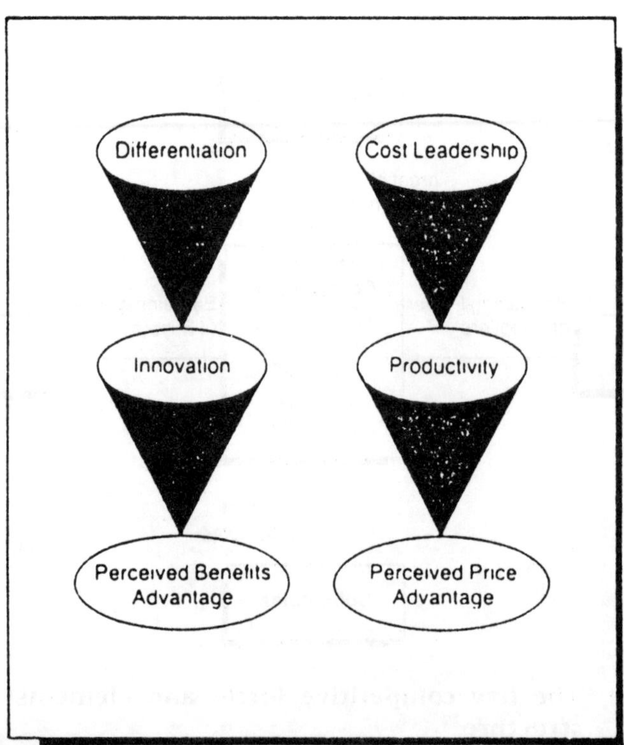

Figure 1.21 Strategic alternatives

Overall cost leadership: aggressive pursuit of an industry-wide lowest cost position relative to competitors.

Differentiation: development of distinctive abilities that are perceived industry-wide as unique. These may be along several dimensions such as product quality, distribution, after-sales service. In marketing terms, this is known as differentiated marketing.

Focus: concentrated effort aimed at securing a competitive advantage in a particular market segment or niche. In marketing terms, this is referred to as concentrated marketing.

In terms of product–market evolution, a firm may change its generic strategy over time by moving from a focused strategy to an industry-wide strategy of either cost leadership or differentiation. Alternatively, a firm may adopt a cost leadership strategy, which changes over time to an emphasis on differentiation.

Figure 1.21 shows the alternative strategic options and Figure 1.22 the trade-offs that occur between differentiation and productivity gains through cost leadership.

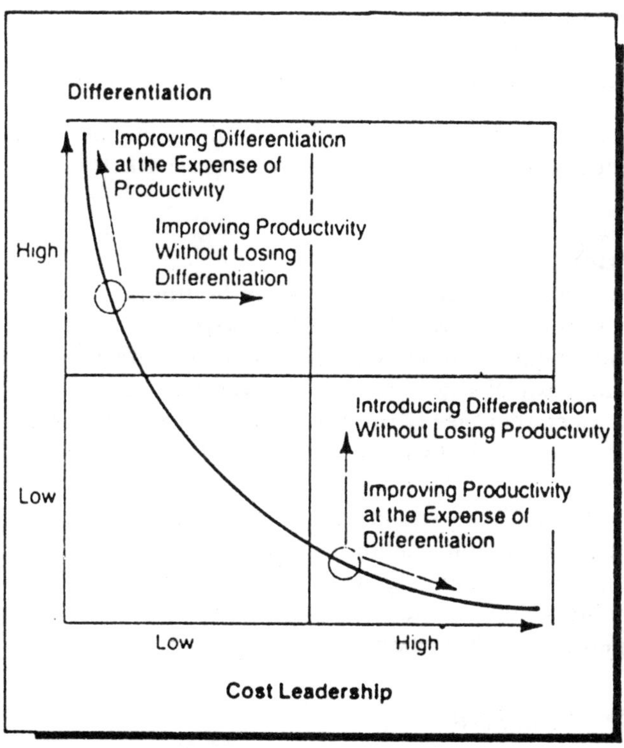

Figure 1.22 Strategic directions

□ *Cost Leadership versus Differentiation*

Cost Leadership

Cost leadership is one of two generic strategies in which a firm sets out to become the low-cost producer in its industry.

Policy choices that tend to have the greatest impact on cost include:

- product configuration, performance and features;
- mix and variety of products offered;
- level of service provided; and
- channels employed (eg. few, more efficient dealers rather than many small ones).

The primary focus of the cost leadership strategy is to use low costs as a route to profitability. It also, however, provides the option of competing on price, should this be necessary.

Although the advantage of a cost leadership strategy is that it provides a source of competitive advantage, particularly for market leaders who can use economies of scale, it is usually not appropriate in markets where:

- there is product parity;
- the leader is already heavily committed to an extensive product range; and
- service and channel distribution are critical factors of competitive advantage.

Although cost management and reduction should be pursued where possible, it should not necessarily be the strategic focus for market leaders in declining markets.

Differentiation

In a differentiation strategy, a firm seeks to be unique in its industry along some dimensions that are widely valued by buyers.

In the gases industry, some segments of which are in decline, BOC has selected product availability as the key differentiator and has positioned itself uniquely to meet that need. In similar industries such as auto parts and accessories, service and distribution are vital differentiators in declining markets.

Product parity usually exists between competitors, and differentiation occurs on availability, service, information provision and price.

In adopting a differentiation strategy, a leader will aim for cost parity with its major competitors, but should reduce costs only in areas that do not affect favourably perceived differentiation.

□ *Coverage versus Focus*

The degree of segmentation of the market and the size of the largest segments, together with the leader's competitive strengths, will determine whether a strategy of coverage, or one of focus, is required for leadership and dominance of the market. Usually, a leader will need coverage of the main market segments and a strategy may be adopted to attempt to combine some segments with the same product offering. This strategy of counter-segmentation may be viable in declining markets as customers decline to a hard core of users. Selection of narrow or wide market coverage forms an important part of competitive strategy. It determines the market scope to be targeted by the business.

□ *Sustainable Competitive Advantage*

The task of competitive strategy is to develop, maintain or defend the firm's competitive position based on a sustainable competitive advantage. The advantage needs to be sustainable because of the considerable investment required to achieve it. Consider the following competitive advantages and their investment requirements:

- the superior product engineering and perception of product quality achieved by Mercedes Benz;
- the brand identity and preference for Coca Cola and Fosters lager;
- the low-cost advantage achieved by Aldi Stores and British Telecom;
- the superior knowledge of the fast foods business held by McDonald's restaurants;
- the scale advantages achieved by Cadbury-Schweppes in the European market.

These represent elements of sustainable competitive advantage developed by these businesses over many years.

□ *Market Structure and Competitive Position*

A firm's competitive position and the market structure in which it operates, acts as a pervasive influence and constraint on its competitive market strategies.

□ *Market Structure*

Most businesses operate in oligopoly market structures defined by a situation in which supply to the market is controlled by a few large producers, the remaining supply being accounted for by small firms. There are a number of sub-structures of oligopoly, however, which are relevant at the product/market level of competitive strategy. These are:

- monopoly dominance;
- joint dominance (duopoly);

- oligopoly dominance; and
- equal oligopoly.

Monopoly dominance refers to a market structure in which one firm has a very large share of the market (ie. share of total industry sales), while all other oligopoly firms each have a much smaller share. In this type of structure, a single firm has such clear share dominance over other firms, that it can, if it so desires, exercise monopoly-like control over both the market and its competitors' strategies. This is particularly evident in price changes. In a market structure of this type, the dominant firm will tend to lead changes in the general level of product prices, with other oligopoly firms following these changes. This is true in the European airline industry, in which the principal national carriers have held a monopoly for decades.

Joint dominance or duopoly refers to a structure in which two companies jointly dominate a market, while all other competitors, as a group, have a small market share. Two types of duopoly dominance occur in practice, one in which the two firms have approximately equal market shares, the other in which one firm has a distinct market share advantage. In both cases, the two dominant firms primarily react to each other's strategies. Either one of the two may be price leader, or it may alternate between them, with other competitors likely to follow changes. The two dominant firms jointly exercise the same types of influences on small competitors, as does the dominant firm operating in a monopoly dominance structure. This type of structure is typified in the UK telecommunications market with British Telecom and Mercury as the principal protagonists.

In *oligopoly dominance,* the dominant firm has a much smaller share advantage over its next competitor than is evident in a monopoly dominance structure. In such cases, the dominant firm's position is more easily challenged by other oligopolists. Nevertheless, it still remains in a position in which it can lead price changes and limit the flexibility of its competitors, particularly through the use of the price variable. The UK car rental market exhibits this structure, in which Budget has a clear share lead.

Equal oligopoly refers to a market structure in which no firm has clear dominance. Characteristically, two or more competitors have similar market shares, which are not sufficient to constitute duopoly or joint dominance. In such market structures, price leadership and other forms of competitive behaviour are much less predictable. It is impossible to arrive at valid generalisations on *a priori* grounds. This market structure exists in the European oriented polypropylene market, in which ICI, Coutaulds, Mobil, Moplefan and others, hold roughly equal shares. Likewise, in the European chocolate confectionery market, the leader Mars holds only a marginal lead. The statistics given in Table 1.7 show an oligopolistic situation both in the UK and in Europe overall.

Meanwhile, the rise of European media outlets such as satellite broadcasting, will change the nature of this and many other markets and a critical mass of

Table 1.7 European Chocolate Confectionery Market Shares (per cent by sales volume)

COMPANY	*UK*	*AUSTRIA*	*BELGIUM*	*FRANCE*	*ITALY*	*NTHLDS*	*SWTZLND*	*GRMNY*	*TOTAL*
Mars	24	4	6	11	1	23	9	22	17
Suchard	2	73	82	13	—	—	17	15	13
Rowntree	26	—	2	17	—	13	—	3	11
Ferrero	2	—	5	6	34	—	—	16	10
Cadbury	30	—	—	8	—	—	—	—	9
Nestlé	3	5	3	10	5	—	17	8	9

Source: Henderson Crosthwaite 1990

Note: Rowntree = Nestlé in UK and Germany

product range will be needed to justify distribution costs and to fund new product launches. Also, the large-scale restructuring of the European chocolate confectionery market is expected to drive costs down and to facilitate even heavier promotional spending on brands.

In addition to those oligopoly structures, a fragmented structure, where market share is divided between many competitors, appears in some markets. In the quantity surveying market, in the UK, no firm holds more than about a 5 per cent market share.

Competitive Position

A firm's competitive position, usually measured by its market share, is also an important determinant of the types of strategies it adopts. The Boston Consulting Group recognises this in their product portfolio theory. The BCG growth-share model views products in terms of their market share relative to the largest shareholder in the market – that is, a measure of relative share.

The relevant measure of position is in terms of dominance. A firm may be in one of three possible positions in the market.

Individual dominance: in which a firm has a significantly higher market share than that of its closest competitor.

Joint dominance: in which a firm and one competitor have approximately equal market shares, which are significantly higher than that of their nearest competitor.

Non-dominance: in which the company has a significantly lower share level than one or more dominant competitors in the market.

Its position, identified in these terms, indicates its relative market power and its capability in managing the market, the competition, the direction the market takes and profitability in the market.

□ *Limitations of Industry Structure Analysis*

The main limitation of this type of analysis, in common with other models discussed, is that it does not specifically take account of the human and behavioural dimensions of competitive strategy. It assumes that competitors will behave rationally with a profit motive and that they understand the dynamics of the market and competition and the consequences of their own strategies. This is not so in many industries. In the building equipment hire industry in the late 1980s, there were many competitors operating at prices below cost at a time when capacity was falling well short of demand. Logic would suggest that prices, margins and profits could all be increased in these conditions – to everyone's benefit in the industry.

□ *Practical Significance*

Industry structure and competitive position impose constraints on the range of viable strategies available to any competitor and their results. Competitive strategies can and do change the structure and position of players in the industry, however, and the objective is to adopt strategies that provide a sustainable advantage to the business within the scope of changing structure and position.

■ Integration of Concepts and Models

Each of the models and analytical tools reviewed in this chapter provides a contribution to strategic formulation. Indeed, there are links between them that provide a more integrated picture of strategic analysis.

■ Product Life-Cycle and Competitive Position

Arthur D. Little has linked various competitive positions ranging from dominant to 'weak' with objectives for changing or holding those positions at different stages of the product life-cycle. Table 1.8 summarises these. Brownlie focuses on two competitive positions: market leader (with dominant market share) and market follower. Guidelines are provided for growth, maturity and decline phases, shown in Table 1.9.

■ Portfolio, Product Life-Cycle and PIMS

Table 1.10 indicates the characteristics of strategies suggested by the portfolio approach and their relationship with the product life-cycle.

Table 1.8 Guidelines for Various Product Life-Cycle Stages and Competitive Positions

	Embryonic	*Growing*	*Mature*	*Aging*
Dominance	All-out push for share	Hold position	Hold position	Hold position
	Hold position	Hold share	Grow with industry	
Strong	Attempt to improve position	Attempt to improve position	Hold position	Hold position or Harvest
	All-out push for share	Push for share	Grow with industry	
Favourable	Selective or all-out push for share	Attempt to improve position	Custodial or maintenance	Harvest
	Selectively attempt to improve position	Selective push for share	Find niche and attempt to protect	Phased withdrawal
Tenable	Selectively push for position	Find niche and protect it	Find niche and hang on or Phased withdrawal	Phased withdrawal or Abandon
Weak	Up or Out	Turnaround or Abandon	Turnaround or Phased withdrawal	Abandon

Source: G. S. Day, *Analysis for Strategic Market Decisions*, 1986, p. 212.

It is important here not to confuse the stage of the market life-cycle with the stage of the individual product's evolution.

Question mark products may be introduced during any phase of market growth of the product category life-cycle. Cash cows may exist in markets that show significant growth, are static or even declining. 'Dog' products may be declining when various segments of a mature market show growth prospects. The BCG model shows the evolution of a firm's own product from introduction through to maturity.

The PIMS findings tend to support the underlying concepts of growth-share, product life-cyle and the effect of learning experience on costs and profit margins. Figure 1.23 shows some of these findings.

Table 1.9 Competitive Position and Life-Cycle Stage

Competitive position	*Growth*	*Product life-cycle-stage* *Maturity*	*Decline*
Market leader (Dominant market share)	Build market share; reduce prices to discourage competition; develop primary demand and channel strength.	Maintain market share; advertise for brand loyalty; product differentiation; price with competitors.	Harvest market share; maximise cash flow; reduce product expenditures such as advertising and selling
Market follower	Invest in Research and Development advertising and distribution to increase market share; concentrate on a particular market segment; advertise for positioning.	Maintain or reduce market share; price to penetrate; reduce costs below the market leaders.	No product expenditure; withdraw from the market.

Source: D. T. Brownlie and C. K. Bart, *Products and Strategies*, 1985, p. 24.

Table 1.10 Portfolio Position and Life-Cycle Stage

Product Classification	*Life-Cycle Stage*	*Product Stage*	*Strategy Guideline*
Question Mark	Growth	Introduction	Investment
Star	Growth	Growth	Maintenance
Cash Cow	Maturity	Maturity	Harvesting
Dog	Maturity	Decline	Withdrawal

■ Strategic Position and Generic Strategies for Competitive Advantage

Four different strategic positions are shown in Figure 1.24. These are based on:

- competitive advantage in terms of differentiation or cost leadership; and
- low or high market coverage.

□ *Low Advantage in Cost or Differentiation and Low Market Coverage*

Here, the business is in a commodity marketing situation, where products are homogeneous, the market structure is fragmented and price competition

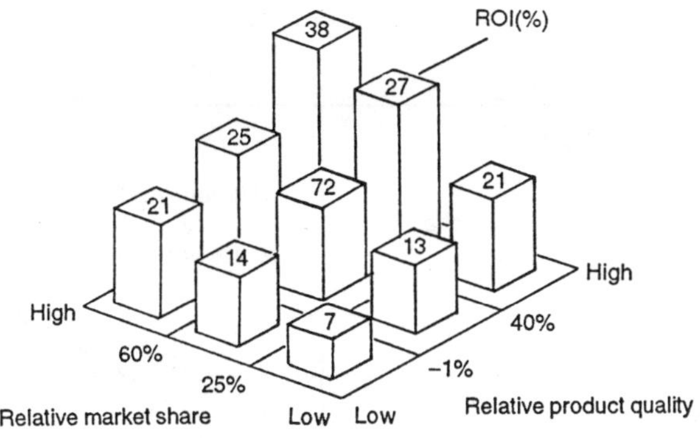

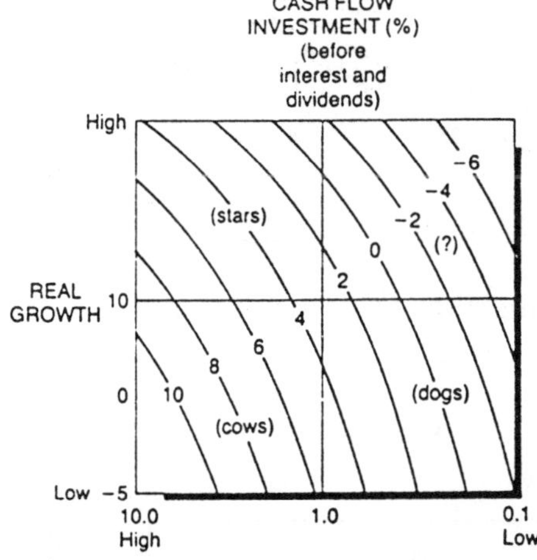

CASH FLOW RATE CONTOUR LINES FOR THE GROWTH-SHARE MATRIX

Market share

13% 27%

Stage in life-cycle			
Early	6	20	33
Middle	11	20	29
Late	15	19	27

Figure 1.23 Portfolio, life-cycle and market share

Source: G. S. Day, *Analysis for Strategic Market Decisions*, 1986, pp. 162, 163 and 187.

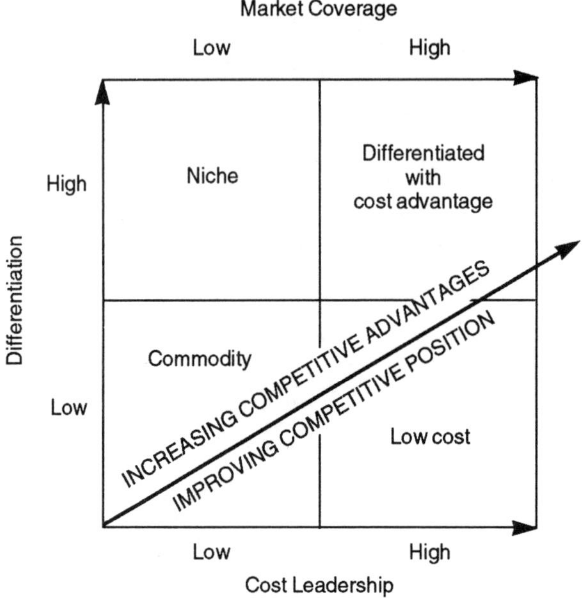

Figure 1.24 Improving competitive position

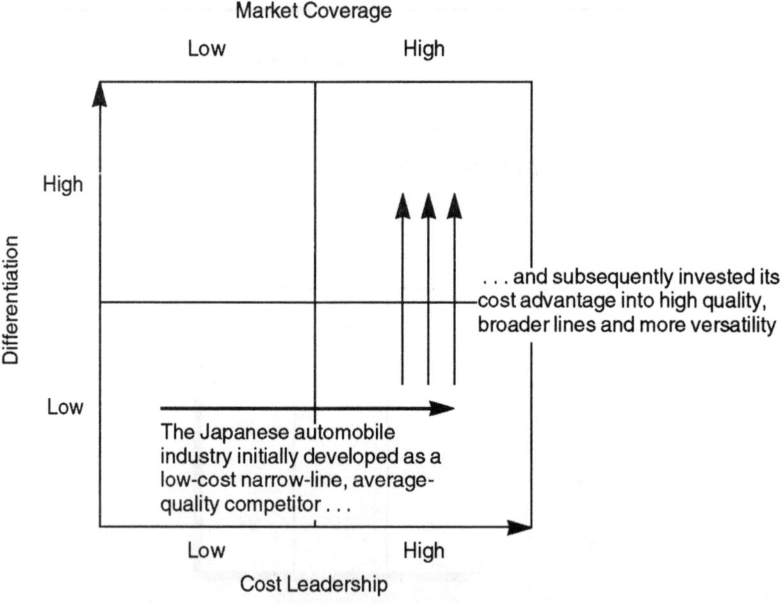

Figure 1.25 The path to competitive position taken by Japanese car manufacturers

features. Profit is usually low. It is desirable, if possible to change this position, unless a cost leadership position can be achieved with resulting market share and profit gains.

☐ *Cost Advantage, Low Differentiation and High Market Coverage*

This is a desirable position if the cost advantage can be protected and sustained. The volume and market share resulting from a high market coverage should yield profit.

☐ *Differentiation Advantage, Comparative Costs and Low Market Coverage*

This is a niche position, where emphasis is necessary to protect and improve differentiation. It is viable for small competitors and for large competitors in large volume segments. Share of the overall market is relatively small.

☐ *Differentiation and Cost Advantages with High Market Coverage*

This is the most profitable strategic position, because the market leader has cost, value and volume advantages over its competitors and can command a price premium, with higher margins than its competitors. This position is dominant in market share terms.

For large companies seeking dominance, competitive strategies should be directed at moving towards this strategic position shown in Figure 1.24. There are, however, different paths from which to choose. The Japanese car manufacturers, such as Toyota, have moved from an imitation/commodity position to cost leadership, then to differentiation with cost advantages as shown in Figure 1.25. There is evidence that smaller companies, such as Honda, have now developed niche strategies aimed at competing in specific market segments. McDonald's started as one of many in the fast foods hamburger business, moved to a niche position with product and service superiority, and then to a high-volume and market share position, gaining cost advantages while maintaining differentiation (see Figure 1.26).

■ Competitive Position

A firm's competitive position is fundamental to the selection of competitive marketing strategies. In this book, a broad view is taken of competitive position.

In essence, the factors involved in assessing competitive position are all those which have an impact on market performance, such as sales revenue, share and company/brand image and on profit performance, such as investment

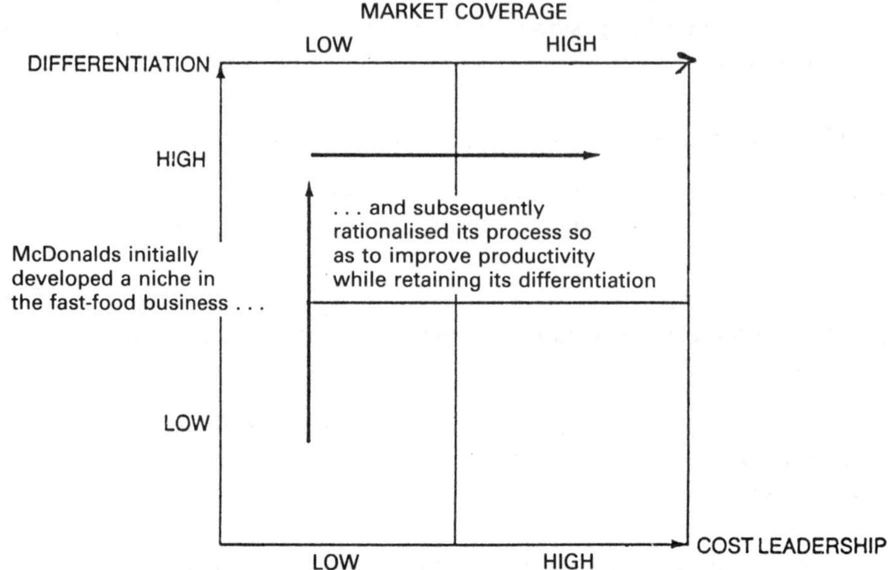

Figure 1.26 The path to competitive position in McDonald's

levels, costs, margins, prices and productivity and can be evaluated against major competitors.

A number of dimensions are important in practice when assessing competitive position and deciding upon strategies to maintain or change position.

■ Market Positioning

This refers to the relevant market's recognition and perception of a firm's position in the market – what it stands for and what its offerings provide relative to those of its competitors'. For example, in the copier market in Europe, Xerox is perceived to be industry leader (the standards setter) and provider of a wide range of high-quality, reliable products supported by dependable after-sales service. Companies and their products become positioned in the market's collective mind on a variety of intangible and functional dimensions, which are used by customers to distinguish them.

Market research techniques are now available to identify corporate and product positionings in a firm's target markets. Perceptions of quality, range, availability, image and other relevant dimensions are measured for competing firms. Positioning studies are used to focus a firm's attention on what target customers believe to be important, to improve areas of perceived relative weakness and to consolidate perceived advantages.

This type of analysis provides direction to improve or reinforce market positioning.

Product and Market Coverage

An assessment of the extent of product and market coverage, points to opportunities for widening or narrowing product range and segment spread. Table 1.11 shows the relative coverage of two competing firms.

Firm A has broad coverage of all except one market segment and has the full range of variants, except in segments one and three. Firm B specialises only in segment 5, with a full range.

Table 1.11 Product-Market Coverage

		Market Segments				
		1	2	3	4	5
	1	A	A	A	A	B
Product	2	A	A	A	A	B
Variants	3	A	A	A	A	B
	4	A	A	A	A	B
	5		A		A	B

Innovator or Follower

The market stance of innovator or follower is determined by the extent and timing of the introduction of new products. Competitors frequently take a deliberate decision on whether to be innovator or follower and structure their research and development functions and marketing departments accordingly. The advantages of being first into a market are well known, but the risks can also be high and the costs of failure great. Long-term competitive position can be strengthened by a record of successful innovations.

Strategic Positions in the Market

The market leader has the position of being first in the customer's mind. Kleenex with facial tissues, Hoover with vacuum cleaners, Heinz with baby food, IBM with computers, Budget in rental cars, Xerox with copiers. This, in the long term, is supported by the highest market share.

In some markets, there are two, or even three leaders, characterised as joint leadership. Other positions in the market are the high-share flanker, who poses as a serious challenger to the market leader, and the remaining positions belong to specialists who focus on market niches.

In many European markets, there is only room for two large mainstream competitors, a leader and an alternative, and the rest are niche competitors, specialising in narrow segments of the market. Viable positions in the market become strategic because they provide a basis for building, maintaining or successfully defending competitive position. These strategic positions are:

- market leader;
- market challenger;
- market follower;
- market specialist.

The general characteristics of each viable strategic position are shown in Table 1.12.

The size and structure of the market and the economics of supply will determine how many viable competitors can exist. For example, the British life assurance industry has hundreds of competitors – a market leader, a challenger and about twenty followers and the rest specialists. In the British domestic airlines industry, however, there is only a handful of competitors. The market size, structure and characteristics provide opportunities for a range of market positionings based on quality, service, price and image attributes.

Table 1.12 Strategic Positions in the Market

Market Leader	
Largest market share Perceived as industry leader Leads industry moves	Covers mainstream market Maintains share Has the largest profit Protects its profit base Major impact on the market
Market Challenger	
No. 2 or 3 in share Perceived as an alternative to leader Innovative and aggressive Seeking leadership	Covers mainstream market Increases share Investing for future profit Major impact on the market
Market Follower	
A significant share Adequate quality lower priced alternative Quick to follow industry moves	Covers largest segments of the market Holds or increases share Cost advantages Limited impact on the market
Market Specialist	
Large share of a small segment Small share of overall market Perceived as a specialist	Specialises in a market niche Holds share Small, flexible and responsive Little impact on the overall market

The relevance of these strategic positions to competitive marketing strategy is to be able to identify what strategic position a company has, then develop strategies to defend or inforce that position, or change it.

■ Market Structure and Shares

The market structure and shares of individual competitors are important dimensions of competitive position, because they set the scope within which change can take place. Table 1.13 indicates a typical range of structures and share positions found in European markets.

The structure and share positions provide some guidance for formulating competitive marketing strategies. In certain conditions, such as a mature market, the dominant leader in a monopoly dominance structure may want to adopt strategies to defend its share leadership and its overall competitive position.

One of the leaders in a joint dominance structure may adopt a leadership strategy to attain clear-cut market leadership. A niche competitor may want to adopt a growth strategy to strengthen its position in one or two segments of the market or to be a leading force in the market.

■ Profitability and Resources

This dimension of competitive position is internal to the company, but should be assessed in relation to competitors' profitability and resources. It flags the company's ability or otherwise to fund and continue support for its strategy in relation to competitors.

Table 1.13 Market Structure and Share Positions

Market structure	Monopoly dominance (one dominates)	Joint dominance (two dominate)	Equal oligopoly (three or more equal share)	Fragmented structure
Market share positions	• Dominant leader (e.g. 50 per cent) • Large non-dominant (e.g. 25 per cent) • Small niche competitors (e.g. 5 per cent)	• Two leaders in share terms (e.g. 40 per cent) • Specialist niche competitors (e.g. 5 per cent)	• Three or more substantial shareholders (e.g. 25 per cent) • Specialist niche competitors (e.g. 5 per cent)	• Market share spread between many competitors (e.g. 5 per cent)

■ Internal Source of Competitive Advantage

Elements such as cost structure, specific skills, responsiveness and other internal characteristics that affect success in the industry, also form another dimension of competitive position. Frequently, as part of a competitive strategy, a business must act on costs, know-how or factors which make the company more market responsive, to enable it to improve competitive position. When Lord King joined British Airways as Chairman in the early 1980s, for example, he realised that his first priority was to get costs and quality into line before marketing could have any impact on the business.

These dimensions of competitive position have quantitative components (market share, profit, resources) and qualitative ones (market positioning, coverage, responsiveness, know-how). The task of competitive marketing strategy is to improve the quality of competitive position and reduce the risk of disaster. Often, this will require action on many or all of the competitive position dimensions. Although there may be a trade-off between profit and strength of competitive position in the short-term, while the firm wants to remain as a strong contender in the market, long-term profitability will be tied to a strong and defendable competitive position.

In most markets, there is room for a market leader, a differentiated number two, a substantial low price positioned competitor, and niche specialists.

■ Competitive Strategies

In practice, an almost infinite number of variations in competitive strategy exist, because of the multi-faceted aspects to be dealt with when changing or defending competitive position and the vast array of different market and competitive conditions existing at any point in time.

In considering competitive position from a strategic point of view, however, there are four main directions which competitive strategy can take:

- developing and building;
- maintaining and holding;
- defending; and
- withdrawing.

The fourth direction, withdrawal, involves harvesting and phased divestment strategies in which marketing's role is to maximise customer goodwill and migrate customers to other products, if that is applicable.

In reality, companies adopt a sequence of strategies that are dependent upon their objectives, competitive position and market and industry conditions.

Competitive strategies for building, maintaining and defending competitive position are addressed according to four market positions of firms:

- dominant position – market leader;
- position of joint dominance shared with a competitor – joint leaders;
- a growing force and substantial share – challenger or follower;
- a growing niche position involving dominance of a narrow segment–market specialist.

This book is organised around these four fundamental competitive positions and a chapter, each with a number of sections, addresses aspects of each position.

Each of these four chapters is organised around the four segments of the Porter matrix as follows:

- *Low cost, high differentiation.* This position has a number of variants, such as: dominant position – market leader; joint dominance shared with a competitor – joint leader.
- *Low cost, low differentiation.* Examples are provided showing why this is a difficult strategy to sustain and why it sometimes leads to failure.
- *High cost, low differentiation.* This is obviously a 'failure' strategy. Examples will be provided showing how some companies slide into this box through neglect.
- *High cost, high differentiation.* This, too, can be a dangerous strategy unless the guidelines provided are followed.

Case histories will illustrate several variants of each position and will demonstrate appropriate and inappropriate strategies for developing, maintaining and defending competitive advantage. It will be clear from these case histories that not only are they not mutually exclusive, but also that companies move from box to box.

The remainder of this book is organised around these four fundamental competitive positions as illustrated in Figure 1.27. Four chapters, each with a number of sections, addresses aspects of each position.

The first case history in this book concerns the radiator market in Europe. It describes a British company operating principally in the UK which has been overtaken by a Pan-European competitor. This case is included because it is typical of the dilemma facing thousands of organisations and illustrates that such firms can pursue a number of the options described in Figure 1.24 which is repeated here as Figure 1.27.

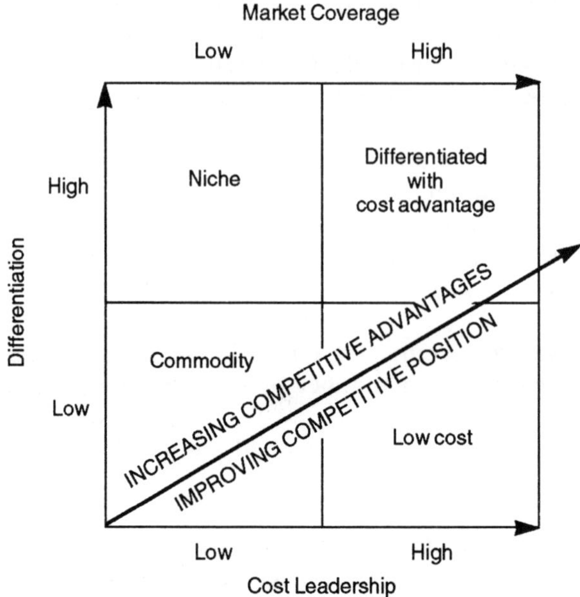

Figure 1.27 Improving competitive position

■ Case Study 1: Myson Radiator Division

■ Background

The Radiator Division's origins go back to the mid 1950s when Bob Myson established the Myson Group based in Ongar, Essex. The Company developed a range of complementary heating products enjoying both growth and financial success, eventually going public in 1969. The Company suffered a downturn in profitability in the late 1970s combined with a loss in confidence in the management, and in 1981 an independent financial group purchased Myson for £15m. This move was followed by a period of rationalisation, coupled with rigorous financial management. After some initial consolidation, following this change of ownership, there was a dramatic improvement in the profitability of the Company. Such was its growing power, that in 1986, Myson bought the heating division of Thorn EMI, a major competitor. This purchase was accomplished for £40m and had the effect of tripling Myson's turnover, virtually overnight.

In 1990, the Company was acquired by Blue Circle Industries for a figure approaching £200m. It now fits into its new corporate structure as shown in Figure 1.28.

The Radiator Division has two manufacturing plants, one at Gateshead and the other in Hull, employing 245 and 97 operators respectively. These, together with the administration staff, (38), give the Company a total work force of 380.

This case study describes how the Myson Radiator Division is challenged to re-appraise its strategic marketing, in order to remain a key player in its field.

■ Radiator Manufacture

There are two basic methods of producing radiators for heating purposes. One is to bring the two rectangular sides of the radiator together and join them by seam welding around all four edges. This method can be adapted for production runs so that, in effect, a continuous length of radiator can be made from feeder rolls of steel, and subsequently 'chopped up' to the desired lengths. However, radiators made this way show the characteristic seam weld on the highly visible top edge.

This is the production process used at Hull, where Myson's product is known as Supaline.

At Gateshead, the radiators are produced by the other method, from one sheet of metal which is folded double. Since the bend is at the top, only the two sides and the bottom edge have to be welded together. Therefore, radiators

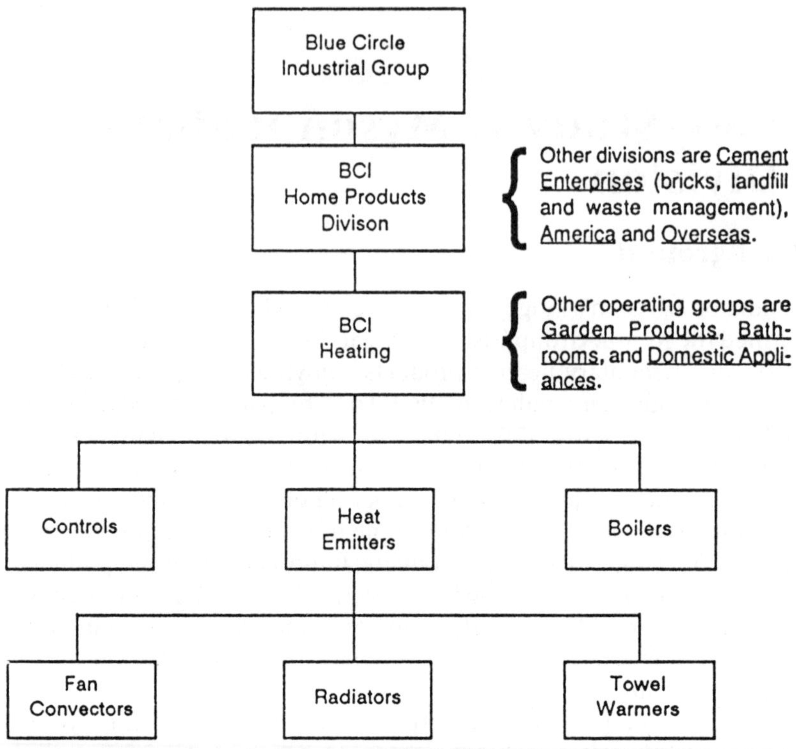

Figure 1.28 Schematic diagram of corporate structure of Blue Circle Industrial Group

made in this way have a non-welded, 'round top' which is claimed to have a significantly higher customer appeal, compared to the 'seam top' alternative. However, this manufacturing process is more labour intensive than that at Hull.

As in most industries, there are some 'tricks of the trade' which are learned with experience. However, the technology and materials used in the manufacture of steel panel radiators could not be described as breaking new ground. They are tried, tested, and largely predictable.

■ The Radiator Market

The UK radiator market has, for a number of years, enjoyed sustained growth. For something like 25 years it has been a buoyant and profitable trading arena.

However, as more and more households have central heating installed, so the potential market for radiators reduces. Current estimates (1993) are that

72 per cent of domestic properties are now furnished with heating systems, so further market growth can come only from four areas:

1. The remaining 28 per cent – However these are predominantly households in the lower socio-economic groupings and give little cause for optimism.
2. Replacements – Radiators generally have long, trouble-free lives. Replacements and extensions of current systems account for only 8 per cent of total volume sales.
3. New housing – The recession of the early 1990s hit building heavily. The only saving grace is that much of the new building that does take place is tending to be for 'executive style' housing, ie. larger and therefore requiring more radiators.
4. Commercial sector(s) – This is an area never exploited by the Company.

Taken together, the first three areas offer little prospect of growth comparable to earlier years. Indeed, the domestic market could, with some accuracy, be described as reaching maturity (see Figure 1.29).

It can be seen from this graph that the UK radiator market peaked in 1988. Equally, over the next few years the total forecast demand is predicted to be in the order of 5.5 million radiators per year.

The commercial market would be a step into the unknown.

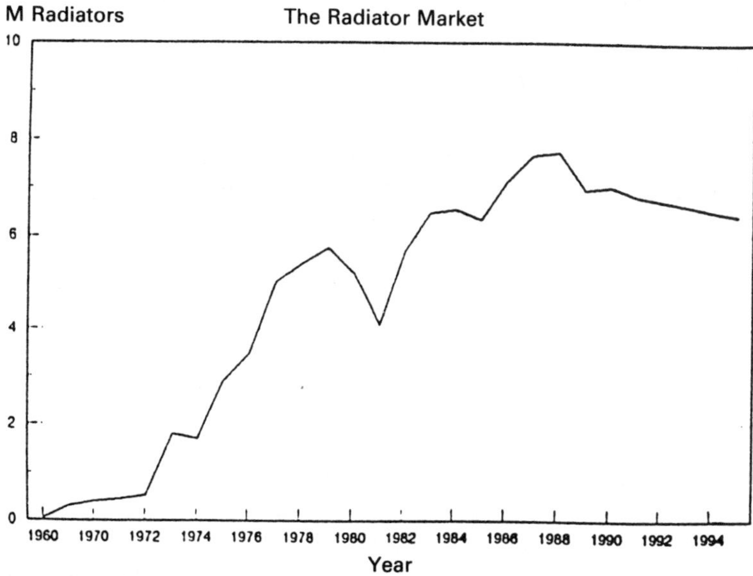

Figure 1.29 UK radiator market, 1960 to date

Table 1.14 Market Share (per cent)

Company	*1984*	*1985*	*1986*	*1987*	*1988*	*1989*	*1990*	*1991*	*1992*
Myson (total)	34.8	32.3	30.2	28.5	26.7	26.0	25.9		
Round top	19.1	17.7	16.9	16.5	15.9	15.8	16.6		
Seam top	15.7	14.6	13.3	12.0	10.8	10.2	9.3		
Stelrad	36.6	37.7	38.9	46.3	48.7	59.5	48.2		
Warmastyle	15.6	16.0	16.0	10.6	10.0	11.5	12.2		
Barlo	6.0	7.0	8.0	7.7	9.0	5.6	6.0		
Others	7.0	7.0	6.9	6.9	5.6	7.4	7.7		
Total (millions) market	6.53	6.27	7.20	7.41	7.72	6.93	6.10		

Source: Myson Radiators

□ *Market Share*

There are some twenty companies supplying radiators to the UK market, who also satisfy the required BSI standards. Of these, the key players are Myson, Stelrad, Warmastyle and Barlo.

Back in 1984, Myson and Stelrad had roughly equal market shares, at around 35 per cent. However, as Table 1.14 shows, since that time Stelrad have steadily increased their market share, largely at Myson's expense.

In order to be able to read 'behind' these figures, it will first be necessary to gain some understanding about the competing companies.

■ Competitor Analysis

Stelrad

This Company's operations include three manufacturing plants in the UK and nine in Europe (where, unlike Myson, it is also a significant player). It has been investing heavily in automating its production process, spending some £40m in doing so. Like Myson, it is also part of a large group, Metal Box.

In the UK it has a capacity to manufacture 4 million radiators per year, whereas current sales are in the order of 3 million radiators.

It plans to increase its market share to 70 per cent by the mid nineties. Its strategy for achieving this would appear to be by very aggressive pricing, made possible by a cost leadership base. Improved quality is also an issue being addressed.

At present, Stelrad's prices for seam top, their only product range, undercut those of Myson's Round Top by 13 per cent and Supaline (Myson's seam top range) by 2 per cent. In addition, Stelrad has the most extensive distribution of any Company, and market research shows that they are the first choice for specifiers, ie. those who authorise the type of radiators to be used in new products and installations.

It is estimated that Stelrad's current return on sales is in the order of 17 per cent.

Warmastyle

Warmastyle is an exclusive agent in the UK for a Belgian manufacturer, Veha. The difference in scale of this Company's operation is best illustrated by the fact that total production capacity is 1.6 million radiators per year, while actual sales are running at about 1.2 million.

Unlike Stelrad, Warmastyle do offer Round Top radiators which sell at 20 per cent less than Myson's equivalent, and 6 per cent lower than Supaline. However, despite competitive pricing, Warmastyle have a poor quality image and a record of long delivery times.

This Company distributes from two recently opened centres. One at Skipton, North Yorkshire, serves the northern half of the UK; the other is at Basingstoke, Hampshire, serving the south. It has a strong and loyal distribution network of mainly small to medium sized, independent merchants.

Barlo

This Company is a two plant operation, at Clonmel (Eire), where the Company originated, and at Leigh, Lancashire. It has a production capacity of 1.2 million radiators per year, but sales only amount to around 0.4 million.

It also prices very competitively, its Round Top being 10 per cent lower than Myson's Round Top and 3 per cent higher than Supaline. It distributes mainly through small independent merchants, and appears to have a market strategy of increasing penetration in the north of England and Scotland.

This Company is in a weak financial position, which could make them vulnerable to a takeover. Moreover, the advanced manufacturing plant at Leigh could become a threat in the hands of a more aggressive and sophisticated owner.

□ *How Does Myson Compare?*

It has been mentioned above that Myson operates with two manufacturing plants. The total capacity available is 2.7 million radiators per year (1.6 million Gateshead and 1.1 million Hull). However, like every other manufacturer, actual sales fall short of capacity, being 1.6 million radiators (1 million Gateshead and 0.6 million Hull).

Myson's Round Top radiators are perceived to be high quality products. The non-seamed top is not only aesthetically appealing, but also provides safety benefits by having no sharp edges as a potential source of injury. As a result, these radiators are widely specified and also have broad distribution base. In contrast, the Supaline range is in direct competition with Stelrad and has no differential advantages.

The business is still profitable, but the margins are far more susceptible to pressure than in the 'golden' years prior to 1988. Round Top provides a 17 per cent net profit on sales, compared with Supaline at 8 per cent. Taken together (remembering there are different volume sales for the two ranges) there is a 14 per cent profit margin on sales.

One significant difference between these competing players is in the area of sales representation. Whereas all main competitors have a dedicated sales force, ie. selling just radiators and any immediate ancillary equipment, Myson is represented by a sales force which operates on behalf of the whole Blue Circle Heating Group.

The issue is discussed in more detail later, in the section headed 'Sales Force'.

□ *Financial Performance*

The Company's financial performance in recent years is illustrated in Table 1.15.

Over this period, sales volume has fallen to 85 per cent of its 1987 level. Net profit has fallen by a similar proportion, 88 per cent. These figures only serve to demonstrate that in a stable or decreasing market, such as that for radiators, it is not easy to increase prices to generate profit. Nor, with such over-capacity for production in the radiator industry as a whole, would such a step be beneficial to maintaining market share.

It is in recognition of this fact that the Company has improved its grip on cost control. By doing so, it has improved manufacturing efficiency, and has also made some savings through the re-location of its Seam Top warehouse, and by closing its Cardiff and Essex factories.

Nevertheless, the figures above illustrate a gradual downward drift that cannot be allowed to continue unchecked. It would seem, therefore, that some new strategic thinking will be necessary if the Company is to reposition itself successfully, vis a vis its competitors.

Indeed, the 1990 sales volume of 1.77 million radiators is forecast to fall to about 1.5 million by 1993, unless some action is taken; to reach the Company's objective of sales in the order of 2.2 million by 1993, a strategic gap of 0.7 million radiators has to be bridged.

Table 1.15 Recent Financial Performance

	1987	*1988*	*1989*	*1990*	*1991*	*1992*
Sales volume (M)	2.072	2.072	1.84	1.57	1.412	1.541
Turnover (£M)	41.17	40.75	36.6	33.8	31.5	31.7
Net profit (£M)	6.27	5.9	4.8	5.5	5.6	4.96
Net profit (%)	15.2	14.5	13.0	16.2	17.7	15.6

Source: Myson Radiators

■ Marketing Review

As a springboard to finding new marketing strategies, the top management team has invested considerable time and energy in reviewing the Company's marketing.

Here are some of the issues which they addressed early in 1991:

Mission Statement
The Company defines its business as: 'We satisfy customer needs for steel heat emitters. Our major market is currently in the UK where we supply all market sectors, primarily through merchant outlets.'

Distinctive Competences
'During the past ten years, success has been achieved by reducing operating costs and maintaining a high market share in certain geographical areas, whilst capitalising on existing brand loyalty. Our two product ranges are complementary. However, our Supaline range competes in a commodity type market (low margins, high volume). Our policy is to have a strategic position with Supaline in this market against the market leader. This will enable the Division to absorb many of its overhead costs in this product range, whilst the high added value Round Top range will enable us to grow the profitability of the Division.'

It is interesting to note that the above paragraph actually says little about the Company's distinctive competences. If they were pushed to be specific, top management would probably come up with a list like this:

- We have maintained a high profile in the UK steel radiator business for 35 years.
- We produce Round Top radiators of unmatched quality.
- We have a small and enthusiastic top management team who are not averse to change.
- We have an experienced and highly committed work force.
- Our understanding of radiator manufacturing is second to none.
- We are equally competent at 'flow-line' or 'small batch' production.
- We have the resources of a large parent Company behind us (like Stelrad).
- We have a good relationship with a significant number of distribution outlets.
- We are a 'no-frills' organization.

While some competing companies might lay claim to some of the individual statements given above, taken together, they do convey an image which is perhaps distinctly 'Myson' and could not be any other Company.

Future Direction
What was known, however, in early 1991, was that the company intended to:

- continue to strive for increased operational efficiency;
- grow the business in real terms;
- develop products and technology which would keep them in the forefront of the industry; and
- become a Pan-European business in the medium to long term.

Product/Market Strategy Analysis

It was agreed by the Company that the critical success factors in the UK radiator business were as follows (given in descending order of importance):

- wide specification base;
- availability (through distributors);
- sales force effectiveness;
- major group support; and
- competitive market price.

Equally, the criteria for establishing the attractiveness of market sectors were agreed as follows, (again in descending order):

- a sector must offer volume growth;
- a sector must be profitable;
- a sector must not be vulnerable (to alternatives, change, etc.);
- a sector must be sizeable;
- there must be minimal competitor activity; and
- a sector must not be characterised by cyclical business patterns.

These criteria were of course 'ideal situations', but they did provide a benchmark against which various market sectors could be compared.

By using a weighted scoring procedure, it was possible to assess the extent to which the Company matched the critical success factors, and the comparative attractiveness of its various markets.

Using this information, it became possible to construct the 'directional policy' matrices shown in Figures 1.30 and 1.31.

This particular analysis shows an imbalance in the spread of the Company's business. Area 5 (commercial) proves to be the most attractive market, but it is the one which least matches up with the Company's strengths.

Conversely, it is in the less attractive markets where the Company plays to its strengths.

Since markets 1, 2, 3 and 4 are not going to become more attractive, certainly, not in the short term, then the Company faces the prospect of investing in new organisational strengths to become successful in the most

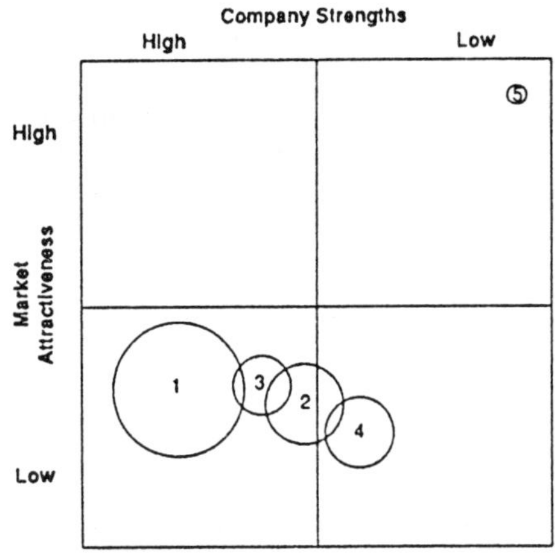

No.	Sector	Actual Sales Volume (1989)
1.	New housing	410,000
2.	Existing private	240,000
3.	Existing public	180,000
4.	Other/DIY	220,000
5.	Commercial	50,000
	TOTAL	1,100,000

Note: The circles are drawn proportional to sales volume.

Figure 1.30 Directional policy matrix – Round Top

Company Strengths
High
Low
High
Market Attractiveness
Low
1
2
3
4
5

No.	Sector	Actual Sales Volume (1989)
1.	New housing	20,000
2.	Existing private	300,000
3.	Existing public	250,000
4.	Other/DIY	80,000
5.	Commercial	50,000
	TOTAL	700,000

Note: The circles are drawn proportional to sales volume.

Figure 1.31 Directional policy matrix – Supaline

attractive market. However, these new strengths, as well as being costly and time-consuming to develop, might well prove to be incompatible with those other markets which constitute the bulk of the current business.

A possible silver-lining to this problem could be that markets 1 and 3 ought to be capable of generating profits to enable investment in market 5, if that solution were to be chosen.

Figure 1.31 analysis shows an imbalance similar to the previous one. It also provides a far less satisfactory overall picture. There would clearly have to be a high level of investment in areas 5, 4 and 1, which are attractive markets, but ill-matched with the Company's strengths.

However, the cash cow (area 3) and the cash dog (area 2) might only be capable of generating funds enough for a selective investment in the other areas. This suggests that management might have to consider withdrawing from one, or even two, of the highly attractive markets for Supaline.

A further option for funding might exist, if the parent group saw the development of these markets to be in its long terms interests and if a convincing proposition was put forward.

New Product Development

The whole of the foregoing analysis has an underlying assumption, that the Company's business prospects are inextricably tied up with its existing products and markets. This is clearly not the case, as we shall see.

It is extremely difficult to develop a new generation in steel panel radiators. If a continuum could be envisaged that operated as shown in Figure 1.32, then most attempts at Myson for developing new products could be placed somewhere near the centre.

There is a continual search for obtaining the optimum radiator configuration, regarding material used and heat output. This invariably involves experimentation with convector fans on the back of the radiator. Worthwhile though it is to seek such product improvements, nobody in the industry can visualise that this route will lead to a quantum leap in radiator design.

Another new development, in the area of improvement/modification, is the introduction of the low surface temperature (LST) radiator. This has been in response to the safety lobby, who recognise that it is possible to suffer burns, if the skin accidentically comes into contact with a hot radiator.

The problem is resolved by placing a vented steel enclosure around the offending radiator. The design of this outer 'case' can give the installed unit considerable customer appeal as well as making it safe.

A third new development option, this time imitating units available in mainland Europe, is the compact radiator. Again, like the LST radiator, this comes enclosed with panels, but also has integrated plumbing and a thermostat control. However, there is a strong suspicion that such a product could prove to be too avant-garde for the traditional UK market. This makes it the least strong contender for serious development.

Thus, of these three options, modified design might provide some short term

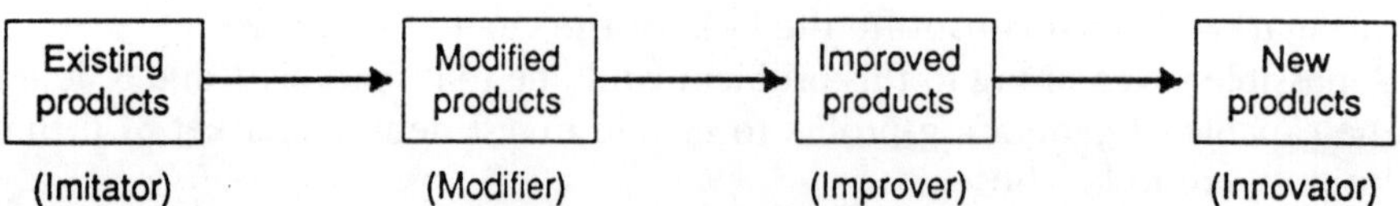

Figure 1.32 Product innovation continuum

differential advantage in performance, or reduce production costs, whilst LST radiators could open up new market segments in schools, hospitals and other public buildings.

These initiatives therefore, may have a role to play in contributing to increasing sales of new products into, essentially, existing markets.

□ *Existing Products into New Markets*

Mention has already been made of the attractiveness of the UK commercial sector, which could clearly be a source of business development.

Another, potentially vast market could be that of Europe. It is calculated that this market accounts for 18 million radiators per year, of which Myson currently supplies 50,000.

However, statistics such as these are not enough. The decision to export as a significant strategic move must be strongly connected to the Company's economic objectives. It is not a decision to be taken lightly.

There are basically two alternative approaches to exporting as outlined in Table 1.16.

Table 1.16 Approaches to Exporting

	Approach 1	*Approach 2*
Time horizons	Short term	Long term
Target markets	No systematic selection	Selection based on analysis of sales/market potential
Dominant objective	Immediate sales for profit	Build permanent market position
Resource commitment	Only enough to get immediate sales	Whatever is necessary to gain permanent market position
Entry mode	No systematic choice	Choice of most appropriate mode
New product developments	Exclusively for home market	For both home and foreign markets
Product adaptation	Only mandatory adaptations ie. to meet legal and technical requirements	Adaptation to meet foreign buyers' preferences, incomes and conditions of use
Channels	No effort to control	Controlled in support of marketing objectives
Price	Determined by domestic full cost with some ad hoc adjustments to specific sales situations	Determined by demand, competition, objectives, and marketing strategy
Promotion	Mainly confined to personal selling or left to middlemen	Advertising, sales promotions and personal selling mix to achieve marketing objectives

Approach 1 above could be termed a sales approach and has no real commitment to serving export markets on a permanent basis. In contrast, approach 2 is a less opportunistic entry strategy, which needs careful planning, and as a result takes more time and effort to introduce. Also, it would be fair to say, approach 2 will bring a more permanent level of success.

The reason for this discursive note, is that it might become tempting for the Company to try to remedy its falling sales situation, by choosing to export via approach 1. While this might bring some marginal, short term rewards, it might also serve to obscure the real issues.

Alternatively, to export along the lines of approach 2 will take possibly three to four years to get the strategy up and running. Therefore, any serious decisions about exporting might need to be made sooner, rather than later, while the Company has time on its side.

■ A Differentiated Product or a Commodity?

One of the key issues facing the Company, whether it markets at home or abroad, in familiar or new sectors, concerns the nature of its product. In particular, two factors of extreme importance are:

- the extent to which it can be differentiated from other products and thereby command a higher price; and
- the relative costs to produce the product.

The interaction of these factors is conveyed in Figure 1.33.

Taking the two radiator ranges in turn, Supaline is largely a 'me-too' product, and is indistinguishable from most other 'seam top' radiators. Thus its differentiation is low. Moreover, in terms of relative costs, the Company's are probably higher than its main competitor Stelrad (who are close to, if not having already, achieved cost leadership in this product range).

In this analysis, Supaline is close to falling into the disaster box. In contrast, Round Top might find itself in or around the 'niche/focus' strategy box.

□ *Options for Differentiation*

Radiators seem almost designed to be commodities. They all need to conform to a range of standard sizes, meet the same regulations, and are completely anonymous objects. However, if the product itself cannot be differentiated, can some sense of individuality be achieved in other ways? To do this it will be necessary to examine the 'product surround'.

The 'core product' can be seen as the radiator itself, with its functional features, style and design.

The 'product surround' is all the other elements that go to make up the total product 'package'. It includes such items as:

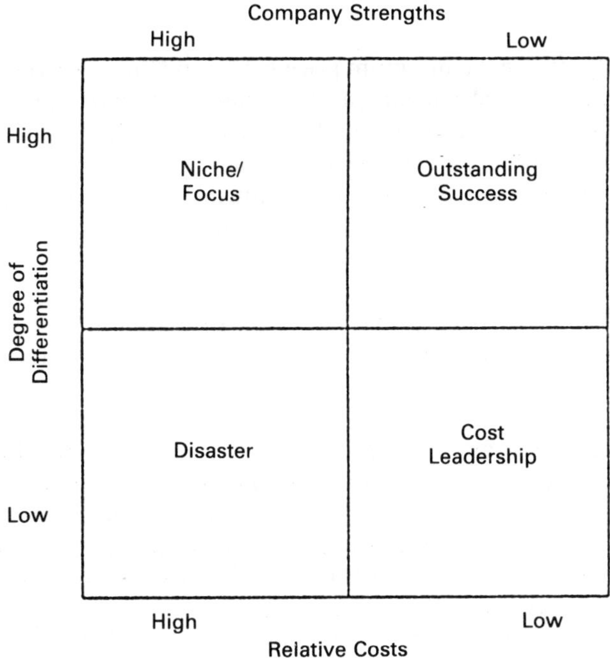

Figure 1.33 Porter's strategy matrix

- price;
- advertising;
- sales force;
- promotions;
- distribution channel(s);
- packaging;
- labelling/brand image;
- Company reputation and image;
- reliability of deliveries;
- quality; and
- auxiliary services
  - spare parts/accessories availability
  - warranties
  - user instructions
  - installation assistance
  - system design service
  - after-sales service
  - distributor support, etc.

Taking each of these in turn, the Company's policy is along the following general lines:

Price

The policy has been to get a premium price for Round Top, in recognition of its added benefits, and to sell Supaline at its highest competitive price.

Thus, there is an element of price differentiation on the Round Top range, whereas Supaline more or less follows the field.

Quantity discounts are given in some circumstances, but these are more or less standard industry practice and do not constitute a differentiating tactic.

Advertising

There is very little media advertising. In fact the Company are very wary about spending money in this area, either on product or corporate advertising.

Sales Force

The sales force, as mentioned earlier, operates in a fundamentally different way from those of competing radiator companies. Figure 1.34 helps to illustrate this point. It shows that they have a total divisional responsibility, rather than being dedicated just to radiators, in the way that competitors' sales forces are.

The sales force is organised in regions, each region matching that of the eleven British Gas regions.

Area Managers are designated to generate sales by specialising in one of the following market sectors:

- merchants;
- installers; or
- specifiers.

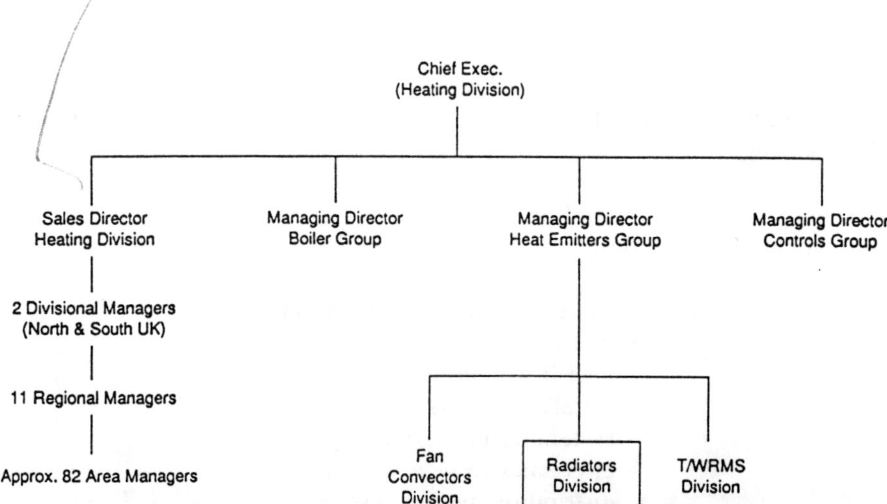

Figure 1.34 Organisational positioning of sales and radiators divisions

The rationale behind this sales structure is that all the Heating Division's component groups distribute their output through the same channels.

Therefore, it is argued, it makes it simpler and more effective for a distributor to deal with one sales representative for all his requirements, instead of one for radiators, another for boilers, and so on.

However, there are practical problems associated with this approach. In total, the Heating Division supplies about 35 different products, each of which can have a number of variations. Thus, the product knowledge required by the sales force is vast. On top of this is the administrative burden of keeping up with price changes, modifications and so on.

Although all sales staff have targets set to sell particular volumes of products throughout the total range, former salesmen have confided that their role was largely reactive, rather than proactive. Sales visits tended to degenerate into servicing calls. Instead of selling, issues about deliveries and stocking problems seemed to take over. With such a wide product range, there would always be something that was causing a distributor a problem.

Targets for those dealing with specifiers are based on the number of calls and on the number of contacts, as well as on end results. However, many of the problems associated with getting to grips with such a wide product range mentioned above, still apply.

Promotions

These have been mainly aimed at installers, to encourage to them to 'buy Myson' from their supplying merchant. Such promotions have involved prizes of holidays or attendance at special events. Despite all this, they could perhaps be described as 'me-too' promotions and have done little to differentiate either the products or the corporate image.

Distribution Channels

Products reach their destination following the route shown in Figure 1.35.

The installer will only hold enough stock for his immediate use, therefore the supply flexibility has to be available at either the factory or at the merchant stage.

Specifiers, such as local authorities, architects and so on, have the power to insist upon what equipment is installed. Thus, the installers approach merchants generally with a particular radiator in mind. On occasions, when there is no specification, the installer will be swayed by his personal preferences, or perhaps by price or availability.

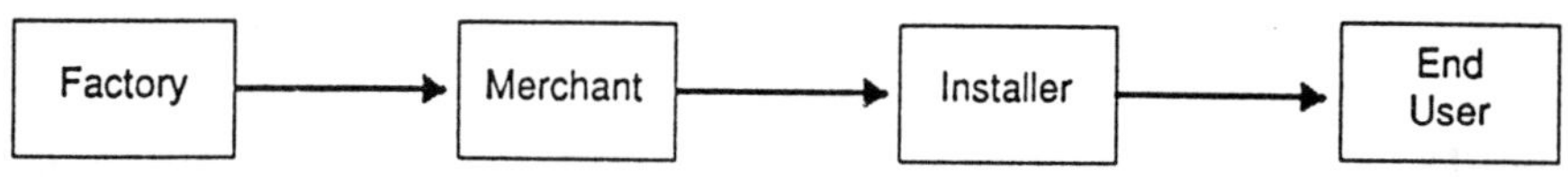

Figure 1.35 Distribution chain

Indeed, with installers generally working to tight deadlines on contracts, availability is often the most critical factor.

Merchants come in all shapes and sizes. Some have extensive national coverage, some have a strong regional representation, and some are small, independent merchants who, typically, might supply within a few miles radius of their base.

The dominant merchant is Plumb Centre, who, along with Cadel, Travis Perkins and BSS, account for the major part of Myson's output. However, as none of these merchants is an exclusive distributor, they will stock competing ranges of radiators.

There is a trend for distribution to polarise between the large national merchants on the one hand, and the small, second-line merchants on the other. While individually the same merchants do not generate vast sales, their collective business is quite substantial and appears to be growing.

Myson's relationship with the major merchants is satisfactory, but as a company they are not as well entrenched as Stelrad. Their dealings with second-line merchants tend to be opportunistic.

Packaging

Radiators are packaged as they come off the production line. This reduces the risk of them getting chipped or damaged thereafter. Individual packaging consists of plastic foam corner protectors to guard the most vulnerable parts of the radiator. A shrink-wrapped plastic envelope is then put over the whole unit. The Company name on the plastic sheet is the only form of identification the radiator receives. Batches of radiators are moved on wooden pallets.

Labelling/Brand Name

No radiators seem to be labelled. Any identification is tied up in the immediate packaging, which is subsequently thrown away.

Company Reputation and Image

While the Company is known and respected in the industry, little conscious effort seems to have gone into seeking some form of differentiation along these lines.

Reliability of Deliveries

The Company's performance here is about the same as most other suppliers. To increase customer service levels even higher would add to costs, without producing any significant benefits.

Quality

Steps are being taken to improve the quality, particularly regarding the overall standards of the painted finish.

Auxiliary Service
The only areas where the Company is differentiated from their competitors is through its design service. This appeals mainly to the building industry and provides a 'bespoke' heating system, complete with drawings and guarantees. Clearly, the project has to be sufficiently large to justify the Company's involvement.

■ Corporate Culture

Corporate culture has been described as the glue which holds the organisation together. Perhaps, this is a little fanciful, but without a doubt organisations have some intangible quality which can be invisible to 'outsiders', but which has considerable significance to those who work within it.

The culture is partially set by the style of the top management; people below observe how this group reacts to crises and in what things they show particular interest. Such activities then become central in organisation life. However, more important than this is the shared organisation experience, the collective learning that accumulates as the Company grows and overcomes problems that beset it along the way.

In the radiator division, there are echoes of its earlier 'lives' still reverberating quite loudly. Much of the pioneering enthusiasm, dating back to its 'international' days, still remains. Moreover, the period of stringent financial management under the investment group has also left its mark, giving rise to what is essentially a 'no frills' organisation.

However, the fairly directive, controlling style of top management which typified much of its earlier phases of development, has now given way to a more participative, delegative style which appears to be more appropriate.

All in all, there is a quiet, positive and optimistic outlook towards the future.

■ Summary

This case study has tried to describe all the pertinent issues which circumscribe the Company and exercise its management. It is possible to summarise most of these in a SWOT analysis (see Figure 1.36).

In looking to the future, the Company anticipates that the radiator market will be unlikely to fall below 5.0 million units per year, at least for the next three to four years. Also, that any external influences such as increases in the price of its basic raw material, steel, changes in interest rates, and so on, will affect its competitors in much the same way as it will Myson.

Clearly, such external changes might affect the validity of profitability forecasts, but should make little difference to the Company's overall competitive position.

It must be remembered that this Company is still successful and surviving at a time when the poor economic situation is sending many others to the wall.

STRENGTHS	WEAKNESSES
A key player Part of a large group Well established Can make seam or round top Flexible production facility Management commitment to improvement Profitable Better 'technically' than Stelrad	Product/market portfolio is unbalanced Market share falling Supaline is a 'me-too' product Little product/company differentiation Prices and profits are getting squeezed Company does not have full control over sales force Not much experience of exporting Not so strong in merchants as Stelrad
OPPORTUNITIES	**THREATS**
Commercial sector has barely been tapped European market New products like LSTs Trend in building towards larger executive housing means more radiators Increase in total sales through second-line merchants	Competitor activity becomes more aggressive Deregulation 1992 will open UK to European manufacturers Barlo taken over by a serious challenger to Round Top Housing sector takes a long time to recover Radiator market actually falls rather than flattens out Move towards commodity market Stelrad have cost leadership Major merchants are becoming increasingly powerful

Figure 1.36 SWOT analysis for Myson Radiators

The only thing that is certain in this case study is that, if it continues with its existing policies, the Company will inexorably fall into decline.

Having said that, its best way forward is by no means clear cut. There are a number of potential options which might be pursued. Here are just some of them:

Should it . . .

- re-appraise its seam top operations?
- pull out of that field altogether?
- consolidate at one plant?
- try to differentiate its products?
- price more aggressively to win a greater market share?
- advertise more?
- develop the commercial market?

- export?
- have its own sales force?
- re-appraise its distribution methods?
- develop an exclusive distribution network?
- fight back to establish cost leadership?
- invest more in developing new products?
- widen its horizons?
- buy out a competitor? (e.g. Barlo)

However, questions come cheaply. It is the answers that are expensive. Nevertheless, an investment in a new strategy is essential if the Company is to win the long success that it seeks.

Remembering that all this takes place against a backdrop of a mature market in which there is a considerable over-capacity for the manufacture of radiators, what would you do if you were running the Company?

CHAPTER 2

Low Cost, High Differentiation Strategies

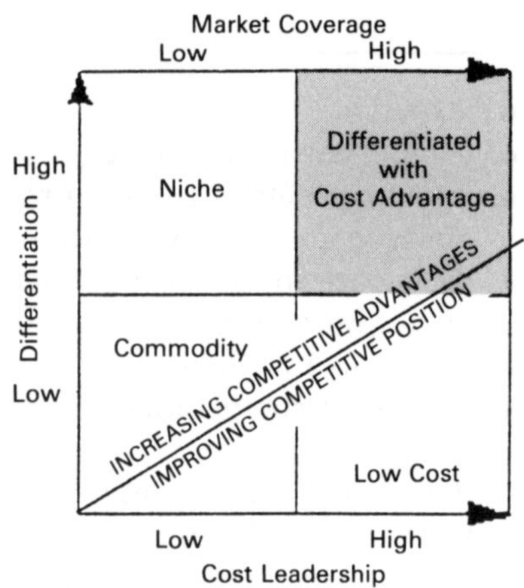

■ Dominant Leader Strategies for Defending Competitive Position Through Low Cost, High Differentiation

■ Section 1: Introduction

Research, experience and intuition, all indicate that the dominant market leaders – the company that stands out above the rest – has significant advantages in the market which it dominates. These translate into the ability to manage the market and the competition and to return the highest profitability in both the short and long-term.

The PIMS project suggests that market share and profitability are strongly related. It reports that businesses with market shares above 40 per cent earn an average return on investment three times that of those with shares under 10 per cent.[1] The importance of share varies, however, between industries and market situations. The PIMS analysis suggests at least two important differences:

1 Market share is more important for infrequently purchased products than for frequently purchased ones.
2 Market share is more important to business when buyers are fragmented rather than concentrated.

Factors such as economies of scale, risk aversion by customers and market power are some of the intuitive explanations of the dominance/high profitability relationship.

The PIMS study also reports that high investment intensity, referring to the capital invested per pound of sales, usually leads to lower rates of return.[2] This suggests that dominant leaders should weigh carefully the needs for investment against competitive requirements and profit impacts.

These relationships are likely to hold in many European markets which are small in size and require significant investment in capacity, distribution and servicing to supply the decentralised national market. This implies that, once dominant, it is important to protect dominance and profit because the successful entry of a third or fourth major force may take profit out of the industry or substantially reduce the leader's profitability.

Leadership in many European markets has been built by being first in the customer's mind: BCL for cellophane, Mars for confectionary countlines, BOC for gas, for example. In the short-term, leaders are almost invulnerable, being carried along by momentum. Leaders should use this short-term flexibility to develop and implement strategies supporting a stable, profitable long-term future.

The dominant leader should reinforce its positioning as the standard – Coca Cola's theme as 'the real thing' and Xerox's reinforcement of 'we invented the product' maintain the positioning of being the original. The leader may need to adopt strategies to improve the product, its service or its distribution, but the focus should be on reinforcing the leader positioning in the market's collective mind.[3]

A strong market leader has the greatest ability in an industry to manage the market and the competition to its advantage by using its market influence and its profit and cash to contain the activities of its competitors and invest in new initiatives. It has a wider range of strategic options than its competitors.

Bloom and Kotler[4] in their analysis of strategies for high market share companies, point out that the company that acquires a very high market share exposes itself to risks that its smaller competitors do not encounter. Competitors, consumers and governmental authorities are more likely to take certain actions against high share companies than against small share ones. British Telecom is increasingly being challenged by competitors in the law courts and through public debate, because of its strong monopolistic position in an increasingly deregulated industry.

Accordingly, market leaders must make their decisions with much more care than do their competitors and consider whether their market share management strategies should be share building, share maintenance or share reduction. Alternatively, market leaders may need to adopt strategies to reduce the risk associated with their high market share. This may include public relations to improve corporate image, industry development from which competitors also benefit, and lobbying to develop closer relationships and support of governments.

Just as the size of a dominant leader's share should be considered and managed in relation to profit and risk, so should it manage the share levels of individual competitors. This may require strategies to limit the share growth of some competitors while enhancing the share growth of others. Market leaders have the opportunity of shaping the competition in the market by the targeting of the strategies they adopt. Costs, risks and profit protection should be considered when formulating competitor targeted strategies.

The dominant market leader will, at different times, consider both offensive and defensive strategies. Offensive moves are those strategic changes the market leader initiates. They may be threatening to competitors where the objective is to take market share and undermine their positions through a frontal attack on selected competitors' markets. They may be non-threatening offensives designed to improve volume and profitability in the industry as a whole.

Offensive strategies include:

- product, packing and service innovations;
- development of new market segments;
- redefinition of the market to broaden its scope and position products more closely against broad substitutes; and
- market development through product variety and distribution strategies to increase usage and widen availability.

Ries and Trout[5] maintain that only the market leader should consider playing defence. Under certain market conditions, the most profitable strategies are those that protect and defend the market share and profit base of the market leader. Under other conditions, it may be more rewarding to adopt market-building strategies.

Defensive strategies include:

- blocking competitors by brand-for-brand matching; distribution coverage and price strategies to reduce their market share and profit potential;
- pre-emption of a competitor's action by being first with a new product or distribution system;
- use of government regulations, tariffs, import quotas or court actions to increase a competitor's costs or deny a market base; and
- rumours about a competitor's viability, service back-up or reliability of products.

In practice, all these strategies are used frequently by leaders to defend their market positions.

Two main types of strategies for gaining maximum coverage and closing competitors out of opportunities, are product proliferation and competitor acquisition.

Market saturation, by offering a proliferation of products to distributors and retailers, limits the opportunities for competitors. British Airways has been successful with this strategy in the airline market, retaining overall leadership of the European market.

A strategy for achieving or increasing dominance is to take over competitor's brands in the same industry. Nestlé have done this in the European confectionery market by taking over Rowntree.

In practice, market leaders adopt both offensive and defensive strategies to strengthen and protect their leadership position. The selection of appropriate leader strategies depends, in part, on existing and expected future industry and market conditions.

As noted in Chapter 1, the structure of the industry itself, its suppliers and buyers have a major influence on the evolution of the industry and its profit potential. Also, the threat of substitutes and new entrants influence the appropriate strategies to be adopted to reduce or eliminate their impact.

The implication is that the market leader should influence the balance of forces through strategic moves, thereby strengthening or defending its position.

Evolution of an industry is affected, too, by the life-cycle stage of its main markets. The large body of life-cycle literature provides marketing strategy guidelines for a market leader at each stage. During the growth stage, it is appropriate for market leaders to adopt offensive strategies, whereas in maturity and decline, defensive strategies may be more appropriate.

The level of market share of the leader and the shares held by its competitors will influence the leader's strategies and its degree of vulnerability to attack. For example, British Telecom's high level of dominance leaves the way open for a viable alternative. Typically, customers resent such a high level of dominance and perceive the leader to be arrogant, unapproachable and rigid in its approach to the market. Usually, any major attractive alternative will be tried and, if it delivers its promise, accepted. In this structure, British Telecom needs to be first with new products and innovations to reduce the risk of substantial share loss and consequent effect of profit.

At the other extreme, a leader may hold 35 per cent of the market, the challenger 20 per cent and other competitors ranging between 10 per cent and 15 per cent. Here the leader's objective will often be to build its market share and competitive position to consolidate its dominance. Aggressive, innovative strategies will be necessary for its achievement.

Somewhere between these two extremes, there are markets in which the leader holds 50 to 60 per cent, with the second shareholders at 25 per cent and other competitors holding 10 to 15 per cent. In the UK, Pedigree Petfoods, a division of Mars Inc., holds 60 per cent share of the petfoods market. In these conditions defensive strategies of blocking, pre-empting and matching competitors are sufficient to protect market share and profit.

The next three sections in this chapter outline the strategic issues relevant to dominant market leaders in different industry and market conditions. The first looks at a mature market and the use of multibrand strategies. Section 3 highlights factors relevant in the growing market dominated by one or a few major companies and section 4 discusses the issues involved in restructuring an industry when the market is expected to decline. In each case the market leaders strive to defend and enhance their competitive positions while seeking to protect their profitability.

Section 2: Multibrand Strategies to Protect Dominance

The world of packaged consumer goods marketing has long been the province for development and maintenance of specialised brands designed to meet the unique wants and needs of segments of a product market. Procter & Gamble has been very successful with brands such as Tide (washing detergent), Cascade (dishwasher detergent), Crest (toothpaste), and Pampers (disposable nappies). The Coca Cola Company has followed its flagship Coke with Tab, Sprite, Diet Coke and the recent turmoil of New Coke and Classic Coke. Each brand is uniquely positioned to occupy a certain location or position in the target market's mind. Most leaders, in packaged goods industries, cover competitive moves by introducing another brand. Each brand adopts a single position strategy. Many companies, such as Coca Cola and Levi, have found it is difficult to move from an established brand positioning – the more so the stronger the brand.

Branding Policies

Branding means the use of a name, term, symbol, design or combination of these, to identify a product or service and distinguish it from competitive products. Brand marketing is a highly integrated, market segment focused, form of marketing based on the delivery of some unique value or benefit to the target market. The product is packaged with a brand image. A number of alternative branding policies are adopted. Selection of a particular policy depends upon corporate polices, the firm's overall share of the market (large or small), the degree of differentiation existing between products in the category and the degree of coverage of the market desired by the firm. The advantages and limitations of each of five alternative policies are noted in Table 2.1.

Table 2.1 Advantages and Limitations of Branding Policies

Branding	*Advantages*	*Limitations*
Corporate, Family, Range Branding	The goodwill accruing to the brand helps all product in the range.	Family name sets the scope for different price/quality positions.
	Advertising, promotion and packaging costs can be spread across a number of products.	The failure of a new produt reflects on the image of the family brand or corporate name.

Branding	*Advantages*	*Limitations*
	Less resistance at trade and end user level to new products using the family name.	
Individual Branding	Where products are different, individual brands highlight differentiation. Can achieve different product positions in one market (eg. high quality/high price brand and low quality/low price brand). New product failures do not reflect on existing brands. Reduces vulnerability from competitive attacks.	Requires a separate marketing budget for each brand. Need a viable market size for one or more brands to be supported. Brands can be locked into declining markets when their benefits are very highly focused.
Combination Umbrella Individual Branding	Can ride on the reputation of family name while identifying specific characteristics of the product. Can engage in both individual brand marketing and benefit from family name advertising.	Family name sets the scope for price/quality positioning of individual products. Failure of an individual brand has some negative impact on the umbrella name.
Private Branding	Gives manufacturer opportunities for full capacity production runs and allows emphasis on cost efficiencies. Requires minimal marketing by the manufacturer.	Lose identity with end market and ability to influence market trends. Lower margins available than for manufacturer's brand. Gives marketing power to distributors.
Generic Branding	Reduces costs of packaging and promotion.	Easily matched by competitors. Promotes price competition.

Davidson suggests four types of branding.[6]

□ *Corporate – Umbrella Branding*

Corporate names are sometimes used as brand umbrellas. Cadbury adopts the policy of attaching its corporate name to individual names of specific products. Examples are: Cadbury's Milk Tray, Cadbury's Wispa, Cadbury's Drinking Chocolate. H. J. Heinz also adopts this policy in its food business, which includes Heinz Soup, Heinz Baby Food and Heinz Baked Beans and Spaghetti.

□ *Family – Umbrella Branding*

A family name is used to cover a range of products in a variety of markets. There will usually be common links in quality levels, packaging style and advertising between products carrying the umbrella name. An example of a family umbrella name is Kimberly Clark's use of Kleenex for its products in facial tissues, disposable nappies and toilet roll markets.

□ *Range Branding*

This comprises a brand name for a range of products that have clearly linked benefits in one major market. Walls' brand of ice-creams is an example of range branding.

□ *Individual Branding*

This comprises a brand for one product type in one market, but may include different sizes, flavours or variants of a basic product. Unilever is an example of a company that prefers the individual brand name as a route to market domination. 75 per cent of their business is in packaging consumer goods for use in the home – mainly food and drinks, detergents and personal products. They include such famous names as Lux toilet soap, Cornetto ice cream, Blue Band and Flora margarines, Brooke Bond and Lipton teas, Surf washing powder, Signal toothpaste and Pond's creams.

Combination branding involving corporate, family or range name with individual product brand name is increasing in Europe because of the growing emphasis on corporate positioning. ICI, Alfa Laval and SKF, for example, use their corporate umbrella as a prefix for all of their brands. In the car industry we see Ford Fiesta, Ford Orion and Ford Escort.

In addition to the four options listed, a firm may decide to supply private brands to its distributors or dealers. This involves a contract supply agreement covering product specifications, volumes, deliveries and price. The private brand is owned by the distributor who determines its market position and provides advertising and promotional support. A variation of this option is the supply of 'generics', in which products have no brand name other than the identification of their contents such as 'washing powder'. Identification occurs through package design and colour. The rationale for private branding or generics is one of reducing unit costs of production, packaging and promotion, so that the product can be sold in volume at a lower price. The responsibility for advertising and promotion rests with the distributor.

Just which type of policy is adopted is sometimes an accident, sometimes trial and error, but in more recent times, is the result of well thought-out brand strategies.

■ The Mars Approach to Branding in the Pet Food Market

Pedigree Pet Foods, a Division of Mars Inc., holds around 60 per cent share of the UK pet foods market. Their canned dog food brands are: Pal, Pedigree Chum, Cesar (a brand designed for small dogs), Chum Puppy, Bounce Chunks, and Chappie. Chappie is the cheapest, Pal, Pedigree Chum, Cesar and Chum Puppy are premium brands, and Bounce Chunks are in the middle price range. They also cover the dry dog foods market with Pedigree Chum Mixer and Pedigree Chum Small Bite Mixer. Frolic is a semi-moist dog food.

Their cat foods include: Whiskas (the brand leader), Kit-e-Kat, Katkins, and Katkins Premium. Sheba is a super medium moist cat food in plastic tubs with foil lids, whilst in the dried cat food sector, Pedigree produce Brekkies.

Pedigree continue to launch new products. For example, in 1989 they launched Katkins Mariner and Pal Partners for the cat and dog markets respectively.

By contrast, Spillers Foods have a 15 per cent market share, although they do lead in the dry dog food meal and mixer sector, with Winalot Meal, Spillers Mixer Plus, Bonio and Cheese Crunchies.

H. J. Heinz has made two separate and largely unsuccessful attempts to enter the UK pet foods market. One attempt to launch Sunkist Nine Lives, a tinned cat food produced in France, was abandoned in 1987 in the face of the seemingly impenetrable strength of Mars' leading brands.

The overall breakdown by value of dog food plus cat food is: Pedigree Pet Foods 60 per cent, Spillers 15 per cent, own label 9 per cent, Quaker Oats 6 per cent, Friskies 3.5 per cent, and other brands 6.5 per cent.

■ The Product Life-Cycle and Brand Development Planning

The stage of the life-cycle of the product category's market and the segment trends provide a guide to competitive brand strategies. Conventional life-cycle theory[7] provides guidelines for objectives and strategy at different stages of market evolution. These indicate the changing nature of marketing strategies at each stage and when efforts should be made to extend the life-cycle and target growth segments of the market.

The brand, however, can transcend the product life-cycle with planned extension, repositioning and periodic updating. Coca Cola has demonstrated this with its variants such as Diet Coke and Cherry Coke and extended usage such as Rum and Coke. Today, brands can be the largest assets companies have, yet their value is rarely reported in the balance sheet. But, frequently, business take-overs and industry rationalisation involve the sale of brands that bring far greater proceeds than those of the tangible assets. Managing the financial returns of brands during their life cycle requires profit planning as an integral part of marketing strategy.[8]

In reality, the brand is an asset in which continuing investment is required. A brand development plan is therefore important to gaining the most from this asset.

■ Brand Development Planning

Davidson suggests a number of steps in brand development planning.[9]

- Understanding your brands: analyse all brands by type, then construct a diagram of the core and extension areas for each one, using research as a guide.
- Determine how all your brands fit: establish which names can be used in combination, why and with what relative emphasis.
- Decide which brand names can be stretched and how: stretch brands as widely as possible into commercially attractive new market sectors and uses, without weakening the brand core.
- Know when to develop new brand names: to justify the costs and the risks, new brand names should only be used for distinctive and superior new products, with which existing names do not fit well.
- Consider licensing your brand name: this can be a profitable route for certain consumer products.
- Cover your tracks: strenuously protect your brand names and symbols.
- Have a five-year brand development plan: this should analyse each brand name and describe its role over the next five years.

■ Multibrand Strategies

Multibrand strategies are used by many of the international packaged goods manufacturers as a means of achieving maximum market coverage through positioning of individual brands in different segments of the market. In Europe, Colgate-Palmolive and Unilever (through its subsidiary companies) have a number of different brands of toothpaste, toilet soap, household cleaning products and washing detergents, covering a wide range of market segments.

A multibrand strategy requires an understanding of each brand in the range – its core attributes and benefits and how far it can reasonably be extended. It is important, too, to determine how all the brand names fit in terms of corporate and family umbrella associations and which names can be used effectively in combination. Development of competitive strategies for brands at the product/ market unit level reflects similar considerations to those at the business unit level. These require an analysis of strengths, weaknesses, opportunities and threats in relation to the product/market, assessment of the position of brands in the market and design of competitive brand strategies that achieve strategic (corporate) objectives, individual brand objectives and objectives for the firm's group of brands (if a multiple brand strategy is adopted).

It is clear that a firm's objectives in relation to a particular product/market play a fundamental role in its marketing strategy. But these objectives and corresponding strategies will be significantly affected by the market conditions, market structure and its own market position.

■ Competitors' Brand Strategies

Competitors' strategies in a particular product market will depend on their positioning, whether it is as market leader, a number two or a niche specialist.

Table 2.2 Brand Strategy Guidelines for a Market Leader in Different Market Structures and Market Conditions

Market structure / Market Conditions	Joint Dominance (2 companies dominant with equal shares)	Monopoly Dominance (Dominant market leader with more than 50 per cent share)	Oligopoly Dominance (Dominant market leader with around 35 per cent share)
Growth	Offensive or pre-emptive new brand segmentation and revitalisation Pre-empt entry of new competitors	Pre-empt or match strategies of all major competitors in order of threat priority	Offensive strategies using new brand and variety segmentation and brand revitalisation
Non-Growth	Match price reductions Low impact revitalisations Product improvement through brand revitalisation or new brand	Brand revitalisation	Low impact revitalisations Downward price repositioning

It will also depend on their priorities in this and other categories and the opportunities for growth and profit. Competitive position and market prospects will determine whether a 'growth', 'maintenance', 'defence' or 'withdrawal' strategy is most appropriate.

At the brand level, it is necessary to decide which brands can be extended. The principle involved is to stretch a brand across segments or markets only to the extent that the core qualities of the brand are not weakened. It is also necessary to determine when a new brand is necessary to penetrate a particular market segment.

Appropriate brand strategies for the leader, follower and niche specialist are different because of their different competitive positions and brand potentials.

An external study of over one hundred brand strategies adopted in grocery markets provides guidelines for market leaders, challengers and specialists operating in different market conditions and market structures.[10] Summaries are provided in Table 2.2 for a market leader and in Table 2.3 for a challenger or specialist.

Table 2.3 Brand Strategy Guidelines for Non-Dominant Firms in Different Competitive Conditions and Market Conditions

Competitive Condition / Market Conditions	Challenger in Duopoly Structure	Specialist in Duopoly Dominance Structure	Specialist in Monopoly Dominance Structure	Challenger in Oligopoly Equal Structure
Growth	New brand segmentation	Product improvement at same price	Premium-priced infiltration with downward price repositioning	Brand revitalisation Premium-priced infiltration with downward price repositioning
Non-Growth	Downward price repositioning New brand/ brand revitalisation	Downward price repositioning	Downward price repositioning	Brand revitalisation and new varieties

Section 3: Maximising Market Potential and Profit as the Dominant Industry Force

A market leader, having more than 60 per cent share in an industry in which remaining competitors are fragmented, plays the major role in market development and determines the level of industry profit. Market leader strategies, under these conditions, must do much more than defend market position. Market expansion and profitability should be major ingredients in its marketing strategy. Strategy development by the dominant industry force should address these issues.

Market Definition

The scope of the market within which opportunities are considered should be viewed broadly. For instance, a dominant marketer of pet food might review its business within the broader scope of pet health, hygiene and nutrition. A leading life assurance company may view its progress within the overall finance and investment industry.

Periodic redefinition of the business within broad boundaries is useful to placing the existing business in context and planning growth opportunities.[11]

Substitution between market sectors becomes evident when the overall market is analysed from a broad perspective.

Market Expansion

Focus by a dominant leader should be on expanding the existing market and developing new markets. In existing markets, strategy is designed to increase the number of customers and increase their use. New markets may occur by geographic expansion and by satisfying new needs, the latter often occurring through changes in the product and technology.

For example, accountants were the main users of lined paper pads that gave them columns and rows for analysis of figures. The use of personal computers and spreadsheet programmes by accountants replaced the paper spreadsheet. Now, new customers have entered the market for spreadsheets software packages – analysts, managers and consumers owning personal computers.

In order to achieve effective market expansion, the dominant leader must incorporate innovative products within its range. Creative market segmentation strategies help to expand markets and increase the use of products. Kimberly Clark's segmentation strategy in facial tissues involved provision of Pocket Pak, Mansize and Kleenex Boutique, which increased the use of disposable tissues.

■ Competitive Issues

A number of competitive issues must be balanced with the market expansion elements of a dominant leader's strategy.

□ *Cannibalisation of Own Business*

The need to achieve market coverage, satisfy different market segments, and defend against threatening competitors, usually results in activities that cannibalise the sales, share and profit of a leader's main products and markets. The objective is to minimise cannibalisation by positioning new products away from the company's main products and markets. This, however, is not usually possible in an environment affected by changing technology.

For example, Sealed Air's uncoated bubbles in Europe rendered almost obsolete their own high-priced, coated bubbles in the packaging market but they had to do it in order to retain leadership in a fast-changing market. Here the task is to retain the firm's customer base and adopted migration strategies that will move customers from the old to the new technology while bringing new customers into the market.

□ *Spawning Competitors*

The very dominance of large companies in some European industries spawns competition through the dissatisfaction of some of the leader's staff, who break away and form their own companies. In the European back-hoe loader parts supply industry, JCB has held industry-wide dominance. Most of its niche competitors are made up of people who at one time worked for JCB. In the industrial gas market, dominated by BOC, most people in the industry have worked at some time for BOC.

These are four aspects which deserve attention in a dominant leader's strategy:

1 The formation of break-away groups who can erode profitable segments of the leader's market.
2 The poaching of experienced and motivated staff by a potentially large competitor as a means of entering the market.
3 The creation of niches for 'friendly' competitors to supply segments of the market which the large firm cannot economically service. In this instance, it is preferable to create co-operative competitors than to leave the opportunities open to hostile firms who may become a threat.
3 The joint development of a new sector of the market as a market expansion strategy. Here, if possible, selection of a 'friendly' competitor enhances the leader's ability to manage the market. It is preferable to have certain known competitors.

☐ *Protecting Market Structure and Share*

The dominant firm's strategy needs to address two aspects of protection:

Maintaining Share Level
Product and market matching of competitors' activities and tactical blocking of supply or distribution, can reduce the competitors' market penetration and slow down their acceptance in the market. This is aimed at maintaining overall market share level.

Protecting Monopoly Dominance Structure
This aspect addresses the need to block the emergence of a second force in the industry. Competitive strategy should be designed to keep the market share, revenue and profit small and equally spread between competitors.

☐ *Managing Competitive Forces while Ensuring their Viability*

A dominant industry force needs to manage its relationships and economic arrangements with suppliers and customers carefully. A variety of suppliers are needed to ensure product, service or raw material supplies, choice, reliability, quality and cost efficiency. These may be local or international suppliers or a balance of both. For example, the dominance of Marks and Spencer in the UK retail sector, depends on hundreds of reliable, low cost suppliers and upon variety, range and stock.

Pricing strategies must focus on the customer's ability and willingness to pay in relation to substitutes and a choice to forego the use of the product or service. By keeping a large number of customers and coverage of all main market segments, the market leader is in a position to manage market trends and expectations.

Most European postal organisations dominate the stamped letter business, but have lost a large amount of potential revenue to substitutes – couriers and electronic data transfers. Within the constraints of their charters, they operate in the courier market and offer public facsimile and other text transfer services. Where possible, early entry into substitute markets that show prospects of growth is important to protecting the leader's customer base. This has happened in the finance and insurance industry where insurance companies have entered banking and banks have launched into the insurance market.

The Chairman of Procter and Gamble, speaking recently about five products that have been leaders on average for fifty years (the oldest was over one hundred years old and the youngest was fifteen), said: 'In our experience, it isn't enough to invent a new product and to introduce it on the market. The real payoff is to manage that brand in such a way that it continues to flourish year after year in a changing and competitive market place'.

'To keep an established brand healthy and growing over the long term, the successful marketer must continually anticipate changes in the market place and must continually improve the product and marketing plans to capitalise on these changes.

'In our business, we are forever trying to see what lies around the corner, we study the ever-changing consumer and try to identify new trends in tastes, needs, environment, and living habits. We study changes in the market place and try to assess their likely impact on our brands. We study our competition, competitive brands are continually offering new benefits and new ideas to the consumer, and we must stay ahead of this.

The successful company is the one which is first to identify emerging consumer needs and to offer product improvements which satisfy those needs. The successful marketer spots a new trend early, and then leads it.'

■ Profit Growth

Most large businesses have 'cash cow' markets. These are large markets in which the firm has strong dominance of the type discussed in this chapter. Profit growth and protection are paramount in these markets. Profit issues to be addressed by the firm's strategy include these:

Cross Subsidy of Other Businesses
British Telecom subsidise many of their existing products, such as telegrams, and new products requiring funding, from trunk calls – STD – nationally and internationally. The future of the business and its ability to fund growth relies on the careful management of these 'cash cow' markets.

Non-Price Competition
Competitive strategies should be directed towards focusing on benefits, solutions and user applications and not on price. Price wars reduce industry margins and ultimately profitability.

□ *Justifying Dominance, Price Structure and Marketing Practices*

Large dominant leaders come under the scrutiny of the Monopolies Commission in the UK, other government agencies, the other EC countries and of course the EC itself. Strategies must address this scrutiny with arguments justifying the cost base, price polices and marketing practices of the firm and the industry.

This is consistent with EC policies that recognise that while it must prevent 'unhealthy' market domination, Europe needs large companies to export and compete internationally. The test is the firm's behaviour in the market place with the onus on the company not to abuse a position of power.

In Europe, these issues are being faced continually as companies seek mergers and acquisitions following the opening of the European Community as one economic market.

□ *Costs and Global Competition*

A dominant market leader sometimes loses sight of costs, because of the lack of direct competition and pricing pressures. ICI Fertilizers faced this situation in the early eighties when it dominated all segments of the UK fertilizer industry. But the domination of the European market, excluding the UK, by Norsk Hydro through acquisitions and their subsequent entry into the British market with a lower cost base, eventually forced ICI to all but exist this industry.

Increasingly, the cost structures of competitors are based on global business, in which the costs of research and development, raw materials and packaging innovation can be spread across a number of international markets.

It is within this context that the dominant leader's costs need management.

■ Interdependent Markets

The relationships between interdependent markets needs to be recognised in assessing future strategies for expansion. In a number of industries, it is necessary to penetrate two market areas simultaneously in order to be successful. In the job market, employment agencies need to penetrate both the job seeker market and the job vacancy market to provide an effective job matching service. Similarly, real estate agents must bring together buyers and sellers of properties. This is a key factor in the advertising directories industry.

■ Politics

Any large dominant company in a large European industry will be affected by government politics – indirectly through economic, legal and social policies, and directly by policies that affect the industry and the people working in it. Dominance, restrictions to competition in the industry, and insensitivity to market wants and staff needs, can result in lobbying by special interest groups, attention by (opposition) members of parliament and direct action by trade unions. This can be damaging to market standing and profitability. Competitive business strategies are necessary to pre-empt problems of this kind.

■ The Special Case of Government Business

Many government businesses compete in the private sector with constraints that have to be built into strategy. These include, for instance, the social obligations for train services supplied in certain areas at great cost. The avenue for complaint through government is frequently and often unfairly used against the British Post Office. But the constraints are facts of life.

The restrictions on employee wages, borrowing from the capital markets and time-consuming purchasing procedures, which affect all government agencies, create bureaucratic structures and limit flexibility and responsiveness of government-owned businesses. In addition, these agencies sometimes receive 'unwarranted' criticism because of their government links. These limitations must be recognised when designed competitive strategies.

■ Section 4: Strategic Issues in Mature and Declining Markets

Discussions of strategy in declining markets usually revolve around harvesting or divestment. There is a range of strategic alternatives, however, depending on the long-term attractiveness of the market and the competitive position and strength of the firm in the market. These may include opportunities for life-cycle extension, or broadening of the business base. Frequently, it will require a redefinition of the business and its focus so that appropriate strategies are effected to re-establish business profitability. The main strategic alternatives are to:

- seek or reinforce leadership position:
- defend or develop a niche position:
- harvest and market by managing a controlled divestment; and
- divest quickly as early in the decline phase as possible.

■ Market Leadership Issues

The decline phase of the life-cycle creates a number of problems for the market leader. These issues need to be addressed by the marketing strategy and involve:

Profitability
The costs of doing business (i.e. overheads) and the product costs associated with a wide range and declining volumes, all require close attention. Pricing strategies, product range and distribution costs need review because of the tendency to overservice a declining market.

Competition and Market Position
Niche specialists carving away market share in speciality segments and narrow range low-pice operators reduce the volume potential of the market leader. The leader's strategy must seek to reduce their impact, while maintaining share and profitability.

Distribution Channel Relationships
The balance of power in the distribution system between manufacturer and distributor is a key issue in declining markets. Speciality distributors such as

petrol outlets or spare parts shops need some rationalisation and strong support by the supplier for their survival. General merchandise retailers will be looking to reduce stock and range width and replace declining products with new ones.

The market leader should seek a distribution or supply strategy which strengthens, rather than weakens, its position of power in the distribution channel. This requires strategic focus on channels and specific strategies to address any changes in structure of the distribution system.

Market Perceptions
In declining markets, the product range is usually well known, and price is an issue in the market at both intermediary and end user level. The market leader should conduct research at both levels to determine:

- residual opportunities and any static or growing segments;
- possible customer migration patterns from old products to new substitutes; and
- new product or market opportunities associated with the decline of the product/market.

■ Market Leader Strategic Directions

In formulating a marketing strategy, the leader in a declining market should closely consider a range of alternative strategic directions:

Cost Leadership versus Differentiation
Cost leadership factors that usually have the greatest impact in declining markets are:

- management and production overheads;
- distribution costs and level of service employed;
- channels employed and margins required by distributors;
- mix and variety of products offered; and
- product formulation, configuration and technical quality.

To have a substantial cost reduction effect, a market leader may need to restructure its entire business and change methods, systems and staff attitudes. In practice, it is difficult to do this quickly, and in some instances impossible. In the highly competitive, post-deregulation airline industry in the United States, the market slump during the early eighties left some highly geared airlines with nowhere to go. With high fixed cost structures, the only alternative, for some, was bankruptcy.

At the product level, the experience of the international telephone companies with the declining telegram and telex services has been to reduce costs, but also to reformulate the offer in a way that better meets selected market segments' needs. An intermediary known as a telex refiler routes text messages via a hubbing system supplied by telephone companies at different strategic points on the globe. Refilers are booming because they are able to offer additional service and convenience to their customers.

Although the advantage of a cost leadership strategy is that it provides a source of competitive advantage, particularly for market leaders who can use economies of scale, it is usually not appropriate in declining markets where:

- there is product parity;
- the leader is already heavily committed to an extensive product range; or
- service and channels of distribution and critical factors of competitive advantage and market acceptance.

While cost management and reduction should be pursued where possible, it should not necessarily be the strategic focus for market leaders in declining markets.

In a differentiation strategy, a firm seeks to be unique in its industry along some dimensions that are widely valued by buyers.

In the gases industry, some segments of which are in decline, BOC has selected product availability as the key differentiator and has positioned itself uniquely to meet that need. In similar industries, such as auto parts and accessories, service and distribution are vital differentiators in declining markets, and differentiation occurs on availability, service, information provision and price.

In adopting a differentiation strategy, a leader will aim for cost parity with its major competitors, but should reduce costs only in areas that do not affect favourably perceived differentiation.

Coverage versus Focus

The degree of segmentation of the market, the size of the largest segments and the leader's competitive strengths, will determine whether a strategy of coverage or one of focus is required for leadership and dominance of the market to be retained. Usually, a leader will need coverage of the main market segments, and a strategy may be adopted to attempt to combine some segments with the same product. This strategy of counter-segmentation may be viable in declining markets as customers reduce to a hard core of users.

Industry and Public Expectations

In a declining market, the dominant leader has a number of stakeholders who hold high expectations: shareholders for profit; staff for jobs; suppliers for continued sales; customers for continued supply; financiers for a return on investment.

If unsuccessful strategies are adopted, these expectations dissolve with the future prospects of the leader in that market. Often, small suppliers and customers fall with the industry leader's demise.

The rationalisation of service stations by the oil companies created a back yard industry of unemployed mechanics, who sought to continue their trades as self-employed vehicle repairers – some successfully, many unsuccesfully.

The unavoidable restructuring of declining and unprofitable industries takes a human toll that is not measured by the company's performance reports. A dominant leader has a social responsibility to plan well ahead and to act as the industry educator if it is to be seen as a worthy corporate citizen. A restructuring strategy, implemented poorly, negates the investment in corporate image identity built up over many years of advertising and sponsorship programmes.

Market Expectations

When the market has reached the decline phase of its life-cycle, it is important to reassess the important aspects of the product to customers. Often, product quality is traded by customers for convenience, availability and service as well as price. The leader should develop the non-price aspects of the offer that are important to target customers.

Distributor Focus versus End User Focus

The company's customer focus may need to be reviewed in terms of the targeting of its product offer. Should it be primarily on the distributor or the end user? Whichever focus is adopted, the specific needs of that group will fashion the design of the strategy.

The relative strengths of the company in relation to its distributors or its end markets will, in part, determine this focus. If very little end user brand awareness or loyalty exists, the economics may dictate a focus on distributors. If the distribution system is weak and high brand loyalty exists in end user markets, the leader may capitalise on this by focusing its strategy on end users and looking for new distribution channels.

What should also be analysed is the change in end user segment trends and in channel segment trends. Cannibalisation frequently occurs between distributor segments because of the prevalence of overservicing of declining markets.

'Push' versus 'Pull' Strategy

Although a marketing strategy may be oriented to a 'push' or a 'pull' approach, normally it contains some elements of both.

A 'push' strategy involves all marketing efforts to be directed towards members of the distribution channel, such as wholesalers, dealers and retailers. Little direct effort is made to create brand awareness in the minds of end users. Supplier and brand preference is created through product quality, availability, service and range, offered at competitive prices to customers.

It involves little end user advertising or point of sale merchandising and no emphasis on product packaging that creates differentiation in the minds of end users. Followed to an extreme, the manufacturer suppliers distributors with private brands and operates a type of 'original equipment' or contract supply business.

A 'pull' strategy relies on consumer awareness and brand preference to 'pull' brands through the distribution channel by end user demand generation. This strategy, on its own, usually requires substantial advertising and promotion budgets over a number of years to have a lasting impact. In declining markets, where there is low brand awareness and low product interest, such as car parts, it is costly and difficult to develop brand preference at consumer level.

Own Brands versus Private Labels
A decision between these two options will depend upon the strength of the leader's brands and the strength of the distributors. Private labelling will tend to be in line with a cost leadership focus and a push strategy. Support of own brands is more in tune with a differentiation focus and a pull strategy.

Target Marketing versus Mass Marketing
The degree of segmentation of the market and the strength and specialisation of competitors will determine the approach taken. This may also be affected by the level of marketing resources available to support the strategy.

Market Penetration versus Diversification
The Ansoff growth model, referred to in Chapter 1, indicates the directional

Table 2.4 Product–Market Strategies

PRODUCT → / MARKET ↓	PRESENT	Product Modification – quality – style – performance	Product Range Extension Size Variation Variety Variation	New Products in Related Technology	New Products in Unrelated Technology
Present	Market Penetration Strategies	Product Reformulation Strategies	Product Range Extension Strategies	Product Development Strategies	Lateral Diversification Strategies
New	Market Development Strategies	Market Extension Strategies	Market Segmentation – Product Differentiation Strategies	Product Diversification Strategies	Longitudinal Diversification Strategies
Resource and/or distribution markets			Forward or Backward Integration Strategies		

options of market penetration, market development, product development, and diversification. These options should be considered by leaders in declining markets.

Diversification may include vertical integration through ownership or franchise of distribution outlets. Market penetration may occur by taking over a direct competitor. An extension of the Ansoff model to include diversification in related and unrelated technologies and into resource or distribution markets, is provided in Table 2.4. When faced with a declining market, options for development and diversification using related technologies should be evaluated, but the higher risk options of diversification into unrelated technologies are also available. Frequently, the route to implementation here lies in joint ventures and acquisitions.

■ Alternative Routes to Profit Improvement

There are three main routes to profit improvement:

- sales growth;
- productivity improvement from changing the balance of assets;
- a combination of these.

In a declining market, sales growth is difficult without asset investment. On the productivity side, using existing assets, the options are:

- reduce costs;
- improve efficiency (asset utilisation);
- selectively increase price to improve margins;
- change the sales mix in favour of higher margin products.

Gaining productivity by changing the asset base involves investment, or divestment, or both.

These routes to profit improvement, shown in Figure 2.1, require different focuses for their achievement – growth, margins and capital utilisation. In declining markets, productivity is usually the primary focus, supported by sales retention and regrowth if feasible.

A classic example of a dominant market leader expanding its sales by using its brand strengths can be seen in the launch of ice-cream Mars bars. Mars launched into what is essentially a mature market by creating new consumers on the back of its strong brand franchise in the chocolate market, thus expanding the market. Mars built on their early success, investing in their own production facility in Strasbourg, broadening the range of Mars ice-creams to include Bounty and Snickers and launching the range across Europe. They are

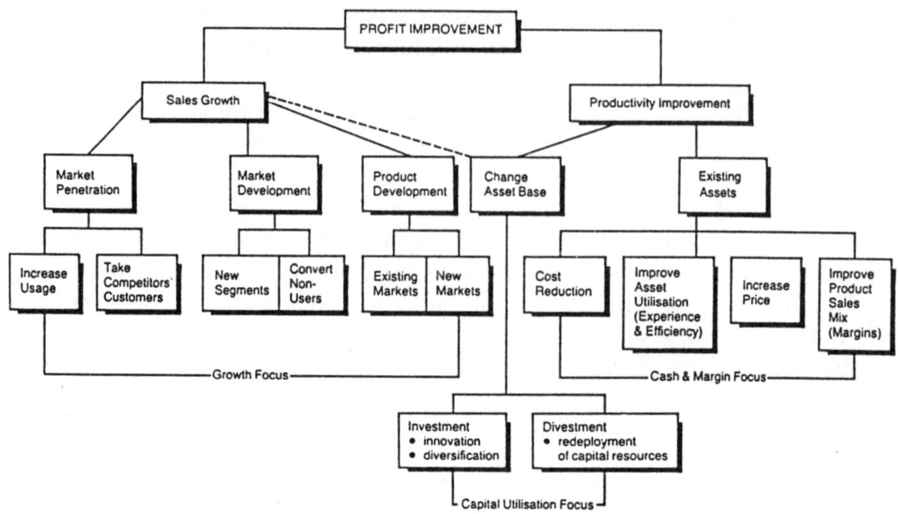

Figure 2.1 Product/division profit improvement options

now in the enviable position of being market leaders in the premium end of both the wrapped impulse and take home multi-pack market segments.

The Mars ice-cream has been a phenomenal success since its launch in the UK in May 1989. It earned £25m for the company in the eight months following its launch. The response has been spectacular, to the extent of Mars having to, at one stage, withdraw promotion to slacken demand. It captured a staggering 10 per cent share of a market it had no previous experience in (ice creams). It has created controversy and destabilised the previous hegemony of Walls and Lyons Maid. It has won awards from consumer groups, industry and marketers alike. This is a distinguished start to a promising future. Spectacular success has since been achieved in most EC Markets.

The company has achieved many of its objectives. It has developed a product which maintains the high quality brand image and its reputation for innovative style. It has created an expanding new market segment, the adult ice-cream eater. It has changed attitudes, encouraging the adult to eat ice-cream and to eat it throughout the year. It has bridged the gap between ice-cream and confectionery, going some way to smoothing the seasonal fluctuation of sales. It opens the future for further diversification of the company's portfolio, from its previous strong bias of confectionery and dog foods, to a whole range of consumer products. The consumer is now used to seeing the Mars brand name in the fridge and freezer.

Mars has succeeded in another stage of diversifying and exploiting its powerful brand image and loyal following. It has always been considered an innovative company with a strong marketing profile. It has again proved worthy of its reputation and has the opportunity in this product of gaining accolade in food technology. The Mars ice-cream story is striking in its achievement. It is a powerful symbol of the consumers' increasing discernment of quality products and the effective use of the marketing discipline.

■ Leader Strategies

If the market leader decides to stay in the market for the long term, despite its decline, a leadership strategy will require a 'package' of decisions designed to restructure the business and its product offering in line with the profitable opportunities available. Two alternative marketing strategy 'packages' are shown in Table 2.5, but several variations of these may be viable in any particular situation.

In each case the elements of the marketing mix must be consistent and specific strategies designed.

For a brief summary of the main options relevant to the top right hand box of Porter's matrix, see Figure 2.2 on page 96.

Table 2.5 Two Strategy Packages

ELEMENTS	*STRATEGY PACKAGERS*	
	Strategy 1	*Strategy 2*
Generic	Differentiation	Cost leadership
Focus	Coverage	Narrow to volume segments
Market	End User	Distributor
Marketing effort	Pull	Push
Branding	Own	Private labels
Segmentation	Targeting	Mass
Strategic direction	Diversification	Market penetration
Route to profit	Investment and regrowth	Productivity and divestment

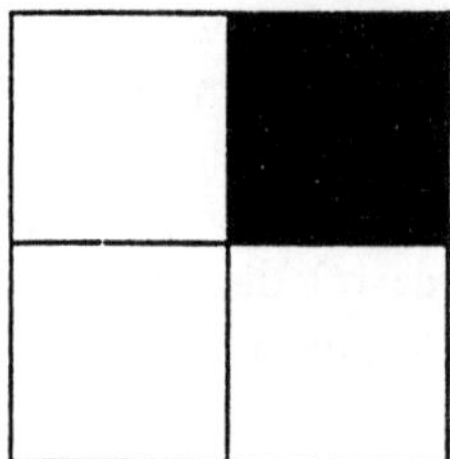

Example: Japanese automobiles, McDonald's fast food

STRATEGY

- Continuous effort to improve differentiation and to reinforce cost advantages: responsiveness, followed with detailed implementation is the name of the game

IMPLICATIONS

- Suppliers management: control and seek cost advantages
- Product design to optimise use of suppliers and assembly
- Process engineering and materials management
- Mass marketing and distribution
- Cost advantages finance differentiation
- Management of implementation makes the difference

Figure 2.2 A 'differentiated, plus cost advantage' strategy is best, but requires superior quality of management

Case Study 2: JCB Defends its Dominance in a Declining Market

The Case of the JCB Sitemaster

Introduction

This case history illustrates how a company can continue to grow and prosper in a declining market through technical innovation and concentration.

J. C. Bamford, Excavators (JCB) is the largest manufacturer of earthmoving equipment in the UK and one of the UK's most successful privately-held engineering groups. Its highest volume product is the backhoe, the familiar yellow excavator with a loader at the front and a small excavator at the rear, for which there is no domestically-produced competition, and JCB is so dominant that the term JCB has become the generic for all backhoes, regardless of manufacturer.

As the backhoe represents the highest percentage of factory output and company profit, its continuing success is of paramount importance to JCB.

The Problem

In 1981 it became apparent that the backhoe market in the UK was in long term decline (see Figure 2.3):

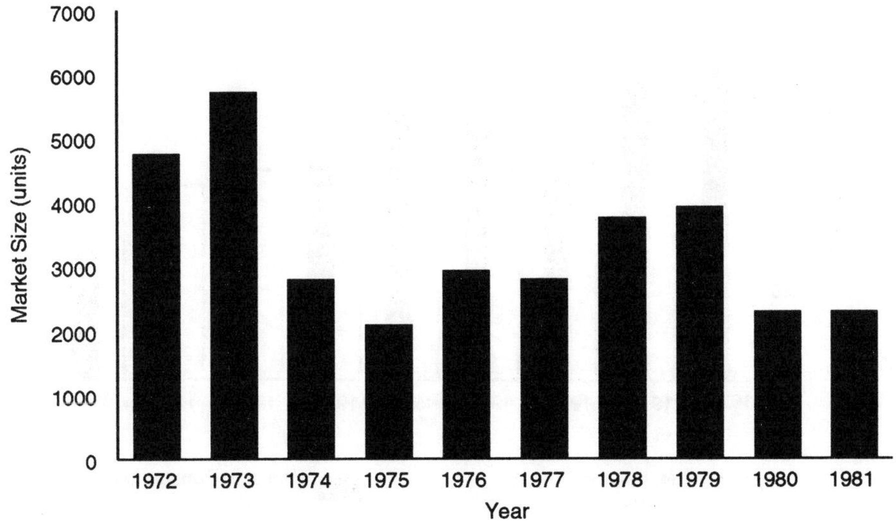

Figure 2.3 Market size for backhoe loaders, 1972–81

- The market had always been cyclic but the 1978/9 peak (see Figure 2.4) was 20 per cent below the 1972/3 peak and it was feared that the next 'peak' would be even worse.
- The world-wide economic recession was hitting the construction and housing sectors very hard and JCB's traditional customers were suffering from a lack of funds to invest in new machinery.
- The recession of the early 80s was forcing down prices and putting severe pressure on profit margins.

Exacerbating this problem was a recent trend towards specialised products, aimed at fulfilling specific requirements. JCB's market research suggested that the backhoe market was saturated and competitors were, therefore, developing niche markets.

The Solution

JCB decided that the on-site versatility of its backhoe was a major factor in its favour and that the ability to use it for more specialised requirements, would represent value and versatility to the customer.

The Company already offered various attachments to the backhoe (forklift, telescopic digger, multi-purpose front bucket, crane attachment and four wheel drive). However, the take-up of these was low, indicating perhaps that customers were unaware of these additional options.

The chosen strategy was to relaunch the backhoe as the 'Sitemaster', the

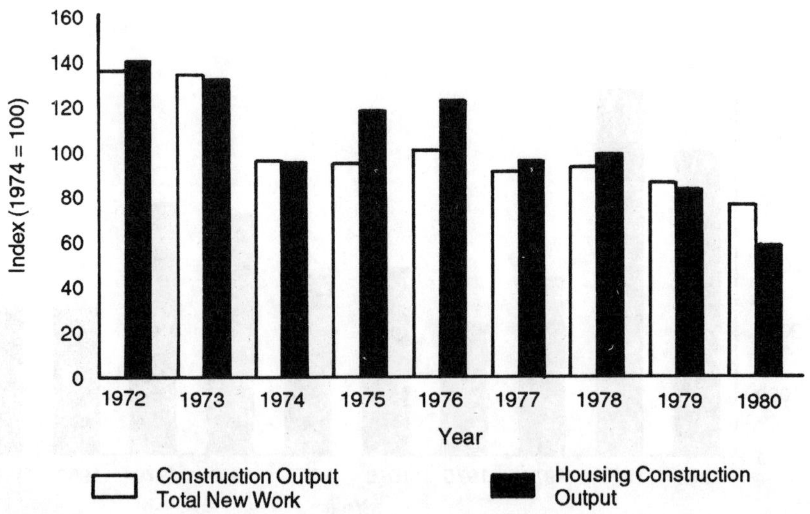

Figure 2.4 Housing and construction

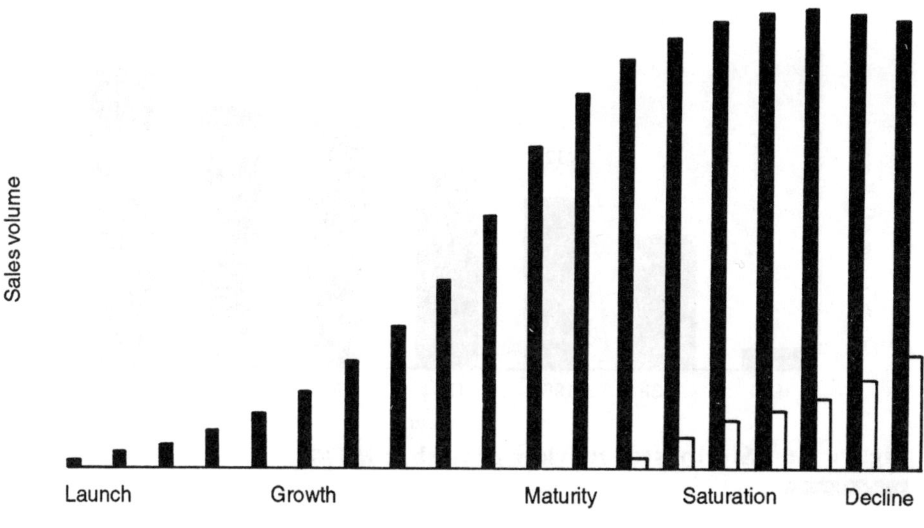

Figure 2.5 Product life-cycle

'One Machine Fleet', to include all options as standard, each being aimed at a specialist site machine, generally used for specific tasks.

In terms of the Ansoff matrix, this was a low risk strategy, involving market development, as the Sitemaster was perceived as a new product, but also entailing market penetration, and extending the backhoe product life-cycle (see Figure 2.5).

□ *The Launch*

The Sitemaster was launched in 1981, with the main thrust of the promotional campaign to make the customer aware of the JCB Sitemaster's investment value as the all-round, versatile site machine which could replace many of the specialist machines on the market, using redesigned literature, key customer targeting, factory vists and extensive training of sales staff and dealers.

Emphasis on strong brand, product differentiation and the reputation for quality and service allowed JCB to command a premium price, while offering excellent value to the customer.

■ Their Success

By 1985, JCB had captured over 45 per cent of the backhoe market (see Figure 2.6) and in addition, the market itself (JCB led the field in this development and its competitors were forced to follow suit), had grown by 32 per cent during this period, largely attributable to the success of the Sitemaster in

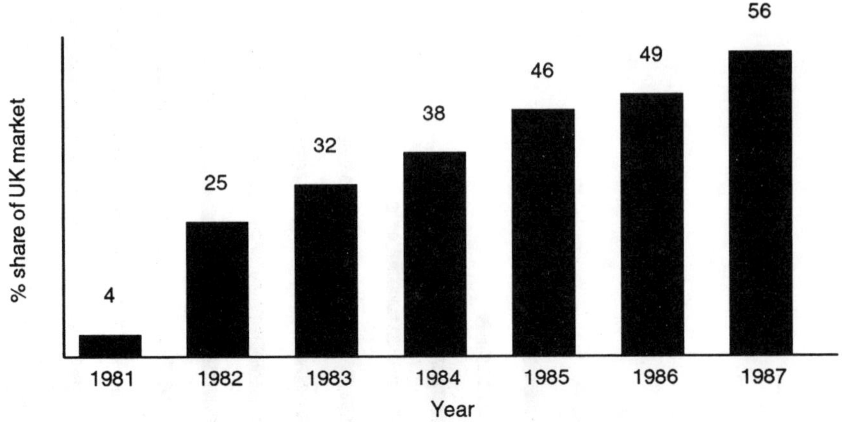

Figure 2.6 Sitemaster market growth, 1981–7

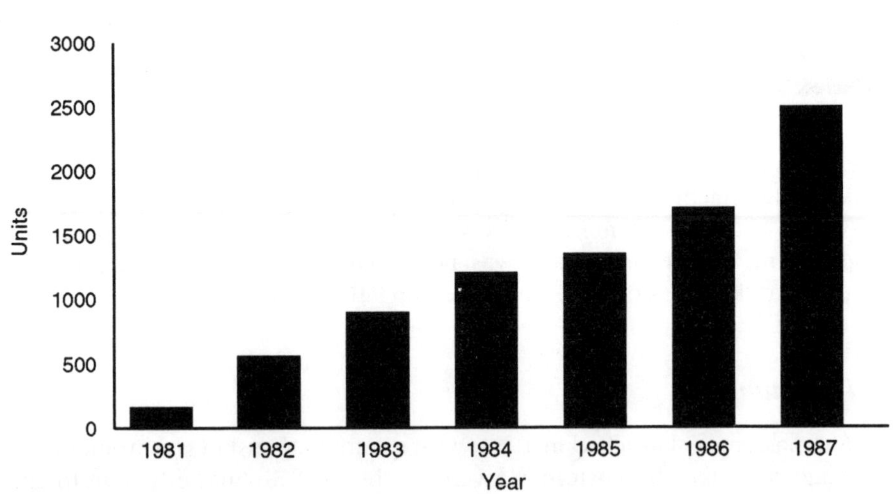

Figure 2.7 Sitemaster sales, 1981–7

redefining and desegmenting the market. In 1985, JCB sold 1,480 Sitemasters, as opposed to 107 in 1981 (see Figure 2.7) – remarkable growth, achieved by combining their unique strengths with the changing requirements of customers.

■ The Broader Picture

In spite of concentrated attacks from US firms and the Japanese, JCB has steadily increased its world market share, and is no longer dependent on its world famous backhoe loader. It is also one of the few construction equipment manufacturers that is profitable. The USA is now JCB's most important export market, in addition to the 30 per cent share of the French and German backhoe loader markets, whilst their telescopic, rough terrain forklift truck is a world leader.

Today, JCB officials proudly compare their performance, not only with US competitors, but also with Japanese companies. For example, JCB's sales, profit and assets per employee are all greater than those of Komatsu, the leading Japanese equipment group.

JCB has also invested heavily in high technology machinery to improve manufacturing productivity. For example, the Company installed a conveyor system for assembling the engine and transmission and then carrying them to the final assembly line, thus replacing labour and forklift trucks, and speeding up the process. Other systems have simplified the handling of parts during stress relieving, shot blasting and painting stages, as well as contributing to higher quality. The Company has also not hesitated to invest in complex manufacturing projects when it felt it could make a better product than it could buy. An example of this is the transmission system for its vehicles.

The result of all these initiatives has been a remarkable increase in productivity, a drop in working capital, and work in progress. In addition, the Company has continued to launch new products in the face of the still-declining backhoe loader market, concentrating on relatively small machines.

With the backhoe loader market growth expected to be minimal by 1992, JCB's entry into the fast growing European market for skid-steer loaders in 1993, did not surprise its rivals. Anticipating the downturn in backhoe demand and building on its strength of product development, JCB had evaluated the opportunities in this relatively fast growing market segment for ten years. The £4 million launch of the innovatively designed JCB Robot, a compact and versatile mini-excavator, developed to tackle smaller jobs, is an important step for the company to secure its dominant position in the excavator market and to generate more recession-proof revenue.

In the traditional highly competitive backhoe market, JCB remains European leader with 40 per cent market share, leading on continual product redesign and improvement to the specification of the range of Sitemasters. Driven by technology, innovation and constant customer consultation throughout Europe, the company's consistent aim is to give value to customers and end users by integrating new features as standard. Computer-aided design has helped JCB reduce the development time from months to weeks, encourage market growth in niche areas and consolidate its position in Europe.

The recent joint venture with Sumitomo has given extra weight to the company's standing in the world market. The combination of Japanese know-how and JCB receptiveness to new ideas has resulted in strong world-wide sales performance, with an export ratio of 70:30. JCB will continue to dominate its chosen markets through product development, judicious alliances and market surveillance.

Case Study 3: Andrex

Defending Market Leadership through Branding

Andrex as a Success

The criteria used for judging marketing success in relation to this case, were the ability of the firm to dominate its market place, satisfy customer needs, and maximise its profit.

Andrex has maintained its share of the toilet tissue market at around 30 per cent for over twenty years (see Figure 2.8). Its next closest competitor, Kleenex, has managed only 12 per cent, while the line denoted by triangles shows the combined share of all own label products.

The satisfaction of customer needs will be examined with the product and innovation. Profit will be examined with price.

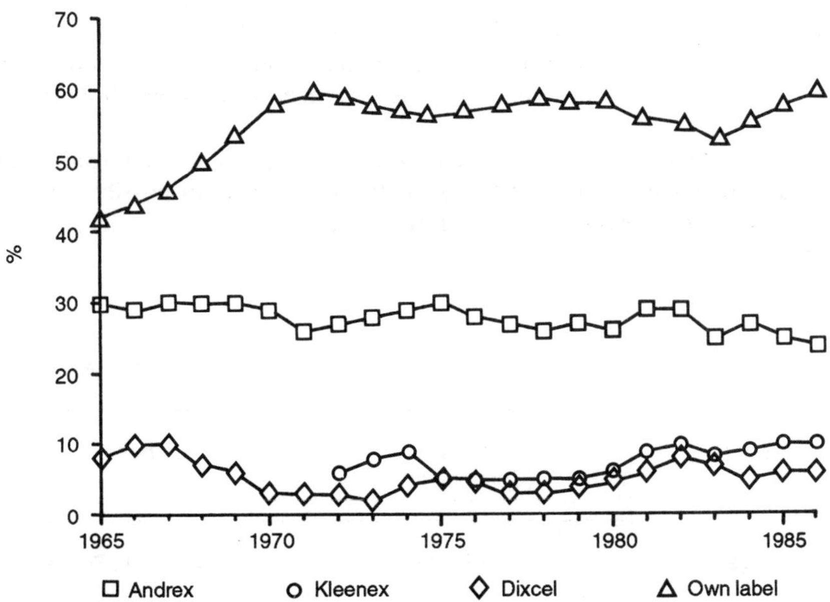

Figure 2.8 Market share of toilet tissue manufacturers

Market Environment and Strategy

Branding

Toilet tissue is a competitive mass market requiring mass production. There is no competitive advantage to be gained from targeting a niche, as a minimum scale of production is needed. Looking at Porter's generic strategies, shown here in Figure 2.9, Scott's choice of branding as a strategy, appears to be logical. The aim of branding has been to differentiate their product and maintain a dominant market position.

Implementation

Product and Innovation

Andrex launched soft tissue in 1956, establishing its position as innovator and market leader. Subsequently, Andrex has seen the need to innovate consistently and upgrade its product to maintain brand supremacy.

Late 1960s	Introduced coloured paper. New display pallets to help retailer.
Early 1970s	Kimberly Clark launched Kleenex, as a direct competitor.
Early 1970s Response	New pack designs; improved colours to match coloured bathrooms; longer rolls.
1980s	Improved softness; larger roll/cheaper per sheet; new nine-pack for convenience/out of town shopping.

Andrex has used innovation to maintain its image as market leader, and meet customer needs. The brand has made this innovation possible, because products have finite lives, whereas brands do not.

	Lower Cost	Differentiate
Broad Target	Cost Leader (Commodity)	Branded
Narrow Target	Cost Focus	Differentiated Focus

Figure 2.9 Porter's Generic Strategies

☐ *Place and Market Power*

Andrex has ensured that its product has always been available in the major outlets. The strength of the brand has ensured that the company continues to get adequate shelf space, as Andrex is ranked by supermarkets as one of the brands that cannot be ignored.

☐ *Promotion – Advertising Strategy*

Andrex has always had the foresight to invest in the brand. From the late 1950s, Andrex has projected a consistent image, using the labrador puppies to create high recall and identification. Advertising has been evenly distributed through the years, maintaining a high brand awareness.

In 1992 over £8 million was spent on advertising, 70 per cent of total toilet tissue advertising.

Despite the different product features emphasised over time, there has been a consistent approach through the brand personality referred to above.

☐ *Price*

Not only has the promotion established Andrex as the leading brand in the market, it has also allowed them to charge a premium price (see Figure 2.10),

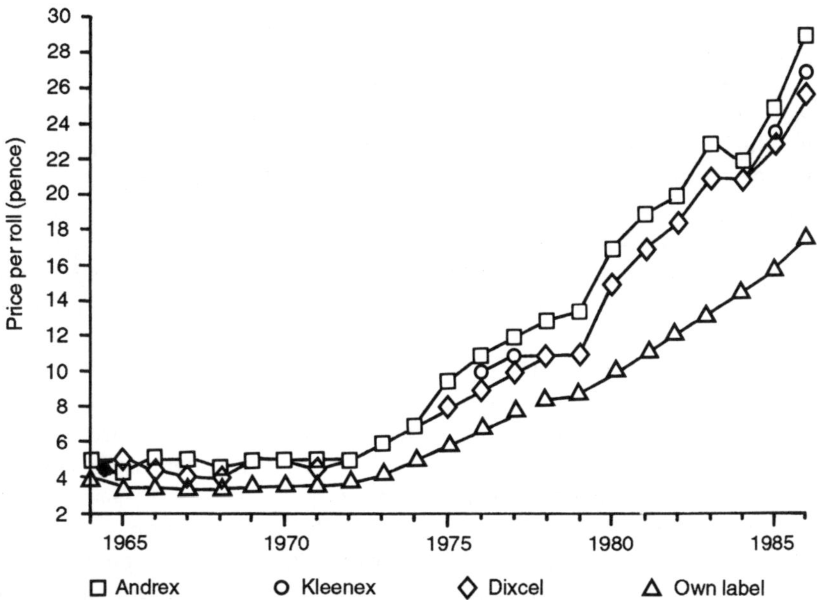

Figure 2.10 Price and competition

which further re-enforces Andrex's image as the premium product. The strategy is thus self-perpetuating.

□ *Profit*

Andrex is priced about 10 per cent above the next brand and with the largest market share, has the cost advantages of large scale production, despite selling at the highest price. Table 2.6 shows how this more than offsets the higher advertising costs.

Table 2.6 Andrex as Market Leader

	1982	*1992*
Market size	£231m	£568m
Andrex share	30% (£70m)	34% (£193m)
Andrex adspend in UK	£4m	£8m

Andrex charges a price premium of 10%, so the additional revenue they earn through the premium more than compensates for their heavy advertising spend.

This ignores the cost saving through large scale production and distribution.

Admittedly, promotion is not the sole cause of the price premium or huge market share, but it is part of the mix that contributes to these factors.

Source: 1982 figures from Mintel March 1983; 1992 figures from various sources

■ Conclusion

The key to Andrex's marketing strategy has been the creation of a premium brand which meets the consumer's needs. Each element of the marketing mix re-enforces and supports the other, ensuring effective execution of the strategy.

Fifty years on, from the early days of Andrex, Scott, the world's biggest tissue manufacturer, has nurtured a resilient brand. Andrex has 34 per cent by value of the UK toilet tissue market in 1992, nearly three times that of its nearest rival Kleenex, and 29 per cent by volume, and has staved off competition from own-label competition through premium price positioning and £8 million plus above-the-line promotion.

The £5.7m television advertising campaign, featuring the Andrex puppy is now in its twentieth-year, and the key to the company's advertising, achieving a higher prompted recall than any other brand.

To date, Andrex is a UK-only brand, but the consolidation of marketing activities into a pan-European account worth £30 million signals a bid to become a pan-European brand, using a common brand name and advertising campaign. However there are problems which may slow down Andrex's ability to penetrate the European market. The predominance of own-label (for example, own label market share in Germany is 67 per cent) and heavy price based competiton will question the rationale for a premium priced branded product.

Brand values have hardly changed over fifty years; an up-market strategy and premium pricing, at 40 per cent above the market average, remains the foundation of Andrex's extraordinary success. Andrex is in fourth place in the league table of UK brands sold through grocers, and this position allows the company to dominate what should be a commodity and price only market.

The strength of the brand continues. Scott recently announced the restructuring of its operation along brand lines to give greater focus to the brand, by creating two business groups with one exclusively focused on Andrex's range of branded products. Fiesta kitchen towels have been relaunched under the Andrex brand umbrella, and new products including the technologically advanced Smart Wipe trade off the brand name Andrex, an essential ingredient to guarantee trial.

Undoubtedly a highly enduring brand, the threat to Andrex's dominance in the UK from the rise of own label brands should be watched carefully.

Case Study 4: Glaxo

A Global Success Story of Product Excellence and the Classic use of Competitive Market Strategy to Become a Dominant Market Force

Introduction

The rise of Glaxo plc from being a modest British company to the world's number two pharmaceutical manufacturer is arguably the most spectacular business success story since the Second World War. Outstanding financial performance mirrors this rise (see Figure 2.11 and Table 2.7).

This has been achieved in an increasingly cost-contained health care environment, in less than a decade, largely because of one drug, the premium

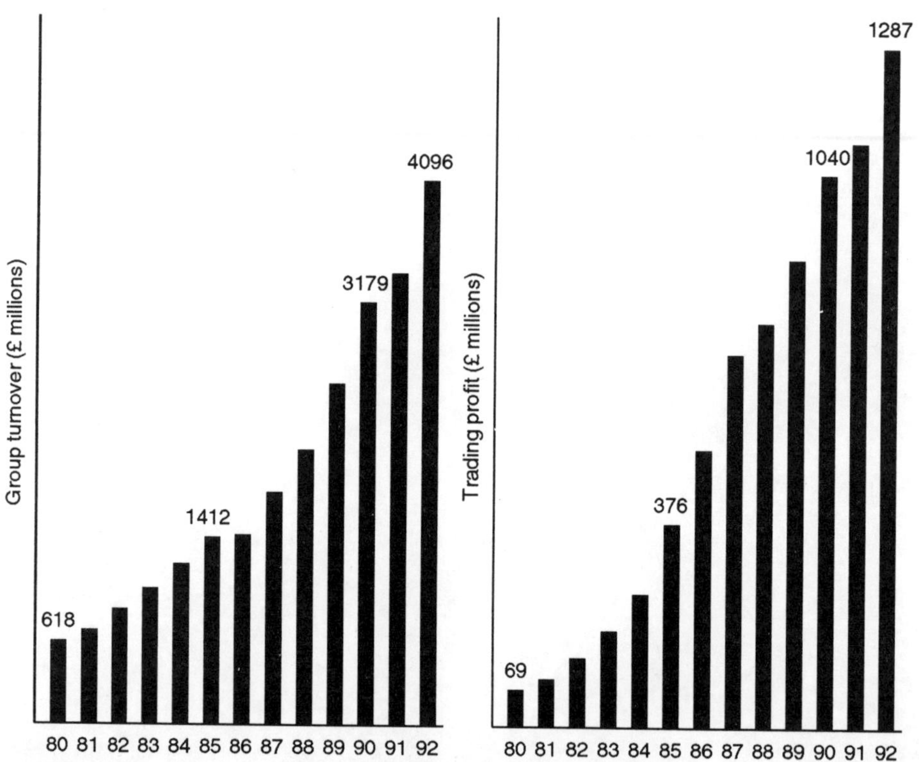

Figure 2.11 Glaxo financial performance to 1992

Table 2.7 Glaxo Financial Performance

	1980	*1984*	*1988*	*192*
Sales	£434m	£915m	£209m	£4096m
Profit before tax	£ 56m	£256m	£832m	£1427m
R&D expenditure	£32m	£77m	230m	£595m
Earnings per share	1.5p	5.7p	19.3p	34.3p
Dividends per share (ordinary)	0.6p	1.6p	6.2p	17.0p

anti-ulcerant Zantac. The success of this drug can be attributed to three factors: leadership, planning and superb marketing. Sir Paul Girolami gave the Company the mission 'to become a world top five ranking pharmaceutical company' – Glaxo exceeded this. Sir Paul has been widely credited with Glaxo's dramatically successful growth. Through planning, executives compressed Zantac's research into six years and launched globally with a 'fast-second' strategy in less than three years, thereby critically extending effective patent-life. Finally, Glaxo demonstrated classic execution of marketing principles: segment identification, life-cycle management, use of the marketing mix, branding, controlled business expansion and emphatic crushing of major competition.

■ Segment Identification

The foundations for Zantac's success were laid in the 1970s with the launch of Tagamet by Smith Kline and French (SKF), an oral ulcer therapy. Prior to 1974, severe ulcers were treated by surgery. The simplicity of Tagamet uncovered a massive, latent patient population. By 1981, Tagamet with annual sales of $800m was the world's best-selling drug. In that year Zantac was launched in competition.

□ *Introductory Phase (1981–1983)*

The Zantac launch strategy was a classic application of marketing strategy. They created a 'halo' of superiority around the Zantac brand; promoted 'perceived' benefits (Zantac did not cause impotence, a fact unscientifically associated with Tagamet); premium priced; used consultant gastroenterologists to influence general practitioner prescribing (WOM concept); and finally, matched competitors' marketing spend. This meant signing co-marketing agreements with prestigious local companies in countries where Glaxo was weak. Key was the US venture with Hoffmann La Roche, effectively doubling the Zantac sales force to match SKF's (see Table 2.8). By the end of the introductory phase, global sales of Zantac were nearly £200m per annum.

Table 2.8 Glaxo Co-Marketing Agreements for Zantac

USA	—	Hoffmann La Roche (Switzerland)
France	—	Laboratories Fournier
Italy	—	Menarini

□ *The Growth Phase (1984–6)*

In a market itself growing at 20 per cent per annum, Zantac rapidly eroded Tagamet's share in nearly all markets. Classical Ansoff principles were used (see Figure 2.12): there was increased market penetration (see Figure 2.13); product development (once-a-day convenience forms); and market development into new segments, such as reflux oesophagitis and gastritis. By 1986, Zantac was truly a global £600m per annum 'BCG-Star', with economies of scale from production centres in the UK and Singapore improving margins to in excess of 40 per cent.

□ *Maturity (1987–)*

A two-competitor, £1.5 billion market, inevitably brought in serious competition. In 1987, the US giant Merck launched Pepcid; it failed miserably, largely

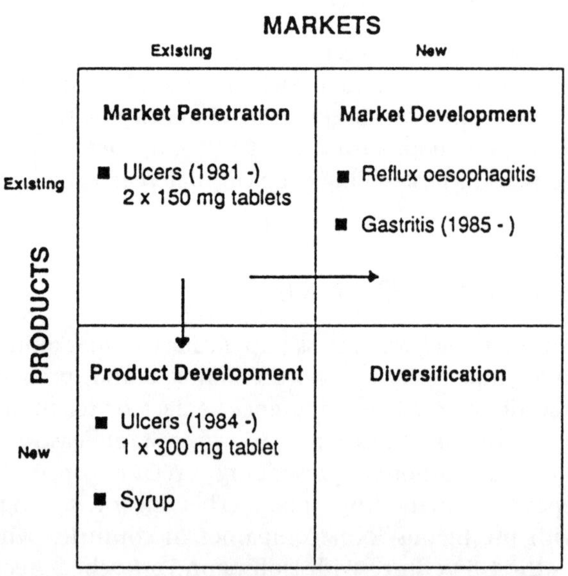

Figure 2.12 Ansoff matrix of Zantac business development

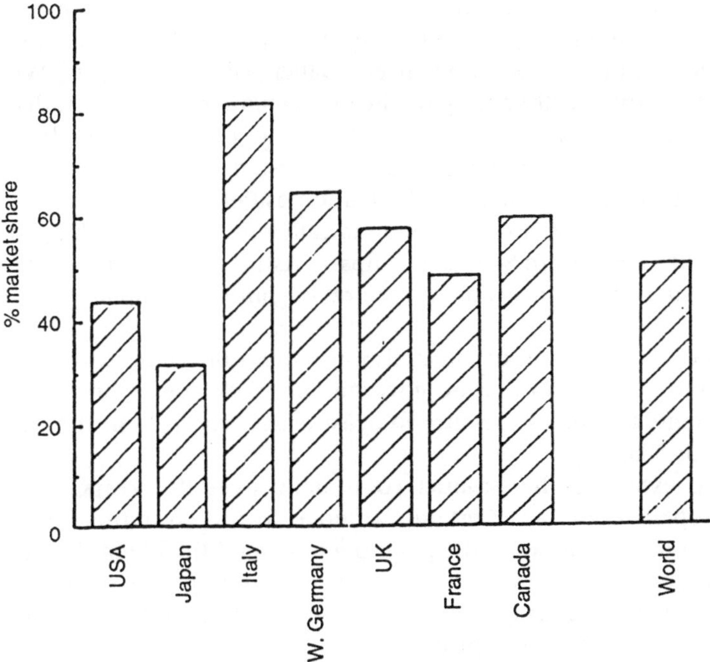

Figure 2.13 Zantac market penetration by country, 1986

because of the dominance of Zantac. While SKF resorted to innovative discounting of Tagamet, Glaxo continued to pursue promotional activities aimed at reinforcing the Zantac brand image. In contrast, Merck undertook expensive 'features-based' promotions – without offering additional product benefits. Doctors were not convinced and reacted against another 'me-too' drug. Glaxo itself was now set to dominate the market.

■ Summary

In 1988, Zantac became the first drug in history to break the £1 billion sales barrier and continues to grow. Other potentially exciting segments are under active development and look certain to carry Zantac's success forward. By 1995 Glaxo may be the world's biggest and most profitable drug company.

There are problems looming on the horizon, however.

Zantac continues to be a significant cash cow product, generating annual sales of about £2 billion, (44 per cent of group sales), 30 per cent of group profits and, as a flagship product, contributing to the image of Glaxo as a successful innovative research company.

But threats to Zantac's supremacy in the world markets take many forms. The original patent on the drug is due to expire in 1995, and the extended patent protection in the US has been challenged in the courts. Without this protection, Zantac will be prey to cheaper generic substitutes. Indeed, the US patent for Tagamet, Zantac's great rival is due to expire in 1994, leading to the probable spawning of competitive generic versions, priced at 90 per cent below Zantac, thus eroding its market share and position.

Zantac is also under attack from a radically different technology in the form of substitute Losec from Swedish company Astra, which many experts claim is superior in performance and therefore is gaining credibility on the world markets.

The recession has had its effect also; premium priced prescription drugs are being squeezed in world wide government crack downs on drug costs and governments are under pressure to delist drugs especially in the US, a critical market for Glaxo.

Having extended the product continually over the years, what are the options open to Zantac? Certainly a move to the Over the Counter (OTC) market would capitalise on the potential to extend the life of the product. But consideration of this strategy has given rise to a split at Glaxo Board level between expanding into OTC sales, and the traditional concentration on research and development of high-priced prescription only drugs. This battle resulted in the resignation of Chief Executive Dr Ernest Mario, supporter of the OTC option.

And without the revenue of Zantac, where will Glaxo's future lie? New products will remain the lifeblood of the company, and the success of drugs launched in the early 1990s, including Zofran and Imigran, is vital to offset the expected decline in earnings. Glaxo's commitment to concentrated research on drugs that are truly efficacious rather than development of a wider range of products, will ensure their influential position.

CHAPTER 3

Low Cost, Low Differentiation Strategies

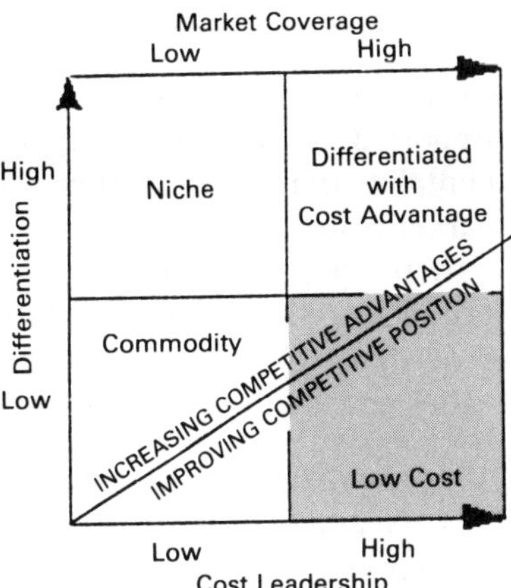

■ Strategies for Leadership in Undifferentiated Joint Dominance Markets

■ Section 1: Introduction

The banking industry is a good example of undifferentiated markets in which a number of large competitors exist, none of whom have a dominant share, but all of whom are seeking a leadership position.

The general principles, discussed in Chapter 2, of offensive and defensive strategies and options for high share businesses, apply to companies holding a jointly dominant position. If the aim is to achieve outright leadership, however, the orientation must usually be offensive.

Hugh Davidson, in his book *Offensive Marketing*, suggests that offence is just as much a matter of attitude as it is of strategy. He proposes seven spokes comprising offensive attitudes:

- *vision* of how the business will change and improve in the future ahead of its competitors;
- commitment to delivery of superior *value* to customers consistently over time;
- *innovation* in every area of the business to achieve improvements in customer value or costs of operation;
- *long term outlook*, which allows commitment to longer term growth and profit goals;
- continuing *investment* to renew and improve all assets, especially new products, existing brands and customer franchises;
- *persistent attack* providing the overall focus of a company's activity on fighting and winning. Any defensive effort is part of a long term plan that will culminate in a fresh attack; and
- *speed of response* to changes in customer needs or in the business environment, and quick counter-attack to competitive thrusts.[1]

Just as a football or cricket team wins consistently with an offensive attitude supported by skill and planning, so companies can develop an offensive mentality that enables them to win consistently and improve share in the market place.

There are a number of different types of offensive strategies which a strong second-placed company or a jointly dominant firm can adopt to obtain market leadership.

Ries and Trout propose three offensive principles:

1 Study the strength of your main competitor's position.
2 Find a weakness in the competitor's strength and attack that point. A competitor, for example, may be delivering poor or slow service because it is large or it has too many customers.
3 Launch the attack on as narrow a front as possible. The principle of force allows a massing of resources to achieve superiority in one area – regional market or market segment.[2]

These principles may be applied to different types of offensive strategies:

- Head-on strategy involves a direct frontal attack to beat a competitor through sheer force. To be successful a firm needs good products, heavy marketing support and substantial financial reserves to enable a prolonged counter-attack by competitors to be rebuffed. Usually a relative advantage in resources, commitment and management focus is required to win a head-on encounter. Ultimately, innovative strategies will be required to sustain a lead in markets characterised by joint dominance.
- Innovation, by being first to provide new products or services that fill existing needs better or uncover new needs, gives a firm an opportunity for leadership in undifferentiated markets. Bernard Matthews has adopted this strategy consistently in the UK poultry market during the past ten years and has become the dominant player in the industry.
- A flanking strategy is made into an uncontested or weakly defended area by the main competitor.

For success, the strategy needs to result in the firm's major competitor losing market share to the prospective leader and frequently to other competitors.

The market structure and share levels of joint leaders have an influence on appropriate competitive strategies.

The level and type of competitive activity typical in undifferentiated markets varies with market conditions. In growth markets, competitors strive to build market share and attain a clear leadership position. In mature markets, emphasis moves to holding and consolidating competitive position with aspects of strategy designed to cover specialists, some of whom may be competing on a price basis.

The three sections that follow analyse the strategies of companies in undifferentiated markets.

■ Section 2: Developing a Market Leadership Position in Service Industries

Most large growth-oriented companies state, as one of their main objectives, the desire to be market leader in the markets or segments they serve.

This section looks at the strategic concerns applicable to developing and maintaining market leadership. A case history of the grocery industry in Europe examines the developments undertaken by certain retailers to take the initiative and establish market leadership in Europe.

■ The Market Leader

To obtain market leadership, a company needs to have a number of characteristics:

- the largest market share in the overall market or major market segment;
- an ability to influence market trends and the activities and results of its competitors;
- a record of leading individually, or with other competitors, in major developments in the industry, such as product innovation, government legislation on standards for the industry, or technological change;
- to be recognised by the market as *the* leader in the industry.

The company must reach a position where it has the greatest ability to manage the market and the competition to its advantage, by using its influence, profit and cash generated to contain the activities of its competitors and invest in new initiatives.

■ Strategic Issues in Service Industries

Companies competing in service industries, in developing their competitive marketing strategies, must consider factors which in product-based industries are less significant. Sectors such as telecommunications, transport, insurance and home repairs are good examples of service industries.

□ *Intangibility*

The intangibility of the service company's 'product' creates particular challenges to the marketer in communicating the benefits to the customer and ensuring that those benefits are realised. British Telecom, for example, provides customers with the capacity to reach information and overseas data banks by way of data communication lines between the customer's computer terminal and the data base. Potential users need to know what data banks are available, how they can reach them, and for what purpose the information can be used. Also service has to be 'used' before it can be assessed and so is purchased on trust.

The intangibility factor means that customers tend to develop purchase behaviour on the basis of three main elements: experience; referrals; and company image.

Experience

Marketing strategies need to focus on making it easy to test a service at minimum risk to the prospect. The customer, once satisfied with the benefits and familiar with the methods of access, frequently becomes brand loyal. Where strategies can be adopted to 'lock the customer in', this reinforces the 'partnership' status of company and client.

In the courier market, companies such as TNT have specialised divisions that provide package deals to retain customers. For large users this may take the form of contractual arrangements. For small users the provision of 'jetpack' envelopes prepaid at different rates according to the number bought are a means of committing customers to a particular service.

Referrals

The development of referrals comes from satisfied customers and, in a service business, highlights the importance of loyal customers. This is a strategic asset from which products and market-building strategies can be developed, and thus protection of the customer base is of major importance.

Image

Service companies must develop a distinct, positive image if they are to achieve leadership in their industries. A study of the financial industry conducted some years ago showed that people believe their banks are unfriendly, bureaucratic, slow to react and oriented more to large corporations. Whether or not this is true matters little, because during the last ten years many individual account holders have moved away from banks to building societies because of what they perceive as negative experiences.

■ Extending the Marketing Mix

Lovelock suggests that service is a process and any service business can be thought of as a system in which many more elements are directly exposed to the customer.[3] In service businesses, people are an integral part of the offering because they can fundamentally affect the service delivery. Wrong advice on an airline booking, for example, has an immediate effect on customer satisfaction.

Magrath suggests that three further Ps should be added to the service marketing mix for strategic marketing purposes:

- *Personnel* have a direct bearing on a service received;
- *Physical facilities* influence the convenience of service, image and 'personality' of the organisation;
- *Process management* involves the tasks, schedules and processes involved in delivering service and affect how the customer receives the services.[4]

Table 3.1 indicates some of the important elements involved in an extended marketing mix for strategic marketing of services.[5]

■ Strategic 'Soft Spots'

In service businesses at least three areas need realistic consideration of how the company is performing relative to its competitors:

Service Delivery Standards

Are the standards what the market is seeking, or are they standards of technical excellence or tradition that are imagined as a part of the culture of the organisation? It is possible to both under-service or over-service the market. For example, the banking industry in many European countries is over-branched, with many branches under-utilised by consumers, who are increasingly finding that they no longer need to use bank branch facilities.

Consistency of Quality

Quality control procedures and monitoring of customer satisfaction are important parts of maintaining an image and a consistent brand position. The decline in quality and reliability of many service sectors in the building industry has been a continuing spur to the do-it-yourself market.

The increasing frequency with which small business owners 'shop around' for an accommodating bank manager within a bank's branch network indicates variability in the quality of service delivered by the various outlets of one institution. (It also suggests dissatisfaction with the service offered by a particular branch.)

Credibility of Promise

The comparative ease with which new service concepts can be devised and packaged sometimes lead to an over-optimistic belief that a particular promise can be delivered. In the banking industry, promotional packages for small firms proliferated during the 1980s, yet the promises have rarely been delivered. Likewise, the promise of excellent service promoted by airlines in the 1990s is rarely lived up to.

Table 3.1 The Marketing Mix for Services

Product	*Price*	*Place*	*Promotion*	*People*	*Physical Facilities*	*Process Management*
Range	Level	Location	Advertising	Personnel:	Environment	Policies
Quality	Discounts	Accessibility	Personal selling	Training	Furnishings	Procedures
Level	Allowances	Distribution channels	Sales promotion	Discretion	Colour	Mechanization
Brand name	Commissions	Distribution coverage	Publicity	Commitment	Layout	Employee discretion
Service line	Payment terms		Public relations	Incentives	Noise level	Customer involvement
Warranty	Customer's perceived value			Appearance	Facilitating Goods	Customer direction
After sales service	Quality/price			Interpersonal behaviour	Tangible clues	Flow of activities
	Differentiation			Attitudes		
				Other customers:		
				Behaviour		
				Degree of involvement		
				Customer/customer contact		

Source: Derived from B. H. Blooms and M. J. Bitner, 'Marketing Strategies and Organisation Structures for Service Firms' in J. Donnelly and W. R. George, (eds), *Marketing of Services*, American Marketing Association, Chicago, 1981.

■ Strategic Dangers

In service industries, there are a number of strategic directions that spell danger. Three important ones are noted here:

Product Proliferation
Competitive dynamics can lead quickly to proliferation of products and services. The banking industry, in their attempts to achieve full market coverage in a fast growing and increasingly competitive industry, rapidly increased their range of products and services during the 1980s. Yet product or service proliferation can easily lead to customer and employee confusion and dissatisfaction, while at the same time increasing costs.

Going Electronic at the Customer Interface
One of the dangers of reducing human contact with customers by using technology is the potential for losing the relationship with the customer and becoming out of touch with the market. Even in today's electronic age, 'human touch' is still important to many people.

Assuming Customer Knowledge
Staff of a service business become so familiar with the services offered, that it is automatically assumed that customers also know. But they don't. Even frequent users do not know all the potential benefits of a service. The marketing stategy should include elements to address this and create new opportunities for repeat business and increased usage of services.

■ Strategies for Leadership

The case history that follows looks at the European grocery retailing market.

Case Study 5: The Single European Grocery Market*

Introduction

According to Theodore Levitt, companies which do not adapt to the new global realities will become the victims of those who do and will subsequently fail. Whilst Levitt may be overstating the case for globalisation, the enactment of some three hundred articles to remove all non-tariff trade barriers intended to create a Single European Market (SEM) makes 'Europeanization' a reality for industry.

The European market is even bigger in terms of population than the two leading world commercial powers of the USA and Japan. However, as can be seen from the gross domestic product figures shown in Figure 3.1, the economy of Europe has been held back by the historical fragmentation of the market into

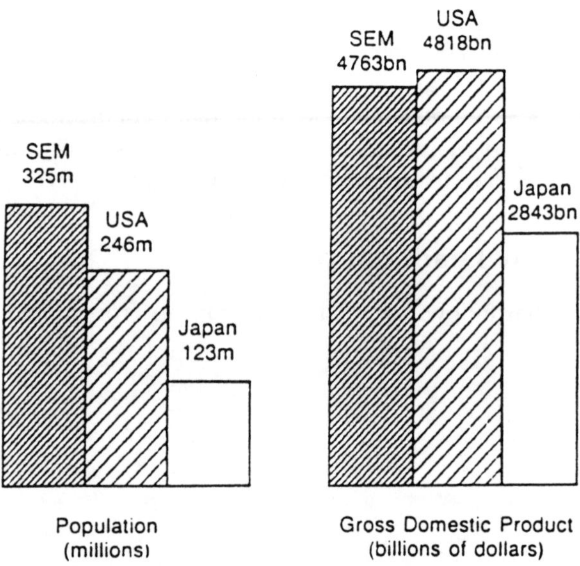

Figure 3.1 GDP and population of the world's leading commercial powers, 1988

Source: OECD[6]

* This case study is taken from a paper by Keith Thompson and Simon Knox of Cranfield School of Management, which appeared in *European Management Journal*, Vol. 9, No. 1, March 1991 and is used with their kind permission.

smaller national markets. The purpose of the SEM is to encourage firms to take advantage of the enlarged market of more than 320m people so that improved economies of scale can drive up productivity and reduce costs.

As the benefits of the SEM become clearer for manufacturing industry, the question arises as to whether the same opportunity exists for service industries such as food retailing. Van der Ster argues that food choice is simply too nationalistic in character for the export or import of store concepts to be successful in the short term.[7] He concludes that it may be the twenty-first century before we can anticipate the emergence of a 'Euro-lifestyle' leading eventually to the development of pan-European store concepts.

Though Van der Ster's view may seem appealing and logical to marketing theorists, the reality of the market is somewhat different.

Many large grocery retailers from France, Germany and the Benelux countries already have an impressive record of cross-border operations within Europe (see Table 3.2). These continental retailers, driven by saturation in their national market and static (or declining) population levels, are planning further expansion within the SEM. The high margins enjoyed by UK retailers provide a tempting prospect for grocery retailers from mainland Europe.[8] Aldi, one of Europe's largest retailers, has already set up operations in the UK. This

Table 3.2 Selected European Representation of Major EC Grocery Retailers

	Benelux	France	Italy	Spain/ Portugal	West Germany	UK
Benelux						
Delhaize	N			R		
GB-Inno-BM	N	R	R			
France						
Auchan		N	R			R
Carrefour		N		R		
Casino	R	N				
Docks de France		N		R		
Euromarche		N		R		
Promodes		N	R	R	R	
West Germany						
Aldi	R	R			N	R
Tengelmann	R				N	
UK						
Marks & Spencer	R	R		R		N

Legend:
N = National Base. R = Representation outside national base.

Source: Adapted from Debenham Tewson and Chinnocks[9]

privately owned West German discount grocer has managed to undercut almost every competitor in every country it has entered in Europe.[10]

It would seem that none of the top British grocery retailers have any shops in continental Europe. However, Marks and Spencer does sell food in some of its overseas stores. Furthermore, Killen and Lees found that UK food retailers have little or no intention of expanding into continental Europe in the foreseeable future.[11]

Reluctance to enter the European market was confirmed by Tesco's Chairman, Sir Ian Maclaurin. In denying rumours of a European takeover bid for French grocers Genty Cathiard, he stated, 'Our research shows that there are still enormous oppoptunities for growth within the United Kingdom and we intend to continue our development here with the greatest vigor.'[12] Sainsburys, the largest UK grocery retailer, has only one overseas subsidiary and that is in the USA. In a recent communication, Sainsbury stated, 'The company chose the USA for overseas expansion rather than extending its operations into other European countries and has no plans to alter this policy.'[13] Thus, the major British grocery retailers reject the idea of expansion into Europe. Their preferred choice for overseas expansion remains the USA; a difficult market in which many British retailers have failed to succeed.[14]

Grocery retailing in Europe is about to undergo a more dramatic change than at any time in the last 25 years. At the very least, the balance of power between grocery buyers and food manufacturers must again be brought into question, particularly if manufacturers are quick to take advantage of the SEM to create pan-European firms. At the same time, UK grocery retailers are likely to be challenged on their home ground by their European peers.

The purpose of this case study is to explore the effects of changes which stem from the SEM in relation to European food retailing. Our strategic analysis has been focused primarily upon the prospects within the UK for European retailers.

■ UK Grocery Multiples and Europe

Viewed in isolation from Europe, it can be seen in Figure 3.2 that the major UK grocery multiples currently conform to Porter's view of market structures, displaying an U-shaped relationship between net margin and market share, with both the very large companies and the niche firms sustaining higher profits.[15] However, as part of a much larger European market structure, the UK's biggest grocery retailers may become only middle-ranking players, since they are considerably smaller in turnover than several of their continental rivals (see Table 3.3). Thus, by confining themselves to only one sixth of the total market, the possibility of UK grocers becoming major players in Europe is simply unrealistic. As the new order emerges and the established competitive structures in the UK disintegrate, UK grocery retailers could become 'stuck in the middle' or, at best, niche marketers relying upon a defence of their geographical segment within the European market to bring the rewards of a

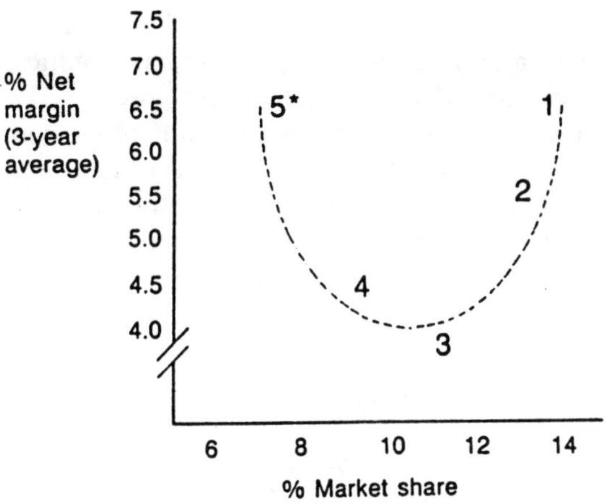

Legend: 1 = Sainsbury; 2 = Tesco; 3 = Gateway; 4 = Argyll; 5 = Asda

*Adjusted for anticipated drop of 25% in profit in half-year report.

Figure 3.2 Structure of UK grocery retailing, 1989

Source: Company reports and *Retail Business*.[16]

Table 3.3 Turnover of the Major European Grocery Retailers, 1987/88

Organisation	*Turnover (£000m) 1987/88*	*Country*
Tengelmann	10.0	W. Germany
Spar Internationale	9.0	—
Rewe Buying Group	8.4	W. Germany
Edeka Buying Group	7.1	W. Germany
Leclerc	6.6	France
Albrecht (Aldi)	6.4	W. Germany
Carrefour	5.7	France
Rewe-Liebbrand	5.0	W. Germany
Dee Corp.	4.8	UK
Sainsbury	4.8	UK
Marks & Spencer	4.6	UK
Tesco	4.1	UK
Intermarche	3.8	France
Promodes	3.5	France
Ahold	3.5	Netherlands
Casino	3.5	France
Argyll	3.2	UK
Asko	3.1	W. Germany

Source: Dawson, J. A. and Burt, S.[17]

focused strategy. However, given the experienced internationalism of some of their European rivals and the progressive convergence of lifestyles throughout Europe, perhaps even that defence is a forlorn hope.[18,19]

The SEM will facilitate a greater European retail presence in the UK and will ultimately result in a Europe-wide retail grocery market in which British retailers will have had no choice but to compete. But when it happens, will the UK's major grocers be looking the other way – across the Atlantic?

Next, we analyse the changes in market structure which are likely to occur in UK grocery retailing as a result of the SEM.

■ The Framework of Analysis

Porter's Structural Framework, shown in Figure 3.3, offers a suitable vehicle for the analysis of change as the UK becomes part of a unified European market. In carrying out such an analysis, we believe that two structural changes emerge as being particularly important in the grocery market: the threat of new entrants into the UK, and an intensification of rivalry. Consequently, these factors are considered in more detail.

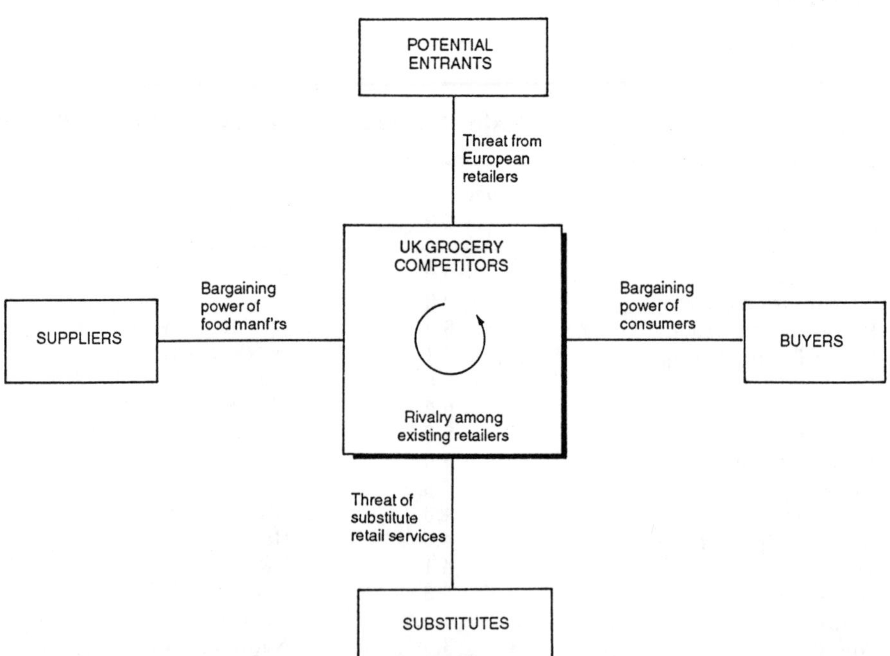

Figure 3.3 Porter's structural framework

Sources: Adapted from Porter, *Competitive Strategy*, 1980.

■ The Threat of New Entrants

□ *Government Policy*

The SEM will open up UK grocery retailing to experienced market entrants from continental Europe. These retailers are large enough not only to overcome the barriers of scale but, because they exhibit a diversity in objectives and style, they also threaten to change the 'rules of the game' in the UK significantly.

The fact that foreign investment is welcomed by the British government is in marked contrast to the protective attitudes displayed by other European countries such as West Germany. Foreign takeovers would be much easier to orchestrate in the UK than in many other EC countries, rendering UK grocery retailers much more vulnerable than their European counterparts. At the local government level, the attitude towards planning controls is much freer in the UK in comparison with procedures in many continental countries.[20]

The response by UK grocery multiples to the domestic European threat has been mainly defensive. Firstly, they have attempted to occupy the high ground in the UK with the best sites and, secondly, they are exploring the possibilities of forming buying groups in Europe in order to balance an increase in supplier size and bargaining power. This hardly seems an adequate response to the prospect of a market which will expand sixfold in population.

□ *Economies of Scale*

While acknowledging that entry barriers for aspiring grocery retailers are generally low, Duke points out that scale barriers are implicit in the need for new entrants to attain competitiveness by acquiring a degree of monopsonistic power similar to that enjoyed by incumbent rivals.[21] The buying power of major multiples enables them to obtain favourable prices which their smaller rivals have no chance of matching. This advantage enables the largest grocery retailers to increase their customer base by offering lower prices leading to a cycle of concentration at the expense of small-scale competitors (see Figure 3.4).

Therefore, to gain enough bargaining power to be competitive in the UK, European entrants will need to acquire a large number of scarce, expensive large-store sites. Furthermore, they must achieve it in a short time span, in competition with existing UK retailers, who are already reporting major difficulties in finding suitable sites.[22] Possibly, the only way for a newcomer with adequate capital to aquire a sufficient number of good sites is by taking over an existing trader. However, companies which are available for acquisition are often only available because they are flawed. Gateway, which achieved third place in the market by 1986, is a case in point. Unable to integrate efficiently the disparate assortment of stores and sites which it had acquired,

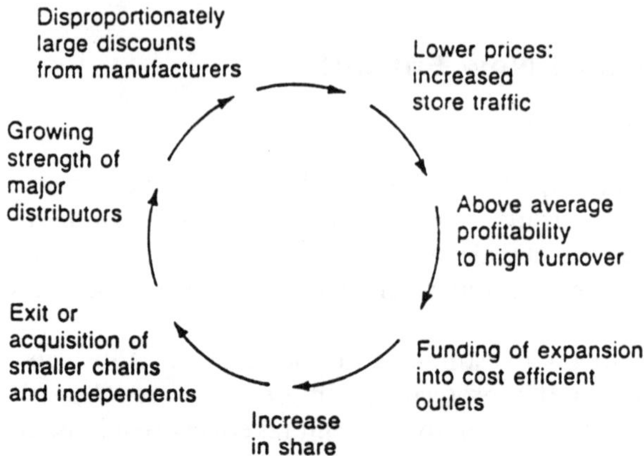

Figure 3.4 The cycle of retail concentration

Source: McKinsey & Co.[23]

the company's performance remained so far below par that eventually Gateway itself was acquired by Isosceles in 1990 (see Figure 3.2).

An alternative strategy for retailers, in their drive to attain economies of scale and monopsonistic power, is the formation of European buying groups. The founding of the European Retail Association in 1989 by Argyll of the UK, Casino of France and Ahold of the Netherlands is a good example of this. The combined turnover of the three members of this association is even greater than the existing buying groups which are such an important feature of European markets (see Table 3.4).

Table 3.4 Comparison of the Turnover of European Grocery Buying Groups vs. the European Retail Association

	Turnover 1987/88 (£000m)	
European Retail Association:		
Ahold	3.5	
Argyll	3.2	
Casino	3.5	
ERA total		10.2
Spar International		9.0
Rewe Buying Group		8.4
Edeka Buying Group		7.1

Source: Dawson, J. A. and Burt, S.

If the SEM makes it easier for producers to move goods across frontiers, it will also be easier for retailers to buy the goods and then move them across frontiers. Buying groups across Europe may operate within the same pan-European market and still not be in direct competition with one another. In such cases it would be feasible for buying groups to co-operate with similar groups in 'paralleling' their sources of supply whereby one buying group buys, not only for its own group members, but also on behalf of a second buying group. Scale economies would not then be confined to the crude use of buying power, but would be big enough to tempt producers into co-operating by offering the prospect of even greater production scale economies as well as entry into new markets.

□ *Access to Distribution Channels*

Continental retailers looking at the UK market may be discouraged to see that their rivals have achieved a very high degree of control over the distribution network. Some 70 per cent of the sales volume of the UK's top seven grocery multiples passes through consolidation warehouses and distribution services under their direct control, frequently through the use of captive sub-contractors using vehicles painted in the grocer's livery. By comparison, the contract fleet's share in France and Germany is 14 per cent and only 3 per cent in Spain.[24] However, deregulation in transport and the completion of the channel tunnel may render the notion of domestic captive-warehousing obsolete for pan-European retailers and, therefore, no longer a barrier to entry into the UK market.

■ Intensity of Rivalry

Self-service grocery retailing in the UK is a mature industry with a relatively high degree of concentration. The pecking order of major competitors is well established, so that even though competition is often intense, it is also orderly. This has resulted in a confident and profitable industry by any international standard.

■ Slow Industry Growth

The major UK food retailers have achieved considerable growth in recent years, but, since expenditure on food has been static, this growth has been at the expense of smaller rivals, as shown in Table 3.5. Growth is currently based upon the development of superstores mainly on out-of-town sites, but industry experts believe that the limit to superstore growth will be reached by 1994/96.[25] A more recent survey by Verdict Research concludes that this date may be optimistic, as the current downturn in UK retail spending has accelerated the pace of retailing saturation.[26] In a static and saturated food

Table 3.5 UK Food Sales by Sector, 1980–8 (Unit per cent value analysis)

	1980	*1982*	*1984*	*1986*	*1988*
Large grocers	40.8	46.5	51.3	55.1	59.0
Small grocers	18.2	16.1	12.6	11.4	10.5
Co-operatives	16.9	14.9	13.9	12.9	11.8
Others	24.1	22.5	22.2	20.6	18.7
Total	100.0	100.0	100.0	100.0	100.0

Source: Adapted from Euromonitor[27] and Mintel.[28]

market, the only way for major grocery retailers to grow will be to take market share from each other. UK supermarket operators will become much more vulnerable, not just because of increasing rivalry in a stagnant market, but also as a result of the entry of large, professional, foreign rivals. These new entrants will already be experienced in operating outside their domestic markets and will be fully conversant with the factors which are necessary for international operations.

☐ *Shifting Rivalry*

Since continental retailers are accustomed to margins which are only a fraction of those in the UK (see Table 3.6) they are unlikely to be deterred by the threat to margins facing UK retailers as a result of intensified competition. As mentioned earlier, Aldi has already opened its first five stores in Britain. More may follow very soon. After all, the purpose of opening up European markets is to increase competition and the UK market appears to offer considerable benefits to French, German, and Benelux retailers. According to research conducted by MORI in 1989, nearly half (46 per cent) of the estate agents in the UK were negotiating with European retailers for high street sites.[29]

Table 3.6 Net Profit as a per cent of Sales of Selected European Grocery Retailers

	1985–86	*1986–87*
Carrefour France	1.2	1.3
Ahold Netherlands	1.1	1.2
Casino France	0.9	1.1
GB-Inno-BM Belgium	0.8	1.1
Delhaize Belgium	0.7	0.8
UK Supermarkets	6.3	6.6

Source: Adapted from Musannif and George.[30]

☐ *Diverse Competitors*

As Porter points out, 'Foreign competitors often add a great deal of diversity to industries because of their differing circumstances and often differing goals'. For instance, Aldi and Tengelmann of West Germany and Vendax International of the Netherlands are privately owned companies not answerable to shareholders. They may, therefore, be prepared to accept a subnormal return on investment to facilitate cut-throat entry strategies. In the diverse competitive environment thus created, players may find it difficult to accurately read each other's intentions and so fail to agree a set of 'rules of the game', thereby leading to uncertainty and sub-optimal performance for all concerned.

☐ *Lack of Product Differentiation*

UK consumers seem to regard retail services as near-commodity, switching loyalties easily if retail offers or service become deficient.[31] With the increasing fragmentation of mass consumer markets as a consequence of consumers adopting more individualistic and experiential attitudes, UK retailers must begin to adapt to the specialist requirements of their consumer groups, and that this product differentiation, which would provide layers of defence against new competitors, is simply not there. Despite many claims that UK retailers are pursuing differentiation strategies, there seems very little difference between the market offerings of the major contenders. The fact is that the single most important criterion in determining the choice of shop is proximity; quite simply, shoppers go to the nearest store. However, the question remains whether this lack of differentiation is due to an absence of any real differences between consumer groups or whether it is due to the lack of a genuine competitive drive for differentiation. Up until now, it is apparent that the major multiples have been able to build their market share in the UK at the expense of smaller competitors and that this has cushioned them from the full forces of having to compete with each other. In an industry that is characterised by openness, enforced by shareholders' requirements and with very little protection from patents of technological edge, it has been all too easy to imitate the successful strategies of peer organisations. Therefore, UK multiples have become increasingly similar, since the real focus of differentiation has been between them and the smaller shops.

However, this scenario is changing; the imminent arrival of major competitors in a market reaching saturation point will intensify competition. New entrants from the continent are likely to hasten the process of differentiation by injecting their own characteristic styles of operation and by seeking out niche markets as a way of gaining a toe-hold in the UK. Consequently, multiple grocery retailers may find it prudent to develop more distinctive identities by seriously endeavouring to relate their market offering to particular customer groups.

■ Bargaining Power of Suppliers

Despite the very large size of manufacturers operating in the UK, their relative power has been diminished due to the fact that the six largest grocery retailers accounted for 70 per cent of the market in 1987. In recent years, the balance of power has rested with the food retailers who have used their power to oblige manufacturers to cut prices, share promotional costs or to supply own label products.[32] The food manufacturers' defence against this has been years of heavy promotional spending to build consumer loyalty through product differentiation.[33] By comparison, retailers' attempts to establish store loyalty have met with little success.

Given the relative ease of moving tangible goods across frontiers compared to the difficulty of moving retailing services (which must be consistently produced and consumed at the point of sale), it is generally agreed that the SEM will benefit manufacturers more than retailers. Fletcher has expressed concern that, if manufacturers choose to develop competitive advantage by forming pan-European organisations, the balance of power could be shifted back towards suppliers.[34]

UK grocery multiples are showing no real inclination to move into Europe as an offensive measure. However, as a defensive strategy, some are banding together to form buying groups (such as the European Retail Association previously mentioned). This may be sufficient to maintain the status quo, since it is apparent that a manufacturer would have to be vast indeed to gain the upper hand over the highly concentrated food retailers of Northern Europe.

■ The Threat of Substitute Services

Although it is easy to dismiss any idea of substitutes for grocery retailers, no doubt the same level of confidence was also felt by businesses in the coal, railway and mechanical cash register industries a few decades ago. Even now there are straws in the wind, such as the return to popularity of neighbourhood shopping. A number of trends are combining throughout Europe which suggest that the needs of a significant proportion of consumers may be more effectively satisfied by alternative retail methods:

1 An ageing population is likely to be less mobile and may show a distinct preference for smaller scale shopping.
2 'Green' consumers who may reject processed, packaged 'supermarket' products as ecologically unsound.
3 The trend towards more working women increasing demand for extended opening hours and fast, convenient shopping. (This should also lead to more men participating in shopping!)
4 A 'cash rich, time poor' society may be prepared to pay premium prices for the convenience of teleshopping and specialogues. Although teleshopping

and other means of direct marketing may not seem the most appropriate medium for fast grocery shopping, they do account for 15 per cent of all household sales of frozen food in West Germany.

■ Bargaining Power of Consumers

The entry by continental retailers into the near-saturated UK grocery market will offer individuals more choice and greater variety, effectively shifting the balance of power further towards consumers.

Athough Porter suggests that knowledge is power for industrial buyers, by analogy it can be the very lack of knowledge in an increasingly complex world which may cause consumers to exercise their power by withdrawing their custom from a store group in the face of the latest food scare. With some 21 million households in the UK, it must be said that retail customers represent a very fragmented force with little individual power. However, it is lack of loyalty to a service which consumers have come to regard as near-commodity, combined with low switching costs and a ready acceptance of imports which makes simple fickleness a threat to UK retailers.[35]

It is unlikely that a new market entrant would rely solely upon a low level of loyalty as a basis for growth. It is to be expected that continental competitors will build upon their existing strengths (such as German staff training and service techniques and French skills in decentralising international store management) to effectively segment the UK market. Their task is being made easier by a convergence of consumers' requirements throughout Europe; Dawson *et al.* have already identified broad trends in shopping behaviour which they perceive as common to all European countries.[36]

■ Concluding Comments

Our analysis has shown that UK grocery retailers will experience an intensification in competition as a result of store saturation and the market entry of highly professional European retailers tempted by the prospect of higher trading margins. The shift in the balance of power back towards food manufacturers, facilitated by the competition of the SEM in 1992, will eventually result in a convergence of consumer tastes and expectations in neighbouring EC countries. The evolution of a pan-European grocery market will occur despite the apparent indifference of UK retailers. In the main, UK grocery retailers have chosen not to participate in the enlarged European market, relying instead upon growth from the US market whilst adopting a defensive position in the UK. The major UK grocery retailers have developed neither sufficient economies of scale nor distinct differential advantage. Consequently, they are at risk of being 'stuck in the middle' as medium-sized players in the enlarged European grocery market. Under these conditions, margins in the UK segment of the European grocery market are destined to fall by perhaps two thirds as they are brought into line with international norms. Furthermore, as medium-sized players, UK grocery retailers are unlikely to remain amongst the most profitable competitors in this sector of the European market. Therefore the major UK multiples must urgently reconsider their position in Europe.

■ Case Study 6: Leadership Issues in The European Cellopp Market

■ Introduction

This case describes the development of the Cellopp market in Europe during the past two decades and suggests a way forward. It is not intended to be a technical note and relies on information in the public domain.

■ Background

The Cellopp market may be described as film materials used in packaging items such as crisps, biscuits, confectionery and bakery products.

Until the early 1970s, the market had been served by regenerated cellulose film (RCF) products. RCF uses wood pulp as its primary raw material, which undergoes a complicated energy-intensive process to produce a continuous transparent film. For the vast majority of applications, the RCF requires a further coating process before it can be used, to enable hot sealing of the film, and to act as a barrier against water vapour and gases to stop the degradation of the packaged food stuffs.

Because of the complexity and capital intensity of the production process, there were only a handful of RCF suppliers in Western Europe, and it was widely rumoured that the RCF producers had operated a very effective pricing cartel until the early 1970s.

However, the RCF producers had become seriously worried by the threat of a substitutional plastic-based material – oriented polypropylene film (OPP).

□ *Substitute Materials*

The technology for OPP was being developed by the giant petrochemical companies – ICI, Hoechst, Bayer, Montedison, Mobil and Shell, and the material that these companies were producing could, it was acknowledged by RCF producers, easily substitute the vast majority of the RCF market. All the RCF producers were clearly in a dangerous long term position as they did not have the technology to produce OPP film or the advantages of vertical integration available to the petrochemical industry. Although the petrochemical companies had no knowledge of the Cellopp market, they soon began to find market penetration relatively easy because of the large price differentials between RCF and the substitutional materials, which worked in their favour.

The OPP producers were marketing a particular product – coated OPP. This material required a coating process similar to that of RCF to enhance the film, with heat sealing and barrier properties. However, there was a further development underway by the petrochemical companies: coextrusion – the simultaneous extrusion of OPP and a heat sealable layer. This one-stage process was inherently cheaper than the two stage process for coated films. However, the coextruded film had one limitation – its gas barrier was inferior to that of coated films, limiting it to particular markets.

□ *Acquisition*

Although the development of OPP films had mainly been in the hands of the petrochemical companies, one of the RCF producers acquired a multi party venture (with one petrochemical company as a member) in 1969. The company's existing name, Shorko was retained and it continued to market its range of coated and coextruded films quite successfully.

However, the gradual erosion of the RCF market began to quicken pace during the 1970s, causing severe price wars to break out and the RCF producers began to incur severe financial losses. As a result, Shorko began to concentrate production on coextruded films, leaving BCL (its parent), to sell the competitive advantage of gas barrier over coextruded OPP. Meanwhile, most of the other producers concentrated on coated OPP.

□ *The Late 1970s*

During the late 1970s the RCF market declined at an ever increasing rate and RCF producers undertook major cost-cutting exercises through product and production rationalisation. However the market acceptability of coextruded OPP had increased and coextruded films were beginning to form a discrete market which needed further capacity in order to fulfil market demand. This, however, did not happen, due to financial constraints.

□ *Market Entry*

In 1978, Mobil Plastics Inc. announced that they were going to set up a plant in Europe using their American technology, with 24000 tonnes per annum capacity by 1982. Mobil's American films, however, were mainly coated types.

When Mobil made their entry into the European market in 1980, they launched a coated film and undercut the price of the competition by a considerable margin – the price of Mobil's coated film equated to coextruded film levels.

The main offensive of Mobil was directed at the RCF market. Their coated films were stiffer than the competition and were a better RCF substitute than most coated films. Through Mobil's aggressive pricing policy and distinctive product, they were able to establish themselves very quickly in the European market.

☐ *Reassessment*

Competitors were concerned at the speed with which Mobil were capable of eroding the RCF market and expansion of OPP capacity was clearly required if Mobil were not to dominate the entire market.

The essential facts about the market were:

- The western European market for OPP was based on the substitution of RCF and on the growth of the European trend of prepackaged groceries.
- The perceived need for gas barrier was declining, hence, there was a high probability that coextruded films would substitute coated film.
- Analysis of competitor activities indicated:
  - ICI was the largest manufacturer of both coated and coextruded films. However, the market leader was taking considerable punishment from Mobil and the company had 'gone quiet' in the market place. Furthermore, there appeared to be no plans for expansion and ICI used a process that the market considered technically inferior, with low line speeds.
  - Mobil (European based and number two in terms of capacity) was leading the market in price. The petrochemical company had ambitious expansion plans and the cash to fulfil these. However, the main thrust of Mobil's activities was in coated films and their coextruded technology was known to be weak.
  - The Shorko operation was expanded in 1983, with the extension of the production facilities at Swindon. This policy gave Shorko the largest production facilities for coextruded film in Europe, and in terms of total OPP film, their capacity was only a little short of ICI and Mobil. During 1984, Shorko acquired a French operation and a new line also came on stream during this period.
  - Moplefan, an Italian state-owned company that was ineffective in most countries outside Italy, was thought to have costly production (over manning), poor quality, and poor process technology.
  - Kalle, part of the giant Hoechst group, appeared to be investing in expansion of another product, PET, which did not compete in the Cellopp market.
  - Bayer's film operation, Wolff, was the smallest of the OPP producers. The technology they deployed had significant disadvantages in terms of production speed, but the company enjoyed a strong reputation for quality and service. Bayer were also expanding other plastics operations, and it was believed that they had insufficient resources to expand Wolff.

However, severe difficulties were being encountered in the industry. As more RCF capacity was closed, more and more purchasers of RCF switched over to OPP films 'prematurely'. This resulted in there being significant undercapacity in the OPP industry. Suppliers had an order book of at least fourteen weeks and had difficulty in coping with a market that simply threw orders at it. Delivery reliability became a major problem in the industry.

Continental Europe had longer distribution cycles (double the UK) leading to the need for films with gas barrier properties ie. coated films. (The distribution cycle is the time from manufacturer to distributor to retailer to consumer). Furthermore, Mobil were particularly keen to play on the perceived need for gas barrier and promoted their coated films on the benefits of the gas barrier film.

At the same time, other major players in the market began to expand. ICI reported that expansion of production was going to be possible via 'debottle-necking'.

Mobil brought forward their expansion plans by approximately six months – presumably to take advantage of the buoyant market.

However, the biggest surprise came from the German companies, who announced that extra lines would be commissioned during 1986 – increasing the capacity estimates for each company by some 8000 tonnes per annum, thus reducing any significant cost advantage of British manufacturers.

□ *1985*

The beginning of 1985 saw a dramatic change in the market. Demand from the trade fell at a remarkable rate and lead times for the whole industry were as short as two weeks.

All companies were taken by surprise at the tremendous slack in the market. Forecasts had pointed to 1986 and beyond being the period of low capacity levels. Furthermore, ICI had been particularly successful at increasing their capacity through the debottle-necking process (ICI were letting it be known in the market place that by 1986 their total capacity would be 50,000 tonnes per annum).

Furthermore, the increase in ICI's tonnage had been achieved with comparatively little capital investment. With the ICI equipment already being well depreciated, it was highly likely their costs were significantly lower than other manufacturers.

ICI were pushing new products into the market, developing market interest in the company. Nearly 70 per cent of ICI's capacity was capable of producing coextruded films, making it almost equal to Shorko's capacity once its expansion was complete.

Prices were being severely eroded, particularly in Europe, although it was felt that the slack in the market was due to film users stock piling in 1984 and that the pipeline effect would be complete by mid to end of April 1985.

Also, in early summertime, the industry's sales usually increased as the snack food trade built up stocks for its busy summer period.

In May 1985 ICI reduced their coextruded prices by 10 per cent on thick films and 15 per cent on thin gauge films.

ICI seemed to be using their competitive cost advantage to reduce their films by the greatest amounts in order to stop the advances of some of the more aggressive competitors.

The financial implications of the price movements were horrifying if these prices were to become the market 'norm'. Whatever modest profits that might have been possible in 1985 had already been eroded by the rise of sterling and the low volumes already experienced would further erode profit levels. The UK price decrease would reduce profits even further if all competitors were to match ICI prices.

In fact, all competing companies reduced their prices in order to compete with ICI, with the result that the status quo was maintained. ICI's dash for market share was frustrated, but at a severe cost to all players. Throughout 1985, prices remained depressed.

Meanwhile, the new product introduction programme of the key players was also tending to maintain the status quo.

□ *End of the Period of Depression*

Very gradually, as 1985 ran its course, order books picked up over the whole product range. Lead times lengthened and feelings of optimism about the future returned. The continually rising demand for packaging film had once again overtaken the suppliers' capacity to produce, and market prices began to rise again, and by January 1987, most suppliers had order books filled some six months ahead. Was this the beginning of a new era of prosperity, or was it merely an action replay of the short-lived boom of 1984?

□ *The Market*

The European market continued to show high growth in 1987, outstripping earlier demand forecasts and increasing by 16 per cent. The UK exhibited particularly high growth, well above what could be reasonably expected of a well developed market, sustained at least in part by exceptionally high levels of sales in the last quarter, ahead of announced price increases.

1988, however, saw growth begin to falter, with order books falling steadily to mid year as destocking once again took place. Although sales picked up from crisis levels mid year through the second half, year on year growth was no more than 3 per cent.

With demand weak in mid-1988, all the major players started to increase capacity. In addition, Italian producers, supported by large subsidies, were installing capacity at an even faster rate. New entrants were emerging, in Italy, Spain, France and the stage was set for substantially reduced levels of capacity utilisation – from in excess of 90 per cent in 1987 to less than 75 per cent in

1990/91 – unless demand growth was higher than the forecast 10 per cent per annum or some capacity was removed.

■ Some Conclusions/Observations

□ *The Capacity Issue*

Central to the ability to market output is the ability to make the product at competitive costs. Thus, in an ever-increasing market such as that exhibited by OPP films, not to have sufficient production capacity is to invite losing market share and competitiveness. That is, of course, unless a strategy of specialisation and 'nichemanship' is pursued.

Evidence suggests that standard film prices tend to fall faster than those of specialised products such as pearlised or metalised films.

The alternative strategy of continually increasing capacity brings with it a cyclical pattern which might be crudely described as 'bursting at the seams', moving to 'investing to ease the load', moving to 'having over-capacity until demand catches up', which then eventually returns to stage one of the cycle, 'bursting at the seams'.

To commission a new line takes about 18 months from the time of agreement to go ahead to it being productive. By way of illustration, let's suppose a supplier increases his production line from five to six. As the new line comes on stream, the production capability increases virtually overnight by 20 per cent. Like many examples, this might be something of an oversimplification because old, inefficient lines might be taken out to make room for the new investment.

Nevertheless, technological advances in new lines bring with them increased processing speeds and so the basic problem remains . . . the supplier can only increase his capacity in discrete steps (which are generally substantial), while demand tends to follow a gradually increasing trend.

□ *Market Prices*

Market prices of OPP have been consistently found to be closely linked to the level of capacity utilisation in the market place. Typically, the added value (sales price less the cost of raw materials) has changed by at least 1½ per cent for every percentage point change in capacity utilisation.

After the last significant weakening in the capacity/demand relationship in 1985, it was seen that the impact of capacity utilisation changes was much greater on standard film than on specials. This is a straightforward reflection of the fact that special films are harder to make, fewer suppliers can therefore make them, and the competitive intensity is correspondingly less.

Foward projections of the short term supply/demand relationship in western Europe show a worsening outlook. Resin prices are up, there is a severe over capacity, and whilst demand is also up by about 10 per cent, this is not enough to cope with available capacity. The impact on prices of standard film, of course, has been devastating.

□ *The Way Ahead*

With prices depressed, it is difficult to justify further investment in capacity, hence the cycle will occur yet again in the early nineties, as demand outstrips supply. But such gains are likely to be short-lived.

The way ahead is far from clear. One way, of course, is to focus attention on shifting the mix of special films to over 50 per cent of output, in order to reduce the impact of the demand/supply/price cycle.

Ultimately, however, the industry will have to deal with the issue of having no dominant supplier who can 'regulate' and 'police' prices and margins.

Therefore, unless some of the competitors voluntarily retire, it would seem that the only way forward is to follow one or more of the following strategies:

- drive R&D relentlessly towards high value-added specials;
- stress service, quality and innovation;
- drive costs down on standard film;
- reduce the impact of the Italian state-subsidised operations before permanent damage is inflicted on the market;
- withdraw;
- acquire another organisation and go for market share growth and cost cutting at the same time.

In summary, there *is* future in this market for those organisations with staying power. But it is likely to go on being unattractive in the short to medium term unless dramatic action is taken by one or more of the players in the market.

■ Case Study 7: Gaining Leadership in an Undifferentiated Market – Ratners Group plc

■ Introduction

Gerald Ratner, in 1984, inherited a company with 120 stores that had a market capitalisation of about £10 million and annual losses of £350,000. He applied radical changes. He took Ratners out of jewellery production, dropped the shops' designer-decor, took the product downmarket, cut prices by as much as half and adopted an aggressive marketing approach built upon the low-price appeal. By 1989, Ratners had 1,700 stores, capitalisation of £500 million and it was clear that Ratners had created a new market.

Sales of jewellery increased threefold in volume terms during the years 1979 to 1989, compared with a 77 per cent increase in the retail price index, making it a fast growing retail sector. The Ratners Group was responsible for this by stimulating the consumer's awareness of jewellery as an everyday purchase and removing the mystique of buying jewellery through their marketing efforts. Although the jewellery market benefited as a whole, Ratners' market share increased from 2.5 per cent in 1984 to 31 per cent in 1989/90 with Gerald Ratner's corporate objective of achieving 50 per cent UK market share.

■ How Success was Achieved

The jewellery market can be compared to the fast food market. Two previously stagnant markets, with little hope of expansion, were turned into rapidly expanding markets due to two companies, Ratners and McDonalds respectively. Ratners used marketing no less effectively than the creators of the Big Mac. Brightly-lit shop windows, open front doors, posters screaming 'lowest prices ever' and '30 days change of mind money-back promise' were deployed to break down the old image of the jewellers as a snobbishly forbidding place. Ratners' method was to make people realise they could buy jewellery on impulse and that it did not have to be a once-in-a-lifetime event.

□ *Market Segmentation*

Ratner recognised the enormous potential of segmenting the market and targeting shops at groups of customers to match their specific needs. A typical jewellers would sell an entire range of products, from Rolex and diamonds to

Swatch and diamante. Customers would be as diverse as a sixteen-year-old buying his first girl friend a pair of earrings to a middle-aged man buying his wife a diamond and sapphire eternity ring. A typical jewellers would cover the market as shown in Figure 3.5.

In order to achieve his stated aim of becoming the leading player in the market, Gerald Ratner embarked upon a series of acquisitions. This was not only to eliminate the threats from competition, but also to provide alternative outlets targeted at different segments of the market. With the acquisitions made up to 1990, Ratner was able to ensure individual coverage of the entire market, as shown in Figure 3.6.

Figure 3.5 A jewellers covering all areas of the market from high price high quality to low price low quality

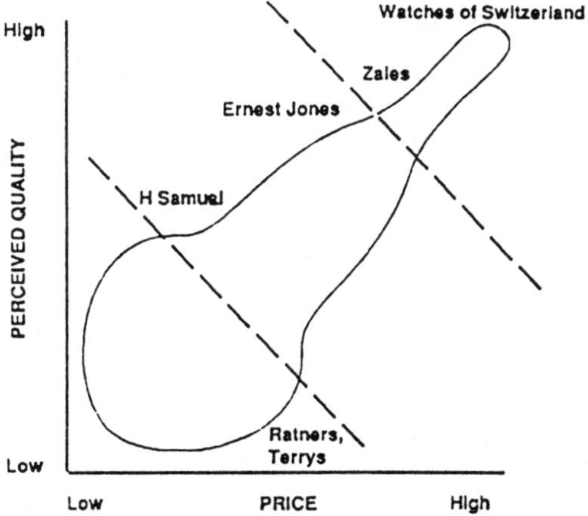

Figure 3.6 Individual coverage of the entire jewellery market

As can be seen, Ratners had segmented the jewellery market into high, medium and low categories. The whole jewellery market had expanded, particularly the lower quality segment, which, as mentioned earlier, had benefited considerably from the cheaper prices and promotional activities of the Ratner stores.

The Low Price Segment (Ratners, Terry's)
Customers were younger, mostly females, wishing to buy cheap, fashionable costume jewellery and were happy with 9 carat, gold plate and zircon stones. Shops were prominently located adjacent to fashion clothes stores, emphasising the accessory nature of the jewellery. Window display advertising was loud and very emphatic, promoting year-round sales and bargains. Low prices were made possible by Ratners' pioneering hollow gold jewellery. Its manufacturers in the UK and Far East used innovative laser-assisted techniques including the production of gold of previously undreamt-of thickness.

The Middle Price Segment (H Samuel)
The traditional H Samuel group was positioned in the middle market, catering for the whole famly, incorporating a wide range of merchandise, including giftware, with an average purchase in the region of under £10.

The High Quality Segment (Ernest Jones, Zales, Watches of Switzerland)
Ernest Jones and Zales specialised in engagement rings and better quality watches such as Rolex, Gucci, Longines and Cartier, targeted at the high priced end of the market, with an average purchase in the region of £50. Watches of Switzerland continued to remain at the top end of the watch business, selling quality names such as Patek Phillipe and Audemars Piquet.

Gerald Ratner's marketing skills were only half the story of the Ratner Group's success. Ratners, Zales and H Samuel's distribution network was driven by computerised electronic point-of-sale (EPOS) stock control systems. Every store fell into one of ten categories of stock level, depending on its flow of business. If an item was out of stock in the warehouse, instead of putting it on the re-order list, the computer flagged it to distribution staff as an item of urgent re-supply. Whilst no longer revolutionary today, at the time, the substantial cost savings and re-supply capabilities were a major contributor to the price reductions inherent in Ratners' strategy.

The Ratner Group's exceptional success is mirrored in the financial figures shown in Table 3.7. These show increasing success until well into 1991.

■ How Success was Lost

Ratner's strategy of acquisition-led growth found favour in the 1980s consumer-led boom, but the consequent slump in high street spending, coupled with an ill-fated Institute of Director's joke about the group's products

Table 3.7 Ratners Group plc Financial Summary, 1988–92

(£000, except per share data)	*1988*	*1989*	*1990†* *53 weeks*	*1991*	*1992*
Sales	360,205	635,160	898,102	1,113,922	1,128,634
Exceptional items			8,531	(2,000)	(97,965)
Profit/(loss) on ordinary activities before taxation	52,742	86,010	130,019	112,057	(122,328)

being 'crap', plunged the company into crisis in 1991, as consumers abandoned Ratners.

Over expansion in the UK and the States, funded by complex and expensive financing together with a depression in sales, resulted in Ratners reporting pre-tax losses in 1992. The company's policy of saturation coverage, and product mix overlap between stores, had led to cannibalisation of sales from one chain to another, a position which was exacerbated by the strategy of sacrificing margins in pursuit of turnover.

The debt-ridden company, under pressure from City and US bankers, was forced to reverse its original sales-led marketing strategy in an attempt to return to profitability. Adopting a radical strategic review resulted in the rationalisation of the group's operations, costing in excess of £100 million, a market repositioning and the resignation of Gerald Ratner as Chairman and then finally Chief Executive in November 1992.

The task of differentiating the three main chains and product ranges, and closing overlapping stores is critical to the group's survival. The back-bone of the company remains H Samuel with 440 shops repositioned to meet the needs of the heartland of mass market jewellery shoppers. Ernest Jones and Leslie Davis, with 195 shops, are refocusing on specific higher spending market areas, and still at the lower end, and with less than 200 shops, shrinking fast, is Ratners.

In 1993, the group has maintained a 30 per cent share of the British jewellery market, but gone is the jewel in the crown, Watches of Switzerland, sold to Asprey for £24 million and Zales which was subsumed into the Ratners' chain. The group retains a strong and profitable presence in America, where it is the second largest jewellery retailer.

Going back to basics, the leaner company now has adopted a trading strategy of margins rather than volume sales in order to extricate itself from the interest charges stranglehold of the City's money men. Gone are the loud window displays and permanent sales banners. A policy of credit and money back schemes and emphasis on quality of service and product now underlie Ratners' new clean, more up-market range. Even so, 1992 trading figures for the most profitable trading period in the year, the two months before Christmas, when traditionally 40 per cent of sales and 80 per cent of the industry's profits are generated, showed a drop of 27 per cent.

At its peak in 1989, Ratners sold 40 per cent of all watches and 25 per cent of all earrings in the UK. But the strategy of high volume discounting was no longer appropriate to the consumer of the 1990s. City analysts do not expect profits from the group until 1993 or 1994. In 1990 the share price reached nearly 300p, with a market capitalisation of £830 million. In 1992, at one point, shares were valued at 9.5p and the company at just £28 million. Time will tell whether the poorly timed joke which incurred such adverse publicity and alienated customers, and the expansionist plans of Gerald Ratner will have proved too far-reaching in their effects.

■ Section 3: Attacking the Market Leader

Experienced marketers often observe that market leaders are constantly under attack and subject to market share erosion by both small and large competitors. This is, of course, true, because the effects of innovation, changing customer requirements, competition and technology, affect the largest market shareholder most heavily, particularly if it attempts to maintain the status quo. Sometimes, competitive attacks on the market leader's position succeed; frequently they fail. This section identifies the strategic principles needed to make an effective attack on the market leader's position and provides a case study of the micro computer market.

■ Competitive Structure of Markets

Most markets have a number of players operating in different competitive positions. The market leader, often the traditional innovator or developer, has the largest share and usually has the largest level of marketing support, such as advertising and sales expenditure. There may be one or two challengers and followers, each with relatively large market shares but clearly behind the market leader. Leading competitors become challengers to the market leader by adopting offensive strategies. The remaining players have small market shares and occupy niches in the market. The appropriate strategies for attacking the market leader differ, depending upon the competitive position of players.

□ *Strategic Principles*

Relevant strategies to be adopted in attacking the market leader are guided by the following principles.

Competitive Position

Ries and Trout,[37] in their book *Marketing Warfare*, suggest three possible strategies, depending upon the competitive position of the challenger and the strengths of the leader.

OFFENSIVE STRATEGY

Here the main consideration is the strength of the leader's position and the ability to attack a weakness resulting from the leader's strength. A leader's wide product range, for example, may dilute the sales force's knowledge and expertise and lengthen the time taken to provide back-up service.

Alternatively, a leader's large investment in product quality or customer service may lift its cost structure to the point where it can be attacked on price. An offensive strategy by a follower should attack the leader's weaknesses and operate on as narrow a front as possible.

FLANKING STRATEGY

An effective flanking attack is made into an area uncontested by the market leader. This may be by developing existing small market segments or creating new ones through innovation. This avoids head-on confrontation with the leader and relies for its success on technical, marketing or pricing innovation, resulting in differentiated offerings to the market.

NICHE STRATEGY

Ries and Trout[38] suggest that most players in a market should be guerillas who focus on a segment of the market small enough to defend and concentrate on slow erosion of a leader's market. This may be done on the basis of price advantage or specialised benefits provided by the firm's product offerings. The niche strategy does not attempt to challenge the leader in the market, but to infiltrate and slowly erode competitors' positions. Chapter 5 deals specifically with growth strategies for specialist niche competitors.

Sustainable Competitive Advantage

The relevance and application of sustainable competitive advantage has been a focus of discussion of competitive strategy in recent years. Porter[39] has been one of the main proponents of this concept. He recognised generic strategies based around differentiation or cost leadership and that the breadth of focus could be industry-wide (ie. broad market coverage) or narrow (ie. market segment or niche). This was referred to in earlier chapters.

The important principle for a company to adopt in attacking a market leader is the development of a strategy that can be sustained, based on a competitive advantage.

In the United States airline industry, Frank Lorenzo of Texas Air Corporation was able to sustain a cost-leadership position by breaking the power of the unions in the industry and operating with labour costs half that of his competitors. The strategy started to take effect in 1981 with the launch of New York Air to compete directly with Eastern Airlines' highly profitable shuttle service between New York, Washington and Boston. By attacking Eastern's profit base, he weakened its overall competitive position and viability. This strategy, reflected in lower priced air fares, allowed Texas Air Corporation to take over Continental Airlines, Eastern Airlines, Peoples Express, and several regional American airlines. However, industrial and operational problems in 1988 made Lorenzo's strategy unsustainable.

Resources

Substantial resources are required for a challenger to mount a sustained attack on the market leader. In particular, financial resources are needed to fund the growth of the business and finance the market coverage required to compete effectively. This includes funds for research and development, market research, advertising and promotion, sales force and distribution coverage and support.

□ *Industry Conditions*

The particular marketing strategies needed by the challenger in attacking the market leader depend on industry conditions. Three important aspects are worth specific consideration: market conditions, competitive conditions and technological change.

Market Conditions

Product life-cycle theory is a useful reference point for identifying different market conditions. Wasson[40] provides a comprehensive account of the changing market conditions with the evaluation of product markets and the general marketing strategies appropriate to each stage of the life-cycle.

During the growth stage, an attack on the leader will require segmentation strategies, development of distribution, and new products to gain market coverage and brand preference. Bowater Scott attacked Kimberly Clark in the growing facial tissue market by offering a variety of pack sizes, colours and used concepts such as portability and decoration which opened up new segments of the market.

In the maturity stage, an offensive on the leader often occurs with the use of price by low cost competitors at a time when the market is much more price sensitive. Another strategy for the follower is to redefine the market and thereby change the range of benefits perceived to be relevant by consumers. In the mature British ice-cream market, Mars defined the market with the introduction of the frozen Mars bar, which gave it an opportunity to attack the market leader, Walls. The strategies of Mars were presented in Chapter 2.

During the decline stage in the life-cycle, the options for the follower are to target the leader's customers by offering lower prices or added benefits of convenience, service and customer support. This is a time when the leader is attempting to milk the market and develop initiatives and investments in other areas.

Day extends the work of Porter by suggesting that the determinants of generic strategies include the price sensitivity of the market and the real or perceived relative differences in product offerings.[41] This is depicted in Table 3.8.

This would suggest that during the early stages of a product's life-cycle the strategies of differentiation and focus are relevant. In the later stages of the life-cycle, overall cost leadership and hybrid strategies are more applicable.

Competitive Conditions

The number of competitors and their relative strengths in market position will determine how vulnerable the leader is to successful attack. If there is one large follower and many low-scale companies in the industry, the leader is able to focus its defensive strategy against one competitor. If two or three large followers are challenging the market leader, however, there is a greater chance of attacks being successful, because the leader is forced to compete on a number of fronts.

Technology

Davidow[42] claims that 'in high-tech you are never safe'. He suggests that a leadership strategy requires large investments both in research and development to develop new products and in marketing to develop the new market.

Table 3.8 Generic Strategies and Market Perceptions

Customer Price Sensitivity		
High	Overall cost Leadership (Obtain substantial cost advantage over major competitors	Differentiation (Seek major quality or structural differences)
Low	Hybrid (Low cost and emphasize differences	Focus (Search for real or perceived differences
	Small	Large
	Relative Differences in Product Offerings	

Source: Adapted from G. S. Day, *Strategic Market Planning*, 1984, p. 119.

These high costs must be continually carried by product lines. The follower copies the leader or obtains a technology licence and spends little money on market development. Davidow refers to 'toothpaste technology' as the result of technology companies being forced to base their products on identical technologies, making their products increasingly homogeneous. With more products being built on identical 'product genes', said Davidow, high-tech products are becoming commodities to satisfy the customer's need for standards of interchangeability and interconnection. The follower strategy in a 'commodity' market gives the firm low overheads, low manufacturing costs and price advantages.

Alternatively, an attack based on new technology can destroy the leader and reshuffle competition. There are many examples of this with start-up companies in the computer industry that succeeded with one new product, then failed because they stuck to it.

In industries where technological change is slow, the follower must attack the leader with price, distribution, service and segmentation strategies.

SEGMENT PRICE TRENDS: THE PRICE PINCER CONCEPT

Trends in relative prices of market segments show different patterns under varied market and competitive conditions. As markets grow and mature, price competition tends to increase and price segments emerge. Relative price movements between segments frequently affect share trends as substitution between segments occurs.

A relative price decline by a significant segment has a 'squeezing' effect on other price segments of the market and is termed here a price pincer movement.[43] This is most effective in gaining segment share in markets in which there is no significant new brand activity. A variety of price pincer patterns can occur under different competitive conditions. These are shown in Figure 3.7.

The trends depicted over time represent the average segment price of products in each of the premium, middle and low price segments. The patterns indicate relative price trends of the three segments. A medium price pincer shows a trend in which the mid-segment price declines in relation to the premium and low price segments. A premium/low price double pincer depicts trends of declining prices of the premium and low price segments in relation to the middle segment. The important trends shown in Figure 3.7 are not absolute price movements over time, but relative price movements.

In the high-tech markets for computer and communications equipment, price pincers can occur rapidly and price relativities between products for the same segment and between segments are a critical issue. Lack of attention to segment price trends can result in large investments in stock sitting in warehouses becoming obsolete.

When operating in a market which has clear price-segment brackets, it is important to track price trends and assess cross effects between products.

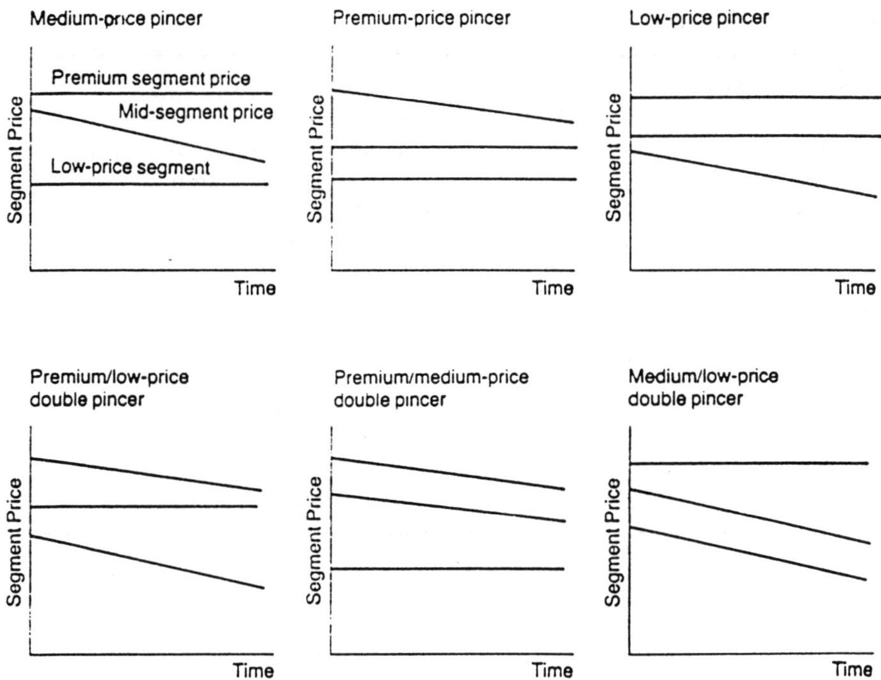

Figure 3.7 Price Pincer patterns

COMPETITIVE STRATEGY DIRECTIONS

In deciding on the strategies to adopt in attacking the market leader, the challenger should consider the principles and conditions discussed. Competitive strategy directions differ according to industry conditions. Some options are presented in Tables 3.9 and 3.10.

Table 3.9 Challenger Strategies in Rapid Growth Markets

Industry Conditions	*Challenger Strategy*
Rapid growth market Many challengers and followers Fast technological change Many segments	Hybrid (low cost and emphasise price advantage) Market coverage Attack leader's weakness New products emphasis Large resource support

Table 3.10 Challenger Strategies in Mature Markets

Industry Conditions	*Challenger Strategy*
	Strategy 1 (Price sensitive market)
Mature market	Overall cost leadership
One main follower	Price advantage
Slow technological change	Market coverage
Established segments	Distribution
	Frontal attack
	Strategy 2 (Not highly price sensitive)
	Differentiation and innovation on non-price factors
	Redefine the market
	Adopt a flanking strategy

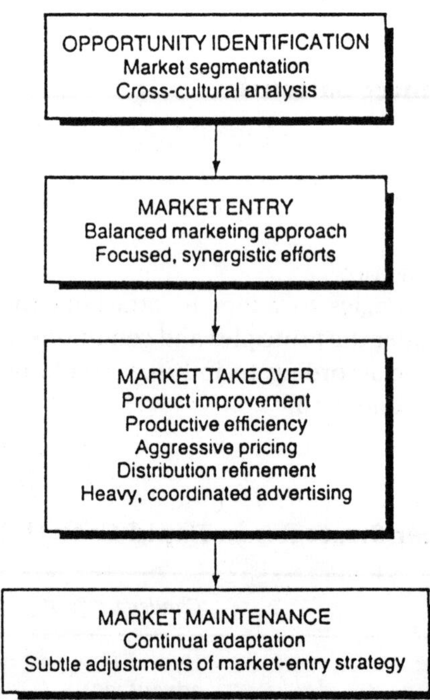

Figure 3.8 The Japanese strategic marketing planning model

Source: P. Kotler, *The New Competition*, 1986, p. 45.

THE JAPANESE STRATEGIC MARKETING APPROACH

Kotler, Fahey and Jatusripitak, in their comprehensive treatment of Japanese competitive marketing, identify a four stage model which they claim, typifies the path taken to market leadership by Japanese corporations.[44]

The first stage, opportunity identification, involves market research to identify unserved segments and to get to know the customer requirements. The entry strategy in the second stage is to find a niche and fill it with products that meet the need. Price penetration strategies are used to move rapidly down the experience curve. A focused strategy and concentrated effort provides the force needed to break in and develop the market.

Share building strategies are part of stage three, 'market takeover', involving product improvements, aggressive pricing and refinements to distribution, supported by heavy advertising. Once leadership is achieved, strategies turn to maintaining share dominance and adaptation to market needs.[45] This sequence is shown in Figure 3.8.

The paths to dominance taken by corporate leaders in the Japanese automobile and motor cycle industries are shown in Figures 3.9 and 3.10.

The Japanese car manufacturers, such as Toyota, moved from an imitation/commodity position to cost leadership, then to differentiation with cost advantages as shown in Figure 3.9. There is evidence that smaller companies, such as Honda, are now developing niche strategies aimed at competing in a

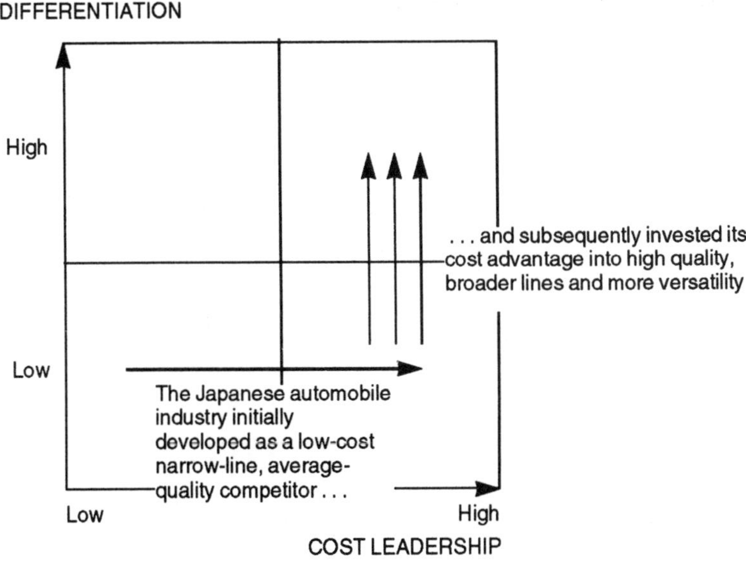

Figure 3.9 Japanese automobiles

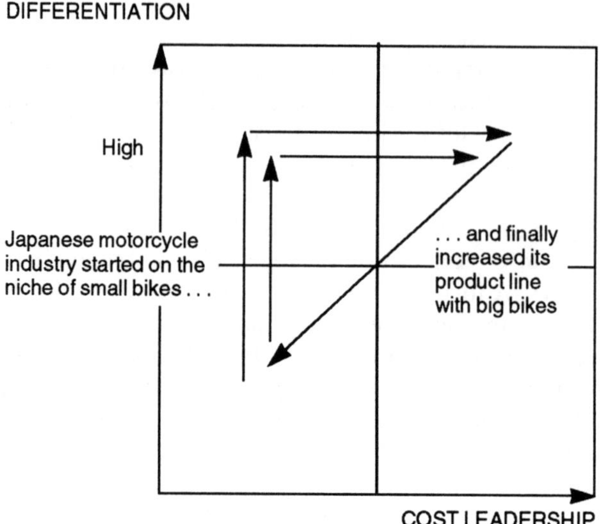

Figure 3.10 Japanese motorcycles

few specific market segments. The Japanese motorcycle industry entered the niche of small bikes, then gained a cost advantage through volume, while retaining differentiation. This became the base for extending the product line with large bikes to compete against the brand leaders in that segment. Figure 3.10 shows the path taken to market leadership.

■ Case Study 8: Amstrad Learns from the Japanese Approach

■ The Attack on IBM in the Personal Computer Market

One of the measures of Amstrad plc's success is that, broadly speaking, turnover and profits doubled annually between 1984 and 1987. Amstrad has described its whole approach to business as market-oriented:

- Identify potential mass-market customers for consumer electronic goods.
- Identify a product which can be adapted for the mass market, and a minimum list of benefits the consumers would want to see in it.
- Settle the lowest possible price and then design the product, for both looks and technology, to meet (and often exceed) the customers' needs within that price.
- Promote the product vigorously, emphasising the perceived benefits and value for money.
- Make the product easily available, when the consumers want to see and buy it: in high street shops.

Amstrad is structured so that it can respond quickly to changes in demand and keep overheads down. The Company has a small asset base, it manufactures virtually nothing itself, and its R&D is limited to designing known and proven technology. Its product portfolio and range are broad and constantly changing.

Amstrad's audio and video products were differentiated on price. For personal computers, it effectively redefined the market by selling business-type computers to the home and small-business user for the first time. It met needs which giants like IBM had not addressed. Its machines were comprehensible, easy to use and affordable – and which innovators like Sinclair failed to attain (high specification and reliability). Amstrad turned an expensive specialist product, available only through limited outlets, into a consumer good which is as accessible as an electric toaster. IBM and Olivetti have both since tried to enter this market.

As befits mass-market products, they are promoted heavily through the mass media. The likely consumers are targeted through television, backed up by newspaper and poster advertising. The advertising budget for the UK alone is more than £20 million annually (10 per cent or more of turnover).

Growth in European markets is increasingly important for expanding Amstrad's bulk purchasing power and the life-cycles of its products (as well as turnover, see Figure 3.11). At first, Amstrad distributed abroad through agents, to save on start-up costs, but has now replaced them in order to:

- have control over distribution and promotion;
- stay closer to markets and customers; and
- develop brand loyalty for products previously sold under agents' names.

The Company can be seen to have grown through a classic succession of product life-cycles (see Figure 3.12). Its policy has carried risks: to reduce target prices, it has had to commit itself to huge orders from its suppliers. To gain

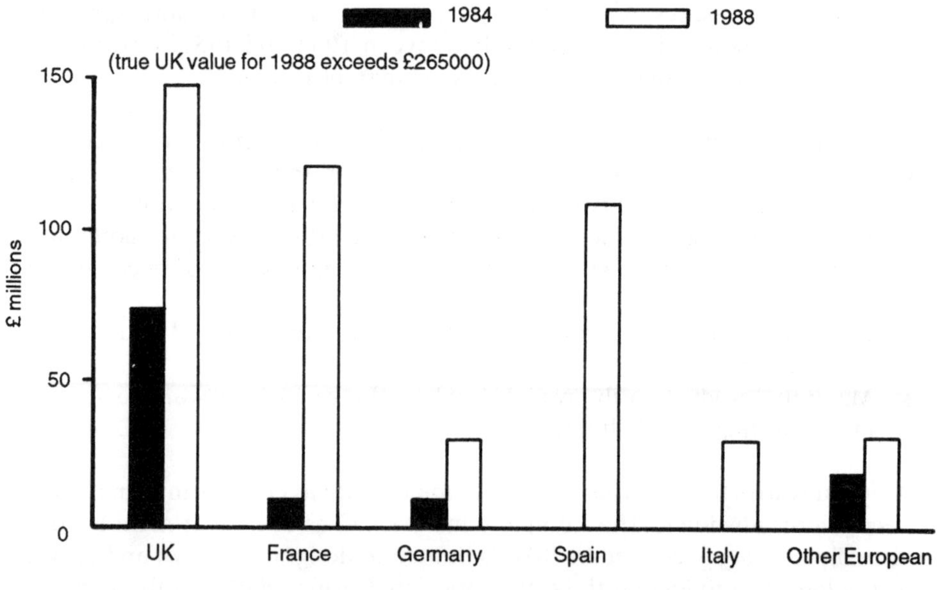

Sales outside the UK accounted for:

- 13% of total turnover in 1984.
- 58% of total turnover in 1988.

In 1987–88 Amstrad's PC range of computers had:

- about 30% of the business market in France
- 30% in Spain
- about 18% in Germany

In 1987–88 Amstrad had over half the home computer market in France. These figures were achieved in under four years.

Figure 3.11 Amstrad's turnover in major European countries, 1984 and 1988

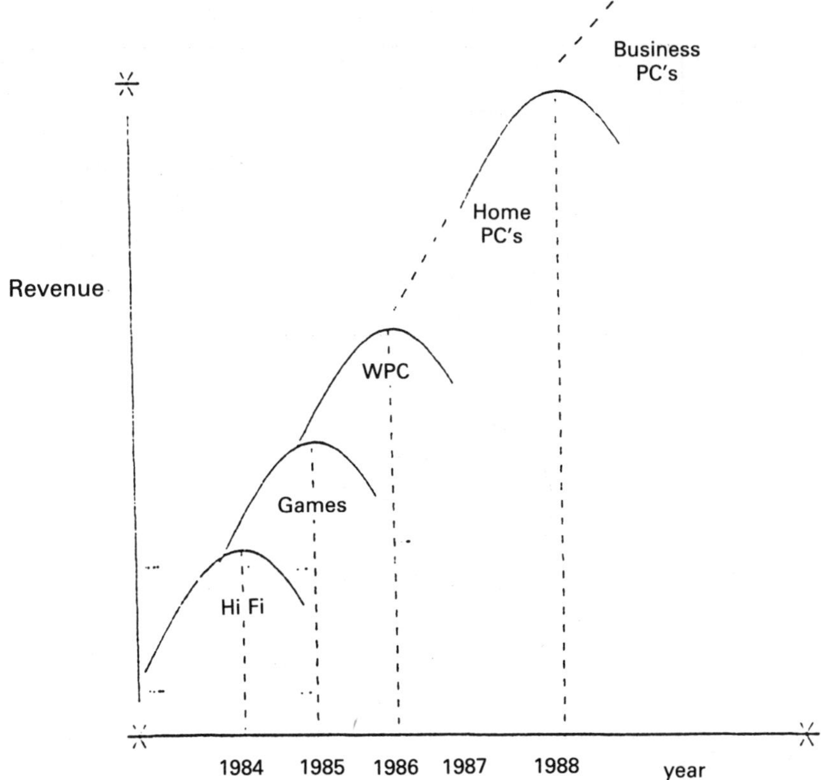

The development of a succession of product ranges and growth in Amstrad's product portfolio are also illustrated in the Boston matrices (Figure 3.13). There are no 'dog' products: any line which shows signs of becoming unprofitable is killed off.

Figure 3.12 The life-cycle of Amstrad products, 1984–8

longer term control and stability, it has entered the established market for business computers (which have higher added value than consumer electronics) and is redefining its image and promotion accordingly. The Company started to promote brand loyalty differentially:

- the Sinclair brand (bought in 1986) for home computers;
- Fidelity (bought in 1987) for consumer electronics;
- Amstrad for business computers.

Amstrad's portfolio is shown in Figure 3.13.

Amstrad, however, was affected like most other computer companies by the growing world recession in the early 1990s and this is reflected in the financial results shown in Tables 3.11 and 3.12.

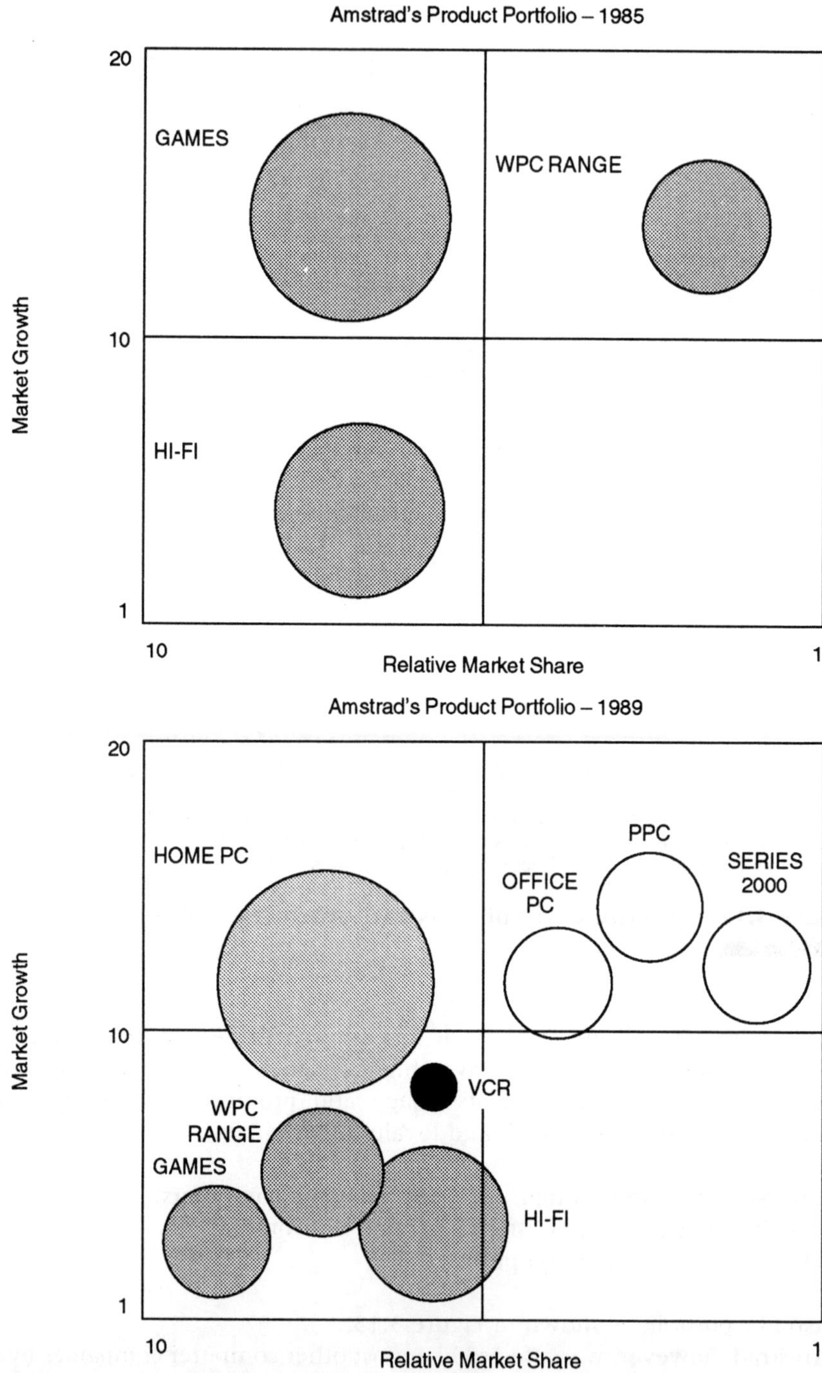

Figure 3.13 Amstrad's product portfolios, 1985 and 1989

Table 3.11 Amstrad plc Financial Performance, 1983–92

	Note	1983	1984	1985	1986	1987	1988	1989	1990	1991	1992
Turnover (£m)		51.8	84.9	136.1	304.1	511.8	625.4	626.3	577.3	528.4	356.6
Profit/(Loss) before taxation (£m)	1	8.0	9.1	20.2	75.3	135.7	160.4	76.6	43.7	20.2	(70.9)
Profit/(Loss) after taxation (£m)	1	5.3	5.7	14.0	52.0	93.4	105.1	51.1	34.3	14.5	(53.8)
Dividends pence/share (incl. tax credit)	2	0.16	0.19	0.27	0.49	0.97	1.87	1.87	1.87	0.53	
Dividend cover (times)	3	10	8	14	27	24	14	6	4	2	–
Profit/(Loss) retained for the year (£m)		5.1	5.0	12.9	47.2	89.6	93.0	43.1	2.3	5.4	(55.5)
Earnings/(Loss) per share (pence)	2	1.1	1.2	2.6	9.5	17.1	19.0	9.0	6.1	2.5	(9.4)
Share capital and reserves (£m)		12.3	29.2	42.2	88.1	179.5	256.2	310.8	311.1	316.5	262.1

Notes:

1. Profit/(Loss) figures other than retained earnings exclude extraordinary items.
2. As adjusted to reflect the 1 for 1 capitalisation issue on 25th November, 1982, the 4 for 1 issue on 4th November, 1983, the 1 for 6 rights issue on 11th May, 1984 and the 4 for 1 capitalisation issue on 2nd June, 1986.
3. Calculated before waiver of dividends for 1983 by A. M. Sugar.

Table 3.12 Amstrad plc Results, 1991 and 1992

Results at a Glance for the year ended 30th June, 1992
Amstrad plc

Amstrad

Turnover by Geographical Destination	1992 £m	1992 % of turnover	1991 £m	1991 % of turnover
UK	141.9	39.8	237.8	45.0
Germany	73.3	20.6	96.0	18.2
France	41.1	11.5	66.3	12.5
Italy	30.1	8.4	31.7	6.0
Spain	24.5	6.9	44.1	8.3
Other European Countries	21.0	5.9	10.9	2.1
Australasia	12.3	3.4	22.7	4.3
Benelux	11.1	3.1	17.3	3.3
Rest of World	1.3	0.4	1.6	0.3
Total	356.6	100.0	528.4	100.0

Turnover by Product	1992 £m	1992 % of turnover	1991 £m	1991 % of turnover
Professional computers	142.1	39.8	230.2	43.6
Satellite receivers and dishes	106.5	29.9	147.0	27.8
Video	70.8	19.9	65.2	12.3
Home computers	16.6	4.7	55.3	10.5
Fax	15.1	4.2	15.9	3.0
Printers	4.7	1.3	13.3	2.5
Audio	0.8	0.2	1.5	0.3
Total	356.6	100.0	528.4	100.0

	1992	1991
(Loss)/Profit on ordinary activities before taxation	(70.9)	20.2
(Loss)/Profit on ordinary activities after taxation	(53.8)	14.5
Net cash	113.8	59.6
Stocks	77.8	175.9
Dividends per share	0.4p	1.4p
(Loss)/Earnings per share	(9.4p)	2.5p
Dividend cover (times)	-	1.8
Net assets per share	46.3p	55.9p

Stagnant growth and poor financial performance in the early 1990s resulted in the need to cut overheads and scale down the business, and prompted a failed board room battle to take the company back to private ownership in the hands of its creator, the ebullient Alan Sugar.

The lifeblood of Amstrad has always been in its products, with the company securing its position in the consumer electronics market by introducing low cost technology products onto the market. But by the early 1990s, the troubled computer and electronics company was in need of a 'blockbuster' product to sell its way out of its problems.

Its core business, by 1992, had shifted to professional computers (40 per cent of sales) and satellite receivers and dishes (30 per cent of sales and 70 per cent market share), with the balance made up from sales of videos, home computers, faxes, printers and audio equipment. The emphasis on the small business/home office sector, prompted by changing working practices and the need for multi-functional machines, offers the largest market growth area compared with stagnant growth in the consumer electronics market.

Personal communicators, or 'personal digital assistants', hand-held note-books which combine the functions of a telephone handset with computer and facsimile machines, and recognise and accept their owner's handwriting, launched in 1993, may prove to be the product to bring the company through the mid-1990s and revive its waning fortunes. Consistent in their policy of providing a low-cost alternative, this Amstrad product, manufactured in mainland China, is the first on the market, and though less sophisticated than potential competitor products from IBM and Apple, proves that the company is still capable of producing new product ideas.

Amstrad claim that this new product will be the world's first in a product sector which some analysts predict could be worth as much as $20 billion a year in sales by 2000. Amstrad also claim that this launch will be the first time a revolutionary product incorporating state of the art technology will be sold at a mass market price from launch.

A similar strategy underlies the thinking behind the proposed launch of a low-priced video phone in conjunction with GEC Marconi. A determined move into the growing telecommunications equipment market will come through an Amstrad subsidiary Betacom.

Following its withdrawal from the highly competitive and fashionable home computer market, Amstrad are likely to continue to reconsider the markets it currently operates in and to concentrate on producing and manufacturing products that will give a significant long term margin. In line with this thinking is the decision to re-enter the audio market. European sales will continue to contribute a significant and growing proportion of revenue (in excess of 60 per cent in 1992). An indication that these strategies are working was revealed with profits in 1993.

Section 4: Repositioning the Business for Leadership

The continual evolution of markets, restructuring of industries through competition and technological change, and the new product/new market activities of business enterprises, all bring about fundamental changes to a company. Writers on strategic planning such as Abell and Hammond,[46] Aaker[47] and Bonoma,[48] emphasise the need for a firm to accept and change in response to, and in preparation for, relevant environmental changes. Porter[49] indicates that effective competitive strategy involves positioning the firm so that its capabilities provide the best defence against the existing array of competitive forces. Abell[50] maintains that the starting point of strategic planning is defining the business. Periodically, this will involve repositioning the business so that it is re-aligned to its changing environment.

In this section, the strategic concepts applicable to repositioning the business are identified and a case study of Tesco portrays a major repositioning strategy by one of the large UK grocery retailers.

Corporate Competitive Positioning

McKenna describes 'dynamic positioning' as three interlocking stages: product positioning, market positioning and corporate positioning.[51] In the first stage, product positioning, a company determines how it would like its product to fit in the market. Does it stand for high-product quality, value for money, or advanced technology? Which market is it aimed at?

The second stage, market positioning, involves the gaining of recognition and credibility in the marketplace. Here, the task is to establish a strong and favoured perception in the target market's mind.

In the third stage, corporate positioning, the company must position itself. This is done, McKenna says, through financial success represented by corporate profitability. A firm's corporate position is also determined by the way it does business, its attitude to its customers, its reputation for service or quality or value, and its new product programme, which provides some perception of its dynamism and innovative stance.

These three stages of positioning provide a link through all parts of the company and connect them all to the marketplace.

Identifying Competitive Market Position

For existing companies, the starting point for strategy development is to identify the company's competitive position. This is done by researching its main markets, and establishing the attributes that are most important to each market. The company is rated on those attributes against its competitors and in relation to the market's perceived ideal rating on each attribute.

In a competitive environment, it is not necessary to match 'perfectly' the desired attributes, but the aim should be to be better in those attributes that are important to the target market. An illustration is provided by competitive positioning research conducted by the *Independent* and *Sunday Sport* newspapers in the UK, the results of which are reported in the case study.

Figures 3.14 and 3.15 show maps of the UK newspaper market in 1986 using different parameters for the *x* and *y* axes.

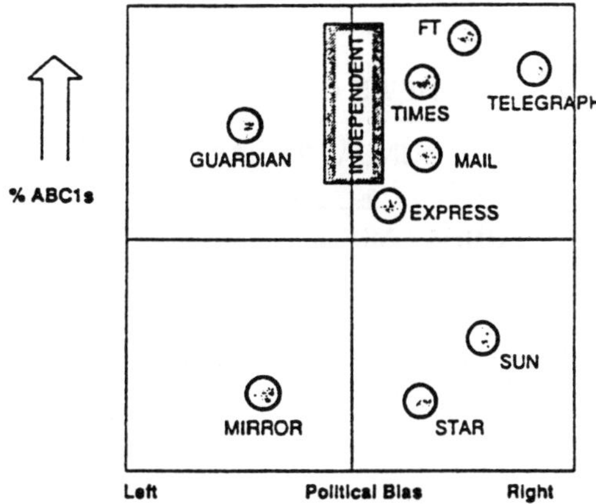

Figure 3.14 Market map, newspapers

Hence, positionings can and do differ in different market segments and they become cemented in the market's mind over time.

When attempting to change corporate market positioning, it is common to find that intangible image factors have a major effect on a company's ability to develop its business. In the retail market, Woolworths in the UK lost its well-established image by attempting to go up market in the 1980s. Consumers were just confused and stopped shopping there. Under new ownership, however, it has succeeded in regaining its former position at the low price end of the market for defined categories of merchandise, consistent with its traditional image.

The strength of the Levi Strauss positioning, representing 'casualness', has restricted the company's diversification into formal clothing using the corporate name. Among others, its venture into formal stylings of suits, sports coats and slacks under the Levi name has been unsuccessful.[52] The company name, if used as a central part of the marketing strategy, establishes the scope for the firm's activities and relationship with the market.

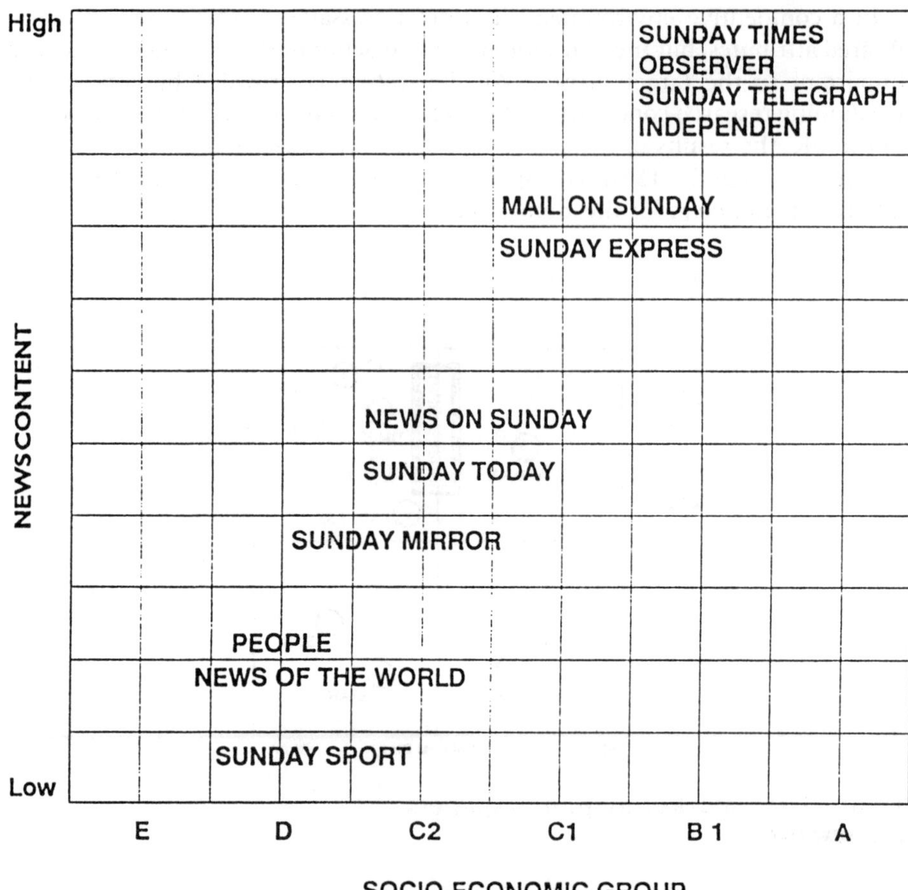

Figure 3.15 1986 market map, newspapers

■ Strategies for Repositioning

Effective positioning and repositioning strategies entail designing products, services and marketing programmes that emphasise attributes or benefits which:

- are important to customers;
- provide a sustainable differential advantage over competitors;
- are in harmony with corporate image.

While a name change may signal a changed or revitalised company, this must be supported by specific strategies that reinforce the image presented. In the early 1980s there was little point in British Airways presenting itself as providing excellent service, when it did not in practice. If this operational change had not occurred, the name change and repositioning attempt would have lost credibility and would have become ineffective as a business development tool.

Computer companies Burroughs and Sperry sought a new name for their merged operations. They looked for a name that reflected the merged companies' 'fresh image and fresh start'. The name Unisys, an acronym for United Information Systems, was chosen. This name served only to confuse the marketplace, having no heritage and reflecting no particular image or orientation. The corporate positions occupied by Burroughs and Sperry before the merger were lost, and the merged company was faced with establishing a position afresh.[53]

Competitive repositioning strategies include a number of points that may be implemented individually or together, depending upon the company's existing position. Some of the options are to:

1 Reinforce and protect/defend important strengths and market opportunities, with the focus on attributes that are important to the market and to the company's profitability; and
2 Eliminate or reduce weaknesses and threats that are important to the market and to the company's viability. A case in point is Ericsson. This Swedish company is a world force in sophisticated telecommunications switches. Ericsson needed resources to develop its position within the telecommunications industry. Peripheral business in personal computers and terminals, were draining both financial and management resources in markets of intense competition and low profitability.[54]
3 Change perception of a performance factor that is important to the market. Advertising or sales effort may be all that is required to inform the market of the company's performance on a particular attribute such as service or product range.
4 Shift the importance of a performance factor. This strategy involves modifying the ranking of attributes in the customer's mind. In the computer market, Apple has attempted, successfully in some segments, to change the top ranking attribute from technical performance to ease of use – an attribute on which Apple leads the industry.
5 Add a new performance factor. In the computer market an example is the attribute of portability.
6 Reduce effort or investment in attributes that are unimportant to the market. Kimberly Clark found that it could significantly reduce the quality of the cardboard core in its toilet paper product without any effect on the market's perception. This resulted in substantial profit improvement.

Tesco's competitive positioning in the UK retail grocery market illustrates a repositioning strategy that was adopted to:

- reinforce its product quality image;
- re-order product quality as the top ranking attribute in the market's perception;
- strengthen its product range; and
- achieve some improvement in price perception.

Other factors to be considered include the cost and payback of a strategy and its financial risk. The potential payback of the strategy will, in part, be influenced by the reactions of major competitors. Therefore, focus should be on factors that competition cannot or will not change and on elements that form the basis of the firm's competitive advantage.

What must also be considered is the segmentation of the market. While a business requires a consistency in its overall positioning, it is possible to emphasise different positioning attributes or benefits in different segments by formulating modified offers and implementing well-targeted communications campaigns.

General guidelines for directing positioning strategies are shown in Figure 3.16. The company holds a position of leadership if it rates better than its competitors on attributes that are most important to the market. Alternatively, if it is worse than its competitors on the most important attributes, this suggests areas where major improvements are required and repositioning strategies are necessary. Similarly, Figure 3.16 provides guidelines for different competitive positions in relation to lower priority attributes perceived by the market. This approach provides a management focus for developing positioning strategy.

■ Strategy Implementation

Major repositioning strategies require close management and realistic time frames. The company's capabilities must be assessed, and detailed programmes started. Some examples of the elements which may require management in the implementation phase of a repositioning programme are outlined below.

□ *Staff Attitudes*

Entrenched attitudes among a large workforce in a business are hard to change and take time. British Telecom has found this with its employees. Major educational initiatives and commercial training programmes were required over a period of years for British Telecom to convert its employees to a business and marketing mentality. Public service-based practices required of government business act to slow this conversion process substantially.

□ *Capital Investment*

Any significant capital investment takes time before it is fully operational and begins to reap benefits. In the airline industry, a simple procedure such as

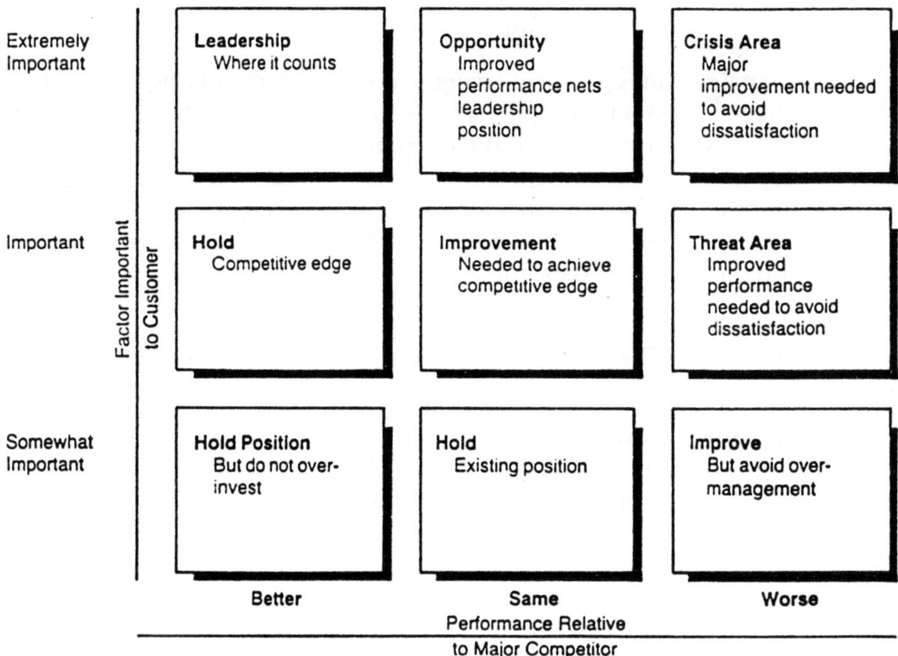

Figure 3.16 Competitive positioning and management focus

flagging frequent business travellers on the reservation and operator computer system requires substantial research of the customer base and extensive reprogramming of the computer system. Procedures and services then must be put in place if the frequent business traveller is to be given priority and additional benefits. All of these initiatives need careful planning, testing and training before full implementation.

☐ *Service Delivery*

Repositioning strategies frequently involve the delivery of a higher level of service or additional service to priority markets. If this is promised through the advertising campaign or the sales force, it must be delivered, or credibility is lost. Frequently, it is the small things that are important to customers. In the hotel industry, it includes addressing the customer by name, rapid processing of customer accounts at checkout, reduction in waiting times for taxis and provision of prompt room service. Often, it requires the company to get back to the basics and ensures that these essentials work well before adding frills.

☐ *Sales Force and Distribution*

As Davidow points out, significant changes in the product offerings and service levels can have a major effect on the sales force and distributors.[55] Programmes to give new skills to the sales force and open up new distribution channels may be necessary for the successful implementation of a strategy. As ITT discovered, with its introduction of connectors for the white goods market in Europe, the sales force did not have the knowledge, confidence or appropriate selling skills to penetrate the market successfully.

☐ *Internal Marketing*

Any major repositioning strategy needs the whole company to be involved and committed to the success of the change. Davidow describes this as a crusade.[56] A programme of internal marketing through all parts of the company is usually a prerequisite for external marketing success.

■ Case Study 9: Tesco

■ Repositioning from Low Cost, Commodity, to Top Right, High Differentiation

■ Number Two Challenging for the Number One Slot

In 1966, *Management Today* proclaimed Tesco to be the UK's most profitable company. It had grown rapidly based on its founder's philosophy of 'pile it high, sell it cheap'. However, by the 1970s it was stuck with its 1960s outlook, losing contact with its customers. It had cramped stores and a poor product range, both in quality and choice. In 1977, it still offered Green Shield stamps, a symbol of the past, its market share was only 7 per cent, its profit margin only 1.8 per cent and its share price was at a low of 20 pence. It was rated a takeover target.

The market had moved on, leaving Tesco complacent and out of touch. Real incomes had increased by 50 per cent since 1958. People were prepared to spend money on quality or luxuries. They wanted the opportunity to buy a lifestyle. More people with cars preferred one-stop shopping, with easy car parking. People wanted shopping to be more pleasant, with a better environment, wider aisles, interesting counters such as delicatessens and a greater choice.

Tesco's initial response to the crisis was a 'knee jerk' reaction to secure survival. They dropped Green Shield stamps, an emblem of Tesco's past, and an important symbol of the new mood for change, and embarked on a price cutting strategy. The breathing space this provided enabled them to consider their longer term strategy. They recognised that with greater affluence, the customer was generally moving up market. Sainsburys ruled alone in this segment. Tesco spotted an opportunity for another player in this area, away from the rest of the pack who were battling for the price conscious segment.

Their market research showed that a substantial majority of consumers had the following priorities in their choice of supermarkets:

1 Product quality
2 Service
3 Store environment
4 Location
5 Price

Tesco structured their new marketing mix around these. Table 3.13 compares the main features of the mix before and after 1977.

With their overall repositioning and revised marketing strategy, Tesco have reshaped their destiny. By 1988 they were challenging Sainsbury for market leadership. Their profit margin was up to 6 per cent and their share price stood at a healthy 135 pence.

Table 3.13 Comparison of Tesco's Marketing Mix Before and After 1977

	Pre-1977	*1980s*
Product	Basic essentials	Quality and extended own brand range Wider choice Luxuries and specialities
Place	Cramped High Street stores Development budget of £6 million per annum	Most superstores of any retailer Out of town Good car parking Spacious layout Development budget of £300 million per annum
Promotion	Green Shield stamps Price based advertising	Robert Carrier Up market image Quality
Price	Top priority Cheapest	Value for money Not absolute cheapest

Tesco has indeed made dramatic gains, with operating profit per square foot up from the 1984 figure of £9.36 to £36.70 in 1990. In 1989/90, a difficult year for the retail sector, Tesco's operating profit per square foot increased by a fifth and its operating margin by more than a tenth, while sales per square foot rose 7.5 per cent and total area increased by only 6.5 per cent. Not even the universally admired Sainsburys could match that performance. Tesco's success is reflected in its latest financial results, shown in Tables 3.14 and 3.15.

Tesco are determined not to rest on their laurels again. They continue to stay close to the customer and match their offer to the customer's needs. Competitive audits are held twice yearly to measure Tesco against the competition in the five critical areas highlighted above. Service continues to be a priority. A 'customer first' training scheme was launched in 1987, and to assess service, incognito Tesco staff visit different stores. Prizes are awarded for the best locations. The entire UK is monitored on a computer to spot demographic trends. By means such as this, Tesco knows that more than 70 per cent of customers are interested in healthy eating, 25 per cent are single people, and 70 per cent of women customers are working. They can therefore continue to match their marketing mix to customer needs.

This is a classic case of repositioning in a growth market to attain joint

Table 3.14 Tesco Financial Record, 1988–92

Five Year Record

Year ended February	1988	1989	1990	1991	1992[1]	Compound growth over five years
Financial Statistics £m						
Turnover excluding VAT	4,119.1	4,717.7	5,401.9	6,346.3	**7,097.4**	14.6%
Operating profit	214.4	276.5	334.0	420.0	**503.3**	27.8%
Operating margin[2]	5.2%	5.9%	6.2%	6.6%	**7.1%**	
Interest receivable less payable	15.3	2.4	9.8	19.1	**65.5**	
Employee profit sharing	(10.7)	(13.6)	(17.2)	(22.0)	**(23.8)**	
Profit before property profits	219.0	265.3	326.6	417.1	**545.0**	26.8%
Net margin[2]	5.3%	5.6%	6.0%	6.6%	**7.7%**	
Property profits	6.6	10.7	35.0	19.1	**0.5**	
Profit before taxation	225.6	276.0	361.6	436.2	**545.5**	25.4%
Taxation	(75.1)	(89.7)	(107.8)	(133.5)	**(149.9)**	
Profit after taxation	150.5	186.3	253.8	302.7	**395.6**	27.2%
Earnings per share[3]	10.37p	11.98p	15.87p	18.37p	**20.43p**	17.2%
Fully diluted earnings per share (excluding property profits)[3]	9.37p	10.98p	13.35p	16.60p	**19.95p**	20.6%
Dividends per share[3]	2.77p	3.40p	4.17p	5.25p	**6.30p**	21.7%
Net worth – £m[4]	867.4	1,031.3	1,254.1	2,159.9	**2,447.0**	28.8%
Return on shareholders' funds[5]	27.7%	27.9%	28.6%	29.4%	**23.7%**	
Return on capital employed[6]	21.5%	22.1%	22.5%	21.2%	**19.3%**	
Net assets per share[7] – pence	59	67	80	112	**126**	18.5%
Productivity £						
Turnover per employee[8]	82,067	89,449	99,400	106,044	**119,246**	8.5%
Profit per employee[8]	4,272	5,243	6,146	7,018	**8,456**	21.0%
Wages per employee[8]	7,809	8,695	10,009	10,579	**12,250**	10.7%
Weekly sales per sq ft[9]	11.00	11.51	12.69	14.12	**14.32**	7.0%
Retail Statistics						
Market share in food and drink shops[10]	7.7%	8.4%	8.8%	9.4%	**9.6%**	
Number of stores	379	374	379	384	**396**	
Total sales area – '000 sq ft	8,220	8,542	9,071	9,661	**10,463**	
Sales area opened in year – '000 sq ft	655	557	787	866	**977**	
Average store size (sales area) – sq ft	21,700	22,800	23,900	25,200	**26,400**	
Average sales area of stores opened in the year – sq ft	34,300	34,800	34,400	41,500	**39,600**	
Full-time equivalent employees[11]	50,192	52,742	54,345	59,846	**59,519**	
Share Price – pence						
Highest	206	169	216	246	**296**	
Lowest	139	129	151	194.5	**207**	
Year End	152	153	196	246	**271**	

Notes

1 53 week period.
2 Based upon turnover exclusive of value added tax.
3 Adjusted in respect of 1991 rights issue.
4 Total shareholders' funds at the year end.
5 Profit before property profits divided by weighted average shareholders' funds.
6 Profit before property profits and interest divided by average capital employed.
7 Based on the number of shares at the year end.
8 Based on full-time equivalent number of employees, turnover exclusive of value added tax and operating profit.
9 Based on weighted average sales area and turnover inclusive of value added tax.
10 Based on Tesco food, grocery, non-food and drink sales and Department of Trade and Industry data.
11 Based on average number of full-time equivalent employees in the United Kingdom

Table 3.15 Tesco plc Financial Performance

	1992	1991	% Increase
Turnover excluding value added tax – £m	**7,097·4**	6,346·3	11·8
Profit before property profits – £m	**545·0**	417·1	30·7
Fully diluted earnings per share (excluding property profits) – pence	**19·95**	16·60	20·2
Dividends per share – pence	**6·30**	5·25	20·0

Financial Highlights

LAST FIVE YEARS

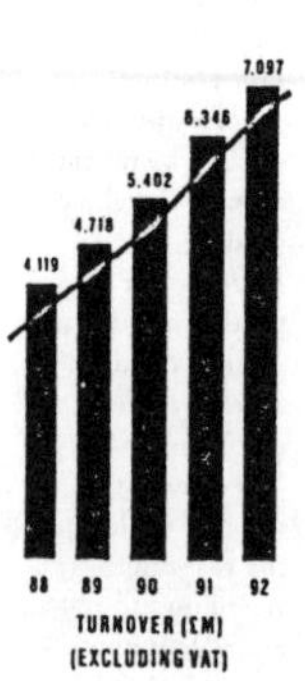

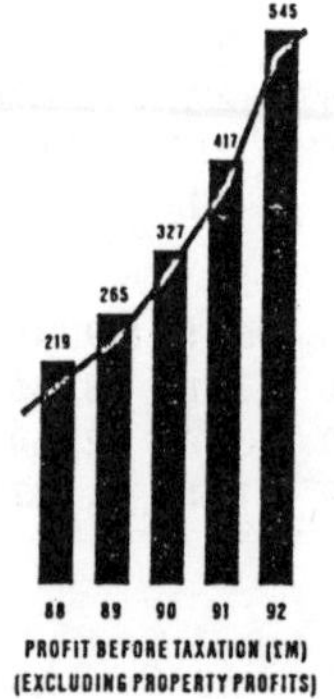

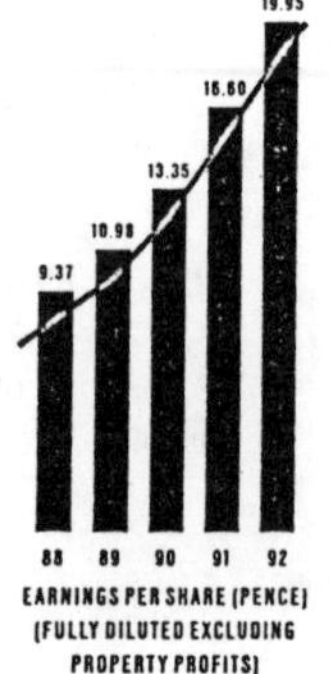

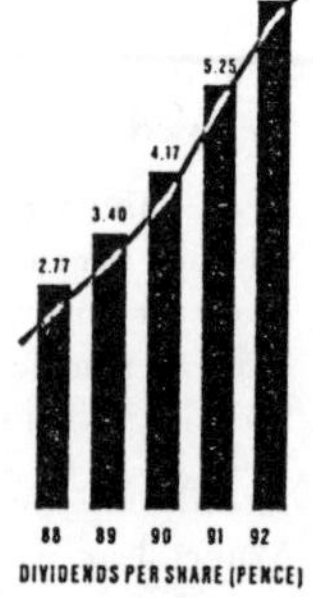

	1992	1988	Compound % increase per annum over five years
Turnover excluding value added tax – £m	**7,097·4**	4,119·1	14·6
Profit before property profits – £m	**545·0**	219·0	26·8
Fully diluted earnings per share (excluding property profits) – pence	**19·95**	9·37	20·6
Dividends per share – pence	**6·30**	2·77	21·7

leadership. In fact, leadership fluctuates between Tesco and Sainsbury, with Sainsbury currently just ahead.

There is, of course, a new threat looming over Tesco. Argyll has made its first tentative forays into the single European market, tying up with Dutch firm Koninklijke Ahold and France's Groupe Casino in the European Retail Alliance to identify and exploit opportunities for cooperation, such as the joint Eurobrand wines and coffees currently under development. The three way alliance has been cemented with cross-shareholdings. The alliance also has a 60 per cent interest in Associated Marketing Services AG alongside seven other European food firms, which acts as a link with suppliers, seeking shared efficiencies.

Such alliances, and the arrival in the UK of French and German retailing groups, cannot be ignored in the medium to long term and must surely bring to an end the 'fortress Britain' mentality of many of the UK's leading retailers.

■ The Future

The real worry for Tesco, therefore, is not its nearest rival Sainsbury, but the threat from both European and domestic food discount stores and the new warehouse club concept, spearheaded by the American company Costco. The cheap and cheerful format, selling branded goods at significantly cheaper prices than the four major grocery retailers, is the fastest growing sector in British retailing and discounters are likely to account for 15 per cent of the grocery trade by 1995. Competition from UK includes the Food Giant supermarkets, owned by Isosceles, Dales (Asda) Low-Cost (Argyll) and Kwik-Save, and from continental Europe, Aldi from Germany and Netto from Denmark.

Tesco, without a foot in this camp, is vulnerable to lost sales. Tesco's current market segmentation is out-of-town superstores, high street stores and metro stores, small city centre convenience shops, pioneered in Covent Garden in London. Previous forays into discount stores with Victor Value were not successful.

To offset the fierce pressure on prices from the discounters, Tesco have adopted a drive for added value services and products, with the provision of on-site petrol stations, in-store pharmacies (following the Sainsbury and Boots link-up) and an emphasis on higher margin items.

The strength of the Tesco brand in the launch of own label and innovative products has helped the company maintain its dominant position in the market. Heavy above-the-line advertising featuring Dudley Moore in a three-year contract, reputedly worth half a million pounds, is part of the second highest promotional spend in the UK retail sector, behind Dixons, at £26.9 million in 1992 (up from £24.3 million in 1991).

With 8 million customers, over 400 stores and 9.6 per cent of market share, Tesco are well poised to continue their strategy of expansion. But they must continue to track the changes in consumer attitudes. From the price conscious early 1980s and the environmentally aware late 1980s, the value for money

1990s and the discount store factor, means that Tesco will face much uncertainty in the medium term, which will test its up-market strategy.

■ Case Study 10: Bernard Matthews

■ Moving from Bottom Left (Low Differentiation, Low Cost) to Top Right (High Differentiation, Low Cost)

■ Introduction

Bernard Matthews started his business breeding turkeys in 1962, and by 1975 he had 70 per cent of the turkey market. To achieve further growth, Bernard Matthews had to develop new products or expand into new markets.

A gap analysis shows how profits could have dropped with time if Bernard Matthews remained a single product business (see Figure 3.17).

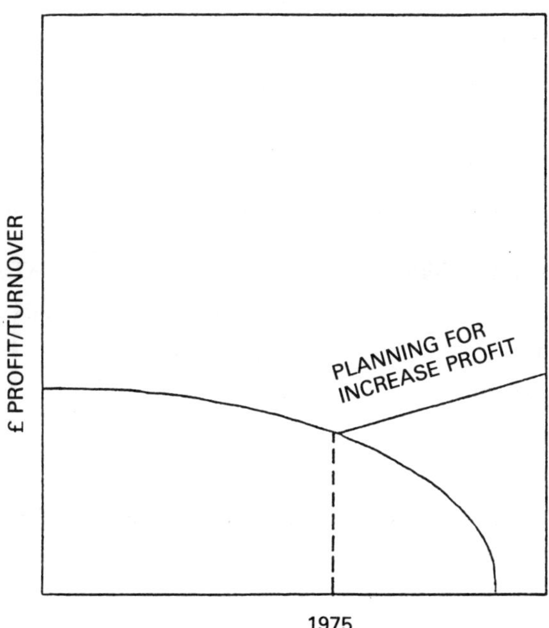

Figure 3.17 Bernard Matthews, planning gap in mid-1970s

Development Strategy

The growth of Bernard Matthews from 1975 was due to a thorough and well executed development strategy. In the early 1970s, profits were threatened by:

- risk of a single product;
- low margins on sales;
- cheap imports; and
- increasing overheads (which were dependent on the cost of feed grain).

In addition, the turkey market was:

- seasonal;
- saturated;
- a commodity market;
- affected by the size of the product, which was not suitable for the average household.

A SWOT analysis shows Bernard Matthews' position in 1975 (see Figure 3.18).

STRENGTHS	WEAKNESSES
High relative market share Technical leadership Bernard Matthew's profile	Single commodity product Seasonal sales bias
OPPORTUNITIES	**THREATS**
New products Added value brands Health conscious consumers	Reduction in size of households Competition – UK – EEC Competition in other meats

Figure 3.18 Bernard Matthews, SWOT analysis in mid-1970s

A Porter matrix shows where Bernard Matthews wanted to go in the late 1970s, from a single commodity product to a range of products with added value (see Figure 3.19).

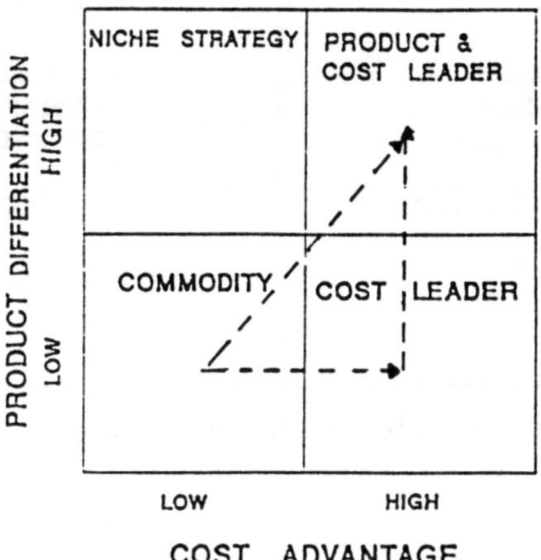

Figure 3.19 Bernard Matthews, Porter matrix

The strategy adopted to achieve growth was as follows:

1 Continue to increase market share in existing products while generating adequate profits.
2 Develop a set of branded products with added value which could be sold throughout the year.
3 Package turkey in small units to suit the average household and sell as a healthy convenience food.
4 Through television advertising convince the public that turkey can be eaten at any time of the year.

■ Marketing Plan

The marketing plan adopted the following policies with respect to the marketing mix:

Product
From 1975, Bernard Matthews launched a steady stream of new products which met the needs of a wide market with a reduced dependence on seasonal sales. The development of these products was assisted by technological innovation in the areas of meat-extrusion and self basting, which were developed in-house. The Bernard Matthews portfolio of products is illustrated in the BCG matrix in Figure 3.20.

Price
The move away from a single commodity product to a range of products with

STARS	PROBLEM CHILDREN
Norfolk Burger Turkey Steak Turkey Sausages	Hamwich Cheese Hamwich Golden Drummers
CASH (COWS) TURKEYS	**DOGS**
Norfolk Turkeys Self-basting Turkeys	

Figure 3.20 Bernard Matthews, Boston Box

added value, enabled Bernard Matthews to compete with a range of convenience foods.

A comparison of price between Bernard Matthews' products and fresh turkey in 1986 is given below:

Fresh turkey	90 pence per pound
Bernard Matthews' convenience foods	193 pence per pound

Place

Bernard Matthews benefited from the shift of meat sales from butchers to the supermarkets, where he had 67 per cent share of the market.

Promotion

A large part of Bernard Matthews' success has been due to high profile advertising, which cost between 6 and 8 per cent of sales. This created a high brand awareness, which not only contributed to increased sales of his products, but also to an overall increase in turkey market size.

Growth

The growth of Bernard Matthews was quite dramatic over a ten year period up to 1986 (see Figure 3.21).

■ Conclusion

The sales performance of Bernard Matthews' products is only a small part of his overall success. His greatest achievement has been to change the eating habits of millions of people. Through his advertising, he has educated people to eat turkey throughout the year, and as a result, sales of turkey have doubled over the last two decades.

More recently, however, he has successfully entered the cooked meats, red

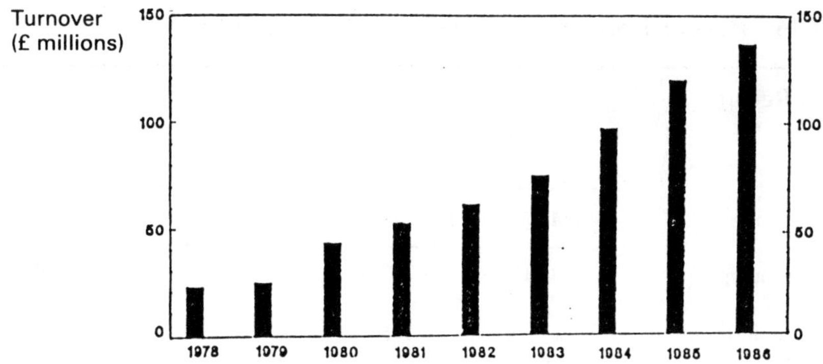

Figure 3.21 Bernard Matthews, sales turnover, 1978–86

meat and fish market, using the same principles as he used in the turkey market.

The testimony of Bernard Matthew's success is that the brand name has become synonymous with turkey products.

New product development has remained an essential feature for future group expansion. Products aimed at children's and convenience meals have demonstrated a keen understanding of the changing UK eating patterns, and products now include commodity and cooked meat and fish products, value added turkey products and whole turkeys. Despite strong pressure from EC and USA imports, leading to financial losses, Bernard Matthews still supplies 33 per cent of the 10 million UK Christmas turkeys.

Exports to Europe, particularly France, currently account for 10 per cent of turnover and are likely to be a central feature of the company's strategy for the 1990s. The acquisition of Hungarian company Savar, with sales in Hungary, Switzerland and Austria provide an established entry channel into the central European market.

The company financial results for 1988 to 1992 are shown in Table 3.16.

Table 3.16 Bernard Matthews Financial Record, 1988–92

Five Year Record	1992 £000's	1991 £000's	1990 £000's	1989 £000's	1988 £000's
Turnover	**144,235**	148,379	150,050	135,758	135,215
Profit on Group operations	**3,912**	13,281	16,130	10,198	10,822
Share of profit of Associated undertaking	**9**	19	31	–	–
Interest	**(583)**	(110)	(623)	(1,088)	(587)
Profit on ordinary activities before taxation	**3,338**	13,190	15,538	9,110	10,235
Taxation	**1,302**	4,510	5,512	3,443	3,509
Profit after taxation	**2,036**	8,680	10,026	5,667	6,726
Dividends	**2,792**	5,609	5,632	3,779	3,133
Retained (loss)/profit for the period	**(756)**	3,071	4,394	1,888	3,593
Balance Sheet					
Fixed assets	**47,254**	46,642	46,140	46,205	45,650
Other net assets	**19,382**	20,940	18,774	14,756	13,423
Shareholders' funds	**66,636**	67,582	64,914	60,961	59,073
Dividends					
Dividends per share (net)	**2.25p**	4.5p	4.5p	3.0p	2.5p
Dividends per share (gross)	**2.9p**	6.0p	6.0p	4.0p	3.33p
Dividend rate (gross)	**11.6%**	24.0%	24.0%	16.0%	13.3%
Earnings per Share					
Earnings per share (before taxation)	**2.68p**	10.56p	12.39p	7.23p	8.11p
Earnings per share (after taxation)	**1.64p**	6.95p	7.99p	4.50p	5.33p

CHAPTER 4

Strategies for Positioning as a Major Force in the Market

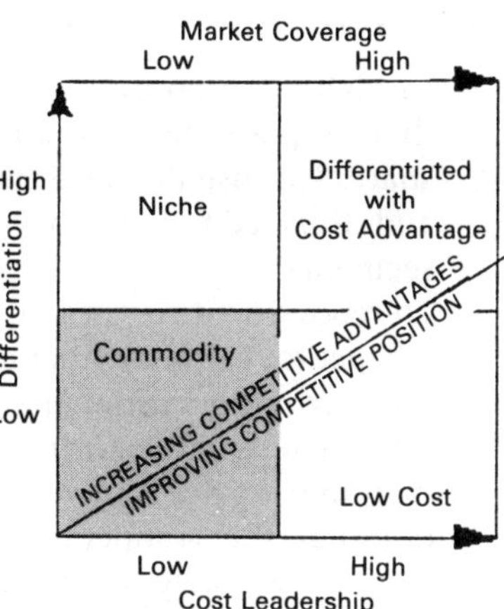

■ Moving Away from the Commodity Low Differentiation, High Cost Position

■ Section 1: Introduction

In some industries, a major new strategy has enabled a challenger to attack the largest shareholders in the market, to achieve a strong competitive position and in a few instances market leadership. To achieve this, a company must be aggressive, well focused on objectives and strategies and adopt the offensive attitudes noted in Section 2.

This strategy is targeted at an uncontested area or a market that is weakly defended by large competitors. Usually, a flanking attack draws a limited response because a large competitor may lack the skills for that market or regard the market as too small. There also appears to be no apparent threat to its dominant position. The strategy attacks the competitor's weakest point with the firm's strongest advantages. As penetration occurs, and the competitive threat to larger companies becomes clearer, it is usually necessary to change strategy to penetrate the market more rapidly so that a defendable position is consolidated.

Four broad positioning strategies represent springboards for the development of a new force.

1 One option is to position strongly in segments neglected by the dominant companies and build those segments as a base for spreading more widely into the main markets.

2 In low-price positioning, a lower price/lower quality product range is offered as an alternative to competitors' higher priced products. Progressively, the quality is added, but the price advantage is maintained to increase market share. This classic Japanese strategy has been very successful for low-cost countries and companies. Toyota cars and Honda motorbikes have followed this flanking strategy.

3 In high-price positioning, the company caters for the premium segment, then re-positions itself and its range at a lower price to build up market share. This usually needs product innovation to support the price premium and thus add new attributes and benefits suitable to specific market segments.
4 To reposition a competitor, it is necessary to indicate something about the competitor's product that makes customers change their minds. A reason is given why the customer should stop buying the competitor's product and buy the alternative. It may be done by creating doubt about the quality or customer service if there is valid cause for customer concern, or by pointing out that the competitor's main advantage is no longer relevant. This strategy is likely to bring an aggressive response from the dominant competitor, and it is necessary to be able to sustain a marketing attack and, if necessary, defend the competitive position.

In his pioneering book entitled *Competitive Advantage*, Michael Porter points out that a competitor who engages in each generic strategy – cost leadership, differentiation and focus – but fails to achieve any of them, is 'stuck in the middle'. This position creates no competitive advantage and usually results in below-average performance.[1] He observes that the temptation to blur a generic strategy and become 'stuck in the middle' is strong for the specialist company focused on and dominating narrow segments of the market when it adopts a broader growth strategy.

When a firm is in the process of changing from a minor to a major force in its industry or market, it must usually change from one strategy culture to another. During the transition phase, it runs the risk of being attacked by specialist competitors and the dominant market leaders. This is a time of vulnerability and the strategic change needs to be made rapidly. If the firm does not make the transition successfully and competitive and environmental forces turn against it, retreating to a niche position may be the only alternative. Sometimes, there is no going back, and the business may be in danger of corporate collapse. Argenti, in his study of British businesses that ended in receivership during the seventies, points out the risks of rapid growth with weaknesses in organisation structure and resources. He identifies the conditions for, and stages of, corporate collapse.[2]

The underlying foundation of an effective competitive strategy lie in the ability of a firm to gain a sustainable competitive advantage. The company seeking to become a major force in the market must assess its resources and its ability to sustain a competitive advantage against a prolonged attack from its competitors.

The risks of a cost leadership strategy threaten the firm when:

- cost leadership is not sustained when technology changes or competitors imitate;
- proximity in differentiation is lost; or
- cost focusers achieve even lower costs in major segments.

The risks of differentiation strategies occur when:

- differentiation is not sustained either through competitor imitation, or the bases of differentiation become less important to customers;
- cost proximity is lost; or
- differentiation focusers achieve greater differentiation in major segments.

The risks of a focus strategy increase when:

- the focus strategy is imitated and the target segment becomes structurally unattractive, resulting in profit dilution;
- broadly targeted competitors attack the segment and its differences from other segments narrow; or
- new focusers sub-segment the industry.[3]

In some industries, structure and barriers to entry may eliminate the possibility of the firm becoming a new force by using a particular generic strategy. A case in point in the UK is the compressed gas market.

BOC holds more than 80 per cent of the cylinder gas business in the UK. It has no constraints on raw material supply, and it has a largely dispersed and fragmented customer base. In the future, the threat of new entrants is low because the capital investment required in gas cylinders and distribution is immense, and there are unlikely to be significant market substitutes.

BOC is in a very strong position to defend its market and ensure it is highly profitable. Its defensive strategies include:

- an extensive distribution system, providing availability and convenience to customers;
- control of hundreds of thousands of customer accounts that maintains direct contact between BOC and users;
- a complex multi-tiered pricing structure that provides for variation in volume, delivery arrangements, cylinder rental and type of gas; and
- production and ownership of cylinders, which is the vehicle for provision of compressed gas.

The compressed gas market is mature, with slow technological change in the industry, and BOC is in a position to protect dominance and maximise profit.

In other industries, however, the three generic strategies can profitably co-exist, providing that competitors pursue different strategies or select different bases for differentiation or focus. Industries in which several major companies are adopting differentiation strategies based on different sources of benefits to customers, provide opportunities for a number of major forces in the market. The personal computer market is one example.

Where the stakes are high, good competitive analysis is a vital ingredient in reducing the risks and increasing the chances of an effective competitive marketing strategy being designed.

The purpose of competitive analysis is to:

- predict future competitive moves;
- identify areas of competitive vulnerability; and
- predict competitive reactions to the firm's strategy.

Diagnosing competitors' motives and commitment to particular markets and inferring strategies from their competitive positions, rate of investment in assets, and the way they define their business and evaluate results, are central to competitive analysis. In particular, attention should be paid to the background, style and personality of the competitor's major decision makers.

A study of the influence of the chief executive's educational background and work experience on strategic decisions shows a positive correlation and somewhat predictable strategic response.[4] It can be expected that senior managers with a financial background focus on profit, marketers are driven by market penetration, share and new products, and technical people focus on product quality and technical excellence. Although top management are usually 'schooled' in a range of management disciplines, their earlier training and work experience provide a guiding orientation.

The conditions favouring entry of a new force in an industry are varied. They can include rapid technological change, industry profit problems, which make leading companies acquisition targets, or significant market opportunities providing market positionings not covered by leading competitors. The market structure also plays a part. Dominance by one or two large competitors can open the door to a new force. A single dominant competitor may have little concern for competitive moves. Where joint dominance by two firms exists, their primary focus is usually on each other.

In each of the following three sections, a new major position has been created in the market. Section 2 investigates a saturated non-growth market and identifies conditions that provide an opening for a third major competitor. The successful strategy adopted using high-price positioning is examined. The Spanish whisky market is used for illustration purposes.

In Section 3 a successful low-price positioning strategy is studied and options for further expansion identified in a slow-growth market. The retailing market is used for illustration purposes.

Section 4 looks at how the restructuring of the marketing process and distribution channels can result in a major new force challenging the leading company. The sources of competitive advantage are also identified. One mini case describes how a company in a commodity market researched the value chain and created a major brand by adding value at appropriate points in the chain.

Two major case studies are used for illustration purposes. One describes a major British player in the UK market being displaced by a smaller company that restructured the market by becoming a pan-European player. The other describes the attack by Virgin Airways on British Airways. Finally, a mini-case describes how a company escaped the commodity trap by taking the branding route to success.

■ Section 2: Creating a Third Force

Many markets in Europe are dominated by two companies, which, between them, hold a 60 per cent or higher market share. A duopoly structure reduces the likelihood of price competition, increases the potential for profit in the market and lends itself to market and brand-building strategies. Frequently, competitors tacitly work together to keep out a third force.

The danger of a duopoly structure is that the two competitors will only focus on each other and not innovate and develop market opportunities. When this occurs, potential is created for the emergence of a third force, which may take several forms:

1. A large company may enter the market from outside the industry or outside the country. The Mars company entered the European ice-cream market in the late 1980s.
2. A small firm may develop and maintain a strong position in the market. Richard Branson achieved this in the UK airline market against the market leader, British Airways, and the aggressive challenger, British Midland. This market was restructured during the eighties.
3. Low-price regional brands, private labels or generics may become a third force and, as a group, substantially affect the market direction and profit return of the two large companies in the market. Local blenders of fertilisers became a third force in the European fertiliser market against ICI and Norsk Hydro.

■ The Strategic Conditions for a Premium Positioned Third Force

A number of conditions are important to the achievement of a strong position in a market dominated by two large competitors. These should be assessed when developing a competitive marketing strategy.

□ *Strength of the Premium Brand's Market Position*

The starting point is to undertake groundwork to develop brand image, exclusivity and aspirational values in the product. This is done effectively in the prestige car market by Mercedes Benz and BMW.

□ *Declining Image of the Leader's Existing Brands*

In markets in which leaders have adopted multibrand strategies and fragmented their marketing effort, the ability to defend their dominance is reduced. This is made worse if major brands are 'milked' and their image declines.

An evaluation of the strength of leaders' brands should be undertaken to identify the appropriate timing for an aggressive attack on the leaders.

□ *Market Responsiveness to Price Repositioning*

Conditions favouring effective downward price repositionings, are saturated non-growth markets, diminishing brand loyalty of traditional mainstream brands and growing price sensitivity between brands. Price experimentation on a regional basis can help the evaluation of price responsiveness.

□ *The Joint Leaders' Competitive Strategies*

The element of surprise is a major advantage to the new competitor. It provides lead time for market penetration to be achieved before strategic retaliation by the leaders. Where the leaders are mainly focused on each other's strategies, or attention is devoted to other markets, and little monitoring is done or concern displayed about the new (or small) competitor, conditions exist for a surprise attack.

□ *Competitors' Cost Structures and Profit Priorities*

An evaluation should be conducted of the ability and willingness of competitors to match price reductions or value offered. Where cost structures provide little room for price reductions or added value at the same price, and profit and cash flow retention is important to competitors in the short and medium term, conditions favour the third force.

□ *Potential for Mainstream Repositioning*

The 'third force' competitor should assess how widespread is the appeal of its premium brand. If it has achieved widespread awareness and appeal, but holds small share because of its substantial price premium, conditions for mainstream repositioning are favourable.

□ *Sustainable Competitive Advantage*

Competitive strategy for repositioning should provide differentiation in image and product/service terms which is not easily matched in the medium term.

Brand building which focuses on a product's unique attributes and benefits is critical during the rapid market penetration phase. Reinforcing premium image through advertising and using distributors and point-of-sale merchandising to indicate value, will develop and retain the brand's wider appeal. Price differentiation which makes it difficult to direct price comparison between brands, should form part of the strategy.

☐ *Sustaining the Attack*

Once committed, the company must be prepared to carry through its attack on the market leaders until its position of a third force is established. This will require the following strategic actions:

- have in place a marketing organisation and commit a budget to match those of the leaders;
- control costs and margins so that increased volume ensures increased profitability;
- adopt a multibrand or multiproduct strategy which enables coverage of all major market segments;
- reposition the brand so that its price premium is narrowed but still maintained at a premium level;
- be prepared to sacrifice the premium position vacated or cover it with a new brand/product offering.

This is a checklist of important questions:

- What position do you own?
- What position do you want to own?
- Whom must you beat to get there?
- Do you have sufficient resources and an organisation to support it?
- Can you withstand sustained retaliation?
- Do you have a differential competitive advantage?
- Can you match your desired future position with appropriate resources?
- When are the conditions right for attack?

■ Case Study 11: Ballentine's (Hiram Walker/Allied-Lyons) in Spain

■ 'Los Mejores Momentos'

Prior to 1982, the Spanish whisky market was dominated by two competitors, J & B Rare, owned by Grand Metropolitan, and Johnny Walker, who together had about 60 per cent market share. Ballentine's, Allied-Lyon's premier brand, entered the market in 1982, appealing to the high price end of the market and repositioned whisky as the fashionable drink.

The meteoric performance of Ballentine's from a position of obscurity has created a new consumer, increased market size (in the period 1982–90 the whisky market grew three fold) and successfully challenged J & B for market leadership and brandy as the national spirit.

The cornerstone of Ballentine's success to date has been the creation of an image of exclusiveness. This theme has been consolidated to make it a permanent feature of the whisky market and not just a temporary phenomenon.

In 1989, approximately 8 per cent of the retail price was spent on promotional activities. The total awareness factors as determined by Spanish market research were 57 for Ballentine's and 75 for J & B (on a scale of 1 to 100). Ballentine's still had to make the necessary investment to improve awareness, but as a relative new entrant in the market, a major breakthrough had already been achieved.

Ballentine's early position as price leader in the market helped to underline the image of exclusivity, and with 75 per cent of its customers in the upper socio-economic groups, price was unlikely to be an overriding factor in buyer behaviour. Price leadership however is not always easy to maintain; latest Nielsen figures in 1993 indicate that Ballentine's and J & B are retailing at the same price.

J & B had been the outright leader for over a decade. However, by 1990 its position had started to look precarious, as is demonstrated in Figure 4.3. J & B put up strong resistance to the Ballentine challenge, but despite large promotional investments, lost is premier position in 1991/2. Together, J & B and Ballentine's have 70 per cent market share.

Sales of the blended whisky suggest that Ballentine's is still in the growth stage of its life cycle and the malt version could be introduced at some future date when the blended whisky market tends towards saturation. Sole distributor and now highly successful joint venture partner, Domecq, has played a vital role in Ballentine's achievement, with a very high weighted distribution penetration.

In 1993, the total market shows continued growth, but at a slower rate, with whisky continuing to be a more fashionable drink. Figures 4.1 and 4.2 graphically demonstrate how in 1982 it was planned for whisky to challenge the traditional brandy for the number one spirit position. By 1993, brandy was no longer the preeminent spirit in Spain.

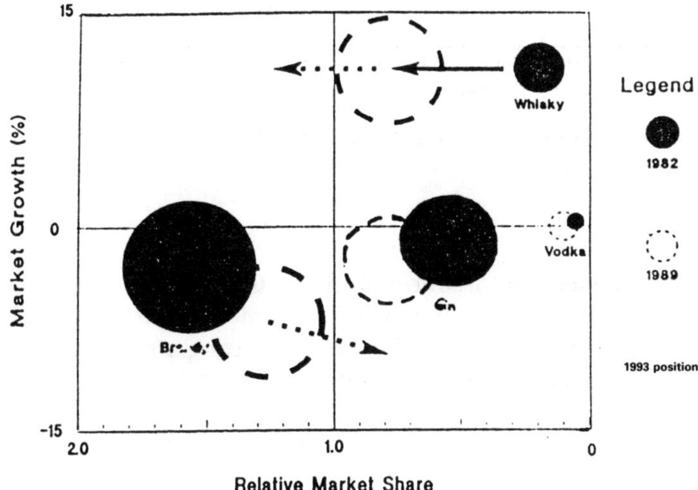

Figure 4.1 Boston matrix: Spanish spirit market from 1982

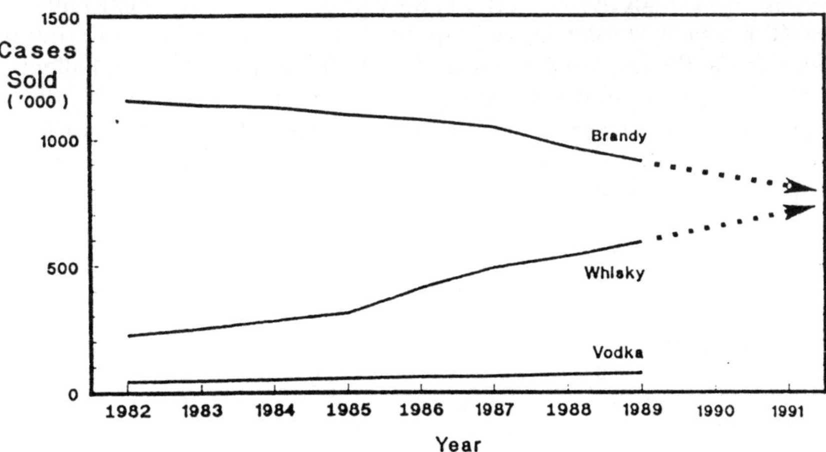

Figure 4.2 Spanish spirit market development, 1982–

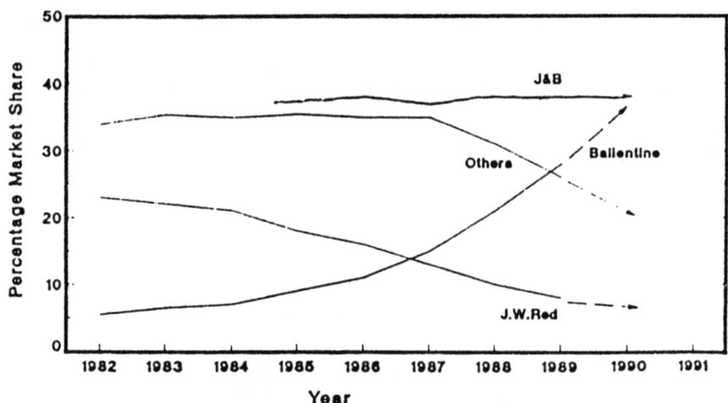

Figure 4.3 Spanish whisky market share, 1982–91

1993 also brings an element of uncertainty to the market; agreement amongst member EC countries has not been reached on consistent excise taxation arrangements. Spain is a low duty country compared with those further north and an imposed rise in duty could be a setback for future market development.

Ballentine's is currently Allied-Lyons' single most important brand and through careful nurturing annually sells over five million cases world wide, is Europe's leading Scotch and a major profit generator for the parent group. It has continued to demonstrate strong market growth in both share and volume as a premium priced brand and is claimed to be Spain's, and France's, biggest selling whisky.

Recent market development strategies include entry of the Mexican market, where the scotch whisky sector is quite small but is expected to grow with Ballentine's at the forefront. Spearheaded by Domecq distribution, Ballentine's will look for long term development of the market.

This case clearly demonstrates how it is possible to become a major force in an established market by satisfying unfulfilled needs, and entering a segment poorly catered for by the existing players.

■ Section 3: Flanking Strategy and Cost Leadership to Position as a Major Force

■ Competitive Positioning

This section focuses on retailing as the basis for illustration. Several aspects of competitive positioning need to be analysed by the retailer.

□ *Positioning Concept*

The concept of the store, which itself represents the product offering, must achieve integration of the marketing mix elements and represent a viable position in relation to competitors. Dickens & Jones, the large department store retailer, has developed a higher quality, high price upmarket position supported by customer service. In contrast, Woolworths has developed a position of being discount, good variety and value for money and has established strength in a limited range of merchandise.

Both the marketing effort of retailers and the experience and perception of consumers establish a consumer-determined market positioning. The issue arising for the retailer is one of increasing its competitive advantage. To achieve this it must develop and defend its relative differentiation. Figure 4.4 indicates how this can be approached, either by developing product-market strengths or by focusing on productivity advantages.

The objective of any retailer is to maintain and increase profitability. Although all of these factors should be managed by retailers, usually at any point in time, focus will be on either product-market led or on productivity-led strategies. For productivity-led differentiation, a tight control on costs and innovations for reducing costs relative to competitors are required. To be successful, segmentation by price requires a sustainable 'low-cost' position. Product-led differentiation requires segmentation by customer attitudes towards service, quality and choice. Both, however, require a customer-based approach.[5] An important aspect in achieving the effect of these strategies is the development of store image.

□ *Store Image*

The total mix of variables determines overall store image. A number of writers suggest that store image is composed of:

- quality, price and assortment;[6]

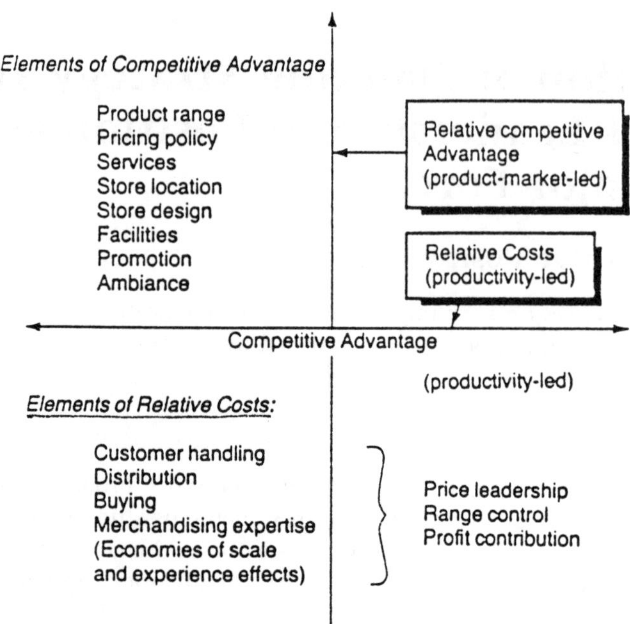

Figure 4.4 Relative differentiation for competitive advantage

Source: D. Knee and D. Walters, *Strategy in Retailing*, 1985, p. 28.

- clientele mix, institutional maturity, merchandise, location, shopping pleasure, transaction convenience, integrity and promotional emphasis;[7] and
- outside attractiveness, fashionability, salesmanship and advertising.[8]

From these factors a list of the components of store image would include:

- characteristics of target market;
- store location;
- product assortment;
- level of prices;
- physical attributes of the store – atmosphere;
- availability of services such as credit and delivery;
- type of advertising;
- type and extent of personal selling;
- sales promotions; and
- civic responsibility and community involvement.[9]

Creating and maintaining a clear, distinct and strong store image requires constant attention to quality of store personnel, uniformity between stores and quick response and action to counter any negative publicity.

□ *Market Segmentation*

Successful retailing today requires a thorough understanding of customers to identify their particular needs. More than this, a retailer must identify the segments in the market and decide which segment or segments to target. Examination of customer profiles often reveals a cluster of features, including demographics, psychographics, buyer behaviour and benefits sought.

□ *Location*

Store location is a big decision in retailing. McDonald's, like other mass markets, conduct demographic, shopping and traffic flow studies to determine appropriate sites. These must also consider the relationship of the retailer with other stores and institutions that generate the target market. For example, McDonald's has locations in heavy traffic areas that allow particular access by children, such as proximity to educational institutions. In contrast, specialty shops cluster as a group in shopping areas and around large retailers in regional shopping centres.

Store location will affect the number of customers attracted and the type of customer, and great care is taken by retail chains in locating stores convenient to the target market. This is designed to maximise sales potential, and minimise sales cannibalisation between stores.

□ *The Dangers of Repositioning*

Once retail chains are well established, it is very difficult to reposition them effectively – that is, to change a retailer's relative position in the market. The store or chain establishes a 'brand' position, attracting loyal customers and the task is to develop and defend it while maintaining relative position.

The temptation to change relative position arises from both a reaction to competition and from the manufacturer-driven nature of some areas of the retail industry. In particular, small retailers are persuaded by suppliers to change position. Also, membership of buying groups by smaller retailers, to combat the buying power of the large groups, can lead to confused positioning or unplanned repositioning.

Another growth option is to widen the positioning of the business to appeal to a wider cross-section of the market. This must be done carefully. Some discount electrical retailers, for instance, have widened their product ranges to include furniture. Marks and Spencer, dominant in apparel retailing in Britain, has successfully added food and home furnishings to its range. There is a limit, however, to the size of any existing geographical market, and expansion can more readily come from new ones. This is illustrated by the Wal-Mart operation in the United States, which has achieved wide market coverage within the States. It operates by having stores in all towns that service a population of 30,000.

Hornes

In clothes retailing in the UK, for example, Hornes has moved from crisis to crisis in its attempt to find a suitable positioning strategy, and has consistently failed.

Hornes has been synonymous with high quality menswear for almost 100 years and until recently one of the few remaining private menswear multiple retailers. Management still lies in the hands of the Horne family, now in its third generation in the Company.

The early 1970s presented Hornes with a number of problems and a changing environment, resulting in a reappraisal of the organisational structure of the Company which had previously been very informal. The new structure comprised three operational divisions: manufacturing, property and trading. The trading division was responsible for the retailing activities of the Company and is the subject of this case.

Between 1971 and 1976, the Company's turnover increased from £5.6 milion to £8 million. During 1974, Horne's senior management decided that marketing activity was required if the Company was to compete successfully in a dynamic menswear market. A marketing manager was appointed and began his duties by appraising the current situation. He found a number of problems, but at the same time he found a considerable number of strengths on which to build.

The Situation – Late 1974

Product Range

The Hornes' product range had remained basically the same for many years. Sales revenue was generated primarily from the menswear range, but also from two coffee bars, two hairdressing salons and a boyswear operation. In addition, Hornes were active in the contract uniform business, holding the Royal Warrant for livery tailoring to HM The Queen. In common with many of their competitors, Hornes offered a credit facility to their customers.

During the late 1960s some changes were made. High fashion merchandise was introduced through two boutique-type outlets, a number of new and refitted branches were opened, and there was some change in the balance of product sales. These developments can be attributed partly to the menswear revolution of the sixties, but perhaps more significantly, to the introduction to the business of the third generation of the Horne family.

However, research showed that Hornes' product range was considered expensive. Average prices were found to be high compared with some similar outlets, although on straight comparisons of like with like, the prices were generally found to be very competitive.

One specific research exercise revealed that the Hornes brand was associated with a quality image which was not necessarily reflected in 'blind' tests.

A number of problems impinged upon the product range. The most important was the presentation of the 34 stores. Some of the branches had not received attention in terms of design (fascia as well as internal) for 25 years. In others, the redesign to suit the late 1960s was not suitable for the 1970s. The dark finishes and associated lighting problems produced exaggeratedly high price images with customers.

□ *Buying Policy Problems*

Possibly the biggest headache was the lack of coordination of the buying activity in order to arrive at a matched and balanced product range. Other problems were associated with this. The general product-orientation of the Company was very much in evidence in this area, together with the complete lack of a planned approach.

Unexpected departures in the buying team and the consequent absence of a planned managerial succession caused severe problems.

Finally, the buyers' performance was judged partly on deliveries to the branches, rather than sales to the customer, and this was not thought to be conducive to Hornes' success overall.

□ *Customer Profile*

The typical Hornes' customer was over 35, from the ABC1 social class groupings, and usually spent more on clothes than average and shopped for quality rather than fashion.

Research on the image perceptions of the Company found that Hornes had an image of good quality and service, and regular customers held favourable attitudes towards the Company. However, there were negative aspects. The perceived expensiveness of the merchandise has already been mentioned. In addition, Hornes' role as a mens' outfitter had resulted in confusion about the product range. Insofar as they had an image, Hornes were associated with shirts and casual wear, rather than with suits and tailoring.

It is worth noting here that the effects of inflation were beginning to make an impact on consumer spending. The traditional Hornes' customer, the ABC1s, were feeling the pinch and this represented a very real threat to the Company.

□ *Promotional Activities*

The promotional activities undertaken at this time were not unlike those of Hornes' competitors. The media selection included the Sunday colour supplements, local press (where applicable) and poster sites at BR and London Transport stations. The creative approach always featured merchandise, with quality at a reasonable price being the major copy point and shopping ambience running at close second. For Hornes, as for its competitors, the summer and winter sales were important promotional events.

Another major feature of the promotion programme was window display. Studio windows were photographed and prints sent to each branch for reproduction displays to be built. Spending on advertising space went up by two thirds from about £59,000 in 1970/1 to £200,000 in 1974/5. Over the same period, the window display budget doubled from £10,000 to £20,000.

As far as advertising was concerned, there were thought to be several major problems. First, Hornes' advertising was indistinguishable from that of its competitors. More important though, was a lack of explicit communications objectives and any attempt to measure effectiveness. Furthermore, no tactics were being employed to broaden the customer base. Rather, the advertising which had been identified in the earlier research at that time was seen to be reinforcing the 'elderly' image.

□ *Sales Organisation*

At about this time, the area manager system began to weaken. The two area managers had been appointed from the most successful of the branch managers. Their basic duties involved ensuring accurate and timely implementation of the detailed head office policy for branch operations. In the main, branch managers were expected to carry out head office policy, and not to develop their own initiatives.

Generally, Hornes' staff were known to be loyal and to have long service. Staff turnover was low. A consequence of this was an increasing average age for sales staff. This did, however, offer the opportunity to maintain a high level of customer service. Associated with this problem, was the fact that because of the skewed sales pattern through the week (some 40 per cent of sales were made on Saturday; the remainder were spread across the week) there was a need to employ part-time sales staff who were often retired people capable of, or willing to adopt the Hornes' approach to customer service.

The skewed sales pattern also provided another dimension to the problem. Research established the fact that customers were unwilling to enter a deserted store unless they had a particular purchase in mind. It appeared that they felt self-conscious about browsing and leaving the store without making a purchase when there were few, or possibly no other, shoppers in the store.

The store image, then, was inconsistent with the product range. The store image was one of conservatism flavoured with middle to old age, but the product range was aimed at a more fashionable, younger man. The advertising programme did nothing to clarify the potential customer image.

□ *Pricing Policy*

Pricing policy was very simple in principle; it was to buy 'right' and to apply a fixed mark-up. For Hornes, *buying right* was mostly assumed to be a matter of applying *flair*. The buyers sought those products which were fashionable without being trend-setting, items which were compatible with a subjectively perceived image.

□ *Product and Distribution*

Owing to the historical management and production set-up, there was little coordination between the hosiery department, the tailoring department and the shoe department. Historically each unit had operated in splendid isolation with little reference to the activities of the others. Hornes manufactured 90 per cent of their shirts and 50 per cent of their tailoring, with all shoes bought out, but sold under Hornes' own label.

The forecasting needs of the Company were decided by taking a 'grand view' on a product group basis: for example the two-piece suits market; the dinner suits market. From the grand view, a historical trend was developed to which an estimate of likely business growth was added; this, when multiplied by an average price, resulted in a forecast for each of the product groups.

Inventory management policy varied by product group. For hosiery, the entire production was allocated to branches on a 'past sales' volume basis. Branches held *all* inventory. Any 'balancing' problems were sorted out informally by area managers. Tailoring products were manufactured and put into a 'base stock' which was used to top up individual store inventory levels. Each store was allocated operating inventory on a basis of historical sales data plus 'management feedback'. The same procedure also applied to shoes.

□ *Distribution Policy*

The underlying problem in distribution was basically a lack of information in terms of quality, quantity and timeliness. For example, feedback was organised on a formal basis of sales activity from the branches. As a result of this, out of stock situations could and probably did occur, but were not recorded. Indeed, no attempt had been made to consider the problems of customer behaviour in out of stock situations.

When an item was specifically requested by a customer, the problem was resolved by informing head office, who, if unable to satisfy the order, would direct the enquiring branch to other branches where stock was thought to be held. If an item could be located in this way, the transfer was made by internal transport and would be pursued even if it took up to two or three weeks to effect.

□ *Competitors and Competitive Activities*

Competitors were seen as 'traditional' and 'non-traditional'. 'Traditional' competitors were as diverse as Simpson, Austin Reed, Dunns, departmental stores, Burtons, John Collier, Marks and Spencer, British Home Stores (BHS) and other variety chain stores.

The 'non-traditional' competitors comprised the 1960s Carnaby Street boutiques who were moving into other parts of London and the provinces, and becoming multiple operations, often located in better and more fashionable areas. As far as their product ranges were concerned, they had become very much the trend-setters. It was significant that collectively, they covered a wide price and quality spectrum.

No significant changes were occurring within the group of traditional competitors. However, the variety chains were expanding their ranges. Marks and Spencer were well-established in mens suits and BHS were adding lines to an already wide range of men's clothing. In addition there was an increasing volume of low priced imported products appearing in almost all UK clothes retailing outlets.

Significant activity was beginning in the multiple grocers. The national chains were expanding their non-food lines in an attempt to increase their overall operating gross margins. Clothing was an obvious product range candidate.

Competitive activities at the time included an extension of customer account credit to two years by the traditional competitors. This was matched by Hornes. To meet the expansion of the boutiques and the development by the traditional competitors of their own boutiques, Hornes again tried to match the competition, but with little success.

Up to late 1974, it could be said that Hornes held a traditional attitude towards marketing. No formal attempt was made to identify the customer or to determine his needs. But whoever he was, he was given service – once he had entered a Hornes' store.

■ Alternative Solutions

On completion of this review of the 1974 situation, the marketing manager was faced with the problem of planning the strategic marketing activity of the Company for the years ahead.

Two basic choices were identified by Hornes. They could try to counter their problems in more or less conventional terms. That is to say, Hornes could re-address their appeal and move towards a more profitable market segment. This would involve moving towards the C1/C2 group from the existing ABs, attempting to lower the customer average age from 35+ down to say 30 and changing the product mix emphasis from leisure wear to focus on suits (usually this purchase determines where other items are purchased).

Alternatively, the Company could adopt a radical approach. Hitherto, clothes had 'typed' people, but recent changes in society had reversed this and increasingly people 'typed' clothes by imposing their life styles onto their clothes purchases. In other words, there was a switch from 'clothes maketh a man' to 'man maketh clothes' or 'you wear what you are'. A radical approach would therefore reject the conventional social class structure in favour of a life style, classless concept.

The idea caught the imagination of management as it offered Hornes an opportunity to differentiate themselves from their competitors. In the event, Hornes chose to adopt this strategy. By so doing, they turned the situation on its head and thereby created strengths out of weaknesses and opportunities out of threats.

■ Life Style Marketing at Hornes

Clearly, the approach selected had fundamental ramifications for operating philosophy. Marketing was extended beyond matching customer needs to corporate resources at a profit, to include an entertainment and social dimension often not considered, but extremely important in retailing. Against this new marketing orientation, the retailing strategy was reconsidered.

□ *Product Planning*

The first step was to centralise the product planning and aim for (and achieve) style and colour coordination. Product planning starts by asking *how* customers use the product, eg. 'What is his life style?' 'What job does he do?', 'How and where do clothes relate?'. Answers to questions of this kind lead to a purchasing plan to supplement the existing buying flair.

While the extent of the product range had not really altered, certain comparative importances had been changing to reflect buying preferences established by research, e.g. the need for a balance between formal and informal business suits had been recognised.

Product planning was started at Hornes by applying subtle changes in product group proportions and groupings. An example of this occurred in the casual wear product group. Hitherto, separate buyers bought trousers, shirts, sweaters, etc. They now bought casual wear to a coordinated plan. Product management concepts were applied to solve problems and the formal adoption of a product management structure had been considered.

Ancillary activities such as coffee bars and hairdressing salons were considered very carefully. The boutique-type operations were closed, as they were found to be totally incompatible with the overall position. School outfitting was evaluated and reshaped. The credit service continued but without extensive promotion. The livery operation was developed as a clothing system which would offer cleaning and maintenance in an overall research/design/supply/maintenance package, separate from normal retailing.

☐ *Pricing Policy*

Product prices were derived from an ongoing review of competitive product/price/quality offerings, modified to include perceived Hornes' benefits of design exclusivity and personal service and of course, based upon customer research on price acceptability.

Quality standards remained, but buyers worked harder with suppliers to achieve lower purchasing prices.

At the same time, a conscious move was made to lower average unit selling prices. This was achieved by shifting the product mix *down market*, to increase the sales of products of *lower* than average price to broaden customer appeal.

☐ *Promotional Policy and the Target Customer Profile: Post-Autumn 1974*

The new marketing approach was based upon the 'self-determined man', not a demographic phenomenon. In fact the move was from 'statistical beings' back to a 'human being'. Life style, not social class, was used for market segmentation.

The promotional theme of the campaign commenced in autumn 1975 was built upon Hornes being a complete menswear store: **'You bring the body, we've got the clothes'**. Because of the need to reposition the Company somewhat down market, the high awareness media were selected for use and included posters, local press, and local radio. Examples of advertising can be seen in Figures 4.5 and 4.6.

Even a short time after the campaign began there were early indications that awareness of Hornes had increased. For example, spontaneous awareness more than doubled among the under-35s – the target group for the campaign. This meant that in towns where Hornes had branches, one third of the under-35s were aware of their presence on an unprompted basis.

☐ *Distribution Policy*

Stockturn in the clothing business was low by comparison with many other forms of retailing. It averaged some four times per year.

Hornes were attempting to develop a target stockturn system on which inventory levels for branches could be based by using the concept of a minimum customer offering. For example, a customer requiring formal evening wear may have *looked* for a dinner suit only, but could be better *satisfied*

Figure 4.5 Examples of advertising used in Hornes 1975 promotional campaign

by a velvet outfit with a wider usefulness. In this way, it was hoped to satisfy the customer *and* maintain high stockturn levels.

The benefits of this approach were thought to be:

- increased customer satisfaction by minimising out-of-stocks;
- increasing customer service by optimising choice;
- maximising return on investment;
- maximising cash flow.

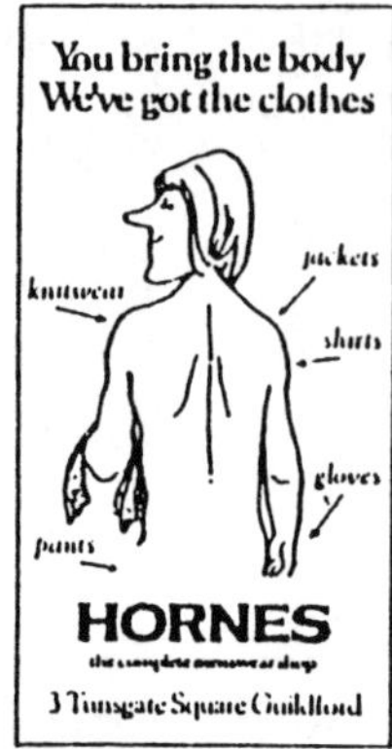

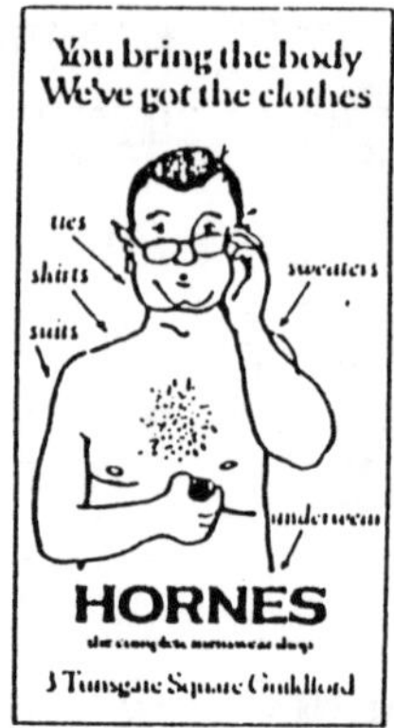

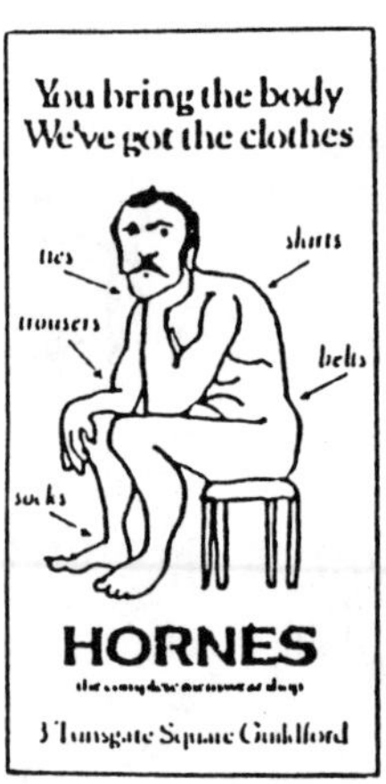

Figure 4.6 Further examples of advertising used in Hornes 1975 promotional campaign

☐ *Store Operations*

An overall design concept was developed for a new store in Manchester, which extended the shop window into the sales area. In Figure 4.7, the central area of the store was used as a 'pre-sales self selection area' and the store inventory kept in adjacent locations.

Consideration was being given to how to develop and reinforce the high customer opinion of the staff and of customer service. Various new approaches were adopted, but were still at a very early stage, and there was still much development required. In retailing, perhaps more than in most marketing activities, constant adjustments to the customers' desires are required, so retailers are always in a state of development.

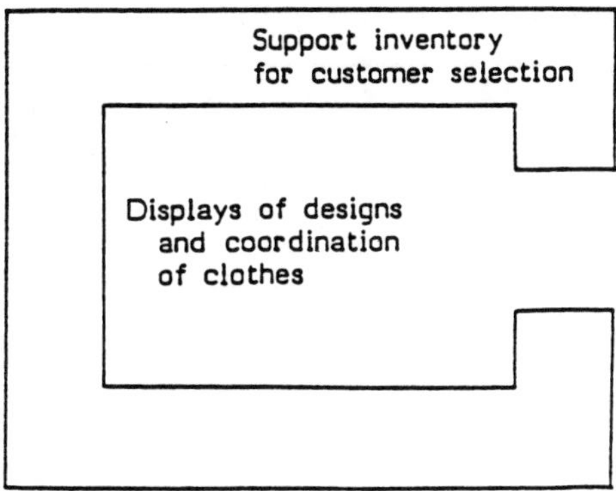

Figure 4.7 Store layout

■ The Eighties and Beyond

The initial success of the new strategy of the late 1970s, which saw overall turnover increase from £8.4 milion in 1976 to £14 million in 1979, was not sustained in the early 1980s. Turnover remained virtually static at around £14 million, whilst the modest trading profits of the late 1970s reversed into mounting losses. See Tables 4.1 and 4.2 for detailed profit and loss figures.

Table 4.1 Detailed Profit and Loss Figures, 1973–83

Year ended		*Turnover £'000*	*Net profit/(loss) before tax £'000*	*Net profit/(loss) after tax £'000*
31 Jan	1973	6,975	430	251
	1974	8,041	558	360
	1975	8,777	410	172
	1976	8.403	319	(81)
31 Aug	1977[1]	15,761	1,102	491
	1978	13,139	972	603
	1979	14,034	357	501
	1980	14,455	40	10
	1981	13,185	(477)	(492)
	1982	13,606	(389)[2]	(487)
	1983	14,700	(668)	(683)

Notes: 1. 84 weeks. 2. Excluding exceptional items: sale of proprty (£1.97 million).

Table 4.2 Profit and Loss Account, 1981–3

	1981 *£'000*	*1982* *£'000*	*1983* *£'000*
Turnover	13,183	13,606	14,700
Cost of sales	(1)	(7,811)	(8,371)
Gross profit		5,795	6,329
Distribution costs	1	(4,189)	(4,638)
Administrative expenses	(13,450)	(2,610)	(3,247)
Other operating expenses		782	893
Interest payable	(222)	(167)	(95)
Exceptional items	12	1,932	90
(Loss)/profit on ordinary activities before taxation	(477)	1.543	(688)
Taxation	(3)	(98)	(17)
(Loss)/profit on ordinary activities after taxation	(480)	1,445[2]	(783)

Notes: 1. Breakdown not available. 2. Loss if sale of property is excluded: £389,000

There is no doubt that Hornes, in common with others in the clothing trade, were badly affected by the recession of the early 1980s. In his annual statement to shareholders in 1983, Mr R. J. Horne recognised that future prospects were unlikely to improve whilst government policy was to reduce inflation and curtail wage increases, thus depressing consumer spending.

Menswear sales are often the first to suffer in times of recession and the last to recover. This is because men can 'make do' with what they already have when times are difficult. Women, on the other hand, try to keep up with new fashions and sales of childrens' wear tends to hold good – mainly because children grow and *have* to have new clothes. However, these markets do tend to be even more price conscious during a recession.

The market was still changing quite rapidly. In the ten years from 1973 to 1983 the expenditure on suits had fallen from 31 per cent of the total spent on men's clothing, whilst expenditure on casual wear had increased from 28 per cent to 58 per cent of the total. Customers were now more sophisticated. Instead of buying trousers here, a shirt there and a sweater somewhere else, they wanted coordinated collections, in which colours and styles matched.

Not all retailers suffered equally in the recession. The Burton Group's Dorothy Perkins and Top Shops were very successful in responding to market trends and in exploiting the purchasing power of the growing number of fashion conscious young people. However, these people were growing older and Burton were beginning to move upmarket with them rather than compete for business from the later school leavers who were less affluent.

Perhaps it was recognition that 'something would have to be done' which led the Hornes Board to recruit Graham Farley to be Group Managing Director in October 1983. Farley had previously been with Burtons for 10 years, most recently as Buying and Merchandising Director of Dorothy Perkins and Top Shops.

A fundamental review of Hornes trading operations was set in hand including a redefinition of the target markets, the introduction of new merchandise ranges and control procedures, and a new shop design. A new merchandising team was set up and John Stenson was appointed Marketing Manager in early 1984.

By mid-1984, things were beginning to move. A shop refitting programme had begun and the first two new-style shops opened in August. The initial results were impressive, with sales increasing three-fold almost immediately. Explaining the background to the new development plan, John Stenson said:

> We had fundamental problems to solve. The market had moved on and we had not kept up with it. Our shops were 'wrong' – for example, we were not geared to 'self-select', and their image was staid and rather elderly. Customers don't like being 'sold to' these days – they prefer to pick what they want without being pestered, as they can in Marks and Spencer.
>
> Our product range and image was confused – the older range was *too* old, more like 40 plus, and the casual *too* young. Our prices reflected equal confusion. Market research showed the average price of a sports jacket was £49 with a range of £39–£59. Ours were priced at £79 – right up at the top end of the market. Our suit prices overlapped the average – some were rather expensive and others were within the top end of the bracket. Knitwear, on the other hand, was quite close to average.
>
> It was clear we had to be more commercial – which is another way of saying we had to compete on price.
>
> However, we decided to make other changes. We wanted to project a new coordinated image, where our shops' surroundings were attractive and indicated quality, whilst our prices were competitive. We realised that the 'bulge' of young people who were Burton's Top Shop market 5–10 years ago were now aged between 25 and 30 and had taken their liking for casual clothes upmarket as their incomes increased. We therefore decided to aim at two distinct groups by age:
>
> - 23–30 coordinated merchandise across the whole product range
> - 35–40+ traditional merchandise
>
> We planned to refit the shops to reflect the new approach. Green slate was used for the shop surrounds, with thick green carpets and oak fixtures inside, with terracotta and yellow colour schemes, and bottle green thick glass window furnishings. The emphasis was to be on natural colours and natural materials. The objective was still to suggest quality and a slightly upmarket image, but we knew customers would be pleasantly surprised by our competitive prices.
>
> We went for more out-of-house branding for the casual wear – French Connection, Sabre, Pierre Cardin, British Van Heusen and Gabbucci, while jackets, suits and trousers were to remain Hornes own brand.
>
> We cleared out all the old range and there was no carry over. The new range consisted of 'coordinated collections', which meant that customers could select a whole outfit, or even a whole wardrobe.

> The first two shops opened in August 1984 – in Bath and Bromley. We did little or no special promotion apart from some local advertising. Account holders (we have about 800 per shop) were invited to the openings but the response was low.
>
> We plan to have thirty of our shops converted to the new style by the end of 1985, and around 80 in the long term.

It remained to be seen whether the new approach would be successful, but the initial results were encouraging. Turnover in the two new shops showed a three-fold increase in the first few weeks after opening, although Hornes expected this to fall back a little to around a 2.5-fold increase.

Hornes drew comfort from the fact that the new custom did not come from existing account-holders, but from new casual customers who were attracted in by the new image. Although the Company appreciated that a re-appraisal of the retailing formula and merchandise discipline inevitably required a significant level of mark-down which would initially affect margins, there was growing confidence that Hornes were back on track for a profitable future.

The new policies were to fail, however, and subsequently further repositioning has not succeeded in rescuing the Company.

The Company lost £1.6 million in 1984, briefly returned to modest profitability in 1985 and was acquired by the giant American retailer Sears in 1987. By 1991, Sears were still complaining of extremely poor performances by Hornes compared with other clothing retailers, and there appeared to be no prospect of an early recovery. So continuing over two decades of confused positioning, leading to confusion in the customer's mind, had led in turn to commercial failure.

■ The Wheel of Retailing

NcNair proposed, from observation of distribution trends, a 'wheel theory' of retailing. He argues that over time a new institution, which is usually a low-status, low-margin and low-cost operation, gains acceptance and attracts competitive emulators. In attempting to differentiate, it adds facilities, increases services, widens its range and progressively becomes a high-cost/high-margin operation and becomes vulnerable to new lower cost retailing concepts.

This is demonstrated, to some degree, in supermarket retailing. The development of supermarkets in Britain replaced the corner grocery shop. Low-cost emulators operating from half-case warehouses and low-cost/no-service facilities penetrated the market. In response, companies such as Tesco have upgraded their stores, widened their ranges, provided more shopping space and raised their prices.

Movement along this wheel does not appear to be inevitable, however.

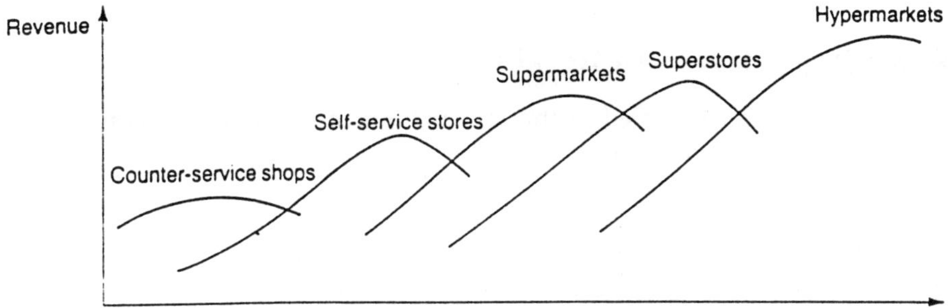

Figure 4.8 Institutional life-cycle effects in food retailing

Source: D. Knee and D. Walters, *Strategy in Retailing,* 1985, p. 40

Kwik-Save, for example, has consistently maintained a low-price 'value for money' position. It is important for retailers to establish where each retailing concept is in its life-cycle. A representation of this in the British environment is shown in Figure 4.8.

Life-cycle theory, as discussed in Chapter 1, should be part of a retailer's strategic analysis to determine market extension potential and opportunities for future growth.

■ Cost and Cost Leadership

The Japanese have shown the lead with strategies based on costs as the key competitive advantage. While maintaining their cost and price advantage, however, they have increased quality, service and reliability, to put themselves in a 'value for money' position. Davidow, in reference to high-technology industries, demonstrates that small differences in costs and margin objectives have dramatic effects on the price a firm must charge in the marketplace. By way of example, if a firm has a 15 per cent cost advantage and has margins objectives of 35 per cent, it will charge a price 39 per cent lower than its higher cost competitor who seeks a 45 per cent gross profit margin.[10] High-price/high-cost suppliers find it difficult to believe that a low-cost competitor can charge such low prices and still make money.

In the retail industry, the opportunity for basing competitive advantage on cost leadership lies in operating efficiencies, maintenance of low overhead costs, bargaining power and skill in buying, and clever pricing tactics. To compete effectively in price-sensitive market segments, the retailer will need good financial and operating control systems and tight centralised management. An eye to cost savings and attention to detail are important attributes of management and staff.

■ Strategic Issues in Retailing

Several issues have emerged in the late eighties to influence the competitive marketing strategies of retailers.

Technology
This affects costs and customer services. Scanning technology reduces operating costs: fewer staff need to label goods, check-outs are faster, stock re-orders are simple and administrative work is reduced. Data are also available immediately on sales trends and consumer reactions to promotions.

The electronic funds transfer point-of-sale (EFTPOS) system is increasing rapidly. This system reduces the number of cash transactions, has implications for in-store strategies directed at impulse buying, and enables marketing data to be collected more efficiently and accurately. Technology for home shopping is in its infancy, but its impact must be considered in retailers' strategies for the 1990s.

Availability of locations
In most major metropolitan areas in Europe, primary retail locations and centres are well established. As demographic patterns and ways of life change, relocation options must be considered. The availability of locations at viable rent levels act as a constraint on the entry of smaller retailers, and on the expansion prospects of chain stores.

□ *The New Flankers*

The rationalisation of petrol distribution has led the oil companies to look for growth opportunities. Petrol companies are learning fast and are beginning to use their prime sites for other forms of retailing.

Price Sensitivity and Cost Management
Price has become a dominant element of the marketing mix in European retailing. The repeated price promotions and seasonal store-wide sales have encouraged European consumers to look for bargains and shop for price. Price-sensitivity is high and a growing concern of consumers with 'value for money' has developed from several decades of price emphasis by retailers.

This means that cost containment and efficiencies are a primary focus of most firms in the industry. The net margins of 1 per cent to 2 per cent of sales achieved by the mass marketers gives a narrow margin for error. Keeping in mind the comments made earlier in this chapter on cost leadership, there is only a small variation in cost and margin ratios required for a retailer to become either uncompetitive or unprofitable.

Government Structure
Government restrictions on retailers' discretion to exercise price differentials

according to location and size of product would have a direct impact on a retailer's achievement of a desired price position and profitability.

Retailers rely on new products and national manufacturer advertising to generate consumer interest and sales growth. Increased restrictions on product labelling such as '100 per cent pure orange juice' and on the description of new formulations, can reduce the sales potential for new products.

Size of Segments

The size and trends of the market and each of the main segments are issues to be addressed by retailers in determining the long-term viability of their competitive position. Continued cost inflation and consumer price-sensitivity alters both the viability of particular market segments and the perceived price positioning of retailers.

Future Competitive Positions in Retailing

The traditional retailing industry in many countries in Europe is in an advanced state of maturity. Ownership is highly concentrated among a few large corporations, with thousands of small retail specialists appealing to localised markets, and in between, a number of narrow range volume-specialist chains competing mostly on a regional basis.

To become a major force in this environment requires a well-planned competitive marketing strategy designed to outflank the dominant players in the field. The wheel of retailing concept suggests these new forces come from the lower end of the market. It is possible, however, that new technology will affect retail patterns and buyer behaviour and that opportunities for entirely new retailing concepts will be with us in the mid and later 1990s.

Case Study 12: Argos

Flanking Strategy and Cost Leadership to Position as a Major Force*

Argos the high street retailer has acquired a grey reputation since its launch in 1973, selling a wide range of goods at low prices through its catalogue. But its less than glamorous image belies a success story that has taken its store total to over 300 in 1993 and a turnover in excess of £1 billion.

The catalogue showroom retailer is the runner-up to Ratners' number one slot as the largest seller of mass market jewellery, with 6 per cent of the UK market. Under the shop-within-shop Elizabeth Duke brand name, it sells the same affordable gold as Ratners and to a similar kind of customer, yet no two retailers could be more different.

Ratners embodied the cheeky stall holder, the unabashed self-publicist. Argos, however is the grey-suited acountant, slow and thorough, with a cautious eye on the books and a calculator constantly at the ready.

Whilst Ratners' success and more recent failure was linked to the personality of Gerald Ratner, personality is the last thing Argos has, or wants.

Market Segmentation

Argos was born out of the sixties phenomenon, Green Shield stamps, with the launch of seventeen stores in 1973. Both businesses were owned by entrepreneur Richard Tompkins, who borrowed the idea of using a catalogue as the retail centre from the USA. Consumers were encouraged, as they still are, to choose their purchases in the comfort of their own home before they entered the store.

The original image was downmarket, with branded goods sold at low prices. Prices were so low, in fact, that many manufacturers refused to supply Argos. The betting shop style stores were spartan, with little of the stock on display and most of it boxed in extensive stockrooms out of sight.

The consumer profile was that of the CD economic profile, *Sun* or *Daily Mirror* reader, and by 1979, when BAT bought the business for £35 million, Argos had reached critical mass with a turnover of £113 million and 91 showrooms.

Repositioning Strategy

Expansion of the Argos brand was limited by the size of the store, its appeal and its catchment area. By the early eighties, Argos was determined to throw off its

* Based on an article by Helen Slingsby in *Marketing Week*, 24 May 1991.

downmarket image in order to improve its consumer profile and thus grow.

Peter Fishbourne, then Marketing Director, says:

'We started out as an out-and-out trading operation, offering a wide range through the catalogue, at low prices. But throughout the eighties, we introduced tracking programmes and decided we had to adjust the business to give it a wider franchise.'

Consequently, under Fishbourne, Argos developed two additional formats to its traditional stores, which have also been revamped. In 1986, the 30,000 square feet Superstores which carry and display the majority of Argos's 6,000 lines, were launched. This was followed a year later by the Best Seller stores, which are smaller than the traditional outlets, carrying 1,600 popular lines. The three formats have now created a classless customer, says Fishbourne, with a much broader appeal, enveloping ABs as well as DEs.

Advertising agency Ogilvy and Mathers' 'Argos takes care of it' catchline, also moved the brand upmarket by emphasising the quality and variety of products on sale. Another element of the campaign was to promote the bi-annual launch of the Argos catalogue, regarded by the retailer's customers as a highlight, backed up throughout the year by specialist supplements, promoting certain product areas.

Argos is currently the UK's leading retailer of keep fit equipment, small electrical appliances, sofa beds and telephones. Argos has managed to race ahead with catalogue showrooms, while others have fallen at the first post. Burton's Linear and Woolworth's Shoppers' World failed very quickly. And even in the US, where the idea was conceived, catalogue showrooms are, say analysts, 'Well past their sell by date'. In fact, Sears, the American leader in catalogue business, announced closure of its catalogue operation in early 1993.

■ Key Factors in Argos' Success

Argos's strategy based on cost leadership has enabled it to gain competitive advantage. A clue to Argos' success in achieving cost leadership is the sophisticated computer systems used to track day-to-day sales at every store. Introduced 16 years ago, well ahead of most other retailers, the IBM mainframe, back at the retailer's headquarters in Milton Keynes, recently doubled in capacity, each night assesses the day's takings and is able to order accurately for each store. Argos also claims that 96 per cent of goods requested will be in stock. Milton Keynes' Store Manager comments 'Customers won't tolerate the fact that we are out of stock, and rightly so. That's the best reason to have the most up-to-date computer systems. With 45 million customer transactions in 1992, the system has to work quickly and effectively and EDI links with suppliers ensure efficient stock processing'.

Ogilvy and Mather Account Director explains: 'Argos' success is based on its thoroughness.' Between 5 and 10 per cent of the marketing budget is spent on market research to monitor perceptions and performance of the stores. All marketing decisions are carefully made on the basis of research and corporate data.

Argos also manages growth with efficiency, making sure that its existing stores are allowed to mature. It has the advantage of low overheads and staff costs because of the nature of the catalogue business. Continuity of management has also enabled Argos to expand without the boardroom wrangling of many retailers. Chief Executive Michael Smith, Directors Fishbourne, O'Callaghan, and Green have all been with the Company for about 17 years.

Argos has engendered a corporate culture comparable with those of Marks and Spencer and Sainsbury, which is at the heart of its success. Top management have led from the front and allowed ideas to percolate through to all Argos staff.

Following its divestment from BAT Industries in 1990, Argos has consolidated its position in the catalogue retailing market, based largely on its strong value for money image and standing as price leader. An independent nationwide survey on price perceptions listed Argos top of the non-food retailers for leading on low prices for all products. It has worked hard to offset cost increases with productivity gains in a hard retailing climate. Now however, it stands somewhat at a strategy cross roads.

Argos has successfully extended the product concept to customers of all ages and class through the three tiered store approach, and has plans to expand at a rate of 25 new stores per year, from 321 in 1993 to over 500 by the end of the decade. However, it is estimated that the established Argos format will be approaching maturity by 2000, and although there are initiatives to extend the concept through shopping over the telephone, there seems to be a limit to its development.

Similarly, market development would appear to be stifled. The concept of catalogue retailing does not transfer well to Continental Europe and expansion to the United States is unlikely.

Argos therefore must sooner or later diversify, but there is a risk attached to this strategy as the company has already found to its cost. Despite lengthy and comprehensive market research, Argos' venture into up-market furniture retailing in the form of the four pilot Chesterman stores, proved to be a classic case of poor timing. Launched during the UK recession of the early 1990s, the stores' poor performance and costly closure were salutary lessons for the normally cautious and disciplined Argos. Any future diversifications will be closer to the core competencies and based on a shorter time span between research and execution.

The demise of the Chesterman experiment has left Argos looking for other UK retailing opportunities; its next foray will no doubt be better considered and timed.

The overall success of Argos is reflected in the financial results given in Table 1.

Table 4.3 Argos Financial Performance, 1988–92

	1992	1991
Turnover	**£1,004m**	£927m
Profit before tax	**£52.9m**	£62.1m
Profit after tax	**£34.7m**	£41.2m
Earnings per share	**11.7p**	13.9p
Total dividend per share	**7.0p**	6.4p

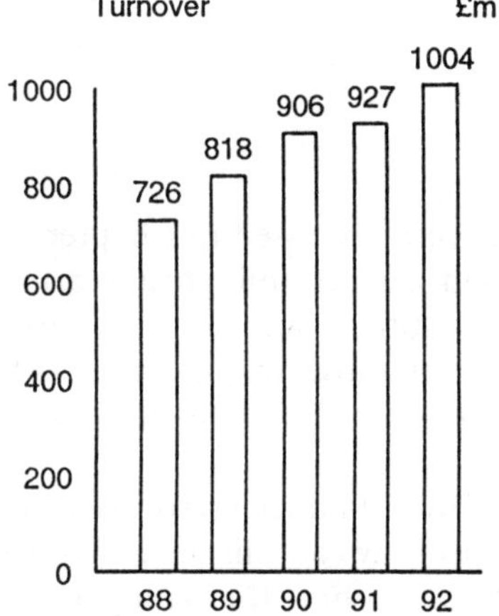

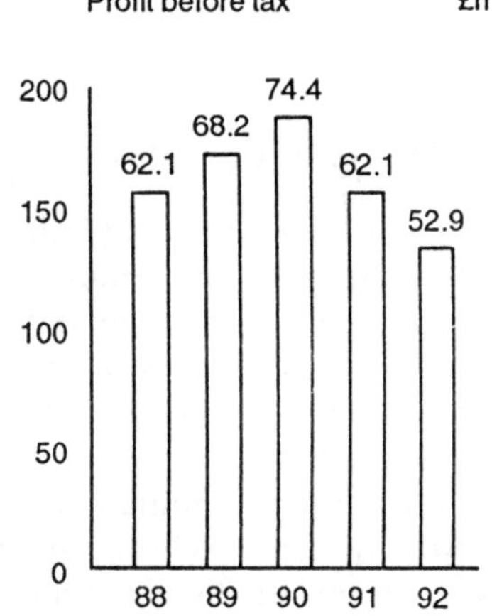

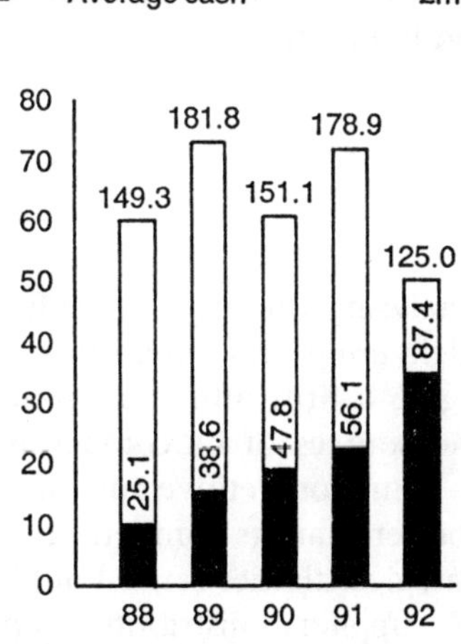

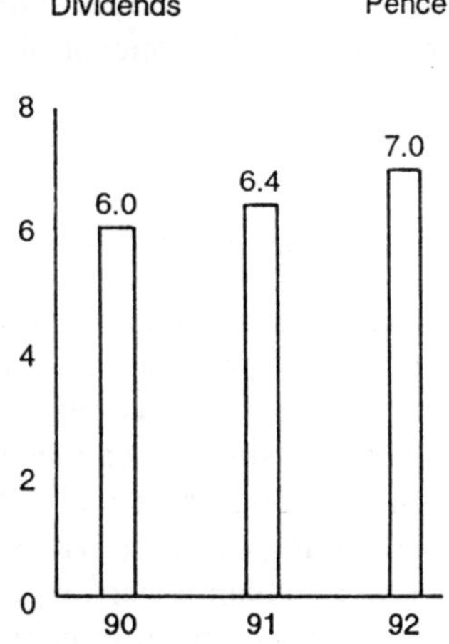

* as at year end

Section 4: Restructuring the Market to Break Monopolistic Competition

To influence the structure of an industry or market, the important elements must be identified and the key competitive forces that determine industry/market profitability found.

Industry Forces

The major forces affecting industry competition were discussed in Chapter 1. The structure of the industry, its suppliers and buyers influence market evolution and profit potential. The threat of substitutes and new entrants influence competitive strategies.[11] One or more of those major forces can restructure the market and change the strategic positions of competitors and their future prospects.

It is clear that a dominant firm has the market power, financial resources and industry influence to bring about a restructure. But how can this be done by a new entrant or by existing small competitors? Either the competitive advantage of the market leader needs to be made obsolete or less relevant, or a significant part of that advantage needs to be obtained by a new force in the industry.[12] Two concepts require analysis to identify how a market can be restructured – the concept of the value chain and bundling.

The Value Chain Concept[13]

Competitive advantage is best understood by analysing the activities a firm performs in designing, producing, marketing, delivering and supporting its products. The value chain is a tool to disaggregate a firm into strategically relevant activities to enable identification of the sources of its competitive advantage – both costs and differentiation. A firm gains competitive advantage by performing these activities more cheaply or better than its competitors. A firm's value chain is part of a larger stream of strategic activities carried out by other members of the distribution channel – suppliers, distributors and customers. It is necessary to understand the links in the chain which provide customer value to be able to restructure the industry to the firm's advantage.

The concept can be summarised as follows:

1 The *value chain* examines all activities a firm performs by disaggregating functions into discrete but interrelated activities from which value stems.
2 Examination of the value chain allows understanding of the *behaviour of costs* within a firm and existing and potential *sources of differentiation.*
3 Value activities are the physically and technologically distinct activities a firm performs, the discrete building blocks of competitive advantage. There are *primary* value activities and *support* activities.
4 Often, the keys to competitive advantage are the *links* or relationships between activities in the value chain. For instance, vertical linkages between buyers, suppliers and ensuing channel activities can lower cost or enhance differentiation.
5 A firm's *competitive scope* is a source of competitive advantage, because it affects the value chain. This may be in terms of: segment scope, the range of products and buyers; geographic scope, the range of regions; vertical scope, the extent of integration; or industry scope, the range of related industries.

■ Application of the Value Chain and Competitive Advantage

A few examples to illustrate the relevance of the concept are:

Customer Access to Financial Services

New technology in the banking and insurance world enhances the accessibility of services to customers and has implications for the traditional structure of the industry. The firms which lead in introducing new services will obtain a competitive advantage.

Here are two examples:

- TSB has moved into the office banking market for small to medium business customers with its Deskbank service. This PC based service will allow customers to manage their bank accounts and make electronic payments. Authorised executives will have smart cards to ensure the security of payment transmissions.

  A computer installation at the TSB will receive and transmit messages between customers and the bank. In addition, it will update customers' accounts and ensure that payments can be transmitted to the customers of other banks.
- NCR, the American financial services company has introduced a 'hole in the wall' system for clients to make applications for insurance policies and pensions. The implication of this use of technology is far reaching in terms of how it eliminates intermediaries such as salesmen, insurance brokers and

the like. Moreover, money that would have been allocated as commission for their services can now be redistributed between reduced premiums or enhanced benefits.

Airlines

It has long been recognised that airline passengers travel for a variety of reasons. Broadly, there are two main segments, business travel and personal.

British Airways is continually experimenting with means of providing additional benefits for frequent business travellers. This involves modifying the cabin accommodation in terms of seat comfort, leg room, meals, refreshments, and steward service. In addition to this, modifications are made to booking procedures and the use of discounts.

The correct formula gives the Company a competitive advantage, however transient this might be.

Preserving Product Differentiation

This is exemplified by the court battles of French wine producers who are determined to safeguard their product from 'copies'. So, for instance, Champagne must originate from that region of France, where the particular soil and climate conditions contribute to its distinctive character.

Similar sparkling wine might be produced elsewhere, such as Spain, but it cannot be called Champagne. Excellent though some of these wines might be, without the prestigious label, they make less impact on the customer, thereby enabling the authentic wine to maintain its differential advantage.

Building Industry

When a large construction product gets underway, the property developer faces the prospect of dealing with a whole range of services, from architects, quantity surveyors, building contractors, civil engineers, electrical contractors, and so on.

A relatively new phenomenon in the industry has been the rise of 'project management groups'. These act on behalf of the developer (thus giving him just one organisation to deal with) and coordinate the work of all others who are involved on the project. By managing the whole process and the interfaces between various parties as the scheme progresses, the project management group make their profits from the added value they achieve at all stages of the construction. For example, if they get the architects to complete their part of the process a week early, the knock-on effect can be magnified as the scheme unfolds.

Telephone Sales

Where products and services are relatively simple or well known, telephone sales can achieve faster results, lower costs and quicker order processing than the use of the field sales force.

■ Bundling and Unbundling Strategies

Bundling is the providing of separable products or services to buyers as a package, or 'bundle'. Delivery and after-sales service, are frequently bundled together and sold as one, although they might just as easily be sold separately.

For example, the chilled food distributors Wincanton Transport, not only run a fleet of low temperature vehicles, which offer guaranteed delivery times. In addition, there are chilled warehousing facilities and the company also undertakes to manage the customer's inventory of chilled foods.

On the other hand, British Airways, in the interests of reliability and general control, have an established network of activities peripheral to the main business, such as engine servicing and repair, and general engineering services. Now BA is considering selling off those activities so that it can remain focussed on its core business of transporting people and freight. Such an unbundling move can help to reduce operating costs and make the company more competitive, in what has become a hostile business environment.

Both bundling and unbundling have their risks. The strategic implications are:

- unconscious bundling may make a company vulnerable to attack;
- a large firm should be prepared to unbundle over time if market conditions change; and
- bundled competitors may represent opportunities for restructuring the industry through unbundling strategies implemented by new competitive forces.

By choosing to 'bundle' or 'unbundle', it is possible to change the basis of competitive advantage in an industry and allow the emergence of new forces.

Bundling can be achieved by putting products or services together as one offer, either across the product range, or down the value chain. *Unbundling* involves grouping parts of the total offer into specialised 'packages' which match the needs of specific market segments.

■ Strategic Implications of Industry Restructuring

When this occurs within an industry, competitors need to take account of new factors in their competitive marketing strategies. Some of the issues of higher importance will be:

The Changed Economics of the Industry

After Rupert Murdoch made his decisive moves in the British newspaper industry in 1985, things were never to be the same again. Not only did he embrace new technology, in the face of strong Trade Union opposition, but he also forsook the traditional home of the press, Fleet Street, to find cheaper production premises out of London's city centre.

The cost advantage of these two moves were such that all competing newspapers had the stark choice of mirroring his strategy, or going out of business.

The Changed Attitude and Aggressiveness of Individual Competitors
For many years, ICI Fertilisers had a fairly comfortable duopoly in the UK market with Fisons. Such was their relationship that ICI virtually controlled both products and prices.

When Fisons pulled out of the fertiliser business and sold their interests to Norsk Hydro in 1988, ICI were suddenly confronted with a big league European player on their doorstep. The changed attitude and astute management of this 'new' competitor was significant in hastening the demise of the erstwhile market leader. Within a few years, most of the ICI fertiliser business was up for sale as a loss maker.

The Changed Strategic Positions of Some Companies
Most industry structures are polarising, so that at one end there are a small number of large companies who between them have the lion's share of the market, while at the other end there are numerous small companies who have found specialist niche markets.

The companies getting squeezed are the medium sized. These do not enjoy the economies of scale and cannot therefore obtain cost leadership. At the same time, they are reluctant to withdraw from markets where they have traditionally traded. It would seem that their only salvation will be to formulate a new strategic recipe.

A classic example is the position of Isosceles-owned Gateway in the UK grocery retail market.

The Changed Costs Associated with Service and Distribution
The emergence of new management techniques such as 'just in time' production, has led to a reappraisal by many organisations of their levels of quality and customer service. This requires a non-nonsense look at distribution channels, the value chain and the trade-offs between costs, product availability and after-sales service.

However, this does not necessarily have to be a cost-cutting exercise. For some companies, an added investment in distribution could provide them with a disproportionate competitive advantage.

■ Case Studies

The case histories which follow are examples of:

- A company moving from a commodity market to a branded market by researching the value chain and then adding value at key points in the chain (Courtelle).

- A company which moved from the top right box (outstanding success) to the bottom left box (low differentiation, high costs) through a failure to monitor industry forces and react accordingly (ICI).
- A company seeking to restructure the market by attacking the leader (Virgin).
- Companies which moved from the bottom left box to the top left box (Pretty Polly and Selincourt)

Case Study 13: Courtelle

Sticking to the Knitting

Introduction

Courtelle is an acrylic fibre used in the manufacture of garments, a key product in the Fibre and Films division of Courtaulds plc. The case concerns the evolution of Courtelle from a declining commodity to a premium product, dominating a selected market.

Criteria for Success

- Courtelle increased sales and market share in a declining market.
- Courtelle increased profits when other manufacturers were just breaking even and material costs were rising.
- Courtelle developed as a brand in a commodity market.

Action Plan

Figure 4.9 shows the decline in the UK Courtelle sales to 1980. Action was necessary if the product was to survive. A marketing audit produced a SWOT analysis as shown in Figure 4.10. The decision was made to concentrate on the knitwear market where their strengths could be utilised and their weaknesses such as the smaller capacity of the plant could be turned to advantage. The following action was taken.

Product
By targeting the knitwear market, the product could be developed to run well on knitting machines and to have the correct 'feel'. Acrylic fibres are normally provided in a base colour and dyed as whole garments. Courtelle developed an on-line dyeing process for the fibre which, coupled with the smaller plant size, allowed a 'tailored product' for each customer, thus improving customer satisfacton. The customers became 'locked into' using Courtelle as they gradually dispensed with their own garment dyeing facilities.

Prices
On-line dyeing is cheaper than whole garment dyeing. The fact that the customer makes a considerable saving on the finished garment by buying Courtelle, means that he is willing to pay a premium price for it. This further reinforces the product image.

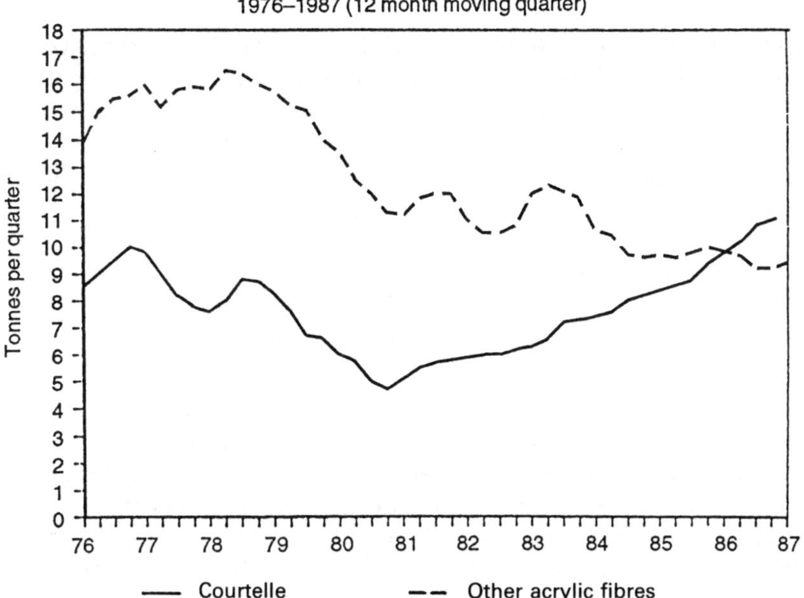

Figure 4.9 Acrylic fibre supply to the UK, 1976–87

STRENGTHS	WEAKNESSES
Knitwear expertise	High cost base
Colour advantage	Unsuitable for carpets and upholstery
Local to market	Shortage of capital
OPPORTUNITIES	**THREATS**
New dying methods	Larger competitors
Colour consistent yarns	Low cost competition
Product tailoring	Declining bulk market

Figure 4.10 SWOT analysis of Courtelle in 1980

Place

Courtelle's head office, in Bradford, is within thirty miles of 90 per cent of its customers, and with the factory also near, distribution costs are low and quick reaction is possible. Technical service is of a very high order; trouble shooters are based at the main headquarters to assist customers with any problems, a very large range of dyes is stocked and computer matching allows the customers' needs to be easily met. A customer support department monitors trends in fashion colours and advises the smaller customers who can't afford to carry out such research.

Courtelle reduced its international effort as it was impossible to achieve the levels of service needed to maintain the quality image.

Promotion

The immediate customer is the yarn mills from where the yarn goes to the knitter and then the retailer. However, instead of promoting to the yarn mills, Courtelle concentrated its marketing strategy on the knitters and retailers, encouraging them to specify Courtelle. Such a case is Marks and Spencer who specify a number of colours to knitters that can only be produced by Courtelle. The image is further developed by sponsoring fashion shows.

■ Conclusion

Courtelle continues to be one of the division's most significant product areas with sales of £166 million in 1992, and high market share. With plants in the UK and now Spain, the producer-coloured acrylic fibre is used in a wide variety of areas from knitwear, fleece and pile fabrics, domestic textiles and cotton type yarns for clothing and furnishings.

Courtelle now dominates Europe's acrylic fibre industry after learning through years of painstaking effort to deliver a wide variety of coloured fibres, while reducing cost. Courtaulds' emphasis on the differentiating factors of this now well known brand helps to support the fibre as a major generator of cash through its above average margins.

■ Case Study 14: The European Fertiliser Industry

■ The Demise of a Market Leader Moving from the Top Right Box to the Bottom Left Box

■ Introduction

ICI, the giant European chemicals group, first became involved in fertiliser production just after the First World War. From that time the division, ICI Fertilisers, experienced periods of growth and profit until by 1980 it controlled almost 90 per cent of the UK production of ammonia, from which nitrogen fertilisers are made.

Not only did this make it the largest producer in Europe, but it had also accumulated technological expertise about fertiliser manufacturer which was second to none.

In 1981 it had a profit of £120 million, contributing a third of the Group's profits; by 1986 it could only break even and by 1991 it was up for sale as a 'no-hope enterprise'.

This case study tries to show how this dramatic turn of fortune came about.

■ Background Information

In the pursuit of increased crop yields, some soil nutrients become used up faster than others. The elements most likely to become depleted are nitrogen (N), phosphorus (P) and potassium (K), collectively known as NPK.

These elements can be replaced either organically or chemically. However, it is claimed that chemical fertilisers have an advantage over organic manures because they are more concentrated and therefore more efficient. Furthermore, chemical fertilisers can be 'tailor-made' to suit specific soil conditions.

P and K fertilisers present little in the way of manufacturing problems, as the technology involved is at a very low level. In contrast N production requires high levels of investment and technical expertise.

ICI made fertilisers containing just one element, or various combinations of NPK. However, because of the very high investment in plant for producing N fertilisers, the Company was interested in exploiting N-rich formulations as much as possible. P and K fertilisers were in many ways secondary products.

■ Historical Perspective

The 1960s had been an expansionist period for the Company. It had set up new fertiliser capacity in the UK and had sponsored plants in India, Malaya,

Australia, South Africa and Canada. (These are now all autonomous operations). Even so, it was not a particularly prosperous decade for the Company, mainly because of over capacity in the fertiliser industry, coupled with the relatively poor profitability of UK farming. In the period from 1969 to 1971, profits were close to zero.

A profound upturn in Company fortunes followed the 1973 oil crisis, which had such a disastrous affect on most of the rest of manufacturing industry. As the price of oil soared, so did the production costs of ICI's competitors who used this as the source of hydrogen in the production of N fertilisers.

In comparison, a virtually fixed price contract for North Sea gas (an alternative source of hydrogen) negotiated earlier by ICI began to yield rich dividends and effectively gave the Company a tremendous cost advantage for this essential processing ingredient throughout the seventies and into the eighties. Not surprisingly, safeguarding the gas contract from political attack became a cornerstone of policy.

This advantage in manufacturing costs was exploited in the market place where the Company became increasingly dominant. By 1980 it had 80 to 90 per cent of the total production of ammonia in the UK (there was competition from only one other ammonia plant) and was certainly the largest producer in Europe, outside the Eastern bloc. From this position of strength the Company pursued a policy of holding prices high and making profits, rather than seeking increased market share. It was afraid of exploiting its monopoly position too openly. Even so, in N fertilisers, the Company had some 60 per cent of the UK market, compared with the 25 per cent share of Fisons, the nearest competitor.

All of this contributed to the Fertiliser Division becoming the veritable jewel in the crown of the ICI Group. In 1981, it contributed over a third of Group profits and the future indeed looked very bright at this time.

Such was the level of confidence within the Company, that it dictated to the industry on prices and increasingly geared its output to what constituted the most economic production runs at the plants. However, the margin between over-confidence and complacency is not very wide. A discerning eye might have spotted some warning signals, nothing too obvious at first, but nevertheless worthy of attention. The danger was not from within the Company, but from outside in the market place.

■ The Fertiliser Market

To describe the UK fertiliser market over the years to 1980 is tantamount to chronicling the fortunes of two companies – ICI Agricultural Division and Fisons.

Fisons was a long established company and highly respected in the trade. It was regarded as having a marketing ear 'close to the ground' and as a result carried a wider range of fertilisers than ICI. However, a significant difference in their history, compared with ICI, was that in the early 1960s a corporate decision was made not to be involved in basic ammonia production. Instead,

Fisons chose to buy ammonia from other suppliers. This decision was coincident with ICI's expansionist phase and it was seen to be mutually acceptable for ICI to build and commission an ammonia plant dedicated to supplying Fisons' main site at Immingham, near Grimsby on Humberside.

From this time onwards, the two companies' destinies were somewhat interlinked. Whenever ICI chose to increase prices, Fisons invariably followed. It was a strategy that suited the two fertiliser giants and their growing dominance had the effect of removing some twenty or so small fertiliser manufactures from the competitive arena. The smaller companies just had not the advantages of the economies of scale of production and distribution afforded to the market leaders.

Thus by 1980, the two companies held 85 per cent of the UK N fertiliser market. The remainder was accounted for by a number of small manufacturers or imports.

□ *Imports*

Just as it suited ICI to have the number two competitor in the home market somewhat dependent upon them for basic raw materials and operating very much in their shadow, so it suited the Company to keep imports to a minimum. No easy task.

However, their major competitors on the Continent were just as concerned in turn to protect their home markets. Thus the European market operated under an uneasy truce, and major producers did not see it as being in their interest to disturb the status quo. The risk of massive retaliation for violating the unspoken code of conduct was too high a price to pay. There was some economics logic in this, since fertilisers are low-price, bulky products and therefore expensive to transport, especially from country to country.

□ *Product Differentiation*

ICI's marketing strategy included a sales force who visited farmers, providing technical advice and expertise regarding soil conditions and ways of maintaining it at optimum fertility. The solution to such problems was, of course, to buy ICI fertilisers from the local stockist, one of a profusion of outlets for ICI, ranging from small individual traders to large private companies which operated nationally.

Thus, in a sense, ICI did not 'sell' fertilisers, but a soil improvement service. Even so, its high straight N fertiliser 'Nitram' was the brand leader.

■ Summary up to 1980

Partly by accident (the fixed price gas contract had been largely opportunistic) and partly by design, the Company were in the advantageous position of having cost leadership and a fairly well differentiated product. Not surprisingly, it was reaping the benefits of this situation.

However, its focus had been almost entirely on the UK, whereas most European producers were far less parochial. Also, a number of events were about to happen which would change the situation and test the Company's ability to respond.

■ The Early 1980s

This period was notable for a number of reasons. Their impact on ICI fertilisers is summarised below.

□ *Change in Demand Requirements*

Farms had become increasingly mechanised and less labour intensive. This meant that farms were beginning to move away from the traditional 50 kg individual bags, in preference for some form of semi-bulk packaging, which did not require man-handling.

Small companies were the first to respond to this new need, then Fisons introduced a half-tonne 'Top Lift' bag which could be easily carried by tractors with a loading arm.

ICI had to respond to the threat that Fisons and other smaller companies now posed. Its hitherto, seemingly unassailable, market share was now being challenged. At first sight another form of 'Top Lift' bag might have sufficed to restore the differential between the two companies. But there were snags.

The somewhat shapeless and bulky 'Top Lift' bags were not stackable more than two high. For ICI with its throughput of some 2 million tonnes per annum of fertiliser, the overall effect would be to reduce the warehouse storage capacity several fold. The prospect of investing in new storage and its subsequent impact on production costs turned the Company against the 'Top Lift' bag. Yet it somehow had to respond to the new and increasing demand for bulk deliveries.

Eventually, in 1984 the ICI response was in keeping with its production engineering traditions. It was called the 'Dumpy' bag and held 750 kg. More sophisticated than the 'Top Lift' bag, the 'Dumpy' was basically a squat cylindrical bag sitting in simplified form of pallet.

The cradle and bag shape ensured that the 'Dumpy' could be stacked high enough to make good use of existing storage facilities at the Company and lent itself to transportation by lorry. The cradle was also designed to accommodate the arms of a fork lift truck and was cheap enough to be considered disposable.

However, the 'Dumpy' never competely matched the competitive advantage on farm provided by the 'Top Lift' bag and ICI failed to keep pace with the growth in this semi-bulk delivery market. Although initial sales were promising, repeat business fell short of expectation and eventually the

Company was forced to introduce an additional range of top lift products in 1986.

☐ *Changes in Competitor Activity*

Despite Fisons' success with 'Top Lift', it had been progressively weakened by its lack of ammonia capacity, its poor production assets and debilitated by the need to supply cash to Fisons's growing pharmaceutical business. By 1980 it was clear that the end was in sight, but for monopolistic reasons, ICI's hands were tied. In 1982 Fisons' fertiliser interest was bought for some £40 million by Norsk Hydro, a Norwegian, State owned company.

It was soon evident that Norsk Hydro was buying its position in the European fertiliser market. In addition to its investment in the UK, Norsk acquired the premier fertiliser producer in Sweden (Supra) and the second largest in Germany (Brunsbuttle), France (Cofaz) and Holland (NSM). Without a doubt, here was a new competitor with ambition and apparently a continental, if not global, strategy.

In contrast, ICI appeared to have no European stategy. Indeed, it could have pre-empted the purchase of NSM, since as a 25 per cent shareholder it had first refusal. It chose instead to turn its back on continental involvement.

In addition to this, two other continental manufacturers UKF and Kemira Oy also bought UK companies and set about making inroads into the N fertiliser market.

If this were not enough, substantial imports reappeared on the UK fertiliser scene. These were principally in the form of urea, an alternative form of fertiliser to ammonium nitrate. Since most of these imports originated from the Eastern Bloc, the pricing was not subject to conventional economic rationale and in effect the material was being dumped at prices with which ICI could not compete.

Not all the pressure came purely from competitors however. The problems surrounding surplus production of many agricultural products in the EEC resulted in lower prices and a decline in farm incomes. The hitherto buoyant European fertiliser market went into decline with considerable over-capacity of fertiliser production in Europe.

The delicate, gentlemanly restraints, regarding exporting to a competitor's country were severely tested by this new economic reality. In the event, the mutual 'hands-off' policies crumbled.

From ICI's viewpoint, this was something of a disaster because their earlier strategy of dominating the market and keeping prices high, made the UK an extremely attractive market for continental producers with surplus capacity, and indeed for manufacturers from even further afield.

To put this development into perspective, between 1982 to 1986 ICI lost about 15 per cent of their market share in straight N fertilisers with the bulk lost to imports.

All of the above factors, uncomfortable as they were, might have been weathered because ICI had such a tremendous advantage over their competitors due to the favourable gas contract that had been negotiated in the early seventies. However, this was coming to an end.

□ *A New Gas Contract*

In 1983 a new contract was negotiated which, in effect, meant that ICI had to increase its raw materials costs by £20 million per year, over a five year period.

At the very time that ICI's main advantage was being eroded in this way, the vagaries of world economics led to a fall in oil prices which in turn benefited competitors who used that source of hydrogen for their ammonia plants.

Appeals to the government for some form of subsidy for the energy prices that the Company had to pay fell on deaf ears. In contrast to this, foreign governments did provide some subsidies to their domestic manufacturers.

□ *A New Threat: Local Blenders*

The topography of East Anglia lent itself to large field sizes and mechanisation. The intensive land use also ensured that it was the area of highest compound fertiliser sales.

The relatively low technology for producing P and K fertilisers meant that someone with very little capital could set up a small 'manufacturing' plant. The raw materials, phosphates and potash could be imported by the ship-load to the East Anglian ports. All that remained for the manufacturer to do was to blend these raw materials in suitable proportions and 'bag' them up.

The equipment required for doing this was not sophisticated, being rather like a cement mixer, and even second hand plant was easy to obtain. The unskilled, often casual, labour necessary for this work and all the ancillary jobs could be readily found. Thus start up costs were negligible.

Not surprisingly a number of 'blenders', as they were called, set up small businesses in old barns, converted hangars and similar readily accessible buildings. Typically the blender would only distribute on a local basis, probably within a 50 mile radius of his plant. To exceed this distance would cause considerable logistical problems.

However, the blender's modest scale of operation, with its low fixed costs, meant that he could make a tonne of compound for some £30 less than ICI.

The impact of blenders was quite dramatic. In 1986, nationally ICI's share of the compound fertiliser market was about 22 per cent. In East Anglia it was only 8 to 10 per cent. In Essex it was even less, only about 5 per cent. Indeed, it is estimated that in these two localities blenders had between them something like 50 per cent of the market.

While blenders were only involved in P and K fertilisers, ICI were not over-concerned. The Company did not see this as a real threat, just a local irritating but explainable phenomenon. However, the more enterprising blenders were quick to latch on to the over-capacity for N fertilisers in Europe. They found it an easy process to import straight N, increasingly as urea, from the Continent, mainly through Antwerp. Without having to invest in new production equipment, these blenders now had the capacity to offer NPK compound fertilisers and straight nitrogens. Thus, collectively, blenders became significant competitors for ICI, albeit on a confined, local basis.

The lower prices offered by blenders, combined with the weakening international market for urea, put so much pressure on ICI's pricing structure that eventually, in mid-1986, it was found to be impossible for the Company to stick to its previous policy of umbrella pricing. Prices were lowered to a level necessary to compete with imports. This step, combined with the higher gas contract, had the effect of transforming the Company into a loss maker once more.

□ *Changes in Seasonal Demand and Discounts*

The use of fertilisers is highly seasonal, and has led to manufacturers offering special prices to encourage an even off-take of production.

However, with the international market becoming increasingly volatile, farmers delayed making commitments on future purchases and instead bought at point of usage in order to take advantage of the best 'bargains' currently available.

Naturally enough, this shift in the purchasing pattern in the industry caused something of a logistics problem at the production end. A 'nightmare' was how one company spokesman described this particular development at the time.

□ *Changes in Distributor Power*

The well-known 80/20 law operates when distributors are measured against throughput. Indeed, one distributor accounted for something like 20 per cent of ICI's sales. So increasingly the bargaining position of major distributors was becoming more powerful, with the net effect of pushing down wholesale prices.

In an attempt to counter 'distributor power', to stop the 'tail wagging the dog' as it were, the Company maintained two separate retail sales organisations, selling direct to farmers under their own brand names, 'Britag' for solid fertilisers, 'Chafer' for liquids.

However, the only way the direct sales operations could take business away from major distributors and keep them in their place was to be more competitive on pricing. This had the effect of pushing down prices or reducing sales of ICI's leading branded products.

■ Summary of the Early 1980s

The Company's long and largely distinguished history in which it had been in the forefront of technological and production engineering developments, had given it impetus and the striving for excellence which carried it to a leading position in the fertiliser industry.

However, all of the factors listed above had the effect on the Company's profits as shown.

- 1981 £120 million
- 1985 £72 million (£55 million of which was made in the first six months)
- 1986 Break-even

Clearly, the Company no longer had the advantage of cost leadership and the breakdown of the pricing 'structure' had the effect of reducing fertilisers to something of a commodity status.

This notwithstanding, the Company was still market leader and had considerable assets in terms of facilities, expertise and staff, coupled with a determination to fight back and recover much of the lost ground.

■ The Recovery Plan (1987–9)

The overall strategy behind this plan was to reduce operating costs and to match products more closely to customer needs, thereby establishing a competitive advantage.

As we shall see, the plan managed to stop the profits slide and get the Company back into the 'black', after two years in the 'red'. This was no mean achievement, bearing in mind the volatile nature of the business environment over that period. Here are the major 'strands' of the recovery plan.

□ *Production Capacity*

Production capacity was trimmed to get it more in line with demand. In addition, old ammonia producing equipment was replaced by a new, more energy-efficient plant which was commissioned in early 1989.

□ *Reorganisation*

This took place in three ways:

1. The organisational structure was simplified in order to reduce the number of levels in the hierarchy, reduce the reliance on 'top down' management, to clarify jobs and responsibilities, and to improve communications.
2. The historically separate sales and marketing functions were integrated in order to get a more coordinated and pro-active approach to deal with customers.
3. The field sales organisation was refocused to generate sales by working with and through a network of chosen distributors. Such a change was achieved with a saving of 25 people from the erstwhile sales force.

☐ *Segmentation*

The traditional way the Company had segmented the market was by splitting it between the products used. Typically, this would be along the lines of Nitram (a high N fertiliser) and compounds. A further split was sometimes made between arable and grass. In some cases, the Company's view of segmentation further broke the market down by the crop being grown in the arable market or by the type of stock being kept in the grassland market. A new structure of the fertiliser consumer was put together solely from taking account of the customer's approach and attitudes towards the purchase of fertilisers and of his farming style. No account was taken of how the *Company* traditionally viewed the market. A marketing plan for ICI Fertilisers was drawn up matching its capabilities with the needs of these new segments. This was the first time a marketing plan based on an analysis of the market had been drawn up.

☐ *New Products*

With the exception of Extran, a high N fertiliser from Norsk Hydro, the only heavily promoted new products to come on to the fertiliser market were from ICI.

In autumn 1988, its first new fertiliser products since 1975 were launched. These were designed for a newly identified market segment, the intensive grassland dairy farmer. This segment had, of course, existed for some time – only its recognition by ICI can be said to be new, especially in the marketing sense. These newcomers had the brand names 'Turn Out' and 'First Cut'. As well as providing the obvious benefits, these products were in addition, characterised by their efficient use of ammonium nitrate. Thus these fertilisers were environmentally 'friendly' because they reduced the risk of polluting the rivers or other water supplies.

An interesting fact about these new products was that, as a result of market research, this was the first time products had been given names reflecting their usage rather than reflecting their chemical analysis. The specific design and subsequent targeting on a clearly defined market segment made both of these products immediate successes, with no obvious risks. Sales of these products in the launch season were in excess of £8 million.

A further launch was a new arable range of compounds which for the first time had been presented as a flexible range under the brand name 'Crop Start'. These were purely P and K fertilisers for use in the autumn – the deliberate omission of nitrogen again had an environmental reason and recognised that nitrogen was usually readily available in the soil in autumn from natural processes.

☐ *Packaging*

The market continued to show a preference for semi-bulk packaging and so the trend for larger pack sizes continued, and although the original Dumpy bag had its faults, it did prove to be popular with some users.

Its successor, Dumpy 2, was also a 750 kg container, but had the facility of top or bottom lifting, i.e. it was more versatile and competed favourably with alternatives. Its more 'squat' profile also improved its storage ability on the farm – a problem with Dumpy 1.

50 kg bags remained a popular size for some users, and were now palletized and 'shrink-wrapped'. An innovation in this field was the use of coloured shrink film on which was printed the product's name.

☐ *Advertising*

Advertising had been very much a 'committcc' affair, with the committee being made up of ICI Fertilisers (ICF) representatives of sales and marketing. Visuals and copy were approved with no reference to the consumer. Each product also had its own campaign, often changed each year, and there was no overall ICIF campaign for its proucts.

In 1988, a proposed advertising campaign for the Company's mainline product, Nitram, was tested opposite the consumer along with some alternative advertisements. The proposed campaign failed badly as it was seen as too clever and complicated, but by including alternative advertisements in the research, a more effective campaign was developed and used. No internal committee played any part in this campaign or subsequent ones. This consumer based approach was carried through to the advertising for the two new products (Turn Out and First Cut) and resulted in recall levels above 60 per cent during their first three months. Advertising for these products also had a similar look to the Nitram advertisements, thus forming the basis of an ICIF house style.

☐ *Distribution*

Another activity which occupied much of the period was that of rationalising the distributor network.

From something in the order of 350, a sharper and altogether more professional network of just 68 distributors was set up. Those chosen were selected with improved customer service in mind so that the external 'trade-off' of service levels versus distribution costs could be better balanced.

It was expected that the number of distributors would continue to reduce, by between 5 and 10 per cent, over the next few years. It was these changes in the distribution network which necessitated the rethink about the role of the sales organisation (mentioned earlier).

Even though all these things were being tackled in the Company, the business environment was continuing to change.

☐ *Imports*

In the period under review, fertiliser prices tended to be higher in the UK than in much of mainland Europe. This meant that although it was bulky and costly to transport over great distances, sales margins achievable in the UK made exporting a viable proposition for some foreign producers.

As a result, imports gradually increased and posed a threat in the declining UK fertiliser market, by making inroads into the major manufacturers' market shares.

Most imports were in the form of urea, which was becoming increasingly popular with end users. A more recent import has been good quality ammonium nitrate, with imports from Eastern Bloc countries tending to predominate over Western European imports.

☐ *UK Competitor Activity*

- Norsk Hydro built a new ammonium nitrate facility. They also introduced a new branded fertiliser called 'Extran'. This had a 34.5 per cent N concentration and was a direct competitor for ICI's 'Nitram', a product which had remained virtually unchallenged for over 25 years.
- Another potentially significant move was that Kemira took over competitor UKF. Although Kemira was a key player in the UK, the company had a poor image in the market place. In contrast UKF had a good image. Interested spectators waited to see how these two distinctive images might be merged in the expanded company.
- Blenders were collectively still an effective competitor. No major producer had the flexibility and closeness to customers that were characteristic of these small 'producers'. Even if one failed another started up elsewhere. The picture was therefore fragmented and transitory, but overall the aggregate effect of blenders, while not increasing, still made an impact on the Company's sales, particularly in East Anglia.

■ Critique of the Recovery Plan

By the end of 1989, the Company was in a healthier position than it was at the end of 1986, and once again in profit, due to the positive actions taken.

But equally, there were still a number of issues which still clouded the sunny picture which were beginning to emerge.

- The fertiliser market continued to decline.
- New European legislation could structurally alter the market more profoundly than hitherto.

- The Company's main competitors in the UK were also leading players in Europe.
- The Company was tied by its history to providing N fertilisers in the form of ammonium nitrate and was fighting a losing battle against other forms of N such as urea and urea compounds.
- Foreign competitors received subsidies not available in the UK.
- As a result of the market segmentation study, it was becoming clear that the consumers' view of the fertiliser market was having a profound effect. For segments in which the Company believed it was strong, the market research had revealed the opposite to be the case. The linkage which had been assumed to exist in the purchase of Nitran and compounds had proved to be unfounded in a number of segments. One danger was that ICIF's traditional agronomic expertise and approaches could well lead to overkill and fewer sales. Also, perhaps the allocation of the Company's research resources needed to be refocused.
- There was still a suspicion that deep down the Company was more concerned about its products and efficiency rather than taking an out-and-out marketing approach which focused on the customer. (It is not easy to change a corporate culture).
- There still seemed to be some ambivalence about the question of whether fertilisers were just a commodity or whether they could be marketed as branded products. In other words, was the competitive edge going to hinge on lower production costs or market and product differentiation? It appeared that the Company sought both.

■ The Onset of the 1990s

A strategic marketing plan was developed for the period 1990–3. The underlying strategy was to maximise profits by selling high N fertilisers. However, the Company only proposed to focus on those segments where cost leadership was possible. In addition it was planned that:

- new products would be developed which met both customers' needs *and* made good use of production facilities;
- distribution costs would be minimised; and
- high plant utilisation would be maintained by exporting to Europe.

At the heart of this strategy was the need to maintain high plant capacity. Without this, the prospect of achieving cost leadership would be untenable.

This strategic marketing plan was accepted by the Board of the Fertiliser Division in May 1990. What had happened to change the Company's fortunes in the last year or so gave them some optimism that the plan was achievable.

However, later in the year the Group Board decided that, although the plan might optimise on the assets of the Fertiliser Division, it did not hold the prospect of building a successful business which would remain viable and provide satisfactory levels of return in the future. It was therefore decided to sell the fertiliser business.

Weakened by the division's drastic rationalisation of the mid-1980s and massive job cuts in 1989, the company's saleability was mixed. Rival firm Kemira put in a bid for the ailing division, but this was blocked by the Monopolies and Mergers Commission, and the cyclical nature of the business and the restrictions imposed by the MMC precluded any more than competitive interest from Norsk Hydro and BASF. By 1993 the business was still up for sale, with no buyer on the short term horizon.

Despite this situation, ICI's most troublesome business appears to be thriving. Although only a shadow of its former self, having slimmed down from 10,000 employees in the 1980s to only 600 in 1992, the company has started once again to generate profits.

However, as before, a significant threat to the division's continued survival will be its capacity to compete effectively against cheaper imports. The former Soviet Union has started to export a 'Niram' substitute, and has already gained 20 per cent of the £600 million market, by selling at 20 per cent below the price ICI was selling at ten years ago. ICI's defence will probably lie in lobbying for an EC-imposed quota or anti-dumping legislation. With the UK being the only European market in which there are no quotas and with farmers consuming more than 5 million tonnes of fertiliser annually, it is still potentially a lucrative market

■ Case Study 15: Virgin Atlantic Airways

■ Attacking the Market Leader*

■ The Current Position

Virgin Atlantic are amongst the extraordinary marketing successes of the last ten years. In this notoriously competitive environment, the Company has established itself as a reputable airline, second only to British Airways in the UK long-haul market, with prime routes, high load factors and excellent service, in a few years. They have achieved their success by offering customers a little more, by remaining constantly visible, by developing a strong brand, and by remaining acutely sensitive to the demands of, and changes in, the market.

Richard Branson, the founder of the Virgin empire, sees the airline as the premier product in his vast portfolio of two hundred companies. Although Branson is determined to make his airline the best quality product in the market, he believes that Virgin Atlantic, in terms of marketing the Group as a whole, is the key.

■ The Market Environment

Virgin Atlantic, founded in 1984, has spearheaded the attack on the Civil Aviation Authority, for, what Branson regards as, the unfair competition between British Airways and his own airline. The case against BA included unfair allocation of slots, monopoly of long-haul flights from Heathrow and undermining of Virgin's position at Gatwick by dumping low price tickets to the US there. He also claimed it exploited its dominant position in airline maintenance by unfairly raising prices for servicing Virgin's aircraft.

The Branson mission was effective. In what Virgin claimed was an unprecedented move in aviation history, the CAA awarded Virgin four additional slots for Tokyo's Narita airport at BA's expense in 1991. Also, on the advice of the CAA, the Department of Transport reconsidered traffic distribution rights at Heathrow, resulting in Virgin flying from this location.

The recession of the 1990s hit the airline industry particularly hard, with both business and leisure travellers cutting back on expenditure. The Gulf crisis further squeezed profits, along with intensifying competition due to the gradual opening up of the UK market, and airlines recorded a drop in passenger levels of up to 30 per cent.

* Based on an article by Franny Moyle in *Marketing Week*, 8 March 1991.

■ Virgin's Success

Virgin's passenger levels, however, barely suffered. The carrier's load factors between January and 15 February 1991 were 71 per cent compared with 74 per cent in the same period in 1990. Branson attributed this to what he claimed was his airline's non-political stance. This had, during the Gulf war, encouraged people to switch from other airlines. But above all, he attributed it to the quality of his product. Demand for Virgin was greater than its capacity before the Gulf war and this was achieved by pursuing strategic route growth, developing a clear product, and by creating a well defined brand with a tangible personality.

Branson's philosophy for success has been based on the need to be the best if you are the smallest. Laker made the mistake of founding a small airline where his competitive advantage was low price. However, low price meant low quality. When majors matched these fares, Laker went out of business.

□ *Repositioning Strategy*

Branson aimed from the start at the high quality segment of the market, but Virgin Atlantic's early marketing strategy could be seen as more of a hindrance than a help in the development of a brand which is now seen as having strong values of quality and service. Early Virgin advertisements featuring rock star Phil Lynott, coupled with Branson's own reputation for running a discount-led retail business, have a resonance even now. Some still see the carrier as a rock 'n roll shuttle. Virgin was set up after Laker's demise and people perceived Virgin as being a backpack airline. Branson also ran an entertainment group, which also added a certain perception. This brand image, along with Virgin's original mistake of operating short-haul flights which were not cost-effective for a small airline, prompted Branson into repositioning Virgin's brand image.

Virgin focused on business travellers, half filling the plane with this type of customer, and thus able to offer lower fares in the back of the aircraft. Virgin concentrated on long-haul flights, creating a type of theatre adventure journey for the passenger, packed with quality and service. Two thirds of Virgin's income now comes from the business sector.

What has captured Virgin's market today has little to do with building a brand through traditional campaigns. The key to Virgin's success has been the creaction of an excellent product which, according to Branson, advertises itself by word of mouth. The Company has also relied heavily on the many column inches generated by the awards its product has won in recent years.

This casual system of reference has been simultaneously supported by tactical press campaigns through Virgin's agency Woolmas, Moira, Gaskin O'Malley. An early campaign poked fun at conventional airline advertising and helped establish Virgin's personality as an airline with alternative ways of doing things.

☐ *Consumer-Orientated Company*

Virgin's Marketing Director, Chris Moss, has masterminded this phase in the airline's development. His view, as is Virgin's in general, is that although upgrading the product means reducing the number of seats, it will engender greater consumer loyalty and encourage more people to pay a full economy fare rather than take a saver deal. Moss's view complements Branson's penchant for long-term thinking as opposed to short-term profit maximisation, and it is this that has made his airline so successful. For example, on its Tokyo routes, Virgin has 60 fewer seats than their competitors; these seats could add £8 million to its bottom line if they were put back. But Branson is building for the long-term and so makes sacrifices in the short-term. This strategy strengthens the word-of-mouth marketing tool that emphasises that Virgin is the best.

Moss has also moved Virgin's advertising away from its mockery of other airlines, towards a more sophisticated approach. The 'girl on the phone' advertisement for first class was the first move towards a glossier style. Strategic brand building, that is no longer reliant on comparison with other carriers such as British Airways, is now the basis for further growth when the route expansion of the airline will be sufficient to support a more global message.

The evolution of a more stylish advertising message, to woo those 50 per cent of business travellers unaware of Virgin's charms, is welcomed by Branson. He sees the communication of the high quality Virgin Atlantic brand as essential in defining the perception of his Group's other products, especially important with brand extension in mind. Having sold his music business for £500 million in 1992, Branson has looked around for opportunities in the airline and associated travel areas.

Branson's ongoing battle with the stranglehold of the national flag carrier remains, with licensed routes blocked by the withholding of take-off and landing slots. There is constant industry and media talk of price wars and, of course, Virgin's moral, if not fully financial, victory in the 'BA Dirty Tricks' case in 1993. Legal battles and out-of-court settlements could result in BA conceding much sought-after routes in recompense for three years of commercial damage. Branson is poised to embark on a £1 billion expansion of his fleet in readiness to start operating these international routes. Surprisingly, BA has emerged relatively untarnished from the 'Dirty Tricks' saga. According to an independent survey, BA has not suffered any real negative effect – with only a 2 per cent drop in the number of people happy to be associated with the company.

Meanwhile, Virgin Atlantic continues to invest in service improvements and strive to retain price leadership. A recent development has been the emergence of a 'mid' class of seats with 6″ more leg room than economy but far cheaper than first class. Virgin maintains a significant position despite having only 4.2 per cent share of the UK international market.

Branson has also started to look again at Europe. With the EC's agreement on the staged liberalisation of air travel, Virgin investigated the possibility of buying bankrupt Dan Air, but the talks ended without result. Instead Virgin has adopted a low cost strategy of a franchise operation, starting with a London/Athens route in 1993, flying in the Virgin livery – a testimony to the power of the Virgin brand. Branson has also declared an interest in setting up bases in other EC countries such as France or Germany from which to run competitively-priced long haul services.

Keen to extend the brand in the travel sector, Branson has also put in a bid to run long distance rail services in the UK when British Rail is privatised in the mid-1990s. He plans to bring the Virgin success factors – quality of service and customer focus – to rail travel.

□ *Future Strategy*

Emerging from the recession of the early 1990s, the market environment remains harsh with traditional profit generators, business account travellers trading down. Virgin Atlantic however remains the key element in the growth of this group. With eight 747s in 1992, the airline is expected to grow to double its current size by the end of the century. An order for four new Airbuses in 1993 demonstrates Virgin's ambitious plans to extend its international network. Flying three million passengers a year (compared with 1.2 m at present) and with a fleet of 16 to 18 large long-haul aircraft flying to twelve major cities, Branson will remain sharply focused on the key profitable inter-continental routes.

Branson sees the fleet's upper limit as twenty. This will enable him to keep the company to a manageable size and with a full complement of strategically profitable routes, the Virgin airline will start to become a truly global brand.

■ Case Study 16: Pretty Polly

■ From Function to Fashion ... From Commodity to Added Value ... From Bottom Right to Top Right

■ Summary

Pretty Polly, owned by the Sara Lee Corporation, the Chicago-based consumer products group, is the leader in the £400 million plus UK hosiery industry, and is currently valued at £110 million. From the early 1970s, under Thomas Tilling ownership, through the 1980s when the company was acquired by BTR and into the 1990s, Pretty Polly has skilfully employed marketing techniques to combat the threat of the commodity trap, establish brand awareness and redefine their product as a high value-added fashion item. In doing so, they have strengthened their position as brand leader in a market under attack by own-label products and increased profitability.

■ Analysis: The Early 1970s

Pretty Polly has had three owners since the 1970s, each adding value to the brand. In the hostile environment of the 1970s, the company had a clear view of its competitive position. Hosiery had slid into a commodity product, the industry was in decline and was facing a number of threats; over capacity, weak pricing, own-label growth, reduced distribution channels and cheap imports.

Faced with declining profits, Pretty Polly identified a gap between its forecast and future requirements; through planning and research, this gap was bridged by productivity improvements and marketing based strategies. In advance of its competitors, the company shut down inefficient capacity, invested in new technology and introduced workforce redundancies. Full use was made of market research to plan marketing strategies; strengths were matched against market needs.

Pretty Polly focused on market penetration and product development as its key strategies. The market was segmented by customer and products developed for each segment (Legworks for 18–24 age group, After Dark for evening wear and Galaxy for grocery distribution). New production processes enabled a higher design input and faster response to fashion trends. The generic product was augmented by the addition of new colours, patterns and styles.

Packaging was redesigned and the Pretty Polly brand name and logo added to all products. A national brand position was established, based upon a family of product ranges supported by the brand name. The company adopted an innovative and award winning approach to advertising; a five year plan

(1975–80) based on television and poster campaigns was implemented and supported by sponsorship and PR.

Pretty Polly did not price cut. Instead they 'added value' to the consumer through innovation in product development and branding. To the retailer they sold the benefits of the range by stressing high retailing margins per square foot. They sought profitability through improved marketing and did not pursue turnover at any cost. Profit in the period 1976–80 grew from £300,000 to £4.5 million.

The company identified the key distribution channels and targeted grocery retailing as the fastest growing sector. Specific brands and marketing mixes were matched against the needs of each channel.

■ The 1980s

The early 1980s saw a slump in performance and profitability, and following the purchase of the company by the industrial conglomerate BTR, much of the hard work of transforming Pretty Polly was carried out by Patrick Austen, the BTR executive, who, moving to the company in 1983, lifted profits from £1 million to £11 m on sales of £125 m. Having maximised its returns through heavy investment in new technology and marketing during the 1980s and no longer considered a core business by BTR, Pretty Polly was able to command a high sale price and was sold for £110 million in 1991 to the American hosiery giant Sara Lee.

■ The 1990s

The purchase is a logical move for Sara Lee, with a tight strategic fit of Pretty Polly with Sara Lee's core business. For the American company, the acquisition of Pretty Polly represents an opportunity to add one of the UK's most successful hosiery manufacturers to its fast expanding European interests. Sara Lee is the world's biggest maker of women's hosiery, and generates most of its profits from products such as socks and underwear.

Sara Lee's recent acquisitions have two things in common; they are all staple purchases and their markets are highly fragmented with own-label goods predominant. Sara Lee will look to get the best value from the brand; it will cut costs, possibly through cheap southern European labour, then offer high-quality branded goods at a low price; the 'value' position. Boosted by significant promotional effort (£3.5 m was spent on the Legacy sub-brand launch) and established distribution networks, Sara Lee's strategy will be to market on a pan-European scale and capitalise on its leading position in Europe, where it already owns the number 1 French hosiery company DIM.

Pretty Polly over the past two decades has become the UK's best known brand in the market, with 69 per cent spontaneous awareness, 25 per cent of all UK sales and 48 per cent of sales in the grocery sector. Strong advertising by the creative agency Bartle Bogle Hegarty and Saatchi and Saatchi, including the girl who replaces her car's fan belt with a stocking and David Bailey 'clock' photography, reinforces the commanding position. The company continues to innovate with sub-brands such as Legacy under the Pretty Polly brand umbrella.

Pretty Polly clearly demonstrates the possibilities of breaking out of the commodity trap and establishing a strong and profitable brand position.

■ Case Study 17: Selincourt

■ Remaining in the Bottom Left Hand Box until Disaster Strikes

Dick Cole, Managing Director of Selincourt plc, looked out of the window of his London office and watched the '7' series BMW gliding out of its parking space and accelerating away from the building. The consultant's words were still ringing in his ears.

'The problem is, Dick, that the moment you begin to show signs of riches to come, you will become takeover fodder with no defences. My advice to you is to consider the possibility of either a management buyout or getting into bed with someone you like – Courtaulds, for instance.'

It was October 1984. As he turned back to his desk, Dick Cole allowed himself a few minutes to dwell on the changes he had effected within the garment and textile group of companies which comprised Selincourt. He had been bought in, from Courtaulds, as Managing Director Designate in 1979, when Selincourt was celebrating its diamond jubilee as a publicly quoted company on the London Stock Exchange. The celebration coincided with the Company's highest ever profits. Prospects looked rosy. But within the year, the onset of the world wide recession had brutally exposed the Company's weaknesses. Problems of keeping new plant going were exacerbated by the need to move existing stock at low margins. Cole soon discovered that cash controls had been minimal. Debt had risen 43 per cent in that first year to stand at a record level of £14.5 million.

After his appointment as Managing Director in 1982, Dick Cole had spent two years steadily rationalising the Group, while, at the same time, coping with the day-to-day problems of keeping the Company afloat. Management changes were made in the subsidiaries, promoting talent from within and bringing in new skills from the outside. To eliminate unprofitable areas, companies had been shut down, reducing the number of subsidiaries from 15 to 11. Cash controls had been firmly implemented and cash management improved. But debt had been serviced at the cost of foregoing dividend payments to shareholders.

A key part of Cole's strategy had been to change the Company's emphasis from a production orientation to a new market awareness. This was the only way the Group was going to be able to respond to the rapidly changing market opportunities in its diverse sales areas.

Now, Cole realised, for the first time in four years he had the chance to look beyond the immediate problems and plan for Selincourt's development, as a Group, in the long term. The Company had tried many directions in the past, under a number of different managements. It was up to him to build on the current strengths of the Group and to devise a strategy for the second half of the 1980s.

■ Historical Background

Selincourt had started trading in 1857 when Charles de Selincourt and Frederick Coleman set up a partnership in the city of London. The Company went public in 1919, but was taken over by the Drapery Trust Ltd. Soon afterwards, it became a subsidiary of Debenhams. The Company's main products were furs, dresses, and tailor-made women's outerwear for both the home and Empire markets. In 1949 Debenhams, predominately a retail group, decided to hive off Selincourt and refloat the Company as a separate unit. For 10 years, Selincourt remained an unspectacular public company. Along with many others, its main objective was to outlive the post war austerity period and look for better times ahead.

□ *The Evans-Mintz Partnership: Expansion by Acquisition 1959–1963*

When Harold Evans, Selincourt's Chairman, first discussed the possibility of a merger of interests with Louis Mintz, there were no minutes, no advisers, just two men talking across a desk and a packet of fish and chips. The two men were to play a central role in the development of Selincourt over the next ten years. After Selincourt merged with the Louis Mintz Group in 1959, the new company claimed to cover the whole field of ladies' outerwear, with a price range which catered for everyone. They also exported to over fifty different countries including the United States and the Soviet Union.

Evans remained as Chairman, Mintz became Managing Director. Their objective was to grow by acquisition, and between 1959 and 1963, no less than 30 companies were acquired. Amongst them were well known names, such as Frank Usher and Garlaine, which were to remain part of the Selincourt Group for many years. As a result of these acquisitions, the Group's products included ladies' fashion wear such as dresses, suits and coats, separates and coordinated casual wear, occasion wear and maternity wear; buttons, fasteners and trimmings; handbags and other accessories; children's clothes; window furnishings and napery. These acquisitions were intended to strengthen the Group's position in all branches of the medium and high class ranges of the fashion industry.

In addition, Selincourt adopted a strategy of forward integration into retailing. They took a 60 per cent stake in Neatawear, a group of 11 shops in the London area, and bought a further chain of 30 womenswear shops. Both concerns were encouraged to continue independent trading and remain free to select merchandise as before.

These acquisitions were financed by a mixture of cash and an increasing number of share issues. The largest acquisition, in May 1963, was a £3.2 million takeover of the ladies' suit manufacturer, L Harris, which owned 5 factories, 9 wholesale showrooms and a chain of 47 'Noel' shops throughout the UK. The purchase was seen as 'natural' because Selincourt shops stocked Harris's suits, while Harris's shops had long sold Selincourt dresses.

□ *Reorganisation 1963–69*

Louis Mintz ran the much enlarged Group on a decentralised basis, except for certain areas. 'While we save a lot of money on bulk fabric buying and centralised manufacturing policies, we don't pool anything which might rob our firms of individuality and incentive. However, the main board keeps in close touch – every member of the Group gets a personal visit from at least one head office Director every week. As for me, I'm always on call and they even ring me late at night with their problems so I can sort them out first thing in the morning.'

But Mintz had not resolved the problems of absorbing so many new companies over a relatively short space of time. The twin problems of reorganisation and integration were blamed for the Group's failure to achieve its stated target for 1964 of doubling profits.

In the event, for the three years from 1964 and 1966, Selincourt pre-tax profits fell. At the end of 1966, Mintz announced a major reorganisation of the structure of the Group 'to improve the efficiency of the Group's activities and, in time, to increase its profitability'. His main aim was to stimulate inter-group trading, which he regarded as an essential element in the growth pattern of a corporation such as Selincourt. The 35 companies in the Group were brought together into seven divisions on a complementary basis. Each company would retain its own board, but would also fall within the orbit of a divisional chairman.

In 1967, the Group sold £1.5 million worth of property and investments to fund its overdraft. Certain companies were not making adequate returns on capital employed; the Group had to be streamlined. Revised targets were set and it was announced that tough measures would be taken with those companies failing to maintain their agreed standard of performance.

In 1968 and 1969, 'unsuitable' and uneconomic subsidiaries were sold off or closed down. Resources were redeployed to maximise returns. The effects of this huge programme of reorganisation and consolidation soon became evident in the Group's improved performance. In 1969, pre-tax profits were up 45 per cent. This was seen as largely due to clearing out the unprofitable companies, a complete turnaround at one of the main subsidiaries and a general tightening of control at divisional level.

Throughout the decade, the retailing operation had expanded by acquisition and had grown to the point where it owned some 90 stores in the UK and 12 in Ireland. By 1968 the retail division was producing 32 per cent turnover and over 20 per cent of profits.

Meanwhile, the export side of the business had also been expanding. In 1961 Selincourt (European markets) had been formed to handle group promotions, distribution and sales in Europe. The marketing effort here and elsewhere was worthwhile. By 1968, export sales topped the £2 million mark, with the largest areas of expansion in Germany, the US and Scandinavia.

Thus after four years of declining profits, by 1968 it looked as if Selincourt, as a group, was back on the rails.

☐ *The Palfreyman Years 1969–1976*

1969 brought an abrupt reversal in Selincourt's fortunes. Pre-tax profits, which were over £1 million in 1968, collapsed to £350,000. This was attributed to difficult conditions in the retailing division. Essentially, it was suffering from a flat turnover and a large rise in overheads, combined with unexpectedly high startup costs of new stores in Scotland.

In May, Evans resigned as Chairman and Ronald Palfreyman took over. Palfreyman had established a reputation as company doctor. His commercial approach, allied with a rigorous system of cost control, had already proved successful in 'rescuing' a company called Contour Hosiery. There were great expectations that this success would be replicated at Selincourt.

Within a year, Palfreyman's presence was clearly being felt. Steps taken included a stringent procedure of stock valuation to speed up clearance, the regrouping of operations to achieve economies in manufacturing and administration and concomitant changes in management. Unprofitable smaller units were sold or closed down. Cutting out the 'deadwood' in the lace and net divisions reduced the number of companies in that division from 11 to just three. On the retailing side, there was a bid to increase the minimal proportions of own-manufactured goods on sale and to cut out the unprofitable lines in the big stores which were felt to be the real trouble spots. Uneconomic shops were sold off, amidst denials that there was any intention of abandoning retailing completely.

Financial control was evidently improved and by July 1970 bank borrowings were at the lowest for 5 years. However, the erosion of reserves meant that the Company's debt/equity ratio stood at 200 per cent.

Despite the denials, there was a progressive divestment of the retail division. In July 1970 the retailing division's Scottish operations were sold off for slightly less than asset value. A further seven shops were sold to the head of Selincourt's retail division. In October, in a £1 million deal, Selincourt sold 50 shops to Dorothy Perkins. Other interests in retailing were also sold off. Selincourt's experiment with retailing was over. The net effect of these disposals was to improve Group liquidity by £2.3 million.

The reorganisation left the Company with subsidiaries which were all trading profitably. Several were poised for growth. One of the garment manufacturing companies set the pace, with two thirds of its output going to Marks and Spencer. This alone represented about 20 per cent of the Group's annual sales.

Palfreyman felt that the success of his consolidation policy provided a springboard for expansion. In May 1972 he announced the intended acquisition of Tricosa, a French company which manufactured fabric and ladies' high class outerwear. Selincourt already held 15 per cent of the equity from a deal completed seven years earlier.

In December 1972, as profits for the year rose sharply on a record turnover of £25 million, Mintz resigned as Deputy Chairman and Managing Director. Organic growth within the Group came from companies involved in both textile and garment manufacturing. The high street boom, fuelled by the Conservative government's 'burst for growth', allowed many parts of the Group to reap rich returns. Plans went ahead for a grand opening of a new plant for Tricosa in France and new factories were built in the UK. Palfreyman was determined to prove that Selincourt could produce sustained profit growth and, at the same time, show that the Group had a prosperous and reasonably settled future in the 'boom and bust' rag trade. Borrowings rose to £7.2 million against shareholders' funds of £3.4 million. The Company was, therefore, again heavily geared at 212 per cent.

But 1973 did not continue the trend of substantial growth. Tricosa made a loss as a result of setting up its new factory in Saumur and the lace and net division had a major upheaval in moving to a new factory in Derbyshire. Palfreyman was undaunted, and in 1974 Selincourt bought a controlling interest in a Scottish knitwear company which manufactured classic and crested sports knitwear in cashmere and lambswool. It made a loss in the same year, partly due to a programme of reorganisation. In addition, Tricosa's losses rose as a result of consumer price resistance in the French market which, in turn, lead to excess capacity at Saumur. However, on the plus side, Frank Usher, internationally known for its ladies' evening wear, produced excellent results and other companies continued to expand their work for Marks and Spencer.

Selincourt had been spending heavily on re-equipment and modernisation of plant, but as yet there was little return on this investment. The '3 day week' and the miners' strike, combined with the first OPEC oil price rise, to cause a collapse in consumer spending. Palfreyman described 1974 as the most difficult year the Group had faced. 1975 brought rising inflation and weak sterling. Interest charges absorbed half the Group's trading profits. While remaining optimistic for the future, Palfreyman stepped down as Chairman in August 1976 and took personal charge of Tricosa. But within a year he had resigned his position and ceased to be a director.

☐ *Leighton and Pick: The Big Years, 1976–1979*

Things were, in fact, moving in the right direction at Selincourt when Lionel Leighton took over as Chairman in 1976 and appointed Dennis Pick as his Managing Director. Tricosa had been turned round from a further loss in 1975 to produce a profit the following year. The Scottish knitwear company reduced its losses and ended the year trading profitably with a full order book. Profits rose to a record £3.18 million. The textile industry was emerging slowly from the worst recession anyone could remember since the early 1950s.

Pick implemented a programme of fundamental reorganisation and substantial capital investment. His policy was to allow each of the 20 companies in the Group greater autonomy than before, while backing them with extra finance. His strategy was to interfere only when there were problems. He believed that for a number of companies in the Group there was 'no real competition'. In 1977 he bought the remaining shares in the Scottish knitwear company, to achieve complete control.

Nevertheless, the targeted profits of £5 million in 1978 were not achieved, although they did rise 8 per cent to £4.56 million. During the year, the Company entered into an agreement with Pierre Balmain to manufacture in France, and market in the UK, US and other selected overseas markets, a product range under the Balmain label. Unfortunately, this new ready-to-wear collection was not a success and the agreement was dropped after the first year. Meanwhile, however, Selincourt had opened a big new marketing centre in Dusseldorf as part of a major export drive to Germany.

In July 1979, the *Financial Times* commented on a 'new atmosphere' among Selincourt directors. 'Instead of pulling for recovery or debt reduction they are now expansionary. Acquisitions costing £2.5 million are now in the pipline.' A rights issue was not ruled out.

In August, Selincourt bought a knitting plant and in October bid, albeit unsuccessfully, for a printer and converter of silks and other fabrics. They also sent a team to Peking to open negotiations for a Chinese manufacturing operation in pile fabrics and nets for curtains.

But, in the latter half of 1979, after the second OPEC oil price rise, the high street turned sour again. This led to serious overstocking and clearance problems. Profits slumped drastically to £2.06 million. With the depressed state of trading and the need to de-stock at low margins, the garment and textile industry was generally plunged into gloom and despondency. Leighton's statement that he expected a sizeable recovery in profits in 1980/1 stood alone in its optimism. One subsidiary, specialising in suede and leathercraft, was forced to close all but one of its shop-in-store units due to severe losses. Elsewhere, other companies in the Group saw profits reduced by up to 90 per cent.

With a high debt ratio, high working capital requirements, high stock levels and excess capacity, the Company was going into the next recession weighed down by every conceivable disadvantage.

☐ *The Collapse 1979–1981*

In spite of Leighton's continued spirit of optimism, sales fell dramatically. In the first half of 1980, garment sales fell by £1.5 million, the textile division's by £0.5 million. Even Leighton had to admit that Selincourt, as with the rest of the clothing industry, was contending with trading conditions of unprecedented difficulty. Full year profits for 1980 fell to £839,000. Borrowing increased by £1 million. The suede and leathercraft subsidiary was shut down at a cost of over £1 million.

Nevertheless, Leighton maintained 'We are now a much leaner and fitter business and poised to take advantage of any revival in the market'. Again his optimism was misplaced. During 1980/1 redundancy and closure costs amounted to £1.6 million. There were 1,600 redundancies throughout the Group. Interest charges for 1981 on a record level of debt of £16.2 million were £2.6 million. This effectively wiped out operating profits for the year.

The collapse had been quick and brutal.

□ *1982–1984*

In April 1982, Sir David Nicolson took over as Chairman and, in July, Dick Cole became Managing Director. The economic climate was inauspicious. Market conditions continued to deteriorate, interest rates returned to near record levels and unemployment rose towards three million, causing a further reduction in consumer demand. Moreover, these problems were not confined to the UK. Similar difficulties were being experienced world wide, and particularly in Germany and France.

Against this sombre background, Selincourt reported pre-tax profits up to £386,000 on a turnover of £64.6 million.

Throughout 1982 and 1983, the new management struggled to keep the Company going. Dick Cole's attention was divided between making sure that the Company could service its debts on the one hand and that it was responding to the dramatic changes in the high street on the other. The first of these priorities meant that dividends to shareholders had to be foregone and every effort was made to reduce the heavy burden of interest payments which were consuming trading profits.

The high street revolution, sparked by the arrival of Next and other newcomers such as Benetton, meant that market awareness was crucial. If Selincourt failed to respond to the changing environment and adopt a market orientation, it could not hope to survive.

Rationalisation and reorganisation was once more the order of the day. During this period, there was an overall improvement in trading results and profitability. But there were still companies within the Group which had to contend with specific problems.

Tricosa had a particularly hard struggle against the austerity measures, imposed by the French socialist government, which had a significant dampening effect on domestic demand. Efforts were made to reduce dependence on the French home market.

The Scottish knitwear company, MacDougall, continued to share the generally depressed state of the Scottish knitwear industry. The market switch away from 'classic' merchandise and the dramatic strengthening of sterling

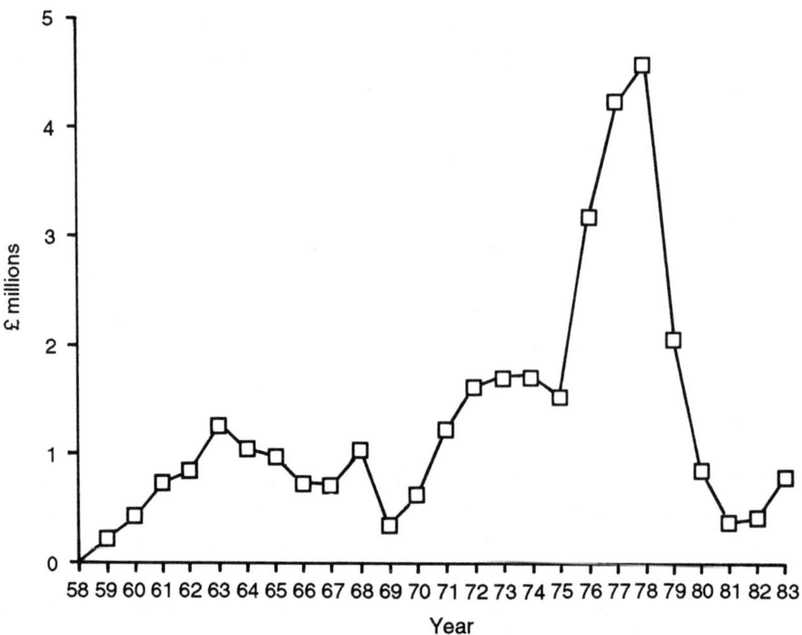

Figure 4.11 Selincourt plc: Pre-tax profits, 1958–83

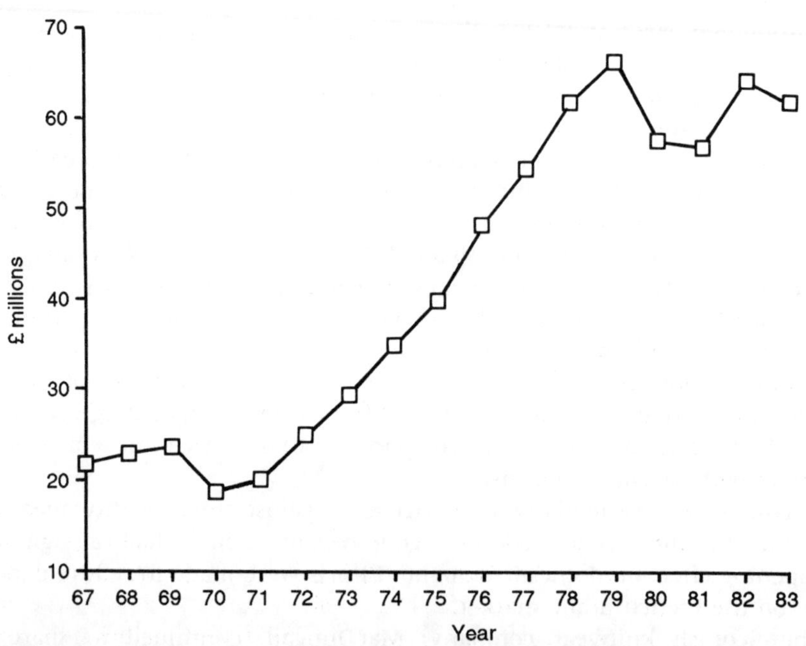

Figure 4.12 Selincourt plc: Group turnover, 1967–83

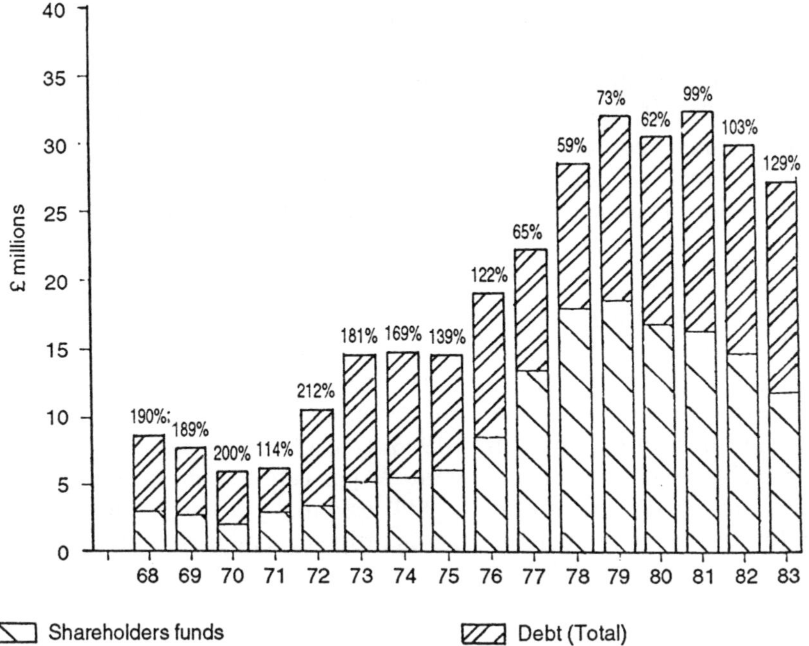

Figure 4.13 Selincourt plc: Debt/equity ratios, 1968–83

both contributed to a deterioration in performance. Options for diversification were considered.

It was the board's belief that the substantial programme of rationalisation and reorganisation would begin to show beneficial results. Sir David Nicolson felt sure that by maintaining levels of capital investment, strengthening management and concentrating resources on marketing, particularly on market research and design input, the turnaround of Selincourt could be achieved.

Gradually, a change of emphasis in the Group became evident. There was no longer a negative stance of retrenchment, but a positive drive to establish new customers and new markets. This stemmed largely from the realisation that they could no longer wait for a major upturn in the economy. The business must succeed on its own terms.

On the marketing front, overall Group objectives included the establishment of closer links with the larger successful retailing and mail order organisations. Marks and Spencer, who accounted for 15 per cent of the 1982 turnover, was one such target. Particular companies were believed to have significant growth potential and a concerted programme of project development was initiated for these businesses.

1983 had been perceived as the year of transition with the twin objectives of profit improvement and cash generation. In fact, pre-tax profits rose to £719,000 on a turnover of 162.5 million.

In the spring of 1984, a recently formed company, Jeff Cooper, and Selincourt GmbH were both closed down. They had failed to achieve the desired results and the cost of further assistance and reorganisation was deemed prohibitive. This left just eleven companies in the Selincourt portfolio. Details of their main activities and an outline of their trading position in 1984 follow.

Garment Manufacturing

Frank Usher

With its international reputation for design creativity, Frank Usher had consolidated its position as front runner in ladies' evening and cocktail wear with a turnover of £4.3 million in 1983/4. It sold to all major UK department stores and upmarket boutiques, with 40 per cent export mainly to western Europe and particularly Germany. Still essentially a family business, it was heavily dependent upon its staff, primarily the designers, for its continued success.

E. & A. Richards Ltd

Split into two divisions, lace and knitwear, E. & A. Richards had doubled profits in the year to January 1984.

Lace Division – Turnover was expected to rise marginally from the £2.2 million achieved in 1983/4, of which 82 per cent was attributable to sales to Marks and Spencer. Recent investment of £250,000 had been made in equipment. To enhance the design side, a lace specialist had been recruited and bursaries in lingerie and foundationwear given at the London School of Fashion and Leicester Polytechnic. Future strategy included continued emphasis on design and product innovation and further investment in production equipment.

Knitwear Division – Designers and manufacturers of fashion knitwear for women, men and children, the division's turnover had risen to £1.85 million, with Next and John Lewis as major customers. A £3.4 million turnover was projected for 1984/5 and capital investment had been set at £1.1 million. With a new computer-aided design department, a stronger product range was being created and it was hoped that a good business relationship could be developed with Marks and Spencer.

Taylor Merrymade Ltd

As designers and manufacturers of separates and coordinated causal wear they made nearly 75 per cent of sales to Marks and Spencer. They intended to expand this outlet considerably and also to develop business with their existing customers Next, Burtons, House of Fraser and Conran as well as with other large specialist retail chains. The Company's main strengths were in long runs in mass production, and, having achieved economies of scale, maintaining them through rigorous management control. There had been substantial capital investment since 1981 and, to attain their ambitious sales targets, further funds had been approved for 1984–87 to expand and improve in-house production facilities.

Tricosa SA

Designers and manufacturers of fabric and ladies' high class fashion outerwear, 50 per cent of the Company's sales were in France while 50 per cent were exported to other European countries and Japan. 1983 had been a difficult year, largely because of problems in the French economy. There was a continued emphasis on product design and innovation to strengthen international appeal along with the desire to develop merchandise acceptable to Marks and Spencer.

Garlaine Ltd

Designers and importers of high quality ladies' outerwear, supplying major high street stores and boutiques, Garlaine was showing marked improvement in profitability. Turnover was expected to rise from the £9.5 million achieved in 1983/4. Brand name 'Linda Leigh' specialising in outsize fashion wear, indicated considerable potential for development, while the 'Parigi' range of occasion wear introduced two years earlier, was proving very successful. Known for its skills in merchanting at the higher value added end of the market, and in design and fabric sourcing, Garlaine nevertheless had to face up to increasing chain store dominance and downward price pressure. It was planned to extend existing ranges and to introduce new brand labels.

Garlaine Australia

Garlaine Australia continued to import and merchant high class European ladies' fashions including Tricosa and Parigi (the latter being made in Hong Kong). It also had contracts with Mondi (Germany) and Liola (Italy). The Company was intending to expand by widening the existing product range and introducing coordinated casual wear.

Concord Fastener Industries Ltd

Manufacturers of fashion belts and accessories. Turnover was projected to grow from £1.6 million, with 60 per cent of sales going to Marks and Spencer. It was intended to double turnover by enlarging the design and sales team and by ensuring market leadership in production and technological efficiency.

Textile Manufacturing

J. H. Walker Ltd/Saluki Fur Fabrics

Manufacturers of single jersey fleece fabrics, silver knit fabrics and pile fabrics. The Company had suffered from frequent management changes – four managing directors in five years – but, following a period of investment and integration, was now restored to profitability. The marketing strategy was based on increased design and technical product development and diversification into related fabric areas for sports/leisure wear and upholstery fabrics. It was hoped that the Company could gain a bigger share of major retailer business, notably Marks and Spencer.

Filigree Textiles Ltd
Manufacturers, dyers and finishers of curtain nets, table napery and associated products as well as printed woven furnishing fabrics and ready-made curtains and blinds. Filigree, after substantial reorganisation, had consolidated its position as market leader in curtain nets. As diversification into other household textiles and products had shown encouraging results, there was to be a redoubled marketing effort, concentrating on the larger multiple retail outlets, including Marks and Spencer.

Jacqmar
Suppliers of piece goods, scarves and accessories under the established Jacqmar brand name. Jacqmar was one of the UK brand leaders in scarves and headsquares and had become the umbrella label for all the fabric business. (This included Walker and Rice which had now shown the long awaited improvement in performance after substantial reorganisation.) Jacqmar itself was currently going through a disappointing period in terms of design creativity, highlighting its dependence on its creative people. But under new management, the intention was to intensify the design effort, increase store presence and develop new products under the Jacqmar label to augment the existing range.

MacDougall of Scotland
Manufacturers of cashmere and lambswool classic and crested sports knitwear. Turnover was expected to grow and £200,000 had been invested in the last two years. Crested sportswear was marketed to sports clubs under the 'Glenmuir' brand. Uncrested knitwear was sold to a limited number of larger UK outlets such as Pitlochry Knitwear, Edinburgh Woollen Mills and Scotch House. There was also a bulk export business in a restricted number of markets such as Japan and USA.

□ *1984*

Dick Cole lent back in his chair. Cutting out the deadwood and encouraging new growth had been a slow and expensive operation and the cost of reorganisation had been immense. There were still problems, including what to do with Tricosa and MacDougall. However, cash flow was now under control and group borrowings were reduced.

As a consequence of brand development, capital investment in new technology, emphasis on design and marketing and a conscious nurturing of relationships with major retail groups, the majority of companies were showing a significant improvement in performance. The Group was now geared to respond to current trading conditions and to follow market shifts and trends. So much for the past, he thought, his problem now was to concentrate on the future.

The garment industry had always been classified as a high risk business, the textile industry less so. The flood of low cost imports into the UK market, along with the consumer's enhanced perceptions of value for money and quality, made it imperative for Selincourt to stress the importance of non price features in their product range. Cole wondered whether there were now sufficient compensatory factors amongst the companies in the Group to enable it to weather both the competition and any future downturn in the economy.

In which direction did the future lie? What were the strengths of the Group on which he should build? In such a fragmented and transient market place, how should he plan a long term strategy? How should Selincourt work as a Group? They had come a long way and it was important to get the next steps right.

The projections were that over the next four years, the debt/equity ratio would get into much better balance, trading profits would start to flow through in decent quantities and profit after interest would show improving returns on capital employed. But, what was the core business? Was there a need to balance the portfolio of companies in terms of risk and reward? Should the group diversify and if so how? Certainly, it needed to be diverse enough to withstand the effects of the fashion and textile cycles. These were all points which he and the consultant had been discussing. There was a Group Managing Directors' conference in November and each of them had been asked to prepare a corporate plan. The conference would provide an opportunity to get a feel for their views of the future.

After that, he would need to sit down and do some planning for the Group as a whole. He had also asked the consultant to come up with his ideas too.

The phone rang, he picked it up. It was a call from the Finance Director who was visiting Tricosa in France. Dick Cole's mind switched back to the present.

□ *1985–1986*

In March 1985, under the new, pragmatic management team which Cole had built up, it looked as if Selincourt had overcome all its problems. After the extensive programme of rationalisation, the board had sorted out its last remaining major headache. The closure of the loss making French subsidiary, Tricosa, meant that the Group was now poised to develop the various projects that had been initiated over the past two years. One of the projects was the development of a whole range of brand name accessories and coordinates, to be marketed by Selincourt in the same way that Chairman Sir David Nicolson had used the Dunhill name to market non-tobacco products when he was

Chairman of Rothmans. As Dick Cole had hoped, sales penetration had increased in major stores such as Debenhams, Dickens and Jones, Harrods, Harvey Nichols, Marks and Spencer, Next and Selfridges. Profits were improving and all the work of the previous three years were reaching fruition.

Then, in April, lightening struck. Jennifer d'Abo, head of the Ryman stationery chain, launched a £17.5 million takeover bid for the Selincourt Group.

Mrs d'Abo had first taken notice of Selincourt when the Company tried, unsuccessfully, to recruit her as a design consultant for its Jacqmar range in November 1984. Because she wanted far greater involvement with the running of the business side of the Group, this initial contact led to inimical discussions about board appointments, capital injections and management style as well as design flair. When it was clear that negotiations had broken down irreparably, Mrs d'Abo found an investment company, Stormgard, which she would use as a 'shell' vehicle for her bid. In partnership with David Dunn, she and a group of five City and Scottish institutions injected £5.3 million of new equity into Stormgard. Dunn, who had previously worked with Thomas Tilling and Hanson Trust, had joined Mrs d'Abo at the time of the Ryman purchase and had subsequently helped to develop that business.

The d'Abo team believed that the fortunes of Selincourt could be rapidly restored with an injection of finance, design and marketing flair and new management. Mrs d'Abo herself was severely critical of what she alleged to be the ineptitude of the existing management, wasting the market potential of some of the best names in British textiles and dress making. She threatened that, when she took over, heads would roll.

Sir David Nicolson mounted a fierce defence of the Selincourt management and accused Mrs d'Abo of oversimplifying the issue of exploiting the Company's potential. In his view, Mrs d'Abo was overlooking the fact that Selincourt was a complex group comprising ten businesses with differing characteristics and operating in specialised market segments. In addition, he was able to report pre-tax profits up from £791,000 to £1.38 million for the year ending January 1985. Moreover, he asserted that Ryman's profits were artificially high, contrived through a change in accounting policy. Instead of their reported profit of £39,724, compared with a loss of £1.73 million the year previously, he estimated a loss of £814,164.

A bitter wrangle ensued. No-one denied that the design flair of Mrs d'Abo allied with the financial expertise of Mr Dunn provided a formidable combination. As for the home team, the best argument in Selincourt's favour was that the present management had transformed the Company from a recession-hit disaster into a respectable business with a marked improvement in profits.

But the years without dividend payments had eroded shareholder loyalty. Ultimately, Mrs d'Abo won. Her final offer valued the Group at around £15 million. When the takeover was complete, in July 1985, Stormgard injected £5.3 million of new funds into Selincourt.

☐ *Stormgard*

Stormgard undertook a thorough review of the structure of the Group, its products and production facilities. The Group was reorganised on a product and geographic basis to create four principal trade groupings. These were fabrics and nets, lace and knitwear, garments and accessories and, finally, fashion.

The revised structure contributed to lower management costs and, by giving greater authority to the four managing directors responsible for the new groupings, achieved a substantial reduction in head office overheads. The board also implemented a system of rigorous cash management with improved debtor supervision and tighter stock control in order to reduce excessive working capital requirements.

In terms of the product range, the emphasis was placed on enhancing the design capability of the Group, whilst rationalising the existing range. A greater priority was to be placed upon presentation and packaging.

The most striking change in the Group line-up was the divestment of Frank Usher in January 1986. It was sold back to the original owners, Mr and Mrs Bruh, who had remained as managers throughout the Selincourt period (1962–1985). They paid £3.2 million in cash and loan stock for the prepurchase; in 1961 Selincourt had paid £600,000. The reason given by Stormgard for the sales was that Frank Usher highlighted the over-representation of the Selincourt Group in the market for occasion wear.

The Group changed its year end to 31 March to take better account of the seasonal nature of the clothing business. The results for the 15 months to March 1986 showed sharply increased pre-tax profits of £734,000 on a turnover of £42 million. The pre-tax figure took account of £141,000 compensation paid to former directors, but also included a contribution of £600,000 profit from Frank Usher. A £4.7 million rights issue during the year had reduced borrowings, but £4 million of stock writedowns and the closure costs were included in the final figures.

In the new fabric and nets grouping, J. H. Walker Ltd and Saluki Fur Fabrics Ltd continued the policy of concentrating on the supply of higher value-added quality fabrics. They achieved stronger sales than previously. New products had been developed for the sports, leisurewear and consumer products markets. Filigree Textiles Ltd produced results which were not so encouraging. However, this was largely due to a depressed market and low margins. The Board planned to strengthen the Company's position in the market by increasing the design effort and rationalising the existing product range.

In the lace and knitwear grouping, E. and A. Richards Ltd saw a marked improvement in turnover and profitability. Consequently, there was a substantial investment in increased production capacity in the knitwear division to meet rising demand and the lace division was directed to the quality end of the lingerie market.

In the garments and accessories division, Taylor Merrymade Ltd increased sales, largely of jackets and skirts, to its major customer Marks and Spencer. To enhance its market opportunities, it strengthened its design team and invested in new production equipment to maximise material utilisation. Concord Fastener Industries Ltd performed satisfactorily, although narrow margins affected profits. The sale of the loss making trimmings division, together with a new product range, was expected to contribute to improved performance in the following period. Jacqmar plc had reported poor trading results in September 1985. Losses had been attributed to an inadequate product range and the failure of the Company to realise the potential of its brand name in the market place. Accordingly, steps were taken to develop a limited range of new products in the upper end of the market and to strengthen branding and hence customer recognition.

In the depleted fashion area, Garlaine maintained its market position. The loss of sales of the Tricosa range was offset by sales of other collections which the Company produced or distributed such as Parigi, Alternatives, Les Aris, Les Lunis, Liola, and Giovannozzi. Market demand for the autumn/winter 1985 ranges was extremely encouraging. However, sales of the spring/summer 1986 range, sold in January to March, were disappointing. This was attributed to poor weather at the beginning of the year and the reduced number of American tourists to Britain. Garlaine Australia had relied heavily for past success on its distribution contract with Mondi. When the German company decided to terminate this agreement, the new Selincourt directors decided to close the Australian operation completely.

The transition period of change and consolidation was over. The new structure placed profit responsibility firmly in the hands of divisional management. Central overheads were reduced, while excessive working capital levels were being tackled. The design team had been expanded and strengthened, capital investment had been directed to areas which could expand into new markets or give improvements in cost effectiveness or product quality.

The Board considered that with a sound balance sheet and the people and products to succeed, the newly rationalised Selincourt Group was poised to take full advantage of any opportunities in the market place.

□ *The Later Years*

At the time of Stormgard's takeover of the Selincourt Group in 1985, prospects looked very promising. Selincourt's management had managed to overcome the problems facing the Company in the early 1980s and was looking forward to strong profits. This optimistic outlook was further enhanced by the promise of the design and marketing flair that Stormgard's managerial team could bring to Selincourt.

But the great hopes that both sets of management had at the time of the takeover failed to materialise. In June, Stormgard unveiled a dire set of results for the year to 31 March 1987, in which profits of £734,000 the previous year turned into losses of £4.67 million.

It has been suggested that Jennifer d'Abo found it difficult to transfer her marketing and design skills from stationery to clothes and textiles. In addition, there was a £239,000 write off at Selincourt, the result of inefficiency according to Stormgard's new Chairman, John Murray. Of Stormgard's £4.67 million losses, stock provisions contributed £2.1 million, £1.6 million of which came from the fashion sector of the Group.

As a result of these disappointing figures Stormgard underwent a severe disposal programme, accompanied by the departure of several key executives, including d'Abo. Following the sale of its stake in Frank Usher in 1986, Stormgard sold Taylor Merrymade and the lace and lingerie manufacturing business along with the fabrics and nets division, comprising Filigree Textiles, J. H. Walker and Saluki Fur Fabrics.

These sales represented the end of the era of problems that followed the acquisition of Selincourt. The businesses sold had been loss makers and highly capital intensive. What remains is a spread of furnishing fabrics, knitwear and accessories companies that are capable of generating profits from a much reduced cost base, together with useful tax losses.

Following Stormgard's disposal programme, the Company was comprised of a healthy portfolio upon which to build. Stormgard returned to profit in the six months to 30 September 1988, making £203,000 before tax. In February 1989, it announced that it intended to recommend a payment of a 0.1 pence final dividend in the year to 31 March, the first dividend payment to shareholders for 25 years.

This was the end of an era which was marked by lack of focus, lack of economies of scale, and poor management. Apart from the Cole years, the events which led to the Group's demise seem to have rolled inexorably towards disaster.

CHAPTER 5

Growth Strategies for the Niche Competitor

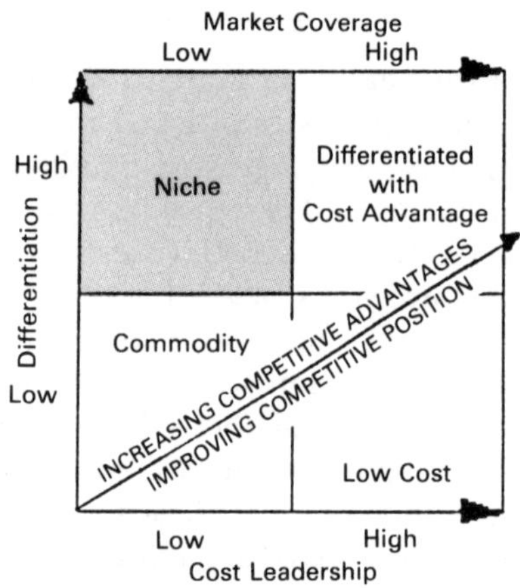

Chapters 3 and 4 analysed the different types of strategies that enable a firm to compete for the mainstream market and develop as a major force in the industry. In this chapter, attention is turned to niche marketing, where the focus remains narrow and specialised in one or perhaps two segments of the market. The company's task is to develop a position in a specialised segment as a strong force in that narrow market, and involves entering segments that are too small or specialised to attract large competitors.

The niche positioning may be an end in itself, or it may be a means to establish a wedge in a larger market. In the latter situation, the niche is the basis for developing a broader flanking strategy into the mainstream market. It is important to distinguish between small brands and companies that have a small share of the mass market and those that have a specialised niche. Davidson suggests questions which help to clarify the distinction:

- Is the niche or segment recognised by end users and distributors or is it a myth?
- Is the niche product distinctive and does it appeal strongly to a particular group of consumers?
- Does the product have a premium price positioning and above average profit in the market?[1]

It is also possible to hold a niche position with a low-price product if it is distinctive and appeals strongly to a particular customer group. Examples include the low-cost locally based solicitor or accountant who services a small local market or a specific industry. A colleague, who specialises as a marketing consultant to the arts industry in the UK, has found a way to service this industry profitably, which is always short of funds, at a cost below normal consulting rates. This is a niche position.

An American study of successful low-share businesses reveals four characteristics which these companies share.

1 They carefully segment their market and select segments where their own

strengths are most highly valued and where large competitors are unlikely to compete.

2 They use research and development funds efficiently by channelling efforts selectively into cost reduction and low-cost innovations.
3 They think small and are content to remain small, with an emphasis on profit rather than market share, and specialisation rather than diversification. They actively take steps to limit growth and diversify cautiously.
4 The chief executive has a pervasive influence on nearly all aspects of company operations, providing the driving force for competitive action.[2]

Some niche marketers, however, having low market shares, are large companies that have developed the skills of operating with many small-volume products. Three large firms that are skilful exponents of niche marketing are Avon, American Express and First Direct Bank.

Clifford and Cavanagh, in their study of American's high-growth mid-size companies, which included discussions with entrepreneurs, extensive statistical analysis of strategic practices and performance and analysis of a diverse range of case studies, report five strategic traits:

1 A focus on *how* to compete as a low-share niche competitor.
2 Emphasis on innovation.
3 Skill at creating and serving niches defined by customers' needs.
4 Ability to identify and build on distinctive strengths.
5 Recognition that the *value* of a product or service, not just its price, spells success.[3]

One way in which a niche competitor can compete is by means of a guerrilla strategy, which comprises a number of elements:

- the use of surprise and in some instances stealth, so that their presence is unknown to large competitors;
- flexibility, allowing speed and providing a moving target; and
- concentration of attacks on ground favourable to the 'guerrilla' company.[4]

This involves attacking a competitor's weak product, his position with a specific distributor, or a small geographical area.

Most of Europe's several hundred thousand small businesses are 'backyarders' operating with low overheads and a small workforce, and concentrating on a localised market. They use guerrilla tactics to survive in the market place. Their narrow niche may be:

- geographical focus;
- demographic focus;
- specific industry focus;
- single product focus (eg. industrial roller doors); or
- positioning at the high or low end of the market.

Ries and Trout propose three principles of guerrilla warfare:

1. Find a segment of the market small enough to defend, so that the firm can be leader of the segment.
2. No matter how successful you become, do not act like the leader. Remain small, flexible and specialised.
3. Be prepared to withdraw from a market instantly. Flexibility of market targeting is required, so that aggressive large resourced competitors can be avoided.[5] It also avoids the prospect of being tied to narrow segments that are in long term decline.

Focus of effort on one regional area is a prevalent strategy for small businesses in Europe because of distances between capital city markets and between city and provincial/rural markets. This is the 'large fish in the small pond' approach and provides regional dominance opportunities for small firms.

The more fragmented the market structure and the less differentiated the product or service, the more difficult it is to find viable market niches. Barriers to entry and scale requirements may also be limiting factors for niche marketing. Conditions favouring viable niche positions include market segmentation in large markets, scope for differentiation, concentration of a few dominant competitors and moderate barriers to entry.

In each of the three sections that follow, growth strategies of niche competitors are analysed in different market and competitive conditions.

Section 1 considers niche strategies in a static or declining market segment in which the niche competitor holds a dominant position.

In Section 2 the issues related to growth strategies for regional brands are explored.

Section 3 addresses the issue of competing against heavily resourced competitors in a growing market.

■ Section 1: Competitive Infiltration Strategies

Much of marketing's focus, reinforced by the high profile of leader marketers such as McDonald's, IBM and Budget (Rental Cars), is on strategies for rapidly penetrating the market, supported by large marketing expenditures in advertising, sales effort and promotion. By far the largest number of companies operating in Europe, however, adopt quite different marketing strategies, based on the premise of gradual, progressive growth in the market place. Most of these firms are relatively small in both financial resources and staff, although many medium size and even large companies in industrial markets and service industries also adopt this marketing approach.

Infiltration Strategies

An infiltration strategy is associated with a slow, but increasing, rate of sales and market share growth and supported by a commensurate build-up of marketing effort. This is contrasted with the rapid penetration strategy in Figure 5.1. Trends in marketing effort associated with these strategies are shown in Figure 5.2.

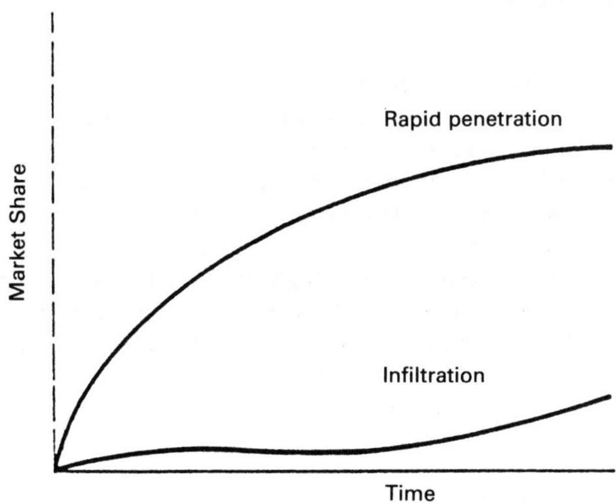

Figure 5.1 Share trends

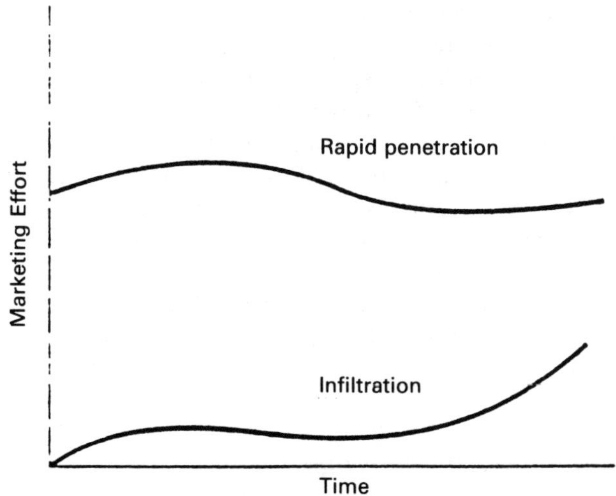

Figure 5.2 Marketing effort trends

A 'market skimming' pricing strategy may appear to be similar to an infiltration strategy, but this represents only one variant. The positioning of the product or the company using an infiltration stragey, may range from the premium to the low end of the market. The essence of infiltration strategy is that it has a relatively low market impact and aims to excite minimal attention of competitors in the market.

■ Strategic Issues

A range of strategic issues face small and medium-sized firms adopting infiltration strategies in the European environment. These result from either the need or desire for change or growth in their industries. For instance, the result of the dramatic slump in the British vehicle manufacturing industry in the 1980s forced the rationalisation and restructuring of car companies, the auto accessory suppliers and the producers for the after-sales market. This forced many small parts and accessories manufacturers to change their strategies in order to survive. In the high-tech electronics industry, there are many small companies seeking rapid and substantial growth. The relevant issues that need to be addressed by these firms and integrated as part of an effective competitive strategy, are different from those experienced by large national and multi-national operations.

□ *Financial Resources*

This factor limits the scope of activities and raises the financial risk to the overall business of any strategy that involves a substantial commitment of funds and management resources.

Concentration of resources in support of one or more specialised market niches, reduces the possibility of 'spreading resources too thinly' and becoming vulnerable to market and competitive forces.

The business definition of the firm should be in line with current and expected future resources and specified tightly enough to provide direction. If the weakness of large firms is to define themselves too narrowly, the vulnerability of small firms is to define themselves too broadly.

These constraints, however, are reduced in their impact if the small firm succeeds in obtaining a larger financial base. This can occur through joint venture arrangements, 'going public', or being taken over by a firm with large financial resources.

□ *Niche or Mainstream Competitor*

An issue facing the firm that wants to grow or one in an industry undergoing rationalisation or restructure, is whether it should seek to enter other specialist niches or mainstream market where the large competitors focus their operations.

Some alternative directions for competitive growth are shown in Figure 5.3. Strategy *X* is a two-phase strategy where phase 1 is designed to achieve dominance in one or two narrow segments of the market and phase 2 involves a move into the mainstream market against the market leader. Strategy *Z* is also a two-phase plan to compete in the main market segments against the market leader. Phase 1 is an infiltration strategy into the main segments of the market.

Phase 2 extends this strategy to confront the market leader by adopting aggressive marketing strategies.

Strategy *Y* is a relatively high-risk strategy for the smaller firm in moving from its narrow market aggressively against the major competitors in the mainstream market.

All three strategies pose the risk of being 'caught in the middle'. This is a position of high vulnerability, where the firm may be attacked by competitors in its original specialised markets and at the same time by the major competitors in the market.

As a firm moves from an infiltration to a rapid penetration strategy, its exposure to competitive reactions increases, and it is important that the firm is able to defend the markets in which it has its major strengths and from which most of its profit is generated. Marketing strategies need to be designed to meet the needs of individual segments and the competitive position that exists in these segments.

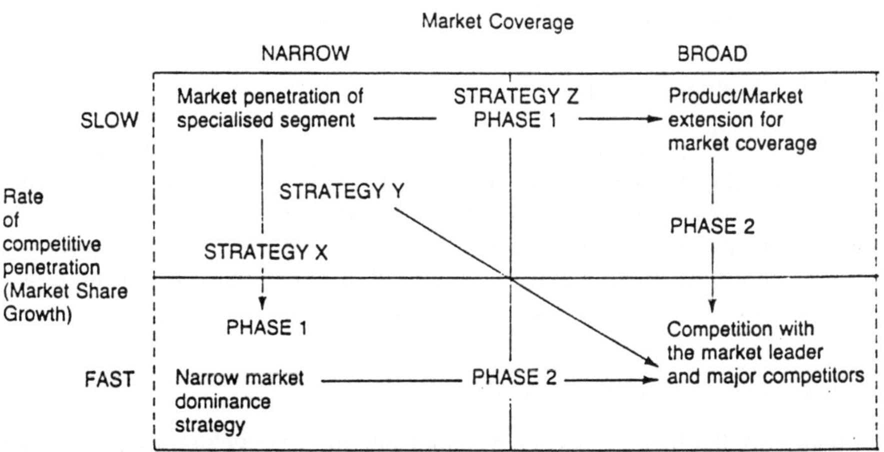

Figure 5.3 Alternative directions for competitive growth for the small specialised firm

□ *Strategic Market Information*

As a firm grows, it tends to lose the 'close to the market' advantage it had when it was a small company with a natural feel for customer needs and perceptions. Growth brings with it operational problems and the growing firm requires a data base of strategic information that enables it to analyse, assess and develop more formalised marketing strategies. Data such as market size and trends, market share, customer perceptions, competitive intelligence and product/ market profitability, become essential for increasing the chances of success in 'the big league'. An understanding of end-user requirements as well as those of intermediaries, needs to be incorporated into competitive strategies.

Most large companies are developing electronic delivery and management systems that enable them to monitor company-client transactions more closely – for example, electronic banking, electronic scanning devices in the grocery trade, and direct computer links with suppliers and customers. Smaller firms have to maintain more tangible communication links and conduct different types of market research that identifies the size, scope and competitive implications of new opportunity areas.

□ *Product/Service Delivery and Organisation*

The successful small firm has a product/service delivery system which meets customer needs. As it grows, there is frequently a fall in product delivery and customer service and the task is to reorganise and restructure a larger business in order to deliver satisfactorily. This often involves changes in the corporate culture, the addition of new people and the loss of established staff who cannot accept or cope with the changed operation of the business from a close-knit family firm to a more formalised corporate structure.

□ *Change of Strategic Position*

Sometimes, the evolution of growth in a small firm changes its strategic position in the market. A niche specialist may progressively become a mainstream competitor and challenger to the market leader. Competitive strategies need to change to cope with this new position. Here, if a too-narrow focus on traditional segments exists, the small firm can miss opportunities and be vulnerable to attack from large competitors.

□ *Integrated Marketing Strategy*

For many smaller firms, a key issue is the challenge of developing an integrated marketing strategy for the first time. This requires consideration of marketing objectives and fitting together the elements of the marketing mix. Key issues, such as the task of developing credibility and an identity in the wider market, determining price positioning, product innovation and new channels of distribution, must be integrated within the competitive marketing strategy.

■ Competitive Strategy Directions

The small to medium firm with limited financial resources has a number of competitive strategies it can adopt. Figure 5.4 suggests the type of strategies that are relevant, taking account of the most important strategic issues raised in the previous section.

The competitive strategy matrix does not suggest all possible combinations, but seeks to provide broad options for strategic direction. The strategic dimensions in this matrix are:

- rate of competitive penetration: slow–fast;
- degree of market coverage: narrow–broad;
- centre of customer focus: intermediary–end-user;
- financial resources relative to competitors: limited–substantial

There are many possible combinations of these factors, but Figure 5.4 indicates four broad strategies where the combination of factors frequently appear in practice. The firm may operate in any one of the boxes shown in Figure 5.4, or may move from one box to another. As firms move from the left side of the chart to the right side, the risk of being 'caught in the middle' increases as does the need for more substantial financial resources to support the new strategies adequately.

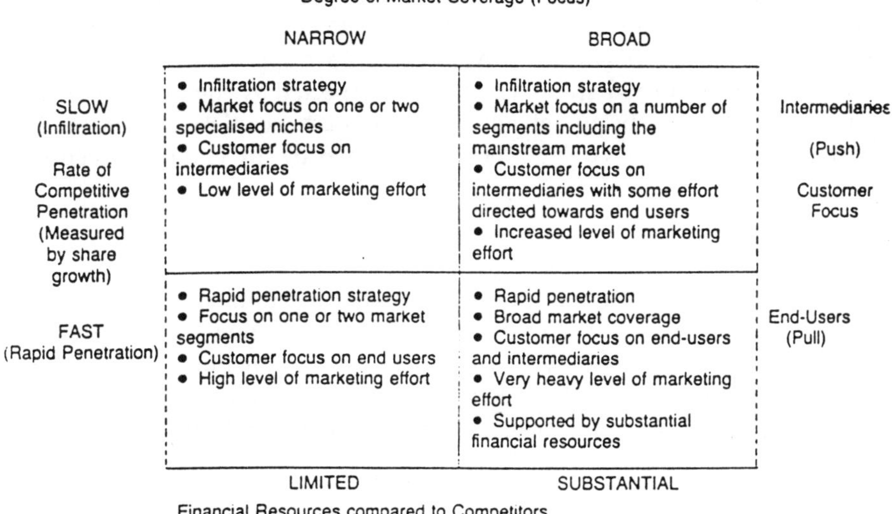

Figure 5.4 Competitive strategy directions for a defined market

■ Case Study 18: Europeanising a Medium-size Company

■ Dominating Niches in the European Chemicals Market*

Brent Chemicals International (BCI) supply speciality formulated chemical and associated systems to solve industrial customers' problems in either their production or maintenance process. It concentrates on a limited number of specific customer industries which currently comprise:

- Industrial metal finishing – the treatment of metal surfaces prior to filling, painting etc.
- Aerospace – the maintenance and non-destructive testing of airframe and aeroengine systems and components.
- Electronics – wet chemical manufacturing processes for printed circuit board and semi-conductor manufacture.
- Inks and coatings – primarily for the packaging industry.
- Printing pre-press services – ie. graphic design and photopolymer flexographic printing plates and rollers for the packaging conversion industry.

Figure 5.5 shows the current breakdown of sales by industry served.

The Company operates internationally, with 45 per cent of sales originated in continental Europe (Figure 5.6). Annual sales are approximately £120m. In world terms BCI is a small quoted company, respected by their customers and competitors alike for the quality of their products, people and service. The corporate goal is to achieve £500m of annual sales by the end of the century.

■ Brief History

In the Second World War, the Brent Manufacturing Company Limited, as it was, worked with Rolls Royce to develop a non-destructive testing system for the new jet engine. This system used a dye in a penetrating fluid to identify pin-prick sized faults invisible to the naked eye in critical engine components. Such faults would cause engine failure in service. Critical parts for the Merlin engine,

* This case is based on material provided by Stephen Cuthbert, Chief Executive of Brent Chemicals International, published in *Long Range Planning*, Volume 24, No. 2, pp. 61–6 and is used with his kind permission.

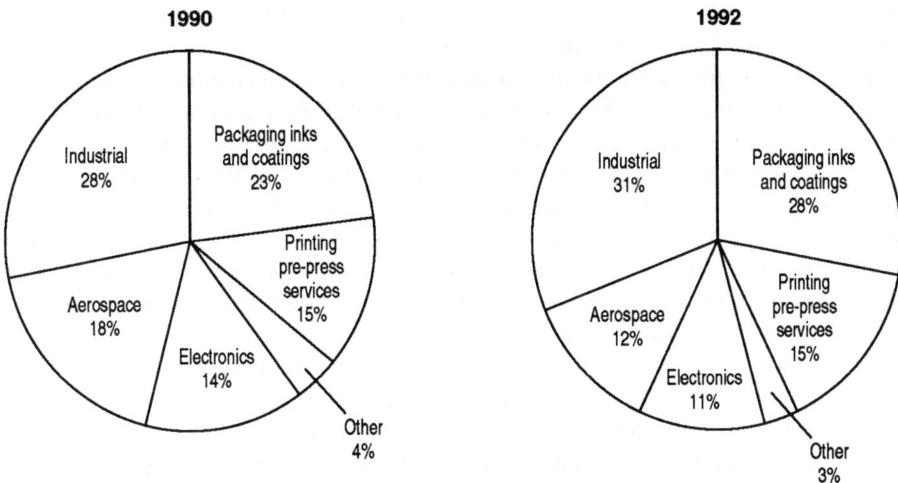

Figure 5.5 Brent Chemicals International plc sales, 1990 (and 1992 after restructuring)

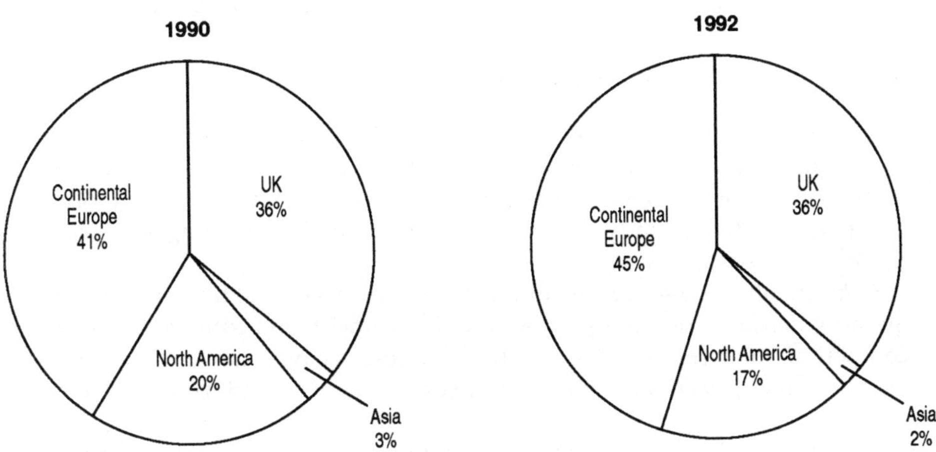

Figure 5.6 Brent Chemicals International plc geographical analysis of sales, 1990 (and 1992)

an important element in the battle for the skies, were also tested using the system, once it had been developed successfully.

Without knowing it, the Company had entered an international market. After the war, British-built aircraft powered by Rolls Royce engines went into service throughout the world. With the engines went the maintenance manuals with BCI's 'Ardrox' product range specified for engine cleaning and testing. A whole series of licensees, distributors and small joint venture companies were set up by Brent Chemicals to service this business in Europe and the major Commonwealth countries.

In 1970 this network was rationalised. Whilst a long term strategy, a suitable structure and profit centre responsibility were being developed in the early 1970s, disaster nearly struck when many European Air Forces began to re-equip with American-built fighters. With the planes came the maintenance manuals with few, if any, Ardrox processes approved. (To maintain the maker's warrantee, an operator could only follow approved maintenance systems). With customer support the Company set about obtaining the necessary American approvals, opening a small greenfield US operation for that purpose. Ultimately it was successful. Today there is a full and wide range of aerospace maintenance products approved for and in use throughout the world. Equally BCI had learned a lesson. The Company was operating in a global niche market, and to survive it had to operate globally too.

Preparing BCI for the single European market meant utilising the multi-national team of managers, sales and technical teams and facilities that were originally developed to support the aerospace activities, and on to which the industrial metal finishing and electronics activities had been grafted. Inks, coatings and pre-press services activities were developed separately in parallel. The company has in recent years grown largely through acquisition.

■ A Clear Focused Strategy

Ten years ago, the Company's strategic plans were little more than a combination of forward extrapolations of past financial results and declarations of corporate intent. With the help of a number of business schools the Company has significantly improved its management's planning and strategic thinking abilities and skills.

Strategic plans now address future customers' needs and how to fulfil them, quantify markets and their growth rates by segment, and contain comparative competitor analyses based on critical success factors, gap analysis, SWOT analyses and directional policy matrices. Objectives and goals are clearly defined.

As a decentralised Group, planning is done both top down and bottom up with the Chief Executive buying in to an operating group's plan, or amending it with them where appropriate by discussion and negotiation.

This process was central to a decision to dispose of two businesses representing in 1989 19 per cent of group sales (Figure 5.7). Automotive body pretreatment and food and beverage plant sanitizing chemical businesses were limited to their respective UK markets with little prospects of successful overseas expansion.

Operating in mature markets with large market shares, they both also had limited upside potential. The corporate strategy demanded that only customers on a global basis (in aerospace and electronics businesses) or at least on a pan-European basis (industrial metal finishing, inks and coatings and pre-press

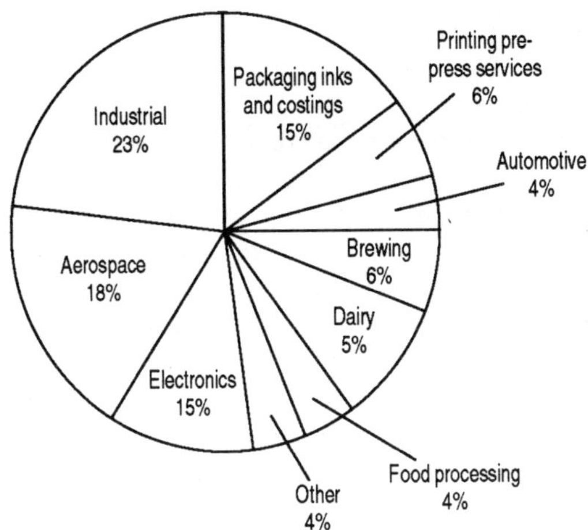

Figure 5.7 Brent Chemicals International plc sales, 1989 pre-restructuring

services businesses) were serviced. The two UK only businesses were succcesfully sold and the £30m realised was invested in building five core business areas, with above average growth prospects.

□ *A Sharp Focus and a Pan-European Structure*

Until 1990, BCI operated in Europe through a series of country-based operating companies which were responsible for the sales of a broad range of products in their own country. Since more and more of the major customers were operating on a pan-European basis; it was decided that the major part of the European business should be restructured into three strategic business units – industrial, aerospace and electronics. Each strategic business unit operates with its own sales, marketing and technical team across Europe. Manufacturing, distribution, finance, information technology and legal functions also operate Europe-wide, reporting to the head of the Brent Europe organisation.

For management purposes, country-based operating companies ceased to exist, although they are still needed for fiscal and legal reasons.

The reorganisation has meant that all managers are forced to think on at least a European scale, and operate as part of a European-wide team.

The former Italian general manager sits on Brent Europe's policy board as a non-executive director to provide a continental perspective. Product development for industrial activities is under the direction of an Italian who has relocated to the UK and aerospace product development for the European market is carried out in France by an all-French team.

Sales people continue to speak Catalan in Barcelona and Flemish in Flanders, but they are now part of specialist European-wide teams focusing on specific markets and applications.

Language communication presents a challenge. Whilst English is the Group's working language, documents are circulated more and more in French, German, Italian and Spanish. A few years ago, all documentation was in English, but loss of meaning and nuance for non-English staff has meant that much more information is translated for improved communication.

The Company specifically looks for language skills when recruiting at senior level. Some senior operating managers speak four continental European languages fluently, and all the senior management group speak, or are learning, a continental European language.

Communications difficulties and cultural differences do exist, but they are dealt with within the organisation and not directly with the customer. This results in giving better customer service, as European or world-wide technical information is made available to any customer in any location, in his or her local language, with any communications difficulties absorbed internally.

One practical point which may be of interest to those studying a similar structure is that too much detailed information was 'pulled' into Brent Europe's UK headquarters in the initial days of operations. This slowed down communications and response times. As the organisation settled down and managers gained confidence in their new line colleagues and new systems and structures, more and more information was being processed and acted on locally.

Interestingly, the two groups that have made the most progress under the new organisation are the oldest and the youngest, aerospace and electronics. The well-established aerospace group has a workforce used to operating in a global market with high inter-dependance between colleagues and customers in various areas of the world. Also, they are for the most part long-serving employees who have known and worked with their colleagues throughout Europe for a considerable time. They regard it as natural and logical to work as a team concentrating on the aerospace market.

The European electronics business has been in existence for less than a decade. It is comparatively small in a new industry which regards national borders as irrelevant barriers in technology terms. The benefits of more tightly co-ordinated operations are obvious to all within the small team. They have risen to the challenge and are enjoying the benefits of operating as a group instead of reporting to non specialist (in their terms) country general managers as in the past.

In contrast, the toughest transition is in the industrial metal finishing area, by far the largest of the three strategic business units; the product range is vast, with some 4500 product pack sizes! In the past each country's sales force focused on different market segments and sold the products it did best with. Until recently due to now defunct licence arrangements, a major part of the product range was only sold in the UK. BCI has a 50 per cent share of the

UK market with an expanding but small market share on the continent, and in the United States.

Product rationalisation (the target was to reduce the product pack size by 66 per cent) and a focus on defined priority areas throughout Europe were seen as essential. Specific agreement to a co-ordinated approach to a number of key market sub-segments on which the sales and technical teams now focus took longer to achieve than planned. Including the planning period, it took a year to effect the necessary changes, and see the benefits begin to flow through.

The new structure is outlined in Figure 5.8. Packaging inks and coatings operations have taken a different route towards the single European market. Liquid inks and gravure applied coatings are sold throughout Europe by the UK and Swiss-based operations, whilst water-based coatings and laminating adhesives for sheet fed work are marketed throughout the continent by the German-based operation. Sales of these products in the UK are handled by the UK operation. To some extent this is a 'half way house', but the sub-segments of the overall market, the associated technologies and the printing methods themselves are distinct. Specialist sales and technical people travel throughout Europe to provide specialist customer service.

Rapid growth, both organic and by acquisition, has resulted in considerable awareness and recognition of BCI's activities in the packaging and graphic arts ('PGA') area throughout Europe. The PGA group has cleverly endorsed this message with skilful use of multilingual public relations, videos, and advertising literature produced to a high standard.

Professionally produced multilingual promotional material is now an important sales tool to obtain the attention of industrial customers and the food

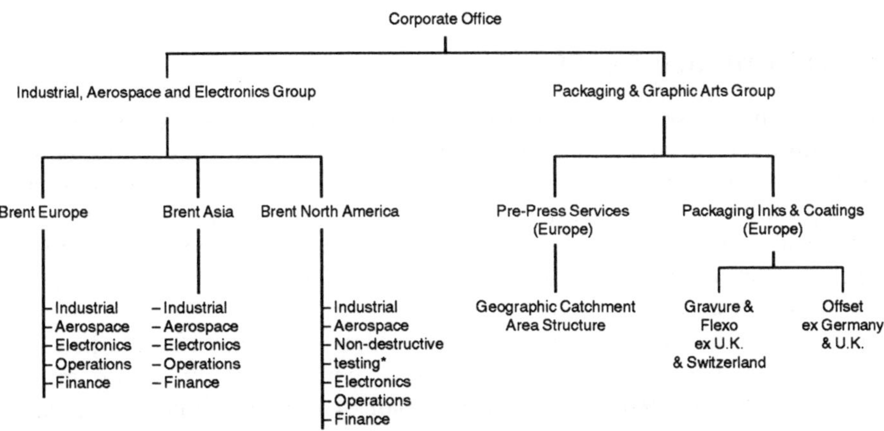

Figure 5.8 Brent Chemicals International plc current structure

Note: Outside North America non-destructive testing sales are largely the responsibility of the Aerospace Groups

packaging sector. Rather surprisingly, the Company and a number of competitors neglected this area for a considerable time.

Because of the need to discuss artwork and graphic design face to face with the ultimate client, the pre-press services sales forces operate within travelling distance of their customers' studios and production facilities. Computer aided graphic design systems are technically capable of being linked together across Europe, but this is not yet commercially justifiable. So pre-press operations operate on the basis of regional centres with satellite branches close to customer clusters, essentially, but not entirely, on a country basis.

To provide an international service BCI has expanded this area by acquisition so that it can now cover a large part of the northern European market with facilities throughout the UK, in Denmark, Holland and Belgium. A chocolate bar wrapper can be produced in the UK with the outer bag wrapper in The Netherlands and the carton in Germany – all must match the standard design and colour scheme. Through its network of companies, BCI ensures a high quality printing plate does the required job, regardless of where the packaging material is actually produced, a good example of satisfying a customer's need on a pan-European basis.

■ The Effect of the 1991–2 Recession

The recession of the early 1990s hit Brent's core industrial markets hard, resulting in a significant fall in profitability. This situation was aggravated by the closure and extensive rationalisation and redundancy costs initiated the previous year. The poor results, however, were partly offset by a rights issue in late 1991 which raised £15.6 million, and produced a strong balance sheet with minimal borrowings.

■ Performance in 1992–3

Building on the solid base of its business in its key markets, aerospace, electronics, industrial, packaging inks and pre-press, Brent's range of speciality chemicals is impressive, including printing inks and chemicals used in aircraft de-icing and essential maintenance, metal finishing and printed circuit boardmaking. With this product experience and expertise, and available funds, the company's position in 1992 indicated the potential to expand and benefit from an eventual market upturn.

The realignment away from low-growth, predominantly UK, markets to a more broadly based international business, with geographical and market spread, is well founded. With well over half of Brent's profits generated by overseas operations, benefiting from sterling's slide, the company has wisely focused on growth areas with long-term opportunities. A key market is the United States, together with the small but growing South-East Asian market, through a wide distribution network, and with contributions from a weaker continental Europe.

■ Expansion by Acquisition

In order to capitalise on the market potential, Brent's strategy for market development has targeted, for acquisition, companies with complementary product/service offerings. Its purchase of Hebro Chemie, German metal finishers, CWC, and Chemical Systems Inc. in the USA, supplying the north American metal finishing industry, will provide synergistic benefits within the Industrial Systems Division.

■ Internal Development

Increased research and development spending and a three-year £20 million capital investment programme provides the Group with an efficient manufacturing technology which meets high environmental standards and promotes strategic advantage. Tighter management direction following the rationalisation programme, including strict overhead controls, a streamlined management structure, manufacturing efficiencies and other cost savings helps to maximise the company's strengths.

The consequence of these measures and market policies is that the figures for 1992 indicated a good recovery from the recessionary dip in 1991. Sales rose from £100 million to £119.8 million, with organic sales increasing by 5% and acquisitions-based turnover contributing 12%. The company's improved performance in 1992 reflected the wisdom of this strategy of expanding internationally by steady organic growth and selected acquisitions in the chosen market sectors.

■ The Way Ahead

Significant investment will be made in the development of environmentally friendly chemicals and the reduction in harmful waste by-products. In anticipation of EC restrictions and strict emission controls likely to be in force by the end of the decade, Brent are working with their customers, in a partnership approach, to find environmentally effective solutions and improvements, demanded by consumers and customers.

Steady growth over the last five years, and a successful riding out of the early 1990s, has put Brent in a strong financial and market position.

Much, however, remains to be achieved, including:

- the creation of a true multi-national team of managers;
- the appointment of Europeans to the Board of Directors;
- the creation of the appropriate pan-European integrated information systems; and
- the ultimate establishment of world-wide business groups, probably first in aerospace. The North American and Far East operations mirror the European structure with this possibility in mind.

The structure, the culture and the focus of the business enables Brent to serve its customers throughout the single European market. In some market areas, there is already a Europe 'sans frontiers'. Other market sectors lag behind, but restructuring and realignment will enable the company to meet its customers' changing requirements and will prove to be more than a match for its competitors. Continuing to stay one step ahead of the customers and two steps ahead of the competition is one of the keys to success and an integral part of Brent's business philosophy.

In addition, the shift in emphasis, from a product based company to the supply of services and non-chemical products, has prompted a change of a visible nature. In 1993, the company's name was changed to Brent International plc. to reflect, more appropriately, the company's future market direction and commitment.

■ Section 2: Expanding Regional Brands

The cost of product development, distribution and advertising is high and rising for new international brands. The failure rate of new brands is high;[6] some companies, such as Kellogg, have a policy of test marketing any new product. Although this reduces risk and potential failure, it adds to the time and cost of new brand introduction.

An alternative to introducing an entirely new brand is to develop an existing brand, as has been done by Rexona in developing Pears, a well established but small soap brand, into a family shampoo brand. Another option is to expand a brand from a strong regional base. In the beer market, Tetley Bitter has been expanded from its original base in West Yorkshire to be a leading brand not only in the UK, but also in international markets.

■ Regional Markets and Regional Brands

Visitors to European countries frequently think of the inhabitants of any one country as a homogenous population. But, each of the regions in each country exhibit differences in climate, culture and attitudes which have fostered the growth and prosperity of home-grown companies marketing mainly to one or two local regional markets. In the UK, for example, the major grocery retailer Sainsburys dominates the South East, whereas Kwik-Save dominates the North West. In almost every industry, in all the countries of Europe, strong regional brands exist and have been traditionally preferred in their home markets.

■ Success Factors of Regional Brands

The basis of success of regional brands lies in their focus on local needs and the concentrated support given to the brand in its narrow geographic market.

Personal contacts, parochial support and knowledge of the market by being 'close to customers' are all important attributes that enhance the acceptance of regional brands. Many have the advantage of being the first product or service in that market and have a 'generic' position in the customers' minds. For instance, Federation beer has dominated the UK North Eastern beer market for generations.

Other regional brands may have been developed later, but have established a specialty position in the market, meeting the needs of a narrow market segment.

■ Expansion Options

Expansion of regional brands to national or international brand status, requires the consideration of alternative growth options. These will be evaluated with reference to a range of factors, including these listed here.

Cost
The cost of expansion and availability of funds will influence the method of expansion.

Product Range
Is the product part of a wider range of products or is it to stand alone?

Selling and Distribution Network
Is there an existing selling and distribution network for national expansion of the brand?

Market Coverage or Focus
Does the product have a high-volume mainstream market position, or is it a specialty positioning with low volume and margins that will influence the growth strategy?

Economics of Production and Product Quality Requirements
The requirements of production demand an assessment of quality constraints and economies of scale factors, as well as location of markets, freight costs and product differentiation needs for different regional markets. Analysis of these factors will determine questions such as centralisation or decentralisation of production.

Financial Backing
A large national company with substantial resources will usually seek rapid growth and integration of the brand within a range of products. A smaller, less resourced firm will usually adopt a more conservative expansion programme. Options such as licensing or franchising may be considered by the smaller organisation.

■ Strategic Issues

The marketing strategy for expansion of regional brands should address a number of strategic issues, some of which stem from their original positioning.

□ *Market Positioning*

The original positioning and heritage of the brand is often its greatest strength. If this can be tied to national market trends and identification of national consumer issues, it represents a strong base for expansion. Tetley's Yorkshire Bitter represented all that was traditional and best about beer drinking at a time when traditional brewing values were being rapidly eroded. It was, then, comparatively easy for Allied Breweries to play on its regional strengths to a national audience. In food products especially, the strength of a particular region is identified in the market positioning of the regional brand. Examples include Buxton mineral waters, Bakewell tart, Cheddar cheese, Holsten Pils, and so on.

The marketing strategy should initially build on the inherent strength and identification of the region as its basis. This means that the image of the region will overlay the positioning of the brand and both the opportunities and limitations that this imposes must be analysed.

□ *Product Quality Control*

Substantial increases in production raise the risk of loss of quality control. Variability in quality and shortages arising from production problems can quickly lose credibility with distributors and end-users.

□ *Mainstream versus Specialty Position*

A decision needs to be made about positioning the brand in the mainstream or in a niche position. Although this decision affects all elements of the marketing mix, it also affects the scope for achieving differing positionings in different markets. A niche positioning in each region provides scope for modification in packaging, pricing, promotion and distribution of the brand. Usually, a mainstream positioning needs heavy and consistent marketing support, requiring economies of scale in packaging, advertising, pricing and distribution, implying standardisation for all regions.

□ *Big versus Small Marketing Budget*

The size of marketing budget required depends on the strategy for expansion. While Castlemaine lager has used a large marketing budget to achieve national distribution, a product such as the board game, Trivial Pursuit, one of the cases included in this section, was introduced with little consumer advertising and achieved more than three million unit sales in Europe within five years.

Similarly, Frank Cooper's Oxford marmalade has expanded dramatically. This positioning is reinforced through its supply of jam for airline passengers travelling first class. Both companies have successfully adopted infiltration strategies supported by low budgets.

□ *Obtaining Distribution*

In the food industry, distribution is a major strategic issue. The dominance of a few retail chains serving the mass market in most European countries, places the balance of power with retailers. Standard requirements for manufacturers distributing in supermarkets, include brand advertising, promotional pricing, co-operative advertising, contributions and incentives for volume sales. Alternative channels require wholesalers to distribute to the fragmented structure of convenience stores, delicatessens, gourmet food shops and health food stores.

The structure and nature of the distribution system, whether it is company owned or independent, will provide opportunities and constraints for expanding regional brands. Trade-offs between consumers' objectives, distributors' requirements and firm's own objectives must be assessed. The types of factors to be considered in establishing channel relationships are shown in Figure 5.9. These relationships require management.

□ *Market Share Objectives*

Focus on the national market requires an analysis of the leading companies in the industry and the distribution channels to the markets, and will determine the most appropriate share objectives and competitive strategy. Weaknesses of the market leader in a particular region may suggest priorities for market penetration. Market structure may indicate a realistic share objective of 10 per cent to 15 per cent in each region rather than an attempt to achieve a 30 per cent share in one large market such as Paris or London.

■ Some Lessons

□ *Danger of Rapid Expansion*

Sometimes, the inherent strength of regional brands lies in their exclusivity, their limited availability and their origin in a small regional market. The mystique of Coors beer was lost when it undertook rapid geographic expansion from its Colorado base to neighbouring American states and to the large Californian market.[7] Quality and service suffered, and its image of exclusivity disappeared.

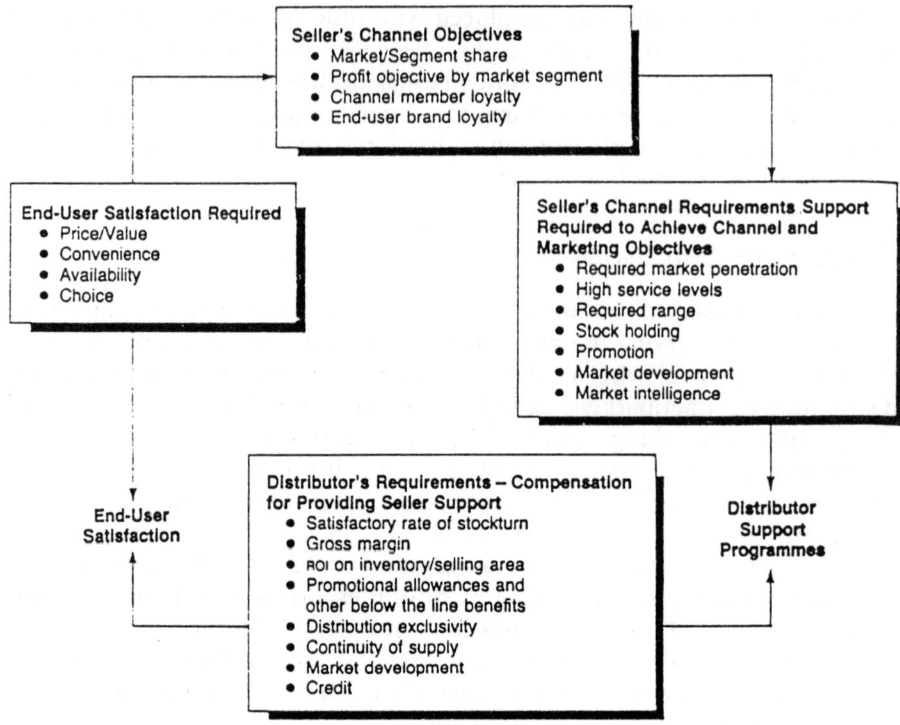

Figure 5.9 Distribution channel relationships

□ *Protect Home Base*

Another danger is for all effort and priority to go into expansion and give little attention to protecting the original market.

□ *Avoid Head-on Confrontation with the Regional Leader*

A fragmented, regionally based market structure often has strong local brands. It is difficult and risky to attack the regional leader head-on as part of an expansion strategy. Differentiated positioning aimed at flanking the local leader usually proves to be the most effective strategy.

□ *A Note on Taste*

In food products, taste is a differentiating attribute, and the relevance of this differs for the brand's original market and its new markets. For the original market, the taste is the basis of the brand, and careful consideration is required if it is to be changed to meet the needs of new larger markets. The experience of

Table 5.1 Infiltration Strategies and Competitor Types

Competitor Type	*Mainstream Competitor*	*Differentiated Specialist*	*Low Cost Specialist*
Strategic Concept	Superior performance/ premium price	Specialised performance/ premium price	Parity performance/ discount price
Entry Strategy Specifications	Premium priced product demonstrably superior in terms of performance Appeals to a relatively small segment of consumers Relatively low share of promotional expenditure in initial years Dual or selective distribution channels with initial emphasis on channel away from mainstream used by high volume competing brands	Premium priced product designed to satisfy specialised needs to a small segment of consumers Minimal share of promotional expenditure Selective distribution using a channel away from the mainstream distribution channel	Product priced at discount but with demonstrated parity performance Minimal share of promotional expenditure Selective distribution using the mainstream channel
Subsequent Strategy Specifications	Downward price repositioning in relation to high volume brands in an attempt to appeal to a larger number of consumers Increased share of promotional expenditure Emphasis on mainstream distribution channel with more extensive distribution	Maintain price premium in original channel of distribution but reposition downwards on price as distribution spreads to mainstream channels Modest increases in promotional expenditure, but with no attempt to compete with high volume brands Broaden distribution to include the major channel used by the product form	Downward repositioning on price while maintaining parity performance in relation to high volume brands Minimal share of promotional expenditure More extensive distribution

Table 5.2 Rapid Penetration Strategies and Competitor Types

Competitor Type	*Large Differentiated Market Leader*	*Large Differentiated Challenger*	*Large Low Cost Leader or Challenger*
Strategic Concept	*Market Dominance* Superior performance/ premium price	*Market Niche* Product/price positioning to specific segment	*Low Price* Lower performance/ discount price
Entry Strategy Specifications	Superior product priced at a premium Extensive distribution using one main channel Dominance share of promotional expenditure	Product/price positioning according to specific market opportunities identified. Pricing strategy may be premium, parity or discount according to product positioning and competitors' market positions Extensive distribution using the mainstream channel Share of promotional expenditure equal or near parity of market leader in the first year	Low and product with a price discount Extensive and/or intensive distribution Relatively low promotional effort directed towards point-of-sale promotion and price specialing; no theme advertising
Subsequent Strategy Specifications	New brand segmentation with downward price reposition-ing to nulify new competitors Intensify distribution Continued dominance of share of promotional expenditure	New brand segmentation (if the market is large enough to support a multiple band strategy and if the market is growing) Intensify distribution Maintain a significant share of promotional expenditure	Downward price repositioning and/or product quality improvement (single brand strategy) Intensify distribution

the Coca-Cola company, with a 'new' Coke is testimony to this point for large brands in traditional markets.[8] But opportunities exist for product variations in other markets to better suit the tastes of those consumers.

■ Alternative Market Penetration Strategies

Expansion of a regional brand into other regions effectively requires a new brand entry strategy for each new regional market. This may involve a progressive region by region expansion, or it may be a full-scale national launch. A variety of alternative penetration strategies were available and their choice will depend upon the type of company and its resources and the rate of penetration desired to achieve the strategic objectives.

Table 5.1, on page 279, provides guidelines for infiltration strategies for the mainstream competitor, the differentiated specialist and the low-cost specialist.

Entry strategy specifications indicate positioning and marketing mix factors during the market development phase, then subsequent strategy changes to broaden the market appeal to increase sales and market share.

Table 5.2 gives guidelines for rapid penetration strategies to be implemented by large companies positioned for mainstream differentiation, cost/price advantage or market niche.

■ Case Study 19: Firkin Pubs – A London Regional Brand

■ The Firkin Concept

Firkin Pubs were founded by a brewing entrepreneur David Bruce in London in 1980s. In a reaction against the policies and monopoly position of the major brewers, Bruce pioneered on-site micro-breweries producing traditional beers, served in a low key environment, targeting the independent student drinker and real ale aficionado. His success with his first pub in 1979 led to a slow expansion of these 'alternative' pubs within the London area over the next decade.

□ *How Did They Attract This Segment?*

Firstly, their product offer matched the consumers' needs. Secondly, they had no competition. No other pub offered the same benefits as Firkin – they had successfully differentiated themselves.

The pubs had on-site brewing facilities, which produced strong beers such as 'Dogbolter' and 'Kneetrembler', some of the strongest beers in London. The on-site brewing was also important – it put the 'real' back into real ales, and was so unique that it became an attraction in its own right.

This emphasis on authenticity was also reflected in the decor. Firkin pubs were unique in character – sparsely furnished, with plain wooden floors, and no jukeboxes, fruit machines or video games.

These machines were replaced by live music – generally a piano player. During the evening, everyone would join in a sing-song, adding to the party atmosphere.

One final difference compared to most pubs was that management really cared about the customer. David Bruce, the founder, spent a tremendous amount of time talking to the regulars, getting suggestions and asking for feedback.

To put all of this into perspective, in most parts of the UK, people who 'go down to the local' and, once there, 'ask for a pint of bitter', are essentially taking what is on offer, with no real thought to either product or location. Contrast that with Firkin customers, who travel some distance, and know exactly what pint they are going to drink once they get there.

So, David Bruce successfully differentiated his pubs; and he wrapped this all up in the cultivation of the Firkin concept. The term 'cultivation' is especially appropriate, because Bruce developed a cult following around his pubs by 'Firkinsing' each one:

- he incorporated the word 'Firkin' into each of the pub names;
- he developed a slogan for each pub;
- he put these slogans on a range of promotional goods;
- he introduced the Firkin pub crawl – a pint of 'Dog' at each Firkin pub; and
- he 'Firkinised' the management ... becoming more involved with their consumers.

This Firkinisation process was so successful that there was virtually no need for outside advertising – promotion was purely by word-of-mouth. For example, a family from East Germany, who, in their first ever journey outside their country, on being interviewed at Heathrow airport, placed a visit to Firkin pubs near the top of their itinerary, which proves how powerful Bruce's whole marketing mix had been.

■ The Stakis Years

In 1990, Bruce sold out the 11 pubs to the Midsummer Leisure group for €6 million, becoming a multi-millionaire in the process. In turn the company was sold on to European Leisure and finally to Stakis, Scottish-based hotel and leisure group. Under these various owners, the chain stood largely still, with little interest in expansion or concept development.

But just as times became tougher for the big national brewers in the UK, so they were for Firkin pubs. Firkin built much of its success on its uniqueness – offering on-site brewing, live music and a 'back-to-basics' atmosphere. By 1990 this was no longer novel. In addition, the static management appeared to be diluting some of the original 'Firkinism' – reducing on-site brewing to only a few sites, introducing video games, and paying less attention to consumer service. Firkin's position in 1990 is summarised in the SWOT analysis shown in Figure 5.10.

Stakis' management under increasing financial pressure looked to the pubs to generate cash, without regard for the differentiating factors that made them so successful in the 1980s.

□ *Strategy Options in 1990/1*

1 Though the London market is probably saturated, Firkin pubs are almost non-existent outside London – a market where Firkin would still be novel. There is therefore great potential in the rest of the UK.
2 If Firkin does not move into other geographical markets, others will. The establishment of a national chain of Firkin-like pubs will eventually threaten Firkin's London stronghold too.

□ *Growth Strategy*

Geographical expansion is imperative. The appeal of Firkin is not limited to London – as evidenced by the high proportion of non-Londoners amongst

Strengths	Weaknesses
Monopolies Commission hostile to big brewers	Dubious name may limit expansion opportunities
Strong and broad cult following	Management complacency
Strong cash flow	Erosion of Firkinism
Financial backing of Stakis Group	Poor location of current pubs
Opportunities	**Threats**
Increasing availability of licenced premises	Lack of direction under Stakis management
Guest beers	Loss of entrepreneurial management
Brewing of lager	Increasing competition from similar
Further growth in London?	Saturated London market?
High growth potential in rest of the UK	Risk of declining appeal of Firkin pubs (analogy of fads like skate boards, etc.)

Figure 5.10 Firkin Pubs SWOT analysis

current regulars. It is probable that consumer need in the rest of the country is similar to London. Opportunities for growth are:

Major Cities

Birmingham, Leeds, Nottingham and Edinburgh and similar cities are suggested. These towns all have large population pools – important, since Firkin only appeals to a segment of the market – and also universities, another strong catchment area. Sites may become available cheaply thanks to the Monopolies Commission, who have forced the major brewers to sell many of their tied houses.

Care should be taken to avoid over expansion in these cities. In addition, they must prevent the classic dip in profits (e.g. from increasing bureaucracy) taken by companies as they expand from small to medium sized enterprises.

The Company's initial success came from close management attention and reaction to consumer feedback. This should be maintained at the new sites – perhaps by using a franchise operation.

Firkin Guest Beers

Another Monopolies Commission proposal, now implemented, is the sales of a 'guest beer' in each pub. Firkin should market its beers to other pubs, while offering to take their beer in return. Note that the sale of a guest lager would also address a key weakness in Firkin's product range.

Foreign Markets

Longer term (once Firkin is established across the UK), foreign markets may prove promising. Sugguested markets are the US, where there is a strong interest in British culture, and continental Europe.

■ Allied Breweries; Future Growth Strategy

In 1991, a heavily debt-ridden Stakis group was forced to divest the fourteen strong Firkin chain for £7 million. In a massive swipe of irony, the Firkin group were acquired by Allied Breweries, (part of Allied-Lyons) one of the major brewers that Firkin pubs were set up to challenge.

Allied Breweries intended strategy would appear to be sympathetic to the chain's origins. 'The Firkin brand is strong and we are committed to retaining its highly popular and individual character. The essential style of the pubs and infamous Bruce's ales will be contined' according to the new managing director, David Longbottom. Their decision, to keep that Firkin chain as it is, is an acknowledgement that Bruce was right and how the major players have been forced to adapt their practices. Allied have no plans to change the concept or the hands-on approach to management. The chain's target market will remain the same – those interested in individualistic ales.

However, where Bruce lacked the resources to develop the chain, Allied have the financial and management muscle to expand regionally and at the same time maintain firm cost controls.

Allied intend to expand the innovative chain, by converting some of their Taylor Walker houses into Firkin pubs, with micro-breweries following the Bruce tradition. The enlarged estate will serve only its own ale brands and guest beers from similar small brewers. Expansion will however be gradual using carefully selected sites as they come available, in London and other major cities, building on existing regional expansion (Manchester, Milton Keynes, Northampton and Derby).

■ Case Study 20: San Serif and Trivial Pursuit

■ A European Marketing Success Story

■ Trivial Pursuit – The American Experience

When Trivial Pursuit was launched in the USA and Canada, it very quickly became a 'cult' game amongst 18–34 year old ABC1s, who saw it as ammunition in the revolt against television and computer games.

Intensive promotion reinforced the perceived benefits of social interaction and educational fun. Enormous unit sales were achieved by the 'stocking up' of retail outlets, who were forced to discount the price. Although household penetration of 15–20 per cent was thus achieved very quickly, sales declined equally quickly and Trivial Pursuit became just another 'here today – gone tomorrow' product.

Horn Abbot, the inventors of Trivial Pursuit, did not want the same thing to happen in the UK and so, after launching their product through Kenner Parker, the games distributor, they licenced the game to San Serif Print Promotions, a UK marketing company, in 1983.

■ San Serif's Strategies for the UK and Europe

The US experience indicated the need to manage carefully the product's life-cycle and therefore in order to turn an overnight success into a long term revenue earner, San Serif followed three distinct strategies (as shown in Figure 5.11):

□ *Market Penetration*

- Quantitative targets were set for awareness (84 per cent in 1987), level of trial (55 per cent) and household penetration (15 per cent).
- Tactical advertising replaced public relations as Trivial Pursuit became inherently less newsworthy.
- Trivial Pursuit trial sessions were organised in schools, trains, wine bars and clubs; competitions and charity games were sponsored.
- ABC1s under the age of 18 were specifically targeted.

Figure 5.11 shows how the product life-cycle of the original Genus edition has been extended to 1988 by these actions.

Markets	Products: Existing	Products: New
Existing	Market Penetration Genus UK 83	Product Development Entertainment Oct 87 Sport Jul 87 Scottish Genus Feb 87 Genus II 86 RPM 86 Baby Boomer 85 Young Players 85
New	Market Extension Genus Italy 85 Genus Eire 84 Genus Belgium 84 Genus Holland 84 Genus Spain 84 Genus Germany 84 Genus France 84	Diversification

Figure 5.11 San Serif's product/market matrix in 1987

☐ *Product Development*

- A new set of general knowledge question cards was released (Genus II) to prolong the interest of those who had already bought the master game.
- The Baby Boomer edition was issued to appeal to the over thirties.
- Special interest card sets were developed to widen the game's appeal. These sets were launched singly and were backed up by specialised promotion: the Fleet Street Sports Writers' Challenge for the sports edition; a West End Premiere at Stringfellows for the entertainments section; a Burns Night for the Scottish edition; and an inter-school challenge for the Young Players edition.

The increased UK sales achieved through the introduction of these further editions can be seen in Figure 5.12.

☐ *Market Extension*

- The larger and nearer European countries were targeted with special emphasis being focused on France and Germany. San Serif initially restricted themselves to those countries where Kenner Parker, their

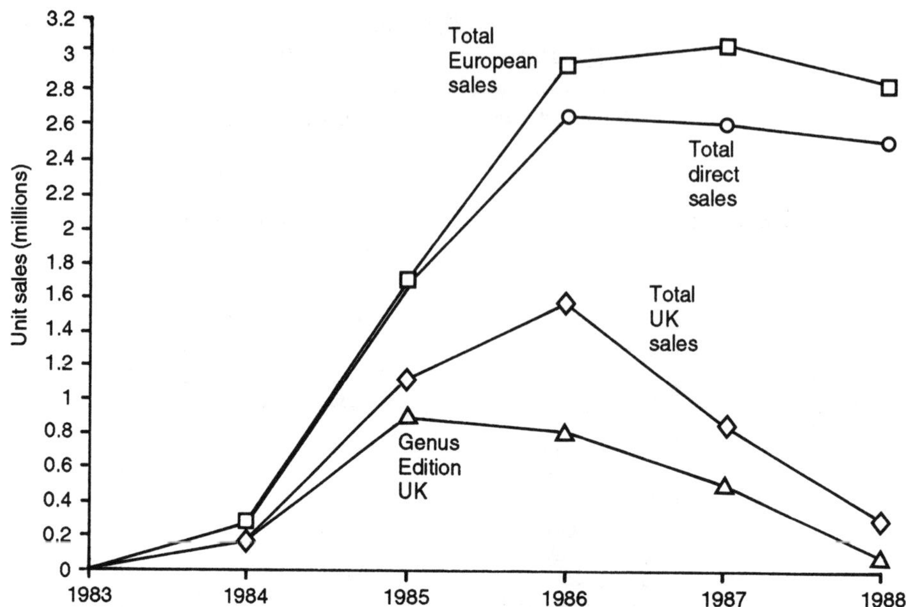

Figure 5.12 Trivial Pursuit UK and European unit sales, 1983–8

distributor in the UK, had an existing network. (These sales are termed 'direct' sales in the accompanying figures).

- Question cards were translated and culturally-specific questions researched.
- In order to reach other, generally smaller, European countries where Kenner Parker did not have a presence, San Serif selected local agents, ('indirect' sales).
- Figure 5.12 shows how expansion into Europe raised the overall volume of sales and Figure 5.13 how the three strategies of penetration, product development and market extension have successfully extended the life of Trivial Pursuit.

How San Serif Got the Mix Right

The major element of the Trivial Pursuit product, the questions, were adapted to match the needs of each targeted segment and each culturally different market. For example, in Spain, both Spanish and Catalan versions were available. Sans Serif was quick to exploit national events and celebrations; thus, a French revolution edition was ready to coincide with the two hundredth anniversary.

Travel, pocket and computer-based versions of the game were developed to widen the number of playing opportunities. A family edition, with adult and

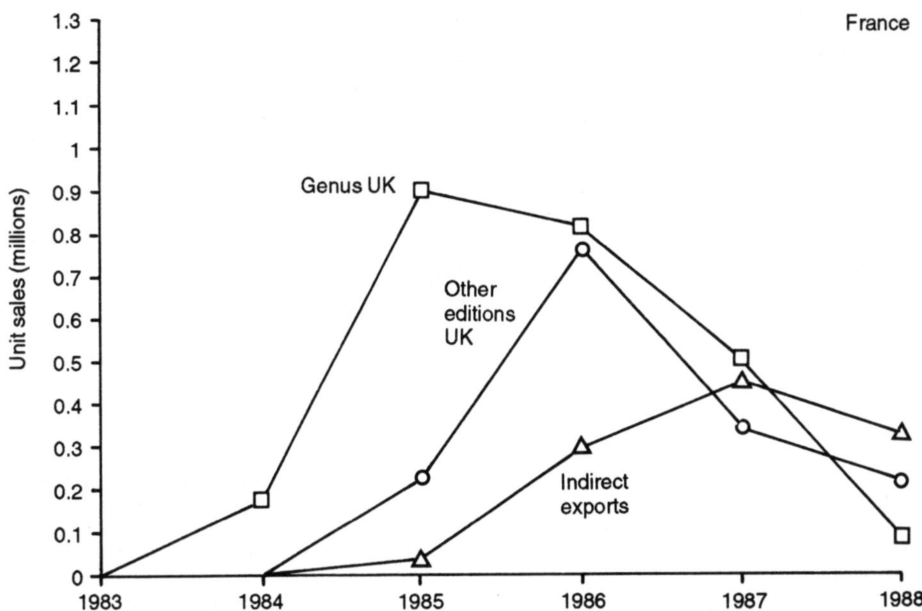

Figure 5.13 Trivial Pursuit's new products and new markets

child question sets was launched which extended the adult game to the family situation and to those children still too young for the Young Players edition.

The premium price at £29.95, was double that of its competitors and this reinforced the up-market image of the game.

To dissuade retailers from over-stocking and then discounting, San Serif closely monitored shipments of Trivial Pursuit throughout Europe. Their closeness to their distributors has allowed them to do this, and even the 'indirect' agents in the smaller countries were obliged to submit all promotional material to San Serif for authorisation.

As each special interest edition was released, new outlets were found. For example, an agreement with a retail chain, Astral, placed the sports edition in 60 sports shops throughout the UK.

San Serif used a mix of multiple media, consumer promotions, trade promotions and public relations to build awareness first, then to convert awareness into trial, and trial into the purchase of a master game, including the board. As the market has matured, the emphasis has changed to encourage the purchase of further question sets.

■ Planning and Monitoring Activities

San Serif set unit sales targets by country and by edition and calculated their promotional spend accordingly. Performance against target was constantly

Table 5.3 Trivial Pursuit: European Unit Sales

	1983	*1984*	*1985*	*1986*	*1987*	*1988*	*Total*
UK	0	174,000	1,122,000	1,578,000	850,000	300,000	4,024,000
France	0	14,000	125,000	413,000	750,000	1,300,000	2,602,000
Germany	0	74,000	282,000	470,000	582,000	432,000	1,840,000
Spain	0	1,000	91,000	129,000	250,000	350,000	821,000
Belgium	0	4,000	18,000	25,000	63,000	64,000	174,000
Holland	0	10,000	12,000	12,000	10,000	27,000	71,000
Eire	0	2,000	12,000	14,000	30,000	15,000	73,000
Italy	0	0	13,000	13,000	60,000	10,000	96,000
Total Direct	0	279,000	1,675,000	2,654,000	2,595,000	2,498,000	9,701,000
Indirect	0	0	35,000	296,000	453,000	325,000	1,109,000
Total	0	279,000	1,710,000	2,950,000	3,048,000	2,823,000	10,810,000
Genus UK	0	174,000	898,000	815,000	506,000	87,000	2,480,000
Other UK	0	0	224,000	763,000	344,000	213,000	1,544,000
UK promotion (£)		137,000	967,000	1,578,000	1,254,000	402,000	4,238,000

monitored, through the close links with distributors, and action taken quickly where variances appeared.

In this way, through the application of accepted marketing strategies, and with a view to detail in the marketing mix, San Serif turned Trivial Pursuit into the biggest selling board game in Europe. Table 5.3 shows the unit sales achieved since its introduction.

In 1990, Serif Cowells, the printing, publishing and leisure group and owners of San Serif, lost its licence to distribute Trivial Pursuit, along with Nintendo games, resulting an almost halving of group turnover and losses in 1991. It retains however the printing and packaging contract.

New versions continue to be introduced; for Christmas 1992, the Annual Edition – to celebrate the game's tenth birthday, containing questions culled from events of 1992 – was launched. The game was a low cost version, without a board.

The success of Trivial Pursuit is demonstrated in the strong revival in the demand for board games of every kind. Board games sales have grown from £114 million in 1988 to £127 million in 1992 with blockbusters such as Trivial Pursuit generating new growth areas.

Technology may be king, but Trivial Pursuit are harnessing it to expand sales. In addition to the three different versions of the full set with board, the travel version and specialist boxes of question cards, sets of questions are now available on CD and cassette. The game will utilise all aspects of multi-media in a bid to keep its attraction in line with leisure trends.

Case Study 21: Derwent Valley Foods Limited

The Creators of the Phileas Fogg Brand

Marketing Success Story or One Product Wonder?

Introduction

Derwent Valley Foods Ltd launched the Phileas Fogg brand at the Olympia food exhibition of 1982. A high quality premium product range including tortilla and corn chips, it was aimed at the adult savoury snack consumer. The product satisfied the specific market needs of the mid eighties and by 1990 sales of Phileas Fogg had reached £15m. The success of the brand was based on three main factors:

- the quality of the product;
- a strong brand, backed by advertising; and
- a good distribution network.

The success of Derwent Valley Foods (DVF) was entirely due to the Phileas Fogg brand. But by 1990, the company was having to face the problems of a largely one product business, which, though a cash cow product, was starting, to mature. There was possibly scope for expansion into new European markets, although this was deemed to be a high risk strategy, because the brand image was not necessarily transferable to a different cultural environment. Additionally, different eating habits made it difficult to predict potential success in these markets.

'Tapas' (tortilla chips with a dip) was launched in 1990 in collaboration with the Taunton cider company; a 'chip and dip' product, initially aimed at the £2.65bn UK pub food market, this was a new market with apparent growth potential. Preliminary indicators were good, with sales of one million units by 1990. There appeared to be scope for transferring the product to the home consumer, using the existing distribution system.

Derwent Valley Foods also manufactured snacks for a number of grocery multiples for sale under their own brand names. This part of the business offered very low margins and therefore future expansion should have to come from development of own brand products.

Despite its successful start, Derwent Valley Foods remained a one product company – heavily dependent on its original range of adult snacks, Phileas Fogg. With a small management team and limited financial resources, would Derwent Valley be able to convert its initial success into future growth?

□ *Product Portfolio*

The problem is clearly demonstrated by the Boston matrix in Figure 5.14. The Phileas Fogg product range was overwhelmingly dominant, but with the product reaching maturity, revenue was likely to start to decline in the near future. In addition, there was a significant lack of new products in the 'problem child' and 'star' sections of the matrix. The only new product hope was Tapas, although it was beginning to become clear that the target sales level of £50m was not achievable.

■ Future Growth

With the high profile success of the Phileas Fogg product range, Derwent Valley Foods had become the focus of attention of many companies, interested in acquiring the brand. Thus the company was faced with a choice of direction for future growth. One option was to sell out to the company with the best

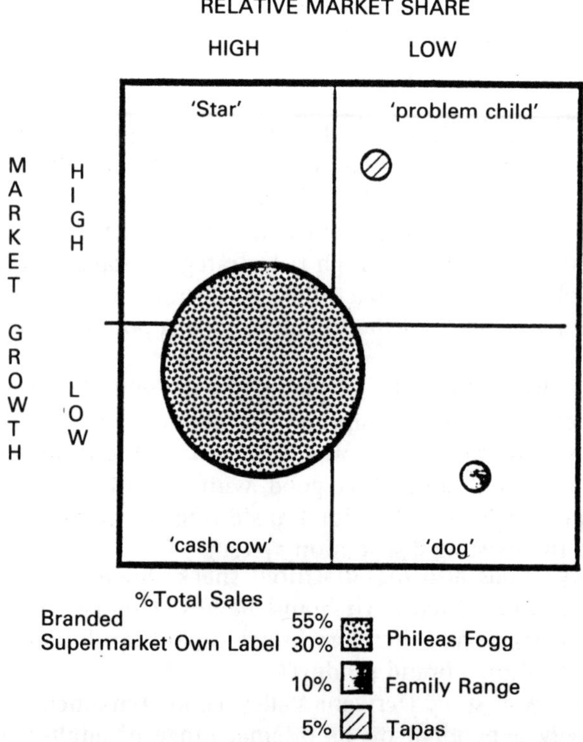

Figure 5.14 Derwent Valley product portfolio

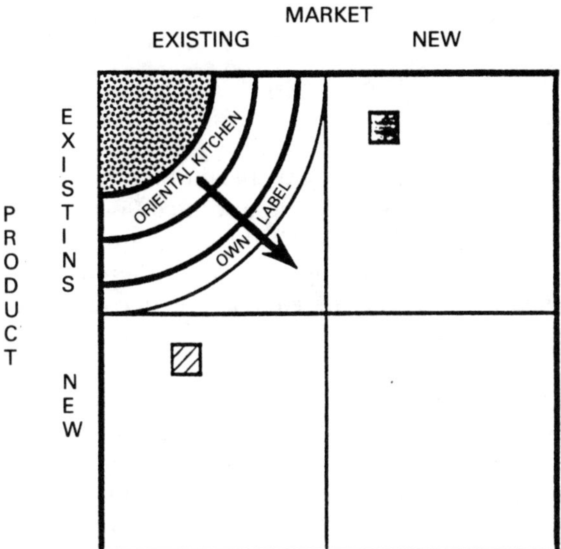

Figure 5.15 Derwent Valley diversification

opportunities for product and distribution expansion (the product was largely unknown outside the South East of England).

Conversely, it could remain a separate entity and focus its marketing objectives on the profitable development of new and existing products, whilst combating competitive launches. Figure 5.15 shows DVF's products in the Ansoff matrix and outlines the strategies that were open to the company in 1990.

Market Penetration

The company could continue to develop the range and grow supermarket own-label to sustain its market position and keep the competition at bay. It could limit its promotional expenditure to periodic television advertising to maintain brand awareness, and retain premium pricing to maximise margins.

Market Extension

Further expansion in the UK could be undertaken together with a thorough analysis of export potential. Joint venture distribution would limit export risk. A possible withdrawal from the low growth, low margin Family range would release funds for a push into more profitable market sectors.

Product Development

The Company needed to develop new product ideas for selective development using its distinctive competencies. The Tapas concept was one such pilot product, that might help to establish a balanced portfolio from which to move into the 1990s.

■ Conclusion

Ultimately the relative size of the company, meant that the founding directors accepted an attractive offer of £24 million from United Biscuits. Realising that a hefty capital injection would be needed if the company was to expand, the directors were dubious of the City's support, and had therefore decided against a stock market floatation. It was considered that growth could only be achieved through alignment with a group with greater resources and stronger distribution channels.

The Tapas concept was never truly successful, and European expansion in 1992 had faltered through limited export experience and distribution, and an inability to find a commercial partner. Similar forays into the US market in 1991 had failed through lack of distribution muscle and inadequate funds. Low volumes and a small sales force had made it difficult to extend distribution much beyond large supermarket chains in the UK.

United Biscuits' purchase of DVF will leave the maker of the quirky and off-beat Phileas Fogg virtually autonomous. Exploiting synergies with UB's snack subsidiary KP, distribution of the range is planned to expand from 8,000 to about 50,000 UK retail outlets, and the strength of UB's neogtiating power could also help to break the solus agreements in the licensed trade. UB also intends to develop Phileas Fogg's sales effort overseas. It is planned to double DVF's sales in 5 years and male Phileas Fogg, with currently only 2 per cent of the total UK snack market, into one of the 5 best selling snack brands.

Innovative and unusual products and flavours, the strong Jules Verne image and distinctive advertising through creative agency Bartle, Boggle Hegarty have made this northern England snacks manufacturer one of the entrepreneurial success stories of the Thatcher era. Almost single handedly, it has pioneered the British market for adult premium snacks, currently worth about £70 million a year and the fastest growing sector of the snacks business.

■ Section 3: Niche Marketing Against Big Budget Competitors

It is not always clear whether a company should adopt a niche marketing strategy or a market coverage strategy. There are many niche positions in markets whereas, in some industries in Europe, there are normally positions only for two or three mainstream marketers. One factor which determines which position to take is the level of resources available to an organisation. If an organisation has small resources compared to its competitors, the most effective marketing strategy is usually a niche strategy. The principles to consider in designing niche strategies with small marketing budgets are outlined in this section.

■ Market Positioning

The links of product differentiation, market segmentation and image are vital to the niche marketer, especially in service industries. An analysis of the needs of different customer groups and an assessment of the positionings of competitors are necessary to determine targeting and strategy.

Selection of segments on the basis of best fit to the product and resource support relative to competitors is a strategic decision. If the wrong selection is made, scarce resources are allocated to markets with the prospect of little return.

The intangibility of services requires marketers to pay particular attention to three factors in their strategies. The first, image, represents the picture and benefits of the service, and needs to be developed with a clear message. Advertising, promotion and selling are important mechanisms for achieving the service's image positioning. The second, experience of the service by the customer, is the means by which an assessment of how well the service meets the need can be made, and if satisfactory, the process of referrals or 'word of mouth' can become a powerful marketing tool. The third factor, delivery of service, frequently involving people as part of the delivery process, is a major element in the creation of satisfied customers.

Close attention to these three factors contribute substantially to the strong niche positions gained by Next during the 1980s. This is one of the cases presented in this section. The case demonstrates, however, that niche success can be transient unless close attention is paid to how these three factors need to change over time as tastes and attitudes change.

■ Selectivity

A small organisation cannot adequately serve all markets. Niche marketing requires application of resources on a selective basis. Selectivity should be applied to service packages, segments, distributors and promotional resources. A portfolio management approach should be taken, with priority given to a limited number of services and markets.

A target marketing strategy provides the opportunity for the development of different positionings in different markets and different images for self-contained segments. The image positioning, however, needs to be clear and distinct in each segment and differentiated from competitors.

■ Life-Cycle Analysis and Strategic Directions

The niche marketer, with focused attention on one or two market segments, must closely monitor market trends and the stage of the life-cycle of its markets. Continued growth may require strategies for extending the life-cycle or entry into new markets. A danger facing niche marketers with their narrow focus, is being 'locked' into markets that are mature or declining. There should be continual assessment of new market opportunities so that flexibility is maintained.

A simple, but useful, tool for analysing strategic directions for the niche marketer is the Ansoff product market growth model. Strategic options range from market penetration to diversification, the latter requiring the development of new products for new markets. Any expansion, however, needs to be from a strong, defendable base.

■ Strategies for Maximising Returns from Limited Resources

Many small organisations engage in 'marketing without funds' – a situation where a marketing job must be done, but there are limited funds. The principle is to rely on and work with others to carry out the competitive marketing strategy – distributors, the media, companies in related markets, and customers.

□ *Unpaid Agents – Customers*

The most effective unpaid agents are satisfied customers. A strategy used by American Express is to encourage existing customers to provide new members, and it is made easy and convenient for the existing member to do so. Methods for facilitating referrals from the existing customers should be a focus of strategy. Alternatively, emphasis may be placed on the existing customers to engender loyalty and repeat purchases. Volvo, which has a small share of the European prestige car market, has adopted strategies that concentrate on developing owner loyalty. These include twenty-four hour service centres to increase customer convenience, showrooms open seven days a week, Volvo credit card for easy payment and regular communications with Volvo owners. These initiatives are designed to forge links between Volvo and its existing customers.

□ *The 'Push' Strategy and Distribution*

Distribution strategy should be a major focus for the niche specialist. The marketer's 'push' strategy puts primary emphasis by the firm on marketing to intermediaries. The selected distributors then create awareness and preference for the product or service.

Incentives are provided to benefit and intermediary by selling the firm's products. In the tourism industry, for example, intermediaries include airlines, train and coach carriers, hotel and resort providers, clubs and associations and travel agents. There are many avenues for adopting a 'push' strategy.

□ *Publicity and Local Sponsorships*

Another avenue includes publicity and local events that can be sponsored at small cost. This can be effective regionally and in country and provincial towns.

□ *Joint Marketing*

Strategies involving marketing through or with related businesses can yield substantial returns from limited resources. This 'piggybacking' approach may include representation at trade exhibitions or joint marketing with another business.

Similarly, in the training market, opportunities exist for joint marketing of specialised computer software products. This is often done, with accounting software packages, which are sold as part of training courses.

□ *Direct Marketing*

This has great potential for the niche competitor. By direct mail or telephone, cost-effective targeting can be achieved, various service packages can be offered to different segments, and appropriate images can be created in several markets.

Direct marketing offers flexibility and caters for relatively small budgets, but it requires skill and experience to implement effectively.

□ *Use of Technology*

Computer and communications technology are opening opportunities at moderate cost to develop and maintain contact with customers more easily. The small firm should look for cost-saving and service enhancing technology as a means of increasing customer access and productive capacity.

This is an important factor in the training and education industry. Word processing and computer power has revolutionised the production of course notes and training materials.

Customer servicing is improved by transferring data by facsimile or between computers from the servicing agent to the client.

■ Innovativeness, Creativity and Speed

The niche specialist with limited resources must also rely on finding innovative and creative ways of communicating with, and capturing, customers. These can be through more personalised contact, faster response, capitalising on spin-offs from competitors' advertising and identifying opportunities in the market earlier than larger competitors. The sales and direct customer employees need an entrepreneurial flair and marketing orientation. The business infrastructure needs to be geared to the market.

These less tangible attributes of the niche specialist are vital contributors to success against large budget competitors.

The first case, which follows, describes the attempt of a German niche chocolate manufacturer to regain market share lost to international competitors. The second case describes the rise and fall of a niche marketer in the clothing sector. The third case describes the successful launch of a national newspaper into a sector regarded by many as already mature and dominated by a small number of long-standing competitors. The final case, Thorntons, describes the continuing success of a niche player in the mature European chocholate market.

■ Case Study 22: Stollwerck AG in Germany*

Hans Imhoff, aged 67, knows more about chocolate than anyone else. He has been eating 'at least one bar a day' for the last thirty years. No wonder that he weighs over two hundredweight!

Imhoff, however, who owns 97 per cent of the shares in Kölner Stollwerck AG, the chocolate empire, (turnover in 1989: DM 709 million; 1,100 employees), knows precious little about marketing. He has always been a mass goods man. Even the purchase of such venerable brands as Stollwerck (1971), Waldbaur (1976) and Sprengel (1979) did not change a thing. Imhoff made his name as a cost-killer, never launching innovations but always 'me-too' products.

Yet for the last few years, the 'Chocolate Napoleon', as he is known in Cologne, has been attempting to reform. Spectacular losses of market share to major Suchard brand Milka, which had been attacking Sprengel in its stamping-grounds in the northern German states Saxony, Schleswig-Holstein, Hamburg, Northrhine-Westphalia and Berlin (see Table 5.4), and a critical McKinsey report forced him to act.

The management consultants ascertained a considerable deficit in the Company's marketing and product policy. They concluded that Stollwerck AG had too many products which were scarcely differentiated from one another, contributed little to sales, had low profit margins, and increased fixed costs.

Table 5.4 The March of the Lilac Cow (Lila Pause): Market shares of Milka and Sprengel chocolate bars (per cent)

Year	*Berlin*		*North*		*NRW*		*National*	
	Milka	*Sprengel*	*Milka*	*Sprengel*	*Milka*	*Sprengel*	*Milka*	*Sprengel*
1985	5.2	6.9	8.0	18.2	14.7	6.0	15.3	6.5
1986	6.4	6.6	8.5	15.5	15.2	5.0	16.6	5.5
1987	9.3	2.0	11.0	16.8	18.9	5.4	19.5	5.3
1988	17.1	1.9	14.8	17.5	22.3	4.4	23.6	5.2
1989	16.1	2.2	17.5	13.9	22.7	4.0	24.1	4.2

Source: G+O

* Adapted by Collin Randlesome from an article in *Manager Magazine*, November 1989, by Walter Hillebrand.

Table 5.5 Market Shares of Competitors in West Germany, 1989

Company	*Brands*	*Market Share %*
Mars	Milky Way, Bounty, Mars, Snickers, Raider	46.9
Jacobs Suchard	Lila Pause, Knusperzauber, Nussini	10.8
Ferrero	Duplo, Hanuta	15.2
Nestlé Rowntree	Kitkat, Yes	9.5

Imhoff took action and appointed Franz Kraus, aged 32, as Director of Marketing in 1988; Kraus was formerly Lila Pause brand manager with Jacobs Suchard.

Kraus's first step was to do his own survey, which showed that market share was modest; Stollwerck's products were not very attractive to retailers; there were hardly any synergies with other products such as Sprengel chocolate creams; profitability was low; products were little known; consumer attitudes were indifferent; and repurchase rate/brand loyalty was low. Competition throughout West Germany was tough (see Table 5.5).

Imhoff's aim was to establish Sprengel, a traditional but faded brand, permanently in the up-market segment, to double its national market share (1989: 4.2 per cent) over the next five years and thus bring Stollwerck AG into a leading position in the chocolate market throughout Germany.

Kraus was promised a budget of DM 24m per annum for the period 1989 to 1994 to sort out Stollwerck's problems.

□ *Kraus's Solution*

Kraus and his team decided on a new corporate design concept, changing everything from company letter-heading, sales booths and company lorries, in an attempt to guarantee what they call 'total brand display'.

Sprengel, Stollwerck's showpiece range, is now displayed in new packaging in bright red in order to contrast with Milka's lilac blocks. It also boasts a new slogan: 'Sprengel – light and sensual'.

It is targeted at well-heeled people over thirty years of age who aspire to a certain standard and style. Posters and television commercials make it clear who is meant here: ageing yuppies.

To address this target group, the marketing team reduced the Sprengel range from over 100 to 40 items and created, together with the research and development team, two new products: Dacapo (fine chocolate sticks) and Tiamo (chocolate creams), thus complementing the tired, old chocolate cream mixtures called India and Maria Theresia.

The launch was supported by advertising at over 7,000 billboard locations and in magazines such as *Stern, Brigitte* and *Für Sie.*

Kraus' solution appears to have been successful. Imhoff described his company's performance in 1992 as 'outstanding', with a 20 per cent increase in turnover to DM 1.2bn. Stollwerck is now acknowledged to be one of Germany's leading chocolate producers, and with significant profits, plans to diversify into biscuits through a Hungarian acquisition and to expand chocolate production at a site in Budapest. Imhoff is bullish about the future of the company, investing DM 75 million in capital and product development.

■ Case Study 23: Next

The phenomenal growth of the Next empire of retail outlets in the UK high street and in the home in the 1980s, offering affordable, stylish clothes to the Thatcher generation, was born from a shrewd identification, by the charismatic George Davies, of a niche market, bridging the gap between up-market designer shops and the price obsessed high street.

■ The Retail Clothing Industry in the Late 1970s/Early 1980s

□ *Introduction*

Next evolved out of the out-of-date Kendall's chain, part of the Hepworth group, which was struggling to sustain a market position. The clothing market, worth £8 billion in 1982, was in overall decline, with growth lagging 7 per cent behind the retail price index (see Table 5.6). Increasing foreign imports, especially from developing countries such as Taiwan and Korea, were helped by a relatively strong pound.

The UK was suffering from an economic recession which was worldwide. This hit the clothing manufacturing industry in the UK very hard, where numbers of people employed in this sector fell from 250,000 to 90,000 in the period covered. Vertical integration was becoming essential to introduce production efficiencies and thereby cut costs.

Fashions were changing much more rapidly than had ever been experienced before and the typical UK clothing retail companies, who were used to much more conservative clothing trends, were finding it very difficult to keep pace

Table 5.6 The UK Retail Clothing Market, 1976–82

	Overall	*Women's outerwear*	*Men's outerwear*	*Retail price index*
1976	100	100	100	100
1977	119	131	112	116
1978	136	145	125	125
1979	159	165	153	142
1980	177	195	159	168
1981	182	201	159	188
1982	190	211	163	204

with developments. This led to much soul-searching, trying to establish who their customers were and what they wanted.

□ *The Womens' Market*

This sector of the clothing market was in fact quite healthy, with growth in womens' outerwear some 7 per cent greater than the retail price index (see Table 5.7 above) and worth £4bn in 1982.

The market was segmented against three key factors – price, quality and fashion as illustrated in Figure 5.16.

Price–Quality
Clothing which balanced high quality at value-for-money prices but without being too fashionable could be seen in the High Street majors such as Marks and Spencer, John Lewis Partnership and British Home Stores.

Quality–Fashion
For the more up-market purchaser who was looking for high quality and high fashion, but was not too bothered about the price, there were the more 'classy' fashion-conscious outlets such as Jaeger, Benetton and the high-class independent fashion boutiques.

Fashion–Price
Catering for youngsters were a string of rather cheap 'instant fashion' boutiques, where quality was rather unimportant – if the fashion lasted for more than one season you were lucky.

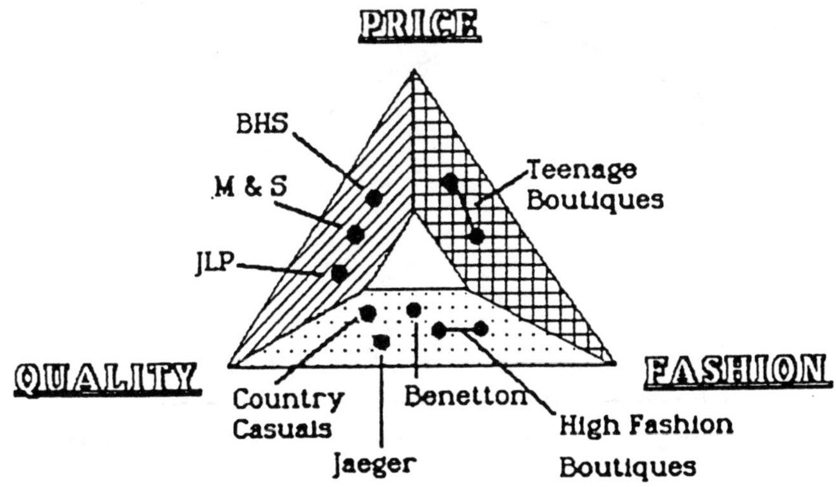

Figure 5.16 Retail clothing – late 1970s/early 1980s

□ *The Men's Market*

This sector was performing very badly, with growth in men's outerwear falling some 20 per cent behind the retail price index, but still worth £2.7bn in 1982. Although there was some market differentiation in the form of Marks and Spencer, Jaeger, Austin Reed and fashion boutiques, by far the largest sector was that of the traditional suit through such outlets as Burton, Collier and Hepworth.

It was becoming clear that the customer was looking for a more casual selection of clothing not catered for at that time and it was for that reason that Burton showed the way by launching Top-Man – a follow-up to its teenage fashion outlet Top-Shop.

□ *Hepworth*

With a product consisting of primarily conventional suits and holding only 2 per cent of the men's clothing market in 1982, Hepworth had been experiencing declining profits over the period 1979–82 (see Figure 5.17).

One of their strengths at the time, however, was the installation of an extensive computer system linking warehouses with point of sale tills, thus enabling very rapid monitoring and control of stock levels at all locations. The stage was set for innovation.

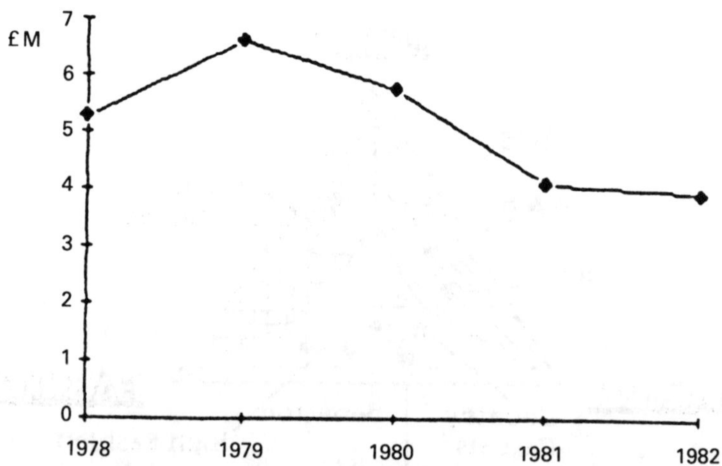

Figure 5.17 Hepworth's profits, 1978–82

■ The Market Gap

In order to establish if a gap in the women's clothing market existed, the following questions had to be answered:

- Where do women buy their clothes?
- What are they looking for?
- What is currently on offer?

Existing outlets could be categorised:

□ *Boutiques*

Catered mostly for teenagers and avoided the 'classic' styles. Their objective was high turnover of rapidly changing fashions. Latest styles were supplied from Paris, with premium price on the designer labels. Items were usually cut from synthetic material with the aim of keeping profit margins high.

□ *Traditional Retailers*

Represented value-for-money through outlets such as British Home Stores. Emphasis was on bulk sales to the consumer and bulk purchases from the supplier. Retailers had a reputation based on pricing and customer policies. The customers were largely older family women, buying conventional indistinctive outfits.

□ *Up-Market Shops*

Sold both 'classic' and 'stylish' items of the best materials and in the higher price brackets. Typical shops were Jaeger and Aquascutum, selling classic quality clothes to a middle aged customer.

Market research identified that a considerable market existed for the average working woman who was prepared to pay above average prices and who was seeking the 'classic' style. A shop that could offer the following would be satisfying a perceived need:

- Quality clothing with a price around 10 per cent higher than traditional retailers.
- Clothing with style, flair and originality.
- An up-market image different from that offered by the traditional retailers.
- Convenience – location and opening hours for working women.

The result was the Next line of clothes, targeted at women with a moderate income, in the 22–45 age group.

■ The Marketing Mix

George Davies joined Hepworth in 1981 when fortunes were flagging. He was given the task of drawing up a brief for the chain of old-fashioned Kendall's women's shops, which Hepworth had just acquired. He was given two months and a possible £1,000 compensation if Hepworth did not like his ideas. He later explained: 'I had just resigned from Pippa Dee and had nothing to lose. I could stick dogmatically to my own ideas, which I had had for some time.' Next emerged very close to his original ideas and he was subsequently appointed Chief Executive.

George Davies identified a gap in the women's clothing market and brought together the ingredients to bridge this gap. He described it as: 'A carefully planned exercise in marketing and merchandising stemming from intuition and experience.'

The concept was simple. Based on the principles of anticipating needs and judicious buying, Next women's shops successfully offered a fashionable collection of women's clothing with co-ordinating accessories for 22 to 45 year olds. The design director and buyers travelled in Europe, USA and Japan to research the forthcoming season's fashion trends and colours. They decided on three or four primary colours. All clothes and accessories for the following season would be patterned and plain in various shades of each colour, so that customers could choose a whole co-ordinated outfit or several mix-and-match outfits. British manufacturers supplied about 80 per cent of the clothes, making it easier to control quality and co-ordinate design in this way. High quality, natural fabrics were used, such as, wool, linen and cotton. The clothes were stylish, with emphasis on good quality, and priced about 10 per cent more than Marks and Spencer, and 50 per cent less than Jaeger.

At their peak, there were 212 Next shops for women in prime High Street positions or shopping centres. The first 79 shops' premises were the transformed premises of the Kendall's women's shops, scattered across the UK.

George Davies wanted to promote an image of exclusive clothes at affordable prices, and he was advised to spend £1m on advertising. However, he decided to advertise in Vogue, spending only £80,000. This fostered the image of Next as 'a cut above' the usual High Street women's clothing shops, with the spin-off of national newspaper coverage.

The shop interiors were intended to create the air of an expensive boutique. Designed by Terence Conran, the shops had an uncluttered appearance; Next could keep low stocks because they used a computerised stock system and an efficient distribution system to replenish stocks. Clothes were arranged in blocks of colour, which was eye-catching and attractive and drew attention to the easy co-ordination of outfits. The well-groomed assistants wore Next outfits. In order to maintain customer interest, each season had three phases, when new designs were produced. All designs were produced internally.

Next kept in touch with customer preferences in a variety of ways. They held cheese and wine fashion shows for 'Club 24' credit card members. Feedback from staff was passed on by managers who met at regional councils, and George Davies and other executives frequently visited Next shops. The buyers were advised by the merchandising director, whose advice on changing trends and customer response curbed possible flights of designer fancy. Next clothes were intended to be stylish, but not outlandish.

The buyers, who all had design backgrounds, worked together with the quality control department, as a team, to ensure a high standard product. The selling staff were usually over 25, of smart appearance and pleasant manner, and motivated by good working conditions and a bonus scheme. There were good opportunities for advancement. Managers were motivated by attending regional meetings and by competitions. Each shop was set target sales for the week, and new staff followed a training programme in-shop for three months.

■ The Early Success of Next

The success of Next in the 1980s can be judged against their financial performance, and the growth in the number of stores named Next (see Table 5.7).

The transition of Hepworth with declining profitability to a dramatical recovery of fortunes with Next's launch in 1982 is demonstrated in Table 5.8, Figures 5.18 and 5.19.

All this was at a time when the economic climate in the UK was far from buoyant. But is it fair to put this revival entirely down to the introduction of Next to the Hepworth's line? Probably so. When the Hepworth's store in Kingston was redesigned and changed to Next, the turnover increased from £8,000 to £31,000 per week!

Table 5.7 Hepworth Group Financial Performance, 1976–1981 (in £m)

	1976	*1977*	*1978*	*1979*	*1980*	*1981*
Turnover	28.6	34.5	42.6	51.3	61.9	75.7
Profit before tax	2.8	3.6	5.2	6.6	5.7	4.1
Gross margin	10%	10%	12%	13%	9%	5%

Table 5.8 Hepworth Group Financial Performance, 1982–8 (in £m)

	Aug 1982	*Aug 1983*	*Aug 1984*	*Aug 1985*	*Aug 1986*	*Jan 1987*	*Jan 1988*	*July 1988*
Turnover	83.4	98.6	108.3	146.0	190.0	372.4	862.1	1085.4
Profit after tax	5.5	7.2	8.6	13.9	17.3	31.2	61.3	62.8

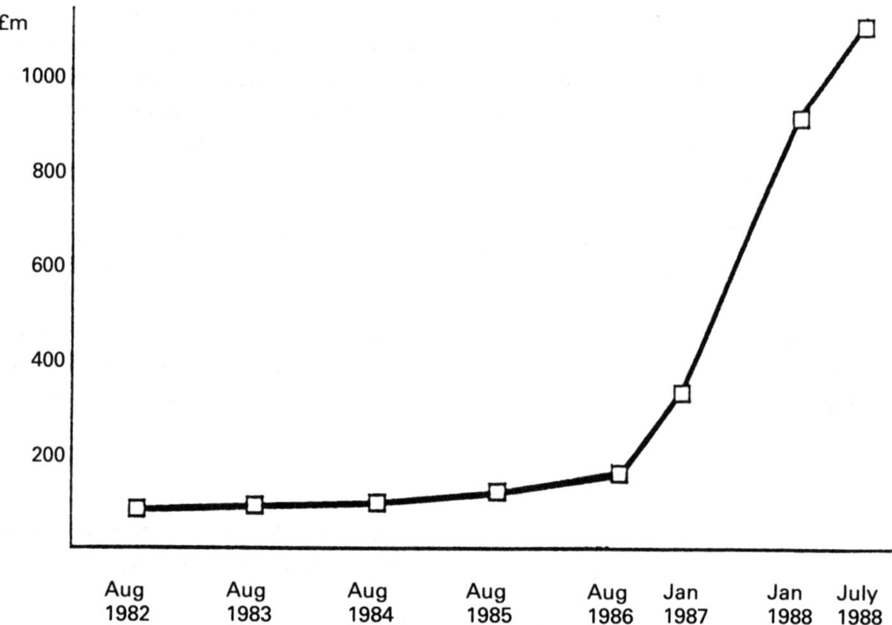

Figure 5.18 Next turnover, 1982–8 (excluding VAT)

In terms of growth of the Next chain, we have seen that the concept was introduced with Next for women. This followed the acquisition of the Kendall's chain, which consisted of over 70 stores. The chain of Next stores grew to over 220 by the end of 1985, when the annual general meeting passed a resolution to reconstitute the Hepworth's company identity under the name of Next. Hepworth's name therefore died on the high street.

The effect that this success had on the traditional clothing retail establishments is equally interesting. Marks and Spencer, the bastion of British retailing, began to see its safe position threatened. For the first time, they were concerned and began seriously looking at their future marketing strategy. Burtons launched Principles in direct competition and a number of other targeted shops were launched, jumping on the bandwagon.

■ The Next Expansion

George Davies continued to be the driving force behind the Next shops. His next concept in the retailing arena was to be Next Department Stores, which he regarded as the 'theatre for retailing', where people could browse around the store at their convenience. This strategy offered customers womenswear, menswear, shoes, accessories, florists and cafés, all under one roof. This also

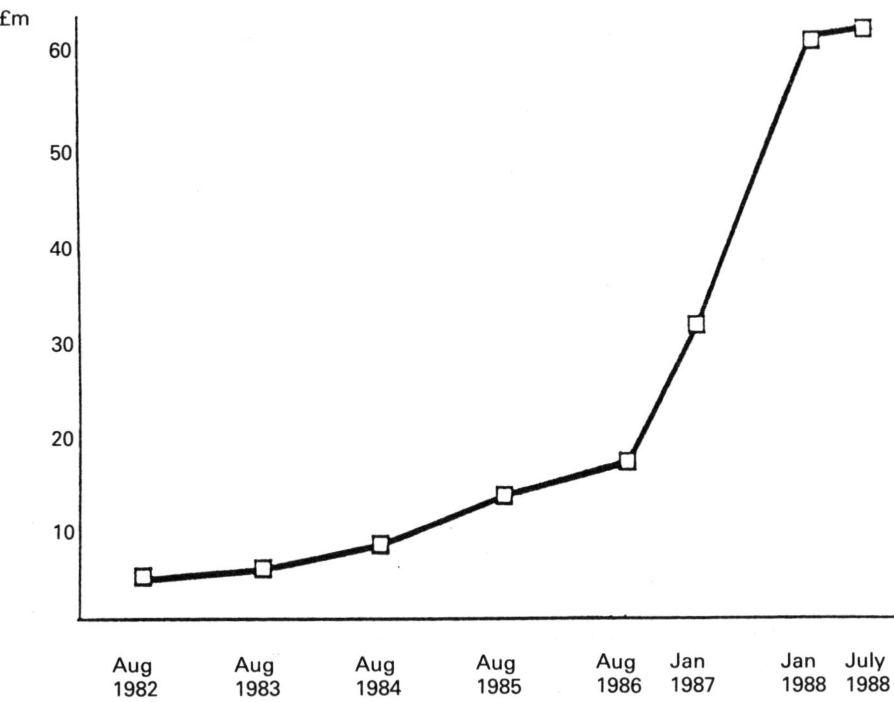

Figure 5.19 Next profit after tax, 1982–8

allowed Next to best utilise their property opportunities. Next Interiors, challenging the might of Habitat, were established in 14 areas. Own brand commodities such as shoes, cosmetics and lingerie were planned, and Next Europe was also on the agenda.

This continual development and introduction of new retailing ideas was intended to continue the momentum, and Company fortunes. This could be thought of as the classical company life-cycle, where maturing products provide the Company with cash to allow new ideas to be tested (see Figure 5.20).

This explosion of stores growth had catapulted the group into the top 100 British companies with a market capitalisation of £1.3 billion. Market penetration had resulted in a dash for high street space, saturation of shops and a confusion of image between Next stores. The core Next brand had become overdeveloped with the womenswear chain mushrooming into too many variations. The mould-breaking Next Directory and the £300 million purchase of the mail order business Grattan had made a bid for the home shopper, but at an enormous cost. With gearing reaching 125 per cent, the group had

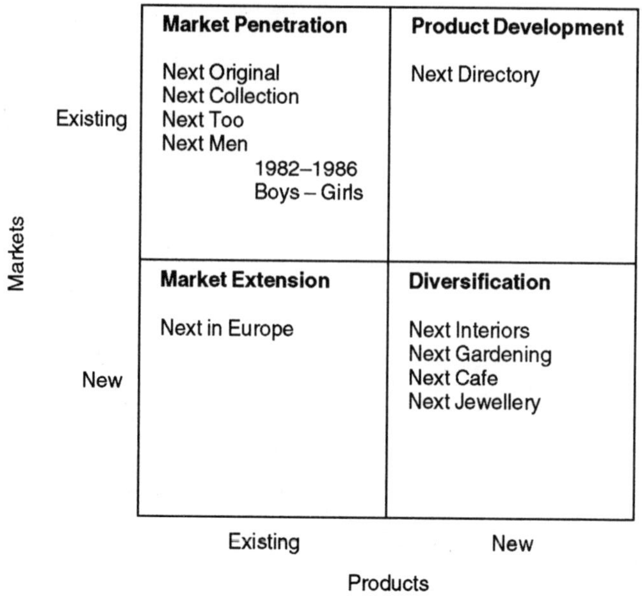

Markets	Market Penetration	Product Development
Existing	Next Original Next Collection Next Too Next Men 1982–1986 Boys – Girls	Next Directory
	Market Extension	**Diversification**
New	Next in Europe	Next Interiors Next Gardening Next Cafe Next Jewellery
Products	Existing	New

Figure 5.20 Next Ansoff matrix in 1988

overstretched itself and was saddled with redemption bills on its convertible Eurobonds. It had also strayed out of its core businesses into financial services and camping holidays.

■ What Happened Next?

When the retail boom of the mid-1980s finally tailed off, the company's position looked very weak. Swift action was necessary and George Davies, the architect of the Next superstructure, was ousted in a boardroom coup. He was replaced by Yorkshire accountant David Jones, who started work immediately with a restructuring programme, selling off peripheral businesses and concentrating on the core business Next Retail. More than 100 shops were closed, Grattan was disposed of at a knock down price of £168 million and closer attention was paid to cost control.

Table 5.9 Next plc Financial Performance, 1988–92

£m	*1992*	*1991*	*1990*	*1989*	*1988*
Turnover	462.0	877.6	1,028.3	1,210.1	1,209.5
Profit before interest	11.1	7.2	38.9	91.8	131.7

Next's fortunes now have come full circle and have signalled a complete reversal with a return to profit of £11 million in 1992 and nearly £39 million in 1993. (For details, see Table 5.9) Whilst its turnover is much reduced (£1.2 billion in 1988; £462 million in 1992), Next has had an enduring influence on the British high street fashion, with a virtually unchanged formula. What George Davies described as 'affordable collectables' – stylish clothes at affordable prices – remain enduringly true to the needs of the market segment.

■ Case Study 24: The Launch of *The Independent* Newspaper

The Independent newspaper, launched in October 1986, is a product which was so well-marketed that it successfully entered and established itself in the market of quality daily broadsheets, considered by many insiders to be closed.

From the outset, founder and editor Andreas Whittam Smith had four goals that he considered indicators of 'success' for his new venture. These were:

1 Circulation (the paper would be purchased in sufficient quantity to break even and be read by the target customer);
2 Quality, of writing, photography and design;
3 Profitability; and
4 Political and financial independence of the paper.

■ The Customer

In 1985 Whittam Smith originally from the *Daily Telegraph* commissioned market research to gather information on the newspaper preferences of a particular socio-economic segment, ABC1C2s, aged 20–45. The market research confirmed Whittam Smith's hunch that a market gap existed for this customer, who, it was found, would be interested in reading a non-partisan, high quality newspaper unlike anything then available in the market.

Results from this analysis revealed what 25–44-year-old ABC1s felt about existing newspapers:

- 80 per cent preferred a newspaper with no loyalty to any one political party and 49 per cent felt that national dailies did not offer balanced reporting.
- 35 per cent indicated that newspapers tried to appeal too broadly. 20 per cent said that they would be interested in reading a national newspaper aimed at 'people of my own age doing my sort of job'.
- 43 per cent thought that newspapers should complement the television and radio news more effectively by offering more analysis and comment.
- 29 per cent could not name a daily newspaper which offered a 'well-rounded read with plenty of general interest articles as well as news analysis'.
- 38 per cent believed that national newspapers should cover regional news and events, but 84 per cent could not name any national daily newspaper which did so.

Extrapolation of the results indicated that 1.7 million ABC1C2 readers of up-market newspapers had changed their paper in the previous year without the stimulus of a new title; that there were 2.2 million such readers who were dissatisfied with their present papers; and that there were 1.6 million such readers who had considered switching papers.

■ The Product

Encouraged by these findings, Whittam Smith set about defining more precisely his potential customer's needs and his product. The paper he envisaged would offer coverage of a wide range of topics from international news to domestic, education and consumer affairs, reported with no political bias. Having raised enough money to conceive, launch and establish *The Independent*, respected journalists were wooed away from established papers, attracted by the prospect of working on a high quality, non-partisan paper, produced and run by newspapermen, rather than wealthy businessmen with a political axe to grind. The layout of the paper was carefully designed, to produce a look that was simultaneously new but familiar, innovative but trustworthy. The potential positioning of *The Independent* can be seen in Figure 5.21.

A newspaper was able to sell two products: the newspaper itself and advertising space within the paper, with both products contributing to turnover. *The Independent* offered advertisers particular benefits, listed below, that were not available from most other papers.

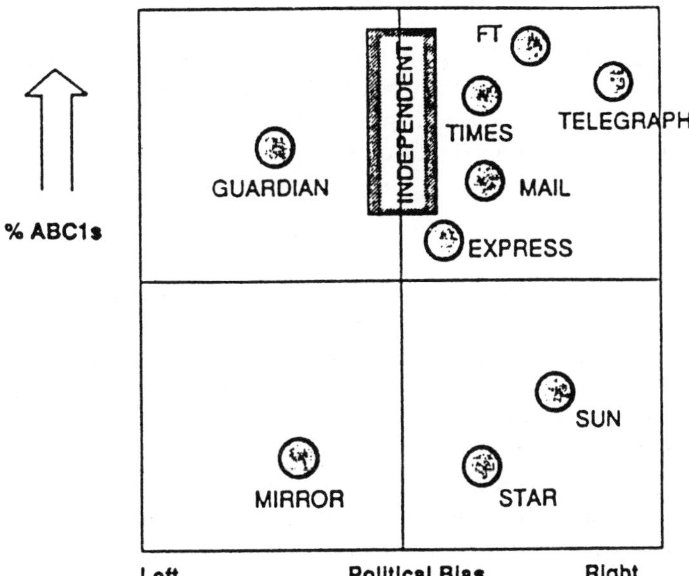

Figure 5.21 Market gap analysis

- *Lost Cost* – cost savings resulting from the use of new technology would be passed on to advertisers.
- *High Spending Readers – The Independent*'s target readership had very high spending power. It was also difficult to reach by other advertising media (for instance ABC1s are very light ITV viewers).
- *A Quality Environment* – in which to advertise quality products.
- *Regional Advertising – The Independent's* distribution system which allowed regional advertising in a national newspaper.

■ Price

The price of *The Independent* at launch was set at 25 pence, which was high enough to position it among the quality dailies. To set the price any higher, however, would have been quite risky for a new product entering a closed market.

■ Promotion

Active promotion of *The Independent* started six months before the first issue hit the news stands. The promotional campaign attempted to generate awareness, interest and trial purchase of the new newspaper. In addition, multi-media (radio, television, print, and posters) advertising was used successfully to communicate the independent character of the paper. The phrase, 'It is. Are you?' (ie. independent) became widely recognised and effectively branded and differentiated *The Independent* from the *Guardian*, the *Times*, and the *Daily Telegraph*. Three million leaflets offering trial subscriptions with money-back guarantees were mailed out shortly before the launch, and telephone and face-to-face interviews were used both pre- and post-launch to get closer to the customer and get detailed feedback on customer reactions.

■ Place

While *The Independent* was, and still is, available to customers in the same outlets as other quality dailies, the methods of printing and distribution adopted to get the product to the customer were revolutionary. Fleet Street typesetters were dispensed with, in favour of direct entry and editing of stories on desktop computers by reporters. Once the issue was finalised, it was electronically transmitted to third-party printers in three locations around England for printing. Whittam Smith believes that by not owning its own printers the newspaper, and ultimately the customer, benefit. *The Independent* does not have to deal with the print unions, enabling it to keep its creative energies focused on its product and customer.

By 1988 circulation had surpassed the 320,000 required to break even and reached around sales 400,000 daily. *The Independent* believed that its actual reach was about 1,005,000 equivalent to a share of about 15 per cent of the quality paper market. The quality of the paper was attested to both by its growing number of customers, and the numerous awards it won, including the Best Overall Newspaper Design two years in a row. In April 1988 the paper was re-financed, ahead of schedule and a profit of over £4.088m was made in that year. A recent MORI poll found that readership was evenly split among the three main political parties, a good indicator of its continued political independence. Financial independence was maintained in keeping with the paper's Articles of Association by prohibiting any individual or corporation from acquiring more than 5 per cent of the share capital.

■ Product Development

With the success of the daily broadsheet, it was inevitable that the company should attack the Sunday market. Whittam Smith has always watched the market with interest and had even taken early tentative steps to buy the *Observer*. However, in 1989, *The Independent on Sunday* was launched and established a small but significant market share of the quality Sundays. As winner of the National Sunday Newspaper of the Year award in 1993 for its 'stylish prose', the paper now averages sales of 403,000, along with the rest of the competition, a long way behind the market leader the *Sunday Times*.

The launch of the Sunday paper and its fight for survival along with the now defunct *Sunday Correspondent* has had a far-reaching financial effect, weakened the firm foundation of the daily *Independent* and delayed the flotation of the company. In 1993, in an attempt to eliminate competition, Whittam Smith put in a firm bid for the ailing *Observer*, but was beaten by the *Guardian*.

■ The future

For the daily *Independent*, the situation has become difficult. The battle for market share is intense, with extra sections and colour magazines being launched by competitors with regularity. With a trend of slow gradual decline in broadsheet and tabloid sales, the fight for circulation and the all important advertising continues.

Under such pressure, *The Independent* has started to lose its direction. With circulation slipping, it took the strange decision to change what has been regarded as its strength – its layout. The radical redesign, launched in March 1993, altered the typeface and introduced the first ever seven-column format. The resultant increase in sales, a modest 5,000 issues, has not been sustained, with average daily sales standing currently at 364,000 (Sept 92–March 93). Its future direction looks unsure.

■ Case Study 25: Thorntons plc

■ Introduction

Established 83 years ago with one toffee shop in Sheffield, Thorntons now has the largest independent chain of quality confectionery shops in the UK, and is famous for its freshly-made luxury chocolates.

This case shows how the Yorkshire family firm's marketing orientation has secured its recent success.

□ *Criteria for Success*

Business performance indicators:

- Sales growth from £36m (1985) to £84m (1992).
- Profit growth from £2.1m (1985) to £10m (1992).
- 1988 stock market flotation eight times oversubscribed.

■ 1980s Strategy

□ *Market Overview*

Thorntons' success stems from a clear overview of the dynamics of the £3bn confectionery market. During the 1980s Thorntons perceived that the £1bn sugar-based sector demonstrated static volume, raw material cost pressure, and a vociferous health lobby.

The £1.94bn non-luxury chocolate sector was characterised by a 70 per cent incidence of impulse purchase. The high levels of awareness necessary to prompt purchase – involving advertising, and intensive distribution – resulted in 75 per cent market domination by the three confectionery giants, Rowntree, Cadbury and Mars. Static volumes and active health lobbies worsened the picture.

In stark contrast, the £60m luxury chocolate sector displayed rapid volume and value growth, together with high profit margins. High disposable income allowed the young, middle-class, predominantly female, target market to trade up, while social attitudes softened to luxury chocolates as an 'allowable all year round self-indulgence'. The sector included a growing gift purchase element. Major competitive activity was limited to Ferrero Rocher.

□ *Niche Marketing*

Analysis based on the Boston matrix (Figure 5.22) enabled Thorntons to take stock of its product portfolio in light of the market dynamics, and to adopt

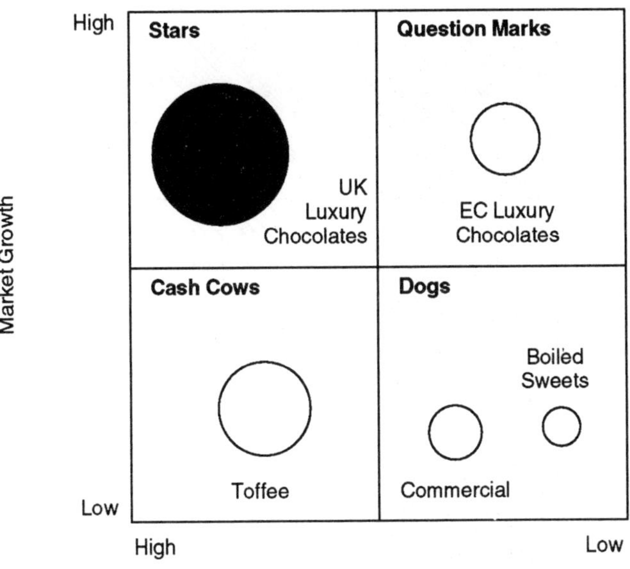

Figure 5.22 Thorntons Boston matrix, 1988

the appropriate strategy for individual product groups. The need to invest for further growth in luxury chocolates was clear.

Also, analysis based on the directional policy matrix (Figure 5.23) confirmed the mouth-watering match between the attractiveness of the luxury chocolate sector, and Thorntons' distinctive competences.

To this high growth, profitable sector, Thorntons could bring product quality, premium image, manufacturing flexibility and vertical integration.

The resultant niche marketing strategy (Figure 5.24) required high differentiation to avoid competition on price. Differentiation by quality was the key for Thorntons, impacting on all marketing variables.

The USP of the product was the quality of the soft centres, made from fresh ingredients such as cream, butter and real alcohol. Uncompromising production standards were enforced in a £9 million, purpose-built factory in Derbyshire.

A unique concept in the retail confectionery market, Thorntons' shops were the only outlets for their branded product (Marks and Spencer were supplied with a reformulated, own-label product to avoid cannibalisation). Control of the distribution chain, including franchised outlets operating to a company manual, ensured conformance to the stringent handling requirements of such critically short shelf-life products. A store-redesign further augmented the quality offering.

Thorntons' promotional strategies included television and poster advertising to exploit the Christmas/Easter seasonality, with a platform based on quality

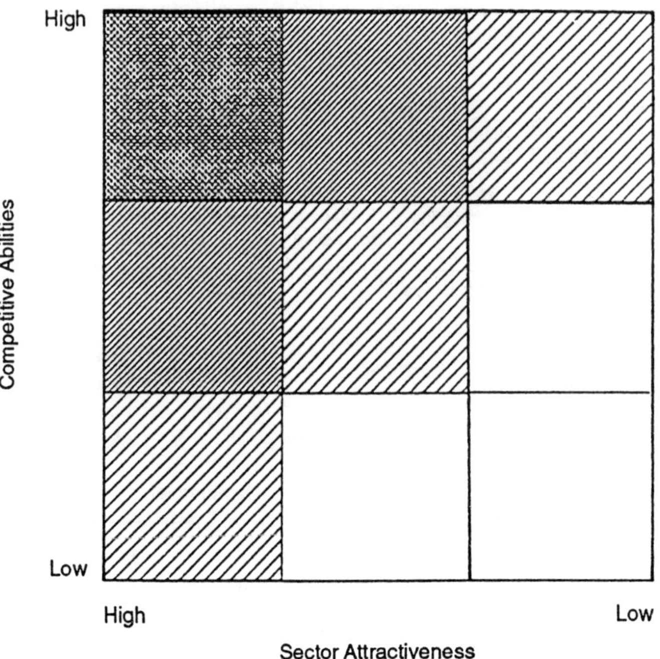

Figure 5.23 Thorntons directional policy matrix

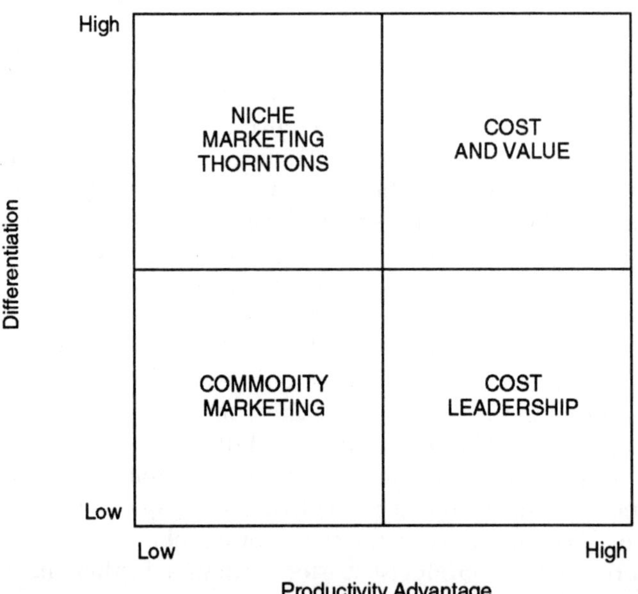

Figure 5.24 Thorntons Porter matrix

and freshness. In-store displays were used off-season to encourage sampling of innovative products, such as Beaujolais Nouveau truffles.

Based on the relative price inelasticity of the product, Thorntons adopted a high pricing policy to reinforce the quality image, and to promote the product's acceptability as gifts.

Thorntons position as a top-of-the-range niche market confectioner has relied not just on the quality of the product, but also on marketing techniques. The device of writing the recipient's name in white icing on the outside of an Easter egg has been part of the company's competitive advantage since the 1920s.

Early distribution was focused on the south of England, but cautious expansion throughout the UK with company outlets and franchises has resulted in a thorough coverage of the country. Thorntons now operate through 395 shops; of these 189 are franchises or mini-franchise units, usually in towns too small to merit a full Thorntons outlet and where the selling space is limited to one counter in a gift or card shop.

■ The Future

□ *European Market Expansion*

The Single market offers a positive opportunity for Thorntons to source and distribute its products. The first acquisition and move into Europe came in 1988 with the £2 million purchase of Belgian confectioner Gartner Pralines. Gartner, based in Antwerp, specialises in high quality chocolates and fresh cream products, sold mainly through patisseries. Thorntons are now distributing Gartner's products through its own UK stores, as well as selling its own confectionery to the Belgian group's existing customers.

But the major push was the purchase of French confectioners Sogeco and La Nouvelle de Confiserie in 1989, and their associated well known brand names. Bringing these companies back into the black has used up much of the company's resources and has taken longer than expected due to different working and sweet-eating cultures.

□ *Product Development*

The company's investment in new product development, such as the new Select range – the ultimate Eurochoc, has meant that the product portfolio remains distinctive and enjoyable to the consumer. Recent moves to produce sugar-free products for Boots represent an interesting development area for the company and a growing market opportunity.

□ *Diversification*

With weather playing a key role in influencing chocolate purchases, the achievement of a weather neutral business remains a key strategic goal.

Table 5.11 Thorntons plc Financial Record, 1988–92

	1992	1991	1990 (53 weeks)	1989 (56 weeks)	1988
	£000	£000	£000	£000	£000
a) Profit and loss account					
Sales					
– continuing operations	84,325	79,911	71,115	58,416	47,915
– discontinued operations	–	–	5,055	5,504	4,582
	84,325	79,911	76,170	63,920	52,497
Operating profit	10,443	11,408	10,008	8,260	6,888
Profit on property disposals	148	713	783	827	667
Net interest receivable/(payable)	(565)	(241)	389	824	(51)
Profit on discontinued operations	–	–	131	178	41
Profit before exceptional items and taxation	10,026	11,880	11,311	10,089	7,545
Exceptional items	(824)	–	–	–	–
Taxation	(2,928)	(3,952)	(3,430)	(3,683)	(2,754)
Profit after taxation	6,274	7,928	7,881	6,406	4,791
Minority interest	–	–	10	–	–
Extraordinary profit/(loss)	–	350	950	–	(440)
Profit attributable to shareholders	6,274	8,278	8,841	6,406	4,351
Dividends	(2,324)	(2,273)	(2,076)	(1,572)	(354)
Profit retained	3,950	6,005	6,765	4,834	3,997
b) Balance sheet					
Fixed assets	52,249	49,526	48,975	34,671	27,254
Net current assets	9,565	6,819	2,062	8,047	8,907
	61,814	56,345	51,037	42,718	36,161
Creditors due after one year and provisions	(13,795)	(11,753)	(11,938)	(4,522)	(3,529)
Net assets	48,019	44,592	39,099	38,196	32,632
Capital expenditure	7,809	7,819	13,161	8,447	7,883
Earnings per share	9.9p	12.6p	12.5p	10.2p	8.7p
Net assets per share	75.4p	70.9p	62.2p	60.7p	51.9p
c) Number of outlets (excluding discontinued operations)					
Retail	218	205	205	188	177
Franchise	177	162	138	117	103
Mini-franchise and chill-cabinets	17	11	–	–	–
Total U.K., Eire and Channel Islands	412	378	343	305	280
France	58	59	64	–	–
Total	470	437	407	305	280

Thorntons' Real Dairy Ice Cream is the company's first step away from its core business and markets. From a modest 7 per cent market share, the opportunities lie in developing distinctive products, closely linked to the confectionery brand image with the same high standards and value for money.

□ *Competition*

Such success in a niche market will inevitably attract followers into the only growth sector of the chocolate market. One of the major manufacturers would have the financial strength to launch a less upmarket product and utilise their intensive CTN-based distribution.

■ Growth in the 1990s

A major corporate review of strategy and opportunities in 1992 resulted in new targets for growth; from nearly 400 outlets to 650 in the UK and 150 in France within five years, the development of the commercial own-label business and further consolidation of the ice cream business through the major multiples. Thornton's growth and profitability in the 1990s will depend on the success of the different strategies undertaken to cope with the vagaries of the UK chocolate business, including investment in EPOS and computerised stock management.

Success will also attract predators. Following the 'bar wars' between Rowntree, Suchard and Nestle, Thorntons must be wary of a take-over bid, from a company keen to exploit their unique position in chocolate manufacture and retailing, especially given the slight weakening of their financial position in 1992 (see Table 5.10).

CHAPTER 6

Competitive Marketing Strategy Experience

The previous five chapters of this book provide a basis for analysing competitive marketing strategies of businesses.

This chapter consolidates this experience by:

- providing a summary of the different strategies confronted by major players in the markets in the case studies in this book;
- presenting a summary of changes in strategic position of companies represented in the case studies; and
- highlighting effective competitive strategies suggested by the experience of firms in the case studies.

An overview of the cases provides different strategy sequences which may be useful as a reference point for the marketing strategist. These include:

□ *Market Leaders and Challengers*

- Myson Radiators challenges Stelrad;
- JCB defends its dominance in a declining market;
- Andrex, defending market leadership through branding;
- Glaxo, a global success story;
- The single European grocery market;
- Tesco challenges Sainsbury (retailing);
- Bernard Matthews (fast foods);
- Ballantines in Spain (whisky);
- Argos (retailing); and
- Courtelle (acrylic fibre).

□ *Loss of Momentum and Position in the Market*

- Leadership issues in the European Cellopp market;
- Hornes (men's tailors);
- The European Fertiliser market, the demise of a market leader;
- Selincourt (fashion);
- Next (fashion); and
- Ratners Group plc.

☐ *Strong Niche Positions Established*

- Amstrad (personal computers);
- Virgin Atlantic Airways;
- Pretty Polly (hosiery);
- Brent Chemicals;
- Firkin pubs;
- Trivial Pursuit;
- Derwent Valley Foods;
- Stollwerck AG, Germany (chocolates);
- *The Independent* (newspaper); and
- Thorntons (chocolates).

■ Changes in Strategic Position

The strategic position matrix first presented in Chapter 1 is used in this section

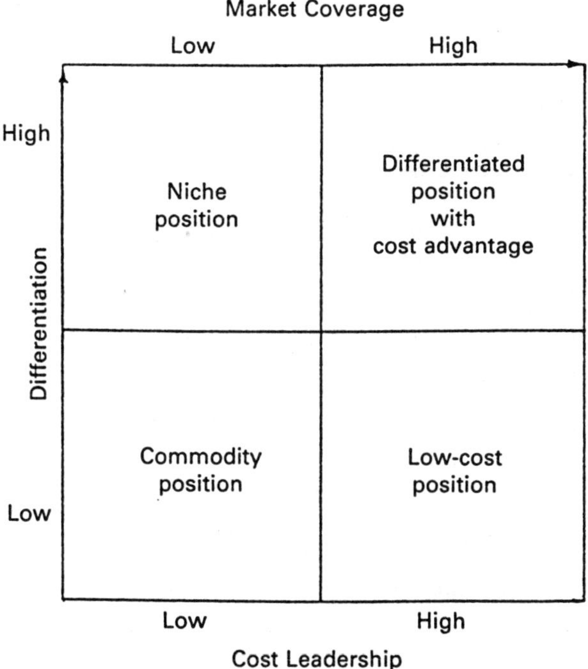

Figure 6.1 Generic strategic positions

to summarise the positions of players in each of the twenty six case study markets. Figure 6.1 shows four generic strategic positions:

1 A commodity position is one in which the company has minimum advantages in differentiation and costs and a low market share with limited market coverage.
2 A niche position is one in which the firm has high differentiation but a low share of the overall market and limited market coverage.
3 A low-cost position occurs when a competitor has cost leadership with a high market share and market coverage.
4 A differentiated position is one with cost advantage – high differentiation, low costs, high market coverage and share.

Figure 6.2 shows strategic directions for improving position by changing relative costs and differentiation.

The simplifying figures (Figs. 6.3–6.14) cannot present a complete picture of the positions of companies and changes made, but they do serve as useful references to establishing the competitive situation and direction of strategic change. The figures are given so that the reader can select and analyse particular case studies.

A figure is presented for each of the twenty six cases studied showing main competitors and the directions of changes in strategic positions.

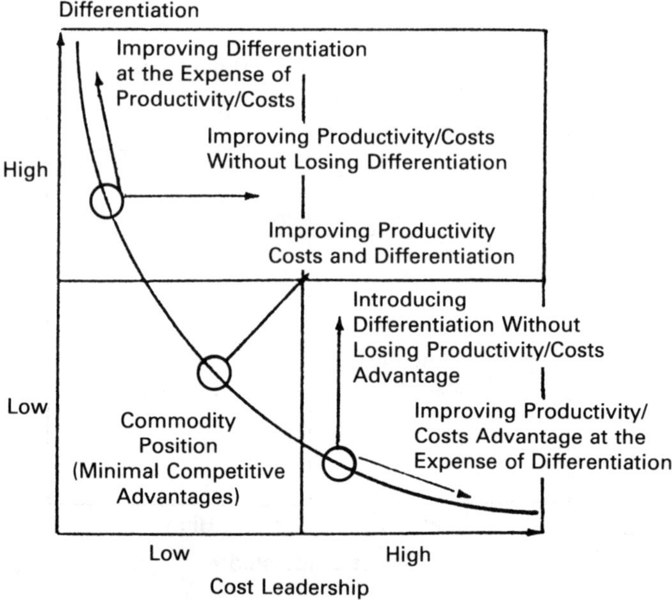

Figure 6.2 Strategic directions

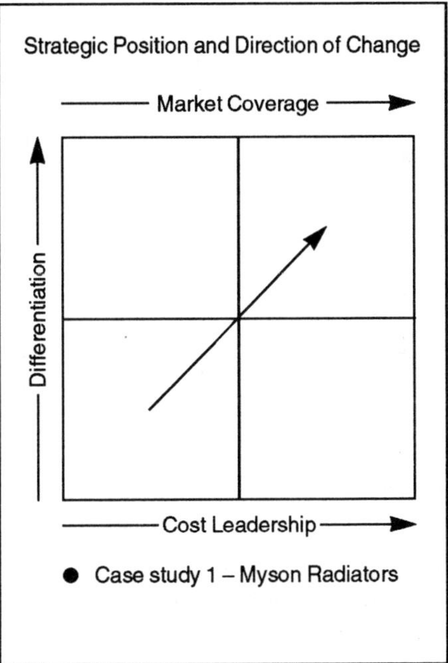

Figure 6.3

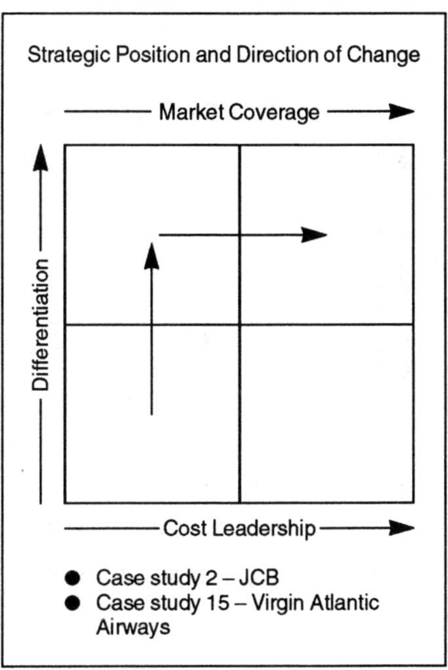

Figure 6.4

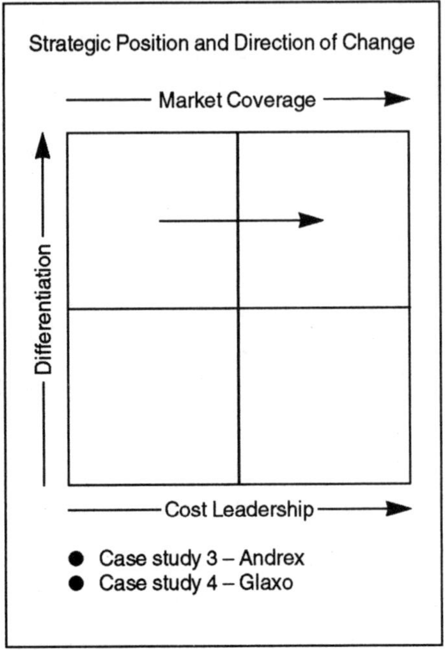

Figure 6.5

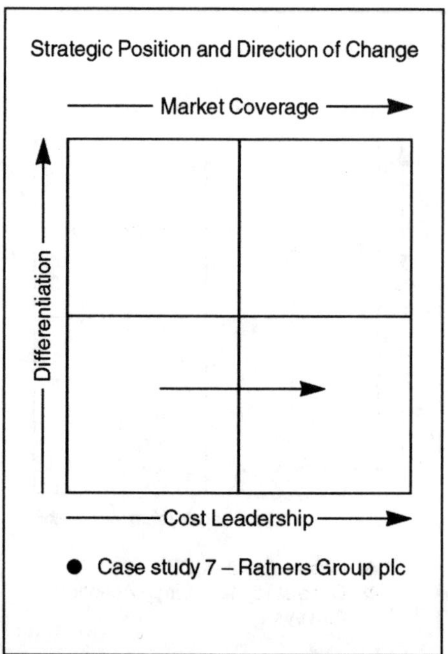

Figure 6.6

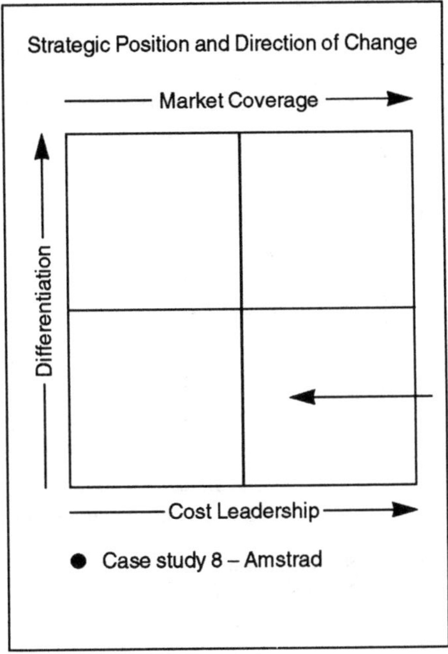

Figure 6.7

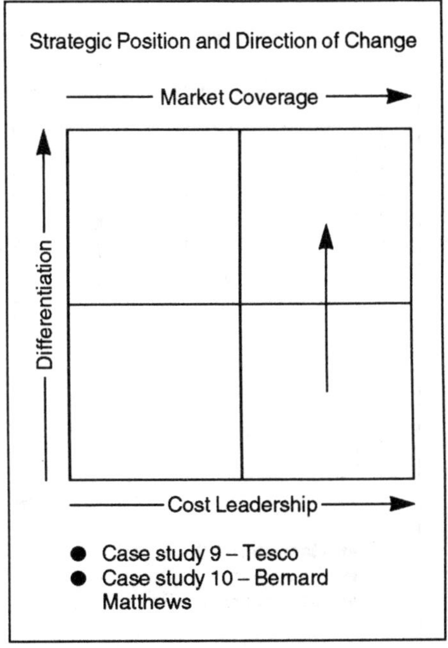

Figure 6.8

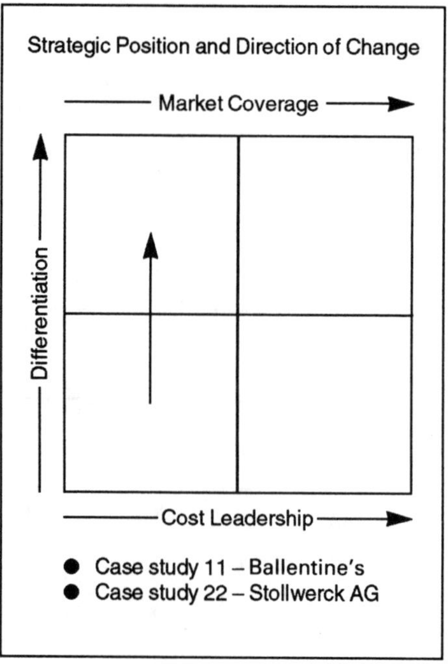

Figure 6.9

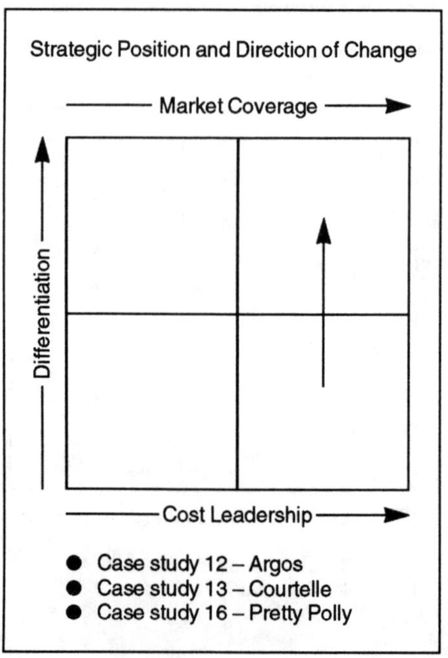

Figure 6.10

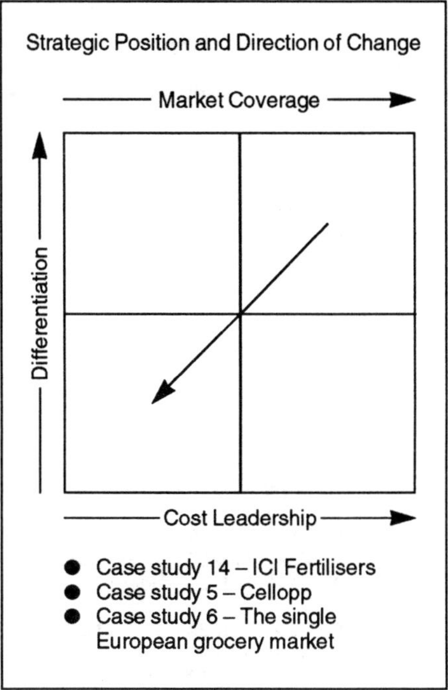

Figure 6.11

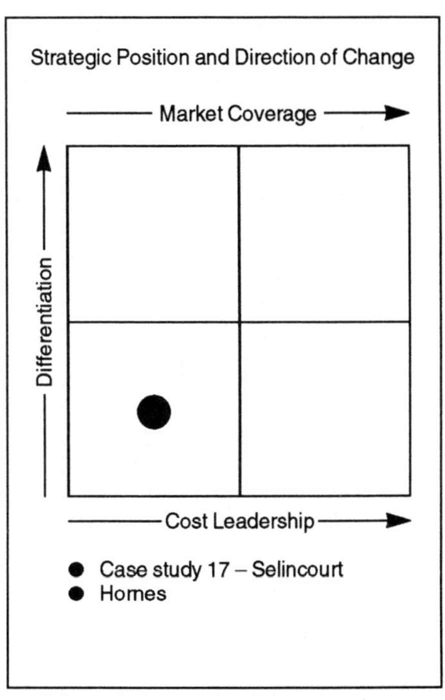

Figure 6.12

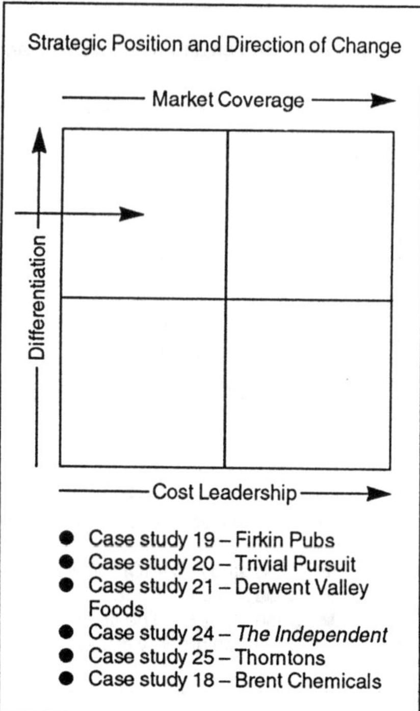

Figure 6.13

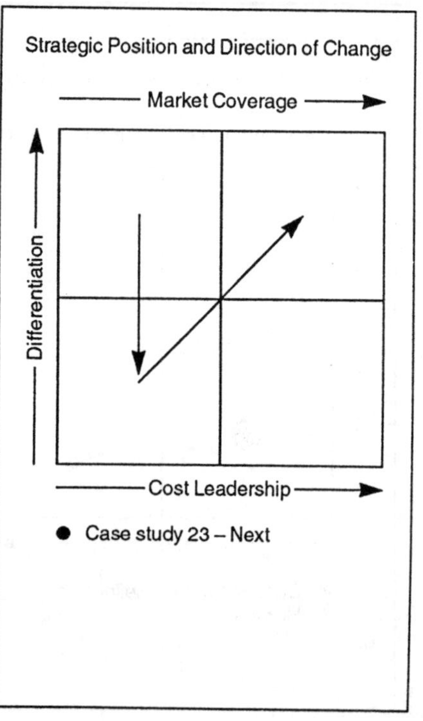

Figure 6.14

■ Strategic Marketing Observations from European Experience

The twenty five case studies presented in earlier chapters reinforce many of the strategic principles observed in other developed economies. Some underlying themes from observations of European marketing practice are summarised here:

□ *General Observation*

For sustained success, it is essential to establish a clear, distinct and defendable competitive position in the market. This may be a position of:

- market leadership;
- joint dominance;
- differentiated alternative – a flanker; or
- specialist – niche competitor.

The firm must determine what it wants to be.

Irrespective of competitive position, attention to costs and ability to be competitive on price is an important defensive capability as competition increases and as technology changes company capacity levels and cost structures. Only those firms that operate in narrow 'prestige' market segments are protected from price competition.

Competitive analysis is an increasingly important activity as a contribution to the design of well-targeted strategies. It is needed to enable realistic assessment of opportunities and threats at a time of increasing global competition and technological change, which has direct impact on the European market.

□ *Observations Specific to Competitive Position*

Market Leader or Jointly Dominant Firm
An alert market leader can defend dominance with pre-emptive strategies, but must invest in innovative strategies to maintain long term leadership or dominance and ensure market profitability.

Dominant firms need to widen their scope of competitive analysis to identify early enough:

- threats from outside the industry in the form of large companies making an entry;
- threats posed by technology widening the boundaries of competition;
- government regulations or polices which allow restructuring of the industry and widening of competition; and
- threats from niche competitors who suddenly change to an aggressive growth strategy.

An underrated threat to the dominant firm is the 'unseen' niche competitor. Even when observed, the 'niche' competitor is misjudged in terms of growth potential and in terms of cost structure advantage.

The Flanker

The flanker operates in the mainstream market with a clearly differentiated and alternative position from the dominant companies or the market leader. To enjoy continued success, the flanker must maintain the position of the differentiated alternative.

The best strategy for taking on the leader is through flanking with innovation that redefines the market in favour of the flanker. Apple is a good example in the personal computer market.

The Niche Specialist

There are usually many opportunities for niche positions in a market, both at the high and low end, regionally and serving specific narrow market segments.

The niche specialist can become a major force, moving from either the low end or the high end of the market. But the transition from specialist to main player must be rapid, or the firm will reap the consequences of being 'stuck in the middle'.

The niche specialist, who does not wish to become a major force in the market, faces problems if its market segment grows to a size where it attracts the major competitors or if profitability draws in new entrants. The specialist must then look for other narrow segments to enter.

■ Summary of Competitive Strategy Principles

□ *Strategy Elements*

Successful competitive marketing strategy requires the design and provision of product offerings that achieve competitive positionings based on:

- attributes/benefits that are important to target customers;
- a sustainable differential advantage over competitors;
- cost/revenue structures that are consistent with strategic and product objectives; and
- harmony with corporate image attributes.

□ *Offensive Strategies*

Attacking the Leader Directly

1 Find a weakness in the leader's strength and attack it.
2 Launch the attack in as concentrated a form as possible.

3 Commit resources to sustain the attack and defend against market leader retaliation.
4 Follow through and consolidate the new position.

Flanking Offensives

1 Move into an uncontested market segment and differentiate.
2 Timing and surprise are valuable advantages to obtain lead time for market penetration.
3 Follow through and consolidate the new position with brand development strategies.

Niche Offensives

1 Specialise in a market segment that can be defended against large competitors.
2 Develop a brand position in the segments served.
3 Be prepared, if necessary, to move to other specialised segments of the market.

□ *Defensive Strategies*

1 Be prepared to cannibalise your own business.
2 Pre-empt, block or match strong competitive moves.
3 Attempt to prevent any battles that will be damaging.
4 Adopt legal actions or industry sanctions to block illegal offensives.
5 Use rumour to advantage.

■ Evaluating Competitive Strategies

The final choice of a strategy depends on judgements about risk, likely outcomes and rewards, resource trade-offs, complex and ambiguous environments and negotiations inside and outside the organisation.

■ Formalised Evaluation Systems

The evaluation stage is a process of testing, refining and retesting strategies against relevant criteria. One checklist of evaluation criteria is that proposed by George Day.[1] He suggests six factors to use in screening the logic of strategy:

- *Suitability*: Is the proposed strategy consistent with the foreseeable environment threats and opportunities? Does the strategy exploit or enhance a current competitive advantage, or create a new source of advantage?

- *Validity*: Are the assumptions about environmental trends and the outcomes of the strategy realistic? Are the assumptions based on reliable and valid information?
- *Consistency*: Are the basic elements of the strategy consistent with each other and the objectives pursued?
- *Feasibility*: Is the strategy appropriate to the available resources? Are the basic elements and premises of the strategy understandable and acceptable to the operating managers who will have the responsibility for implementing them?
- *Vulnerability*: To what extent are projected outcomes dependent on data or assumptions of dubious quality and origin? Are the risks of failure acceptable? Are there adequate contingency plans for coping with these risks? Can the decision be reversed in the future? How long will it take? What are the consequences?
- *Potential Rewards*: Are the projected outcomes satisfactory in the light of the provisional objectives for the business? Are the adjustments to the objectives acceptable to the stakeholders?

The process of evaluation proposed by Day is depicted in Figure 6.15. This shows a limited set of distinct strategy options being screened, then some eliminated or revised and finally matched against the provisional objectives of the business.

This type of screening approach is used in business, particularly for the evaluation of new products. Businesses such as British Telecom, which develop and launch a large number of new products, has developed tailored screening systems to reduce the options to a small number of opportunities and business strategies.

In the normal course of developing competitive marketing strategies, however, formalised evaluation systems are not used by many European businesses. This is one of the least developed aspects of strategy.

■ Practical Issues in Strategy Evaluation

Experience in reviewing a large number of marketing strategy plans at the business and product-market level of analysis, suggests a number of factors to watch when evaluating a strategy.

□ *Lack of Market Analysis*

Many plans include voluminous market data, but frequently little real interpretation for strategy. Lack of market analysis may also occur because of unreliable data or gaps in important information. In particular, the identification of segments and the effect on the market of expected competitive actions, and not tied down.

In these cases, explicit assumptions should be made and their strategic implications noted. To clarify the issues, the consideration of alternative scenarios and their assumptions may be useful. This highlights the degree of uncertainty or risk of the particular strategy.

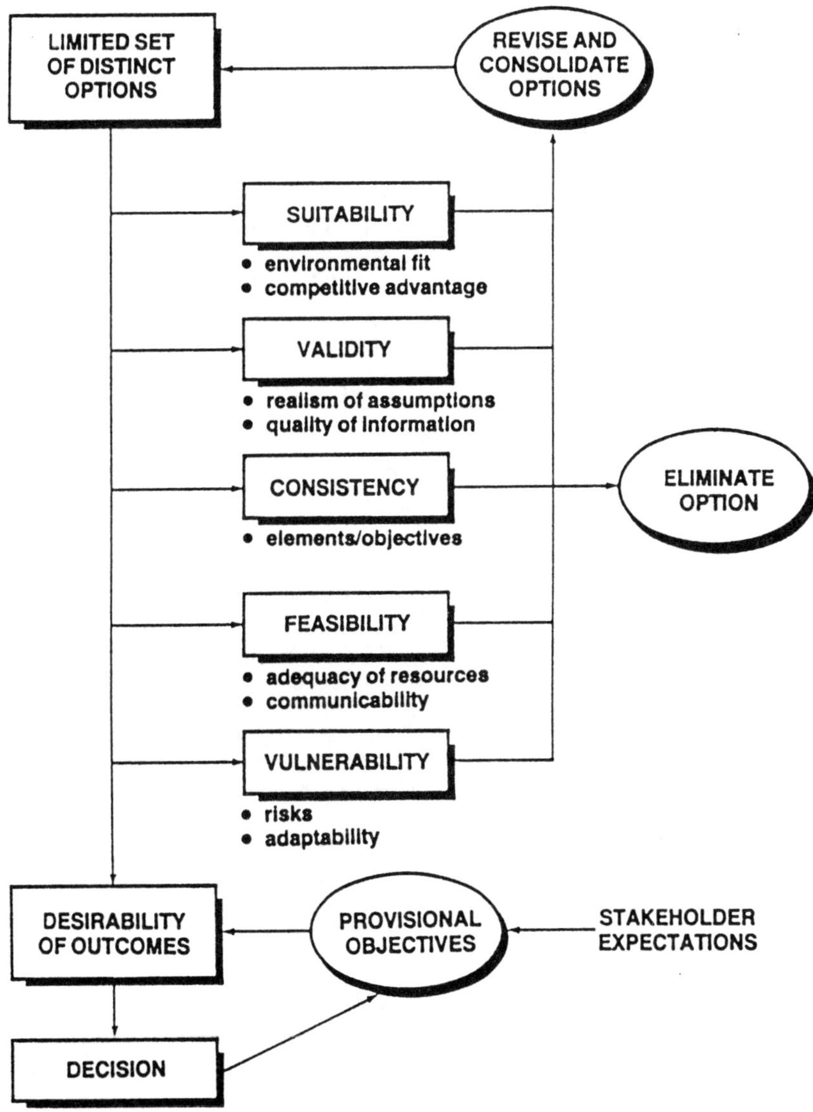

Figure 6.15 Evaluating strategic options

Source: G. S. Day, *Strategic Market Planning*, 1986, p. 169

☐ *Over-estimating the Impact of Marketing Effort*

Marketers have a positive and opportunistic attitude to business. This can lead them in part to unrealistic expectations of the effect of marketing effort. The issues of competitive marketing strategy discussed in earlier chapters need to be clearly in mind when evaluating the likely results from marketing expenditures.

☐ *Under-estimating the Capabilities of Competitors, Especially Small Ones*

This usually occurs because of limited strategic information on competitors, owing to gaps in competitive intelligence. The importance of competitors and likely reactions to particular strategies need to be assessed. If the success of the preferred strategy rests on the reactions of a competitor, additional competitive intelligence should be obtained.

☐ *Limited Consideration of the Pros and Cons of Strategic Options*

A useful way of evaluating preferred strategy is to note pros and cons and compare them with alternative strategies. This process usually acts to modify and strengthen the final strategy decided upon.

☐ *Little Analysis of the Cross-effects between Products and Markets*

This should be attempted, even qualitatively, because it makes explicit the potential problem of unintended cross-effects with the company's other products or markets.

☐ *Problems of Conflicts of Opinion in the Business*

Conflicts occur most frequently in pricing decisions because of the direct interest in price of senior management, financial managers and marketers. Pricing is usually a key part of any competitive marketing strategy. Other conflicts may occur in relation to required resource support or on the timing of strategy implementation.

☐ *Lack of Matching of Required Resources to Support the Strategy*

Lack of commitment or conflicting demands on resources can doom a strategy. Alternatively, a strategy may require a level or type of resources to succeed that cannot be provided by the firm. Realistic assessments of these factors should be made.

☐ *Insufficient and Superficial Financial Analysis*

This is a major weakness found in many competitive strategies. The profit effects on the company and its competitors from planned strategies, are frequently not analysed in any depth. Computer-based spread-sheet analysis and financial modelling readily allow sensitivity analysis and financial risk assessment to be undertaken.

In addition to these, unrealistic forecasts, biases of decision-makers and incorrect assessment of corporate capabilities, are risks associated with strategy formulation and evaluation.

All of these practical problems should be considered when evaluating a strategy. An assessment of weaknesses in these areas and what impact they might have, should form part of the input for the final judgements and evaluations made on the likely success of the planned strategy.

■ Future Developments in Strategy Evaluation

The intensity of competition and change is placing greater pressure on the marketer to develop and implement competitive marketing strategies that will achieve the company's objectives over time at acceptable risk. It will place more importance, for the strategist, on being able to evaluate strategies before they are implemented.

There are a number of avenues being developed in the United States and Europe to help the marketer in evaluating market strategy alternatives and in selecting appropriate strategies. The ultimate purpose is to increase the chances of a marketer achieving company objectives and reduce the risk of making costly marketing mistakes.

The developments which appear to provide fruitful prospects are:

- the analysis of pooled business marketing experience;
- strategic marketing decision support systems; and
- marketing strategy simulation games.

Each of these harnesses computer power to assist the marketer to gain experience in strategy evaluation.

☐ *The Analysis of Pooled Business Experience*

The basic premise underlying the pooling of business experience is that the conduct of a large series of strategy experiments on companies in a similar competitive position will provide guidelines on successful and unsuccessful strategies. This approach has been adopted by the PIMS programme, which has been reported on in earlier chapters.[2] Strategic analysis of this kind is another contribution to the strategy evaluation process. Development of industry-specific models will allow more of the particular conditions to be included in this type of analysis.

□ *Strategic Marketing Decision Support Systems*

Day, in his review of strategic decision support systems, refers to the growing availability of interactive personal computer hardware with abundant memory and user-friendly software, and parallel developments in communication technology. The capacity of these systems to organise and make available data that yield strategic insights, and the need for managers to make decisions more quickly in a consistently shifting competitive environment, means that the conditions are right and the need is pressing.[3]

Keen and Morton characterise decision support systems in the following manner: 'The impact is on decisions in which there is sufficient structure for computer and analytic aids to be of value, but where managers' judgement is essential.'[4] The pay-off is in extending the range and analysis capacity of managers' decision processes.

The relevance for managers is the creation of a decision support tool, which remains under their control, does not attempt to automate the decision process, impose solutions, or predefine objectives.

Examples of marketing decision support systems include the *Brandaid* model, which is used for evaluating marketing mix options.[5] This uses a combination of historical data analysis and field experimentation to develop a basic forecast. The model then takes account of management judgements on responsiveness of market demand to price, promotion and advertising, which are used to assess the sales and profit effects of changes in the company marketing mix. The model is also used to determine the effects of a competitor's change in strategy, given alternative responses by the firm.

Exmar is a computer-based expert system developed at Cranfield School of Management in conjunction with NCR. It assists in the process of developing strategic marketing plans. Another Cranfield knowledge based system, which evaluates new product ideas and prepares for launch, has also been developed.

Stratport is a model designed to evaluate portfolio strategies and suggest an optimal allocation of marketing resources across strategic business units.[6] Using a combination of data and judgement, the relationships between market share and marketing investment are established and relationships between capacity expenditure, working capital and experience arises for costs and prices. In practice it is difficult to obtain these relationships, but the model can help identify a few attractive resource allocation strategies that can then be considered in depth. Similar models such as *Ansplan*, developed by Igor Ansoff, have refined this process.[7]

General Electric has been a pioneer in this field. It initiated what became the PIMS project, and developed in-house a large range of computer-based decision support systems. Of particular note are the models developed by GE's

Corporate Marketing Division of the market share change effects in six strategic variables. Each, of three models, is generic to a broad category of industrial market structure and has been calibrated using the PIMS data base.[8]

These models are being used not for predictive purposes, but for evaluative planning purposes. In one application a business with a large share in a growing market believed it could maintain share over a four-year period without any increase in marketing effort. Using the relevant share change model, it was inferred that the business could lose five share points if they were to pursue a 'no change' marketing strategy. The purpose of this planning aid is to suggest to the manager when it may be necessary to rethink the strategy, when a required rate of share growth is way out of line with an expected rate of share growth.[9] These types of models appear to provide benefits in assisting marketing strategies and planners to evaluate strategic options.

A starting point is to develop a data base of all main products and brands and track their histories as a means of retaining success and failure lessons for future reference and as a basis for strategic analysis.

□ *Marketing Strategy Simulation Games*

The most widely used marketing strategy game in USA and European business school marketing strategy courses, is *Markstrat.* It makes extensive use of product positioning analysis for the formulation of dynamic competitive strategy.[10]

Simulation games are very useful as a means of learning from experience at low cost. They put the student or manager in a position of running a company or a product line and benefiting or suffering from the consequences of the decisions made.

New games are becoming available for the practitioner and student to gain from this type of experience in various aspects of marketing and business.

■ A Final Comment

Reliance on computer-based models is hazardous. They can, as calculators have to an extent, blunt our faculty for thinking. Competitive marketing is a human endeavour that requires judgement, a sixth sense, a mentality and a 'feel' for what makes sense in the market place in which we operate.

Systematic analysis and computer-based support provide a variety of important ideas to weigh against our judgement and experience and to synthesize within our strategic thinking. The field of study is changing, as is the competitive environment. This book attempts to widen the strategic experience of the reader, with a particular focus on the European marketing environment. Increasingly, the difference between companies competing in a market with similar resources, skills and information will be the design and implementation of their competitive marketing strategies.

CHAPTER 7

Uses of Case Studies to Enhance Learning

The twenty-six cases in this book can be used in a variety of ways to enhance learning by the marketing strategy student and practitioner.

■ Case Analysis and Evaluation of Strategies

Each of the cases can be analysed by addressing some or all of the following strategic issues:

- Conduct a SWOT analysis of each important competitor in the market.
- Evaluate the past strategies of each main competitor and highlight the features of each strategy. Indicate how each competitor could have improved its competitive position.
- What key strategic issues must be addressed by the strategy of firm *X*: market issues; competitive issues; external environment issues; or internal issues?
- Suggest alternative plausible scenarios of the future relevant to this market and select the most likely one upon which you will base your strategy. State your assumptions.
- What strategic options are available to firm *X*?
- What marketing objectives and strategies do you recommend: short term (one year); medium term (three years); or long term (beyond three years)?
- List specific marketing activities to implement in the short term.

This type of analysis can be done with reference to your own experience.

■ Study Strategy Sequences and Changes in Competitive Position

Insight can be gained by analysing the sequences to strategies adopted by main players in the case study and the results they achieved. A detailed competitive analysis, which may require the collection of more information on each competitor, can be useful in enabling the strategist to predict more accurately the types of future strategies likely to be adopted. This will also provide insight into the potential for changes in competitive position of specific competitors.

■ Update the Case Study

Having developed your own assessment of appropriate strategies for the firms in the case study, given assumptions about their objectives, a useful exercise is to bring the case up to date and compare the strategies adopted by firms with your own recommendations. Where possible, assess their results and changes in competitive position.

This adds to your ability to evaluate strategies before their implementation.

■ Comparisons between Markets

Using the cases in this book, useful comparative analysis can be made between industries and between markets.

For example, airlines may be compared with brewing or retailing, manufacturing industry to consumer goods. There are many parallels that can be drawn between industries on the basis of competitive marketing strategies for companies in different competitive positions. Select one or more case studies to compare with your own industry or market and analyse the similarities and differences and draw out what can be applied to current and future strategies.

■ Tertiary Level Courses on Marketing Strategy

The cases provided are designed to provide a variety of industries and different strategies. The book can be used for final-year undergraduate business and marketing students and for postgraduate students in at least three main ways:

- as the text and case book running in parallel with a marketing or business simulation game;
- as a supporting case study text to a strategy book which is used as the primary reference; or
- as the text and case book supporting a case analysis course, which also requires field project work by students.

■ Executive Short Course Programmes

Short courses, designed as refreshers for business executives, can include the concepts and cases to reinforce strategy principles and strategic situations, relevant to the industries and markets represented by the seminar participants. This is equally applicable to in-house seminars and public programmes.

Participants can work in syndicate groups to develop strategies for companies in the case studies, that parallel their own market situation or that of major competitors.

■ Further References for Building Marketing Experience

Developing our experience with reference to the marketing experiences of others can occur systematically by reading about a variety of practical strategic situations. These can be found in a number of different types of books and journals.

□ *Case Studies*

The field of case study development pioneered by Harvard Business School as a valuable learning tool needs more application to the European environment. There are many American case books providing strategic experience of US and international companies. The Case Clearing House at Cranfield holds most American case studies, as well as hundreds of excellent European case studies.

□ *Books on Concepts and Cases*

A variety of books are available which provide case study examples of the concepts employed. Two good examples are Urban and Star's book, *Advanced Marketing Strategy,*[1] and Jain's *International Marketing Management.*[2]

□ *Documentation of a Company's Strategies and Evaluation of its Performance*

Business and marketing strategies of individual companies can be found in the business press, business journals and a variety of books.

One very useful recent publication is by Hartley: *Bullseyes and Blunders – Stories of Business Success and Failure.* It compares the strategies and performances of two companies in the same industry, one successful, the other a failure, and indicates what can be learnt from their experiences. Sixteen companies in the American environment are evaluated.[3] Hartley has followed this with *Marketing Successes*[4] and *Marketing Mistakes.*[5] Hendon's book on *Classic Failures* is also instructive.[6]

Another book by Sheth, entitled *Winning Back Your Market: The inside stories of the companies that did it,* provides short case studies on how companies extend markets and the uses for their products. He provides what he terms 'star-making strategies', ranging from repositioning to finding new applications and redefining markets.[7]

These books provide invaluable insights for marketing students and practitioners.

☐ *Company Stories*

Insights on competitive marketing strategy can be gained by reading books written about corporations. The IBM Way by Rodgers[8] and *The Real Coke, The Real Story* are examples.[9]

☐ *Marketing Strategy Books by Business Executives*

These are usually very practical and provide a wealth of examples. Three excellent publications in this area are *Marketing Warfare,*[10] *Offensive Marketing*[11] and *Winning the Marketing War.*[12] These provide short case examples in support of their propositions.

■ Analysis of Marketing Cases – Guidelines for Students

There is no one method that applies to all cases, but the following steps indicate the area to be covered. Some aspects will be more or less important in different cases.

☐ *Situation Analysis*

Note the significant marketing facts in the case; for examples, where is the company now? where is it heading? where should it be heading? what are the strengths and weaknesses of the company? what are the opportunities and threats in its external environment?

State any assumptions being made.

☐ *Problem Definition*

Define the main issues or real problems facing the company and lay these out, where relevant, as one or more principal marketing problem and break each main marketing problem into sub-problems.

☐ *Analysis and Evaluation of Options*

Develop the options open to the company to solve these problems.

Analyse and evaluate the most feasible alternatives in terms of stengths and weaknesses, costs and benefits of each.

Assess the option of 'doing nothing'.

☐ *Other Information that should be Obtained*

Specify the further data you think should be obtained and the analysis required.

☐ *Recommended Courses of Action*

Make recommendations giving reasons.

■ A Note on the Process of Analysis

The analysis of the case study is the most important part of your report. The reasoning whereby the recommended course of action is arrived at carries more weight than the actual decision.

The analysis consists in part, at least, of studying the problem from many different aspects and of attempting to foretell the probable effects upon, or reaction of, the many factors which influence the success or failure of a certain course of action.

1 As the analysis proceeds, alternative courses of action or possible solutions to the problem will come to mind. These must also be examined and their feasibility appraised in much the same way as in the original problem. As the analysis progresses, you may discover that the problem as originally stated requires modification, or that the whole approach to the case needs to be changed.
2 To be complete, the analysis must take into consideration not only the strong points of each argument presented, but also the weaknesses of each. The analysis of one set of factors will indicate a different solution. It is important to recognise the alternative in advance.
3 Occasionally, some assumptions must be made. These should be logical and set forth clearly. Do not make unnecessary assumptions or assumptions which are contrary to facts already given in the case.

Based on the analysis, arrive at one or more decision on the proper course of action to be taken in order to solve the problem. If, as is customary, more than one solution appears to be reasonable, choose the one which, all factors considered, seems to contain the greatest strength and the fewest disadvantages. Be sure that your arguments are based upon the facts in the case, upon logical and clear-out reasonings and upon such assumptions as are made.

■ The Case Study Method of Learning

☐ *Benefits of Case Studies*

Studies cut across a range of companies, industries, and situations to provide an exposure that is far greater than anyone is likely to experience in day-to-day routine. You can build your knowledge of a range of management subjects by dealing intensively with problems in each field. You will come to recognise that the on-the-job problems with which you will deal as a manager are not unique to your company or even your industry. You will thus develop a more professional sense of management.

Perhaps the most important benefit that comes from using cases, however, is that they help you to learn how to ask the right questions. An able business leader once commented, 'Ninety per cent of the task of a top manager is to ask useful questions. Answers are relatively easy to find, but asking good questions – that is the more critical skill.'

If discussion questions are suggested in connection with the preparation of a case, that does not pre-empt the task of identifying the key problems. You must still ask yourself: What really are the problems this manager has to resolve? So often, we manipulate facts and figures without defining the problems.

Case studies help considerably to sharpen analytical skills. You will work with facts and figures to produce quantitative and qualitative evidence to support recommendations and decisions. When challenged by instructors and colleagues to defend your arguments, you develop increased ability to think and reason rigorously.

In addition, cases and case discussions provide a focal point for an exchange among students of the lessons of experience. Such discussions provide a vehicle for reassessing the lessons of experience and gaining increased learning from them.

Cases are useful for developing sets of principles and concepts that can be applied in practice. We consider each case by itself. But out of each will come important concepts and approaches. Taken together, a series of cases should develop for each of us some key ideas that can then be applied in specific managerial situations.

There is one final benefit we seek to achieve by using business case studies: to suggest the sense of fun and excitement that comes with being a manager. You may see a number of situations in businesses that you do not wish to be in. But you should come to sense that being a manager is a great challenge – intellectually, politically and socially.

□ *How to Prepare a Case*

There is no one way to prepare a case. But as a guideline the following approach is suggested. You can take it from there and develop your own methods.

- Go through the case almost as fast as you can turn the pages, asking yourself, 'What is the case about, and what types of information am I being given to analyse?' In particular, look at the first and the last few paragraphs and glance over the tables and figures.
- Now read the case very carefully, underlining key facts as you go. Then ask

yourself, 'What are the basic problems this manager has to resolve?' Try hard to put yourself in the position of the manager. Develop a sense of involvement in the manager's problems.
- Note the key problems on scratch paper. Then go through the case again, sorting out the relevant considerations for each problem area.
- Develop a set of recommendations supported by analysis of case data.

☐ *Some Key Steps Expanded*

Problem Definition
Developing a statement of the questions that should be answered is critically important. In cases, the explicit problems are often stated in the opening paragraphs and at the end. But you may find pieces of the problem scattered throughout the case. Sometimes the problem is crystal-clear; sometimes aspects of the problem may be implied in the middle of the case. It is useful to pick these statements up, note them on your scratch paper, and then try to make some order out of them before you seek answers.

Problem definition is also a matter of delineating a suitable framework which to deal with what may be posed in the case as an immediate question. For example, the manager in the case may be asking, 'What should be our advertising strategy?' That could be the tip of the iceberg, and the more fundamental problem might be. 'What should be our target market segment, and how do we develop an overall strategy for reaching it?' It becomes possible, then, to deal with the specific query regarding advertising strategy within the framework of the broader question. Thus, problems should be defined in a way that:

- resolves the immediate (explicit) issues; and
- deals with aspects of the business about which the immediate problem raises implicit issues.

The problem scope, however, should not be unrealistically and unmanageably broad. For example, it is tempting sometimes to raise the broad question: 'Should we really be in this business at all – or in some other?' Much of the time, however, the manager in the case is not in a position to redirect the company's business. Moreover, the case may not provide sufficient data to deal meaningfully with such a broad problem. In problem definition, then, it becomes important to take account of the scope of control and authority that the manager in the case has.

Good problem definition, then:

- names the immediate issues and defines them in a way that calls for action-oriented answers;
- puts these issues in a proper marketing strategy context, that is, the broader issues; and

- deals with these problems from the perspective of an individual manager, recognising all the responsibilities and the scope of authority, as well as the limitations associated with that position.

Case Analysis

At this point in your preparation, it will be helpful to jot down relevant areas for analysis, one to a page. Areas for analysis are different from the problem statement. For example, if the problems are, 'Should we broaden our product range? Who are our target markets? Which competitors pose the greatest threat?' the areas for analysis might include:

- trends in the market place;
- buyer behaviour;
- corporate and product positioning; and
- competition.

Facts in the case can be marshalled to help you understand each area and to draw some meaningful observations and conclusions. These can, in turn, provide the basis for answering the questions that have been laid out. Inevitably, your analysis will generate arguments that seem to lead to different conclusions. All the evidence may not point in the same direction. It is important that you recognise conflicting considerations, weigh the evidence carefully, and decide what in your balanced judgement is the best course of action.

Having arrived at a decision, you must be able to state your recommendations clearly and to support them with arguments developed from your examination of the analytical areas, using tables and figures where it is helpful to back up your recommendations and proposed plan of action. Then, to complete the work, state any relevant ideas you may have regarding how your plan of action is to be implemented.

A good answer has the following qualities.

1 It deals explicitly with the specific problems posed in the case and within the context of the broader strategy issues.
2 It is well supported by sound analysis and arguments that recognise the pros and cons of taking any recommended course of action.
3 It includes ideas for implementation.

A complete treatment of the case problem will include a consideration of the alternative possibilities that might exist even if these, too, should be rejected.

Finally, one important characteristic of a good answer is that it seems to you to make sense. If it does not make sense, it is probably wrong.

Case Discussions

Up to now, your best results will come if you have worked by yourself. The next step is to meet with your discussion group, present your arguments to the members of this group, and hear theirs. The purpose of the discussion is not to develop a consensus or a group position. It is to help each member to refine, adjust, and develop his or her thinking. It is not necessary, or even desirable, that you agree.

The purpose of individual and group preparations is primarily to make you ready to learn in class. The greater your command of the case facts and the more ideas you have about the case problems, the better prepared you are to take in, react to, and learn from the ideas of others in the class.

In class, your instructor will usually let you take the case where you wish. He or she will then prod you to explore fully the avenues of investigation down which you have started and will lead you into a consideration of other areas that you may have missed. Finally, if the case calls for it, the instructor will require you to make a decision. At the end, he or she may summarise the discussion and draw out the useful lessons and observations that come from the case problem and from class discussion comments – or ask some members of the class to do it.

The classroom is a place for you to express, support and defend your conclusions and recommendations. We learn through controversy and discussion. The effective use of cases as a learning vehicle depends heavily on class participation. Through interchange and constructive controversy we build analytical skills, develop judgement, and gain conceptual understanding. There is, then, a burden of responsibility on each student not only for his or her education but also for the learning of all other students.

Perhaps the greatest pedagogical benefit of the case method is that it generates a high degree of involvement in the learning process. People tend to learn the most from those things in which they are most deeply involved. But it follows, too, that there is little that can be learned from even the best cases without solid preparation.

Discussion in class is also an effective way for you to think rigorously and to develop skills in communicating, in thinking on your feet, and in responding to questions under pressure. Talking in class, expressing your own views, and defending them are all part of a distinctive experience. Seemingly rigorous and tension-building when you are doing it, class participation, in retrospect, becomes one the most valued parts of the educational experience.

As important as talking is, however, listening is more important. It is easy to become so preoccupied with what we think that our minds close to the thoughts of other participants in the discussion. It is just as important in class to be open-minded and willing to shift positions as it is in business. The measure of your individual progress in any one case discussion is not based so much on your own after-class assessment of whether your ideas were 'right'. Instead it is more useful to ask, 'How much did I take away from the class that I did not know when I came in?'

Notes and References

1 Competitive Marketing Strategy: Concepts and Application

1. D. A. Aaker, *Strategic Market Management*, Third Edition, John Wiley & Sons, 1992, p. 10.
2. G. S. Day, *Strategic Market Planning: The pursuit of competitive advantage*, West Publishing Company, 1984, p. 49.
3. D. A. Aaker, *op. cit.*, p. 23.
4. M. H. B. McDonald, *Marketing Plans: How to prepare them, how to use them*, Butterworth-Heinemann, 1989.
5. For example, M. E. Porter, *Comparative Strategy: Techniques for analysing industries and competitors*, The Free Press, 1980.
6. P. Kotler, L. Faney and S. Jatusripitak, *The New Competition: Meeting the marketing challenge from the Far East*, Prentice/Hall International, 1986.
7. R. D. Buzzell and B.T. Gale, *The PIMS Principles: Linking strategy to performance*, The Free Press, 1987, pp. 6–15, 30–35.
8. K. Andrews, 'Corporate Strategy: The essential intangibles', *McKinsey Quarterly*, Autumn 1984.
9. M. Lubatkin and M. Pitts, 'The PIMS and the Policy Perspective: A rebuttal', *Journal of Business Strategy*, Summer 1985, pp. 85–92.
10. G. S. Day, *Analysis for Strategic Market Decisions*, West Publishing Company, 1986, p. 60.
11. C. R. Wasson, *Dynamic Competitive Strategy and Product Life-Cycles*, Challenge Books, 1974.
12. G. S. Day, 1966, *op. cit.*, pp. 91–2.
13. G. S. Day, 1986, *op. cit.*, p. 90.
14. C. R. Wasson, *op. cit.*, pp. 247–8.
15. A. Meenaghan and P. W. Turnbull, *Strategy and Analysis in Product Development*, Volume 15, No. 5, 1981, MCB Publications Ltd.
16. D. T. Brownlie and C. K. Bart, *Products and Strategies*, MCB University Press, Vol. 11, No. 1, 1985, pp. 25–6.
17. B. A. Weitz and R. Wensley, *Strategic Marketing: Planning, Implementation and Control*, Kent Publishing, 1984, p. 132.
18. Boston Consulting Group, 'Perspective on Experience', The Boston Consulting Group, Inc., 1970 and G. S. Day, *Analysis for Strategic Market Decisions*, West Publishing Company, 1986. A review of cost and price dynamics and the issues involved is given in chapter 2, pp. 25–56.
19. W. H. Davidow, *Marketing High Technology: An insider's view*, The Free Press, New York, 1986, p. xvi.
20. W. H. Davidow, *op. cit.*
21. An extensive review of the growth-share matrix is found in G. S. Day, 1986, Chapter 6.

22. D. T. Brownlie *et al.*, *op. cit.*, p. 14.
23. H. I. Ansoff, *Corporate Strategy*, Pelican Books, 1968, pp. 127–31.
24. D. T. Brownlie *et al.*, *op. cit.*, p. 14.
25. R. D. Buzzell and B. T. Gale, *The PIMS Principles: Linking strategy to performance*, The Free Press, 1986, pp. 7–15.
26. R. D. Buzzell, *et al.*, *op. cit.*, chapters 5–10.
27. M. E. Porter, *Competitive Strategy: Techniques for analysing industries and competitors*, The Free Press, 1980, pp. 31–3.
28. M. E. Porter, *Competitive Advantage: Creating and sustaining superior performance*, The Free Press, 1985.
29. Further elaboration of general strategies and market coverage is found in G. S. Day, *Market Driven Strategy: Processes for Creating Value*, The Free Press, 1990, pp. 165–8.

■ 2 Low Cost, High Differentiation Strategies

1. R. D. Buzzell, B. T. Gale, and R. G. M. Sultan, 'Market Share – A Key to Profitability', *Harvard Business Review*, January–February, 1975, pp. 95–106.
2. R. D. Buzzell, and B. T. Gale, *The PIMS Principles Linking Strategy to Performance*, The Free Press, New York, 1987, p. 10.
3. An extensive review of the multifaceted aspect of positioning is presented by A. Ries and J. Trout, *Positioning: The battle for your mind*, McGraw-Hill, New York, 1986.
4. P. N. Bloom and P. Kotler, 'Strategies for High Market Share Companies', *Harvard Business Review*, November–December, 1975, pp. 63–72.
5. A. Ries and J. Trout. *Marketing Warfare*, McGraw-Hill, New York, 1986, pp. 55–66.
6. H. Davidson, *Offensive Marketing: Or how to make your competitors followers*, Penguin Books, UK. 1987, pp. 294–6.
7. An extensive account of product life-cycle theory and its application is provided by C. R. Wasson, *Product Management: Product life-cycles and competitive marketing strategy*, Challenge Books, lllinois, 1971.
8. L. de Chernatory and M. H. B. McDonald, *Creating Powerful Brands*, Butterworth-Heinemann, Oxford, 1992, pp. 226–7.
9. J. H. Davidson, *op. cit.*, pp. 300–1.
10. L. R. Brown, 'An Empirical Study and Evaluation of Marketing Strategies Adopted in Competitive Consumer Markets', University of NSW, unpublished PhD thesis, 1975.
11. The importance of defining the business in a way which provides scope for expansion is dealt with at length by D. F. Abell, *Defining the Business: The starting point of strategic planning*, Prentice-Hall, New Jersey, 1980.

■ 3 Low Cost, Low Differentiation Strategies

1. J. H. Davidson, *Offensive Marketing: Or how to make your competitors followers*, Penguin, UK, 1987, pp. 70–85.
2. A. Ries and J. Trout, *Marketing Warfare*, McGraw-Hill, New York, 1986, pp. 68–73.

3. C. H. Lovelock, *Services Marketing,* second edition, Prentice-Hall International Inc., London, 1991, pp. 13–15.
4. A. J. Magrath, 'When Marketing Services, 4 Ps Are Not Enough', *Business Horizons,* May–June, 1986, pp. 44–50.
5. D. W. Cowell, *The Marketing of Services,* Heinemann, London, 1984, p. 70.
6. OECD (1990) Main Economic Indicators, Paris, June.
7. Van der Ster, W. (1989) 'Food Retailing in the 1990s: a Dutch View', Albert Heijn Conference, Noordwijk, Koninklijke Ahold nv, Zaandam, Netherlands.
8. Davies, R. L. (1989) 'A Checklist of Development Opportunities and Constraints – Britain versus the Continent', in *Responding to 1992: Key Factors for Retailers,* Oxford Institute of Retail Management, Templeton College, Oxford, pp. 45–54.
9. Debenham Tewson and Chinnocks, special report (1989) '1992 – The Retail Dimension', Debenham Tewson and Chinnocks Ltd., London.
10. 'Aldi Reverses Policy to Compete in the UK', *Marketing,* 1 March 1990, p. 3.
11. Killen, V. and R. Lees, (1988) The Future of Grocery Retailing in the UK part II, *Retail and Distribution Management,* Nov/Dec, pp. 27–9.
12. Maclaurin, I. (1990) *The Times,* 3 January.
13. Sainsbury (1989) Private Communication to the Researchers, 11 December.
14. Ogbanna, E. (1989) 'Strategic Changes in UK Grocery Retailing', *Management Decision,* Vol. 27, No. 6, pp. 45–50.
15. Porter, M. E. (1980) *Competitive Strategy,* The Free Press, New York.
16. Retail Business, Quarterly Trade Reviews, No. 12 (1989) Grocers and Supermarkets, Economist Intelligence Unit, London, p. 12.
17. Dawson, J. A. and S. Burt (1988) 'The Evolution of European Retailing vol. II', The University of Stirling Institute for Retail Studies, pp. 40–2.
18. Salmon, W. J. (1989) 'Multinational Food Retailing in the Nineties', Albert Heijn Conference, Noordwijk, Koninklijke Ahold nv, Zaandam, Netherlands.
19. Mintel (1989) *Retail Intelligence,* vol. 1, Economist Intelligence Unit, London, pp. 2–33.
20. UBS-Phillips and Drew (1988) *Europe 1993: Breaking Down the Barriers,* (eds. Foyil, D. and Seward, B.), UBS-Phillips and Drew, London, p. 58.
21. Duke, R. C. (1989) A Structural Analysis of the UK Grocery Retail Market, *British Food Journal,* vol. 91, no. 5, July/August, pp. 17–22.
22. Key Note (1988) *New Trends in Retailing,* Key Note Publications Ltd., London, pp. 4–8.
23. McKinsey and Company (1987) in *The European Food Marketing Directory,* Euromonitor Publications Ltd., London, p. 5.
24. Special Report 'Consumer Marketing in Europe', 4 May 1989.
25. Killen, V. and R. Lees (1988) The Future of Grocery Retailing in the UK part I, *Retail and Distribution Management,* July/August, pp. 8–12.
26. Verdict Research (1990) *The Space Report,* Verdict Research, London.
27. *Euromonitor* (1987) *Retail Trade UK 1987/88,* Euromonitor Publications Ltd., London, p. 47.
28. Mintel (1989) *Retail Intelligence,* vol. 4 'Superstores and Hypermarkets', Economist Intelligence Unit, London, pp. 4.29–4.34.
29. MORI (1989) *The Retail Property Market,* (a study commissioned by Argos Distributors Ltd), MORI, London, p. 20.
30. Musannif, Y. and F. George (1989) 'Focus on European Retailers', Bank Paribas Capital Markets Ltd., London, in 'Responding to 1992: Key factors for retailers',

Treadgold, A., in *Retail Trends in Continental Europe*, Oxford Institute of Retail Management, Templeton College, Oxford, p. 41.

31. *Euromonitor* (1987) 'Grocery Distribution in Western Europe', Euromonitor Publications Ltd., London, pp. 24–31.
32. de Chernatony, L. (1986) 'Consumer Perceptions of the Competitive Tiers Available Within Specified Product Fields', in *Managing Marketing*, (eds. Cowell, D. and Collins, J.), Proceedings of MEG, Plymouth.
33. Whitaker, J. (1983) 'To Spend or not to Spend?', *Nielson Researcher*, 2, pp. 1–14.
34. Fletcher, J. (1989) 'UK Retailers Will be Bound for Europe', *The Grocer*, 15 April, pp. 52–4.
35. *Euromonitor* (1987) 'Grocery Distribution in Western Europe', Euromonitor Publications Ltd., London, p. 25.
36. Dawson, J. A., S. A. Shaw and J. Rana (1988) 'Future Trends in Food Retailing: Results of a Survey of Retailers', *British Food Journal*, vol. 90.2, pp. 51–7.
37. A. Ries and J. Trout, *Marketing Warfare*, McGraw-Hill, New York, 1986, chapters 8 and 9.
38. Ries and Trout, *ibid*, chapter 10.
39. M. E. Porter, *Competitive Strategy: Technologies for analysing industries and competitors*, The Free Press, 1980, chapter 2.
40. C. R. Wasson, *Dynamic Competitive Strategy and Product Life-Cycles*, Challenge Books, Illinois, USA, 1974.
41. G. S. Day, *Strategic Market Planning: The pursuit of competitive advantage*, West Publishing Company, St Pauls, Minnesota, 1984, p. 117.
42. W. H. Davidow, *Marketing High Technology: An insider's view*, The Free Press, New York, 1986, p. xvi.
43. The term 'pincer' is defined by the Oxford Dictionary as 'operation involving the convergence of two forces on enemy position like the jaws of a pair of pincers' (*The Oxford Universal Dictionary*, 1965).
44. P. Kotler, L. Fahey, and S. Jatusripitak, *The New Competition*, Prentice-Hall, 1986, chapter 3.
45. P. Kotler, *et al.*, *ibid*.
46. D. F. Abell, and J. S. Hammond, *Strategic Market Planning: Problems and analytical approaches*, Prentice-Hall, New Jersey, 1979.
47. D. A. Aaker, *Strategic Management*, New York, John Wiley & Sons, 1984.
48. T. V. Bonoma, *The Marketing Edge: Making strategies work*, New York, The Free Press, 1985.
49. M. E. Porter, *Competitive Strategy: Techniques for analysing industries and competitors*, The Free Press, 1980, p. 29.
50. D. F. Abell, *Defining the Business: The starting point of strategic planning*, Prentice-Hall, Englewood Cliffs, New Jersey, 1980, chapter 2, pp. 11–25.
51. R. McKenna, *The Regis Touch*, Addison-Wesley, San Francisco, 1985, pp. 13–18.
52. N. Shoebridge, 'Levi Pulls its Jeans Back Up', *Business Review Weekl'*, 13 March 1987, p. 100.
53. N. Shoebridge, 'When only the Right Name Will Do', *Business Review Weekly*, 27 March 1987, pp. 71–3.
54. *Australian Business*, 10 February 1988, p. 34.
55. W. H. Davidow, *Marketing High Technology: An insider's view*, The Free Press, New York, 1986, pp. 79–85, pp. 4–10.

4 Strategies for Positioning as a Major Force in the Market

1. M. E. Porter, *Competitive Advantage: Creating and sustaining superior performance*, The Free Press, 1985, p. 16.
2. J. Argenti, *Corporate Collapse: The causes and symptoms*. McGraw-Hill, London, 1976.
3. M. E. Porter, *op. cit.*, p. 16.
4. L. R. Brown, 'An Empirical Study and Evaluation of Marketing Strategies Adopted in Competitive Consumer Markets', unpublished PhD thesis, University of New South Wales, 1975.
5. D. Knee, and D. Walters, *Strategy in Retailing: Theory and application*, Philip Allan Publishers, 1985, pp. 29–30.
6. D. L. James, R. M. Durand, and R. A. Dreves, 'The Use of a Multi-Attribute Attitude Model in Store Image Study', *Journal of Retailing*, vol. 52, Summer 1976, p. 30.
7. E. A. Pessemier, 'Store Image and Positioning', *Journal of Retailing*, vol. 56, Spring 1980, pp. 96–7.
8. R. B. Marks, 'Operationalisation of the Concept of Store Image', *Journal of Retailing*, vol. 52, Fall 1976, pp. 44.
9. This list is adapted from B. Berman, and J. R. Evans, *Retail Management: A strategic approach* 2nd edn, Macmillan Publishing, New York, 1983, p. 356.
10. W. H. Davidow, *Marketing High Technology: An insider's view*, The Free Press, 1986, pp. 184–6.
11. M. E. Porter, *Competitive Advantage: Creating and sustaining superior performance*, The Free Press, 1985, pp. 5–6.
12. M. E. Porter, *Competitive Strategy: Techniques for analysing industries and competitors*, The Free Press, 1980, pp. 29–30.
13. This section is based on the work of Michael Porter, 1985, chapter 2.

5 Growth Strategies for the Niche Competitor

1. H. Davidson, *Offensive Marketing: Or how to make your competitors followers*, Penguin, UK 1987, p. 168.
2. R. G. Hamermesh, M. J. Anderson, and J. E. Harris, 'Strategies for Low-Share Business', *Harvard Business Review*, May–June, 1978, pp. 95–102.
3. D. K. Clifford, and R. E. Cavanagh, *The Winning Performance: How America's high-growth midsize companies succeed*, Bantam Books, New York, 1988, p. 36.
4. J. H. Davidson, *op. cit.*, pp. 168–9.
5. A. Ries, and J. Trout, *Marketing Warfare*, McGraw-Hill, New York, 1986, pp. 101–8.
6. Studies of success and failure rates and their causes are reported in P. L. Link, *Marketing of Technology: An Australian perspective*, Nelson Wadsworth, Melbourne, 1987, chapter 5; J. H. Davidson, *Offensive Marketing: Or how to make your competitors followers*, Penguin Books, UK, 1987, pp. 332–44. Also see N. Shoebridge, 'Product Failures', *Business Review Weekly*, 24 October 1986, pp. 50–65.
7. R. F. Hartley, *Bullseyes and Blunders: Stories of business success and failure*, John Wiley & Sons, New York, 1987, chapter 15.
8. T. Oliver, *The Real Coke, The Real Story*, Pan Books, London, 1986.

6 Competitive Marketing Strategy Experience

1. G. S. Day, *Analysis for Strategic Market Decisions*, West Publishing Company, St. Paul, USA, 1986, pp. 115–16.
2. R. D. Buzzell, and B. T. Gale, *The PIMS Principles: Linking strategy to performance*, The Free Press, New York, 1987, p. 36.
3. G. S. Day, *op. cit.*, chapter 8, pp. 217–18.
4. P. G. W. Keen, and M. S. S. Morton, *Decision Support System: An organisational perspective*, Reading, Mass., Addison-Wesley, 1978.
5. J. D. C. Little, 'Brandaid: A Marketing Mix Model Part 1: Structure and Part 2: Implementation, Calibration and Case Study', *Operations Research*, vol. 23, no. 4 (July–August), 1975, pp. 628–73.
6. J. C. Larreché, and V. Srinivasan, 'Stratport: A Decision Support System for Strategic Planning', *Journal of Marketing*, vol. 45, no. 4 (Fall 1981), pp. 39–52.
7. Ansplan is now commercially available to companies in the United States, also in Australia through the School of Marketing, University of New South Wales.
8. This was reported in a paper presented to a Conference on Marketing and the New Information/Communication Technologies, C. M. Hills, and J. J. McIvor, 'MDSS'S at General Electric: Implications for the 90s From Experiences in the 70s and 80s', Harvard University, July 1983.
9. These models and their purpose are found in G. Hillis, J. Cook, R. Best, and D. Hawkins, 'Marketing Strategy to Achieve Market Share Goals', in H. Thomas and D. Gardner (eds), *Strategic Marketing and Management*, John Wiley & Sons, 1985.
10. J. C. Larreché, and H. Gatignon, *MARKSTRAT: A Marketing Strategy Game*, Scientific Press, Palo Alto, California, 1977.

7 Uses of Case Studies to Enhance Learning

1. G. L. Urban and S. H. Star, *Advanced Marketing Strategy: Phenomena, Analysis and Decisions*, Prentice-Hall, London, 1991.
2. S. C. Jain, *International Marketing Management*, Third Edition, PWS-Kent Publishing Company, Boston, 1990.
3. R. F. Hartley, *Bullseyes and Blunders: Stories of business success and failure*, John Wiley & Sons, New York, 1987.
4. R. F. Hartley, *Marketing Successes*, Second Edition, John Wiley & Sons, New York, 1990.
5. R. F. Hartley, *Marketing Mistakes*, Fifth Edition, John Wiley & Sons, New York, 1992.
6. D. W. Hendon, *Classic Failure in Product Marketing*, NTC Publishing Group, Chicago, 1992.
7. J. N. Sheth, *Winning Back Your Market: The inside stories of the companies that did it*, John Wiley & Sons, New York, 1985.
8. F. G. Rodgers, *The IBM Way: Insights into the world's most successful marketing organisation*, Harper & Row, New York, 1986.
9. T. Oliver, *The Real Coke, The Real Story*, Pan Books, London, 1986.
10. A. Ries and J. Trout, *Marketing Warfare*, McGraw-Hill, New York, 1986.

11. H. Davidson, *Offensive Marketing: Or how to make your competitors followers*, Penguin, UK, 1987.
12. R. Duro, *Winning the Marketing War*, English Language Edition, John Wiley & Sons, New York, 1989.

Bibliography

Aaker, D. A. *Strategic Market Management*. John Wiley & Sons, 1984.

Abell, D. F. *Defining the Business: The starting point of strategic planning*. Prentice-Hall, Englewood Cliffs, New Jersey, 1980.

Abell, D. F. and J. S. Hammond *Strategic Market Planning: Problems and analytical approaches*. Prentice-Hall, Englewood Cliffs, New Jersey, 1979.

Ansett, R. G. and R. Pullan *Bob Ansett, An Autobiography*. John Kery Pty Ltd, Melbourne, 1986.

Ansoff, I. *Corporate Strategy*. Penguin Books, 1968.

Argenti, J. *Corporate Collapse: The causes and symptoms*. McGraw-Hill, London, 1976.

Berman, B. and J. R. Evans *Retail Management: A strategic approach*. 2nd edn, Macmillan Publishing, New York, 1983.

Bonoma, T. V. *The Marketing Edge: Making strategies work*. The Free Press, New York, 1985.

Boston Consulting Group. *Perspective on Experience*. The Boston Consulting Group, Inc., Boston, 1970.

Brownlie, D. T. and C. K. Bart *Products and Strategies*. MCB University Press, Vol. 11, No. 1, 1985.

Buzzell, R. D. and B. T. Gale *The PIMS Principles: Linking strategy to performance*. The Free Press, New York, 1987.

Clifford, D. K. and R. E. Cavanagh *The Winning Performance: How America's high-growth midsize companies succeed*. Bantam Books, New York, 1988.

Cowell, D. W. *The Marketing of Services*. Heinemann, London, 1984.

Davidow, W. H. *Marketing High Technology: An insider's view*. The Free Press, New York, 1986.

Davidson, H. *Offensive Marketing: Or how to make your competitors followers*. Penguin Books, UK, 1987.

Day, G. S. *Strategic Market Planning: The pursuit of competitive advantage*. West Publishing Company, New York, 1984.

Day, G. S. *Analysis for Strategic Market Decisions*. West Publishing Company, New York, 1986.

Gilmour, P., D. L. Rados and D. M. T. Gibson *Australian Marketing Casebook* 2nd edn, University of Queensland Press, St Lucia, Queensland, 1988.

Hartley, R. F. *Bullseyes and Blunders: Stories of business success and failure*. John Wiley & Sons, New York, 1987.

Keen, P. G. W. and M. S. S. Morton *Decision Support System: An Organisational Perspective*. Addison-Wesley, Reading, Massachusetts, 1978.

Knee, D. and D. Walter *Strategy in Retailing: Theory and application*. Philip Allan Publishers, New York, 1985.

Kotler, P., L. Fahey and S. Jatusripitak *The New Competition: Meeting the marketing challenge from the Far East*. Prentice-Hall, Englewood Cliffs, New Jersey, 1986.

Larreché, J. C. and H. Gatignon *Markstrat: A Marketing Strategy Game*. Scientific Press, Palo Alto, California, 1977.

Link, P. L. *Marketing of Technology: An Australian perspective.* Nelson Wadsworth, Melbourne, 1987.

McDonald, M. H. B. *Marketing Plans: How to prepare them, How to use them.* Heinemann, London, 1984.

McKenna, R. *The Regis Touch.* Addison-Wesley, Reading, Massachusetts, 1985.

Oliver, T. *The Real Coke, The Real Story.* Pan Books, London, 1986.

Porter, M. E. *Competitive Advantage: Creating and sustaining superior performance.* The Free Press, New York, 1985.

Ries, A. and J. Trout *Marketing Warfare.* McGraw-Hill, New York, 1986.

Ries, A. and J. Trout *Positioning: The battle for your mind.* McGraw-Hill, New York, 1986.

Rodgers, F. G. *The IBM Way: Insights into the world's most successful marketing organisation.* Harper & Row, New York, 1986.

Sheth, J. N. *Winning Back Your Market: The inside stories of the companies that did it.* John Wiley & Sons, New York, 1985.

Wasson, C. R. *Dynamic Competitive Strategy and Product Life Cycles.* Challenge Books, New York, 1974.

Willis, G., J. Cook, R. Best and D. Hawkins 'Marketing Strategy to Achieve Market Share Goals' in *Strategic Marketing and Management,* Thomas, H. and Gardner, D. (eds). John Wiley & Sons, New York, 1985.

Weitz, B. A. and R. Wensley, *Strategic Marketing: Planning, Implementation and Control.* Kent Publishing, London, 1984.

Index